Charles & Diana

Charles

Ralph G. Martin

& Diana

G. P. PUTNAM'S SONS · NEW YORK.

G. P. Putnam's Sons
Publishers Since 1838
200 Madison Avenue
New York, NY 10016

Published simultaneously in Canada by
General Publishing Co. Limited, Toronto.

The author gratefully acknowledges permission from
Chappell & Co., Inc., to reprint lines from "I've Danced
with a Man" by Herbert Farjeon and Harold Scott,
copyright © 1928 by Ascherberg, Hopwood & Crew, Ltd.
Copyright renewed, all rights in the U.S.A. controlled by
Chappell & Co., Inc. International copyright secured.
All rights reserved.

Library of Congress Cataloging-in-Publication Data

Martin, Ralph G., date.
Charles & Diana

1. Charles, Prince of Wales, 1948– . 2. Diana,
Princess of Wales, 1961– . 3. Great Britain—
Princes and princesses—Biography. I. Title.
II. Title: Charles and Diana.
DA591.A33M36   1985   941.085'092'2   [B]   85-12150
ISBN 0-399-13094-2

Book design by Joe Marc Freedman
Printed in the United States of America
1 2 3 4 5 6 7 8 9 10

For my dear friends
Phyllis Grann and Sterling Lord,
who wanted me to write this book . . . .
And to my old friend Howard Katzander,
who always lived his life to the full,
and to my dear cousin Harold Charno,
who also knows how to wink at the world.

Prologue

he whole world wanted a Cinderella story.

It needed one. It was a time of nuclear fear, bitter wars, economic trauma. The great world leaders had passed from the stage and their replacements were minor league, unexciting. People wanted something to titillate their imaginations, stir their souls, pull them out of themselves. They wanted a grown-up fairy tale about a handsome Prince who finds a beautiful Cinderella and makes her his Princess, and they live happily ever after.

And, suddenly, they had one. It was almost too perfect. The Prince *was* handsome, his Cinderella was not only beautiful but fresh and unsophisticated and even—although it was impossible to believe—pure. The world followed their courtship as if it were their own. Every tiny snippet of information became an international headline. Photographers were offered impossible sums for obtaining improbable pictures. "Cinderella" was seen on more magazine covers, more television broadcasts, reported on in more newspaper headlines than almost any other human being in our time. The ancient pageantry and splendor of their marriage ceremony was watched by more than 750 million people in every part of our planet.

And how did it really begin?

The myth is that it all began in the middle of a ploughed field at Sandringham when she was sixteen and he was twenty-nine. The two of them propagated the story by telling it themselves. If indeed as young adults they were introduced there, it was of little consequence. In fact, in a vague way they had known each other all their lives. The true story—the *real* beginning, the *real* romantic spark of electricity between them, the real Cinderella story—didn't come until three years later, in 1980, during Cowes Week.

Cowes Week takes place the first week in August when the strip of channel called The Solent, between the southern coast of England and the Isle of Wight, becomes a forest of sailing masts. Some 700 yachts of all sizes from all over the world assemble to take part in a series of races. And thousands of people come to crowd sleepy little Cowes to catch a glimpse of the glamorous Royals. Because for 150 years, this time and place has been a pleasure playground of European royalty.

Sitting in the Solent like a glittering blue jewel, always just freshly painted, is the British royal yacht *Britannia*. Probably the most famous ship in the world, the *Britannia* has the elegance of a floating palace—art treasures on the walls, Persian carpets on the polished floors, a glassed-in veranda, a reception area for 250 guests, a dining room that can seat sixty, a twenty-six-piece Royal Marine Band. This is a ship that has visited some 600 ports, circled the world seven times. For royal guests, there's a royal barge acting as a ferry and even a Rolls-Royce available for shore duty.

One such guest that Cowes Week was a titled teenager, nineteen-year-old Lady Diana Frances Spencer.

She had come as the guest of Sarah Armstrong-Jones, the daughter of Princess Margaret, and this was Diana's first time on the royal yacht, her first time at Cowes. The staff swiftly appraised her and assumed that this young lady was meant as a playmate for Prince Andrew. Things did not work out that way.

Prince Andrew was away most of the day on a ship called *Spanish Lady*. His father, Prince Philip, an expert helmsman, was on a 40-foot ocean racer, the *Yeoman XXI*. During Cowes Week, Prince Philip was in his element. The Queen remained at home with her beloved horses and dogs, and it was Prince Philip's standard that flew atop the *Britannia* mast.

The only member of the royal family in a deep funk was Prince Charles. The Royals had just returned from the Queen Mother's eightieth birthday ball, where he had escorted the current passion of his life, stunning Anna Wallace. Theirs had been a prolonged affair, and there were many who felt that this was the one he finally might marry. But, that night at the ball, Prince Charles felt a responsibility to circulate among the 400 guests, and he left Miss Wallace simmering alone at their table.

One much-repeated myth was that Anna Wallace had turned down her chance to be his Princess by publicly denouncing him at the ball when he finally returned to their table. The fact was that she had swept out of the ballroom and out of his life, in tears, long before he returned. And the final decision on their relationship had been made earlier by the royal powers. But it still hurt.

So there he was now, scudding on the sea on his windsurfer, bitter and brooding. Watching him from the deck of the *Britannia*, Lady Diana Spencer decided that she, too, would go windsurfing. She was an expert surfer and swimmer, and she and the Prince were soon weaving around each other, both full of fun. A sudden maneuver by Lady Diana pitched the heir to the throne into the sea. They both laughed. "I like to laugh," she often said. And the Prince sorely needed some laughter.

Afterward, as they lounged aboard ship casually dressed, they were at ease with each other, sharing memories of their intertwined families at Sandringham. Lady Diana had the gift of the quick, unexpected remark that made him smile. She was the kind of young woman he particularly liked: tall and willowy, with graceful legs, long blond hair and a sparkling personality. More than that, she had a fresh directness, a warm smile and an absolutely contagious laugh.

Later that day there was a spin in a speedboat, a barge trip to the village of Cowes. Its streets had been transformed into a kind of carnival jam-packed with younger "yachties" in rugby shirts, oil-skins, yellow waders or mismatched Wellingtons; older men dressed in double-breasted navy blue blazers with white trousers and proper yachting caps; lovely young women sporting oversize sunglasses and skinned into undersize jeans and tight T-shirts emblazoned with saucy slogans. Weaving in and out of pubs and clubs, shouting greetings at each other, they displayed a loud camaraderie.

Returning to the *Britannia*, everybody dressed for dinner: black tie and starched shirt for the men and the most décolleté evening gowns for the women. The Royal Marine Band played a mix of the most popular music, the soft lights shimmered like candles, and the conversation among the sixteen seated at the dinner table was an eager chatter of gossip and jokes. Later somebody recalled the high jinks of Prince Philip and Prince Andrew, who had imitated apes by swinging their arms and making guttural noises. After dinner, there was a sing-along around the piano. Somebody noticed that Charles, who kept close to Diana, had lost his earlier glum look and now seemed bright and cheerful.

The scene was splendid and the mood was right. He might have reminisced about the first time he sailed on the *Britannia*, during its maiden voyage. He was then a five-year-old headed for Tobruk with his sister to rendezvous with their parents, who were returning from a six-month world tour. The captain had let him keep a life belt as a souvenir, and he had kept it in his room for the longest time. He might have told her of the fun he had, years later, putting old-fashioned car horns under the seat cushions to startle his guests at a party. But he would not tell her that those parties were for various girlfriends.

There was not too much time to reminisce because there was a party that night at a state prison that had been converted into the posh Royal Squadron Yacht Club. Charles might have pointed out a cottage opposite the castle where his great-grandfather, Edward VII, had kept his mistress, the actress Lillie Langtry.

Those who noticed them that night on the dance floor observed that they weren't talking much at all. They danced closely on the slow numbers, oblivious to the crowded floor. Diana was a superb dancer. It was one of her primary interests at school, and ever since. As she put it, "I like movement."

They stopped in at other parties that night, and made a quick detour to a disco. En route, some of them enjoyed the jellied eels at a dock stall called The Smuggler's Den. About the eels the counterman claimed, "It's their aphrodisiac quality, sir."

In the moonlit hours aboard ship, before sleep, the romantic aura could not have been more perfect. On such a night, on a similar royal yacht, during a Cowes Week more than a hundred years earlier, an ancestral cousin of Lady Diana had confided to a friend of an American beauty he had met aboard, "If I can, I mean to make the dark one my wife." The man was Lord Randolph Churchill and the woman, Jennie Jerome.

Many of the guests went home the next day, but Diana stayed on.

The myth is that the romance began in the middle of a ploughed field in Sandringham when she was sixteen and he was twenty-nine. But this is the way it *really* began.

Charles & Diana

n fact, Diana Frances Spencer was not quite Cinderella. It was true she lived in a nondescript block of flats, wore jeans, cycled to work, took care of other people's babies—and even cleaned their houses. It was true that she was just as anonymous as any other teenager standing on line for the Number 11 bus to Pimlico. But it was also true that her blood was as blue as that of any Royal. If she could claim no giants of history among her ancestors, they were still part of the backbone of British aristocracy.

The Windsor and Spencer families were tightly interwoven through generations of royal service and friendship—and were even distant cousins. Both of Diana's grandmothers had been ladies-in-waiting to the Queen Mother; Diana's father had been equerry to King George VI, and then to his daughter, Elizabeth II. Diana's father and the Queen had known each other since they were children.

Nevertheless, it was mostly another myth that the Spencers and the Royal Family, who were neighbors at Sandringham, always popped into each other's houses, and that all the young princes were always splashing happily in the outdoor Spencer pool.

First and foremost, nobody *ever* pops in on Her Majesty, the Queen of England, without a proper invitation.

The Spencers were invited to the Queen's home, a half mile away from the Spencer house, for tea and lunch, and an occasional dinner. And the Queen especially came to tea at the Spencers'. If she was riding by on her horse and spotted one of them, she surely stopped to chat. As for the stories about the princes swimming in the Spencer pool, the Royal Family stays at Sandringham mainly in the month of January—hardly the time for outdoor swimming in England.

The fact was that the Royal Family always had an invisible moat around their homes and their lives, and the Spencers were among the first to recognize it. This is part of the mystique of monarchy.

"You can only be born an aristocrat," said Princess Gloria von Thurn und Taxis, "you cannot become one. You can wear aristocratic clothes, you can put on an aristocratic accent and you can mix with aristocratic friends—if they are willing to mix with you. But you will always be a fake and they—the real aristocrats—will always know it."

"The history of English aristocracy is a history of illegitimacy," said Harold Brooks-Baker, managing director of *Debrett's Peerage*. Historically, this is known as being born "on the wrong side of the blanket." Five lines of ancestral Spencers trace back to illegitimate children of Charles II, another to an illegitimate daughter of James II.

The early Spencers knew how to marry well. The original Spencer fortune made in the fifteenth century came from a man who bypassed the local markets and sold his sheep for a fatter profit to the butchers and wool merchants of London. The Spencers were soon among the richest families in England. Their sons married heiresses and their daughters married men with titles. The first titled Spencer received his title from Charles I, who owed him money. Other kings, James I among them, appeared to have sold titles in job lots. Even 200 years later Prime Minister William Pitt the Younger declared, "Anyone worth 10,000 pounds a year is worth a peerage."

A titled family soon had a family crest, a family motto, and a proper manor house. The Spencer motto was: "God defend the right." Their first manor house was burned to the ground in the civil war between the Royalists and Oliver Cromwell. The next one was a massive red-brick building with a moat around it called Althorp (pronounced "Alltrup"). It was in Northamptonshire and had belonged to the Abbott of Evesham in 1486.

Althorp was a princely place. The Spencers soon filled in the moat, converted a central courtyard into a grand salon, planted orange trees, built a racetrack, and bought enough rare books and art to make theirs one of the great collections in Europe.

Spencers became Lord Chamberlains, Knights of the Garter, Ambassadors to Paris and Madrid, and one First Lord of the Admiralty, among other things. No single one of them was worth a book or a statue. The Spencer who probably did the most with the least was the third Earl Spencer. A happy nonentity at Harrow, spectacularly unsuccessful at Cambridge, he was a shy, awkward young man, a painfully agonizing speaker, who somehow became Leader of the House of Commons, House Secretary, Chancellor of the Exchequer, even a potential Prime Minister. He was so deeply concerned with the wretched condition of the working class that he became a major force behind the passage of the first Reform Bill in 1832. What brought him so far was not his brain, but his character, his natural directness, and his charm. In describing his contribution to government as "indispensable," Prime Minister Melbourne called him "the tortoise on which the world rests."

The Spencer women have a legacy of formidable female role models. The best of them were strong-minded, independent, dazzling types. Georgiana, daughter of the first Earl Spencer, was only seventeen when she married the Duke of Devonshire. She was known as the "Duchess of Dimples . . . the face without a frown . . ." and she called her husband "The Dog." She soon had a string of lovers including famous actors, artists, a future Prime Minister, and the portly Prince of Wales, nicknamed "Prinny," who became George IV. When Georgiana became pregnant in 1785, Prinny visited her with such paternal interest "that it excited some emotion in Georgiana's husband, the Duke." In her fifty-first year, Georgiana wrote, "I am courted, followed, flattered and made love to, *en toute les formes*, by four men . . ."

Her sister Henrietta, who became Lady Bessborough, refused the same Prince of Wales many years later, describing how he "threw himself on his knees and clasped me round, kiss'd my neck before I was aware . . . sometimes sobbing and crying . . . vows of eternal love, entreaties . . . *I should make my own terms!* . . ." She said no to him, but yes to many others.

Young Diana Spencer was probably most interested in her namesake, the granddaughter of the fiery, remarkable Sarah, Duchess of Marlborough. The earlier Diana was only six when her mother died in 1715, and the Duchess of Marlborough was determined that she would grow up to marry the Prince of Wales. It almost happened. The earlier Diana, too, was a tall, lovely young woman, whom everybody called "dearest Di." Prince Frederick, deeply in debt, was delighted at the prospect of such a beauty, with a dowry of 100,000 pounds. Arrangements were almost completed when the Prime Minister scotched it. He had other plans for the Prince. Perhaps it was just as well because the Prince was not otherwise a creditable catch. A mock epitaph read: "Here lies Fred, who was alive and is dead."

Diana later became the Duchess of Bedford, and her brother became the Duke of Marlborough, ancestor of Winston Churchill. Another brother inherited Althorp and the Spencer estates. She herself died of what was diagnosed as "galloping consumption."

The American connection of Diana Frances Spencer does not trace back to the *Mayflower*, but reportedly does include George Washington (to whom the Queen Mother is also related).

The first of the family to emigrate to America came in the 1630s, settling originally in Connecticut, then spreading out to the midwest and far west. At least one member of the family served as a soldier with Washington. All this qualifies the latest Princess of Wales to be considered a Daughter of the American Revolution.

Besides Washington, Princess Diana is also related to seven other American presidents: John Adams, John Quincy Adams, Millard Fillmore, Rutherford B. Hayes, Grover Cleveland, Calvin Coolidge, and Franklin D. Roosevelt. The common genealogical root is Diana's great-great-great-grandfather, Joseph Strong, a Yale graduate in 1788, a Philadelphia surgeon, and a first cousin to both patriot Nathan Hale and a signer of the Declaration of Independence. The son of a Revolutionary soldier and patriot, Dr. Strong was Princess Diana's "gateway ancestor" to New England.

The Strong descendants, all distant kinsmen of Princess Diana, include a large group of notables from presidents to actors and other celebrities: Cary Grant, Humphrey Bogart, *Washington Post* editor Ben Bradlee, Amelia Earhart, Margaret Mead, Lydia Pinkham, Adlai Stevenson, Arthur Schlesinger, Jr., Cornelius Vanderbilt II, and even Benjamin Spock, whose book on baby care the Princess has surely consulted. President Ronald Reagan is connected genealogically through his ancestors Isaac Sheldon and Mary Woodford.

According to David Williamson of *Burke's Peerage*, there are genealogical connections with a large and varied group including opera star Enrico Caruso, film idol Rudolph Valentino, General George Patton, and Nelson Rockefeller. Humphrey Bogart and Diana are seventh cousins. The Windsors and the Spencers share a common descent from King Henry VII and his wife, and Diana is similarly a seventh cousin once removed of Prince Charles.

The Spencers' American connection flourished from Frank Work, a half-Scottish clerk from Chillicothe, Ohio, who became a millionaire stockbroker, and was worth some $15 million at his death in 1911. Work was incensed at American heiresses marrying money-hungry European peers—called it a "hanging offense"—and threat-ened to disinherit any of his children who did. It was not uncommon for newspaper ads to announce English peers who were willing to marry "at once, a very wealthy lady; her age and looks are imma-terial, but her character must be irreproachable."

Work's independent-minded daughter, Frances, promptly mar-ried the third Baron Fermoy. Several years and several children later, she divorced him to marry an untitled Rumanian chauffeur. One of her children, Maurice, later returned to England and claimed the Fermoy title. He became a member of Parliament, settled near San-dringham, and represented the town of King's Lynn.

Princess Diana's maternal grandfather, the fourth Baron Fermoy, was a Harvard graduate who served as an American Army captain in France in World War I. His mother, Diana's great-grandmother, Frances Burke Roche, was one of Mrs. Astor's "400" prominent socialites and died at eighty-nine in New York City.

Fermoy was forty-six when he met and married twenty-year-old Ruth Sylvia Gill, a young Scottish woman from Aberdeenshire. She was a brilliant pianist studying at the Paris Conservatory. King George V offered them a lease on Park House, near the royal estate in San-dringham. On the very day the King died in 1936, Queen Mary told her husband that Ruth, Lady Fermoy, had just given birth to her second daughter, fair-haired and blue-eyed Frances Ruth Roche.

Park House is large enough for a growing family. Edward VII built it as an overflow place for his guests and staff. The brick struc-ture had ten bedrooms with extended space for servants and garages, and it overlooked the royal parkland and the royal cricket grounds.

Lord Fermoy and the new King, George VI, were close friends who went shooting and played tennis together, and even teamed up in ice hockey games against visiting Americans. The two men were hunting together the day before the King died in 1952. Fermoy himself died three years later, whereupon Lady Fermoy became Lady-in-Waiting to Queen Elizabeth, the Queen Mother.

At the time, Lady of the Bedchamber to the Queen Mother was Cynthia Hamilton, Countess Spencer. She would become Diana's other grandmother.

The Countess Spencer was one of those classic British beauties with golden hair and clear fair skin. She was the daughter of the third Duke of Abercorn. Before she married Albert Edward John ("Jack"), seventh Earl Spencer, she had been heavily courted by the Prince of Wales—long before he met Wallis Simpson.

The seventh Earl Spencer, a godson of Edward VII, was a rude, forbidding man who occasionally carried a shotgun when he answered the door. He earned the nickname of "the curator Earl" because he knew the history of every picture, every piece of furniture and plate at Althorp. When a visitor arrived, Earl Spencer would check his shoes for dirt, then follow him with a duster. Distant cousin Winston Churchill once arrived to research his biography of their common ancestor, the Duke of Marlborough. When the Earl saw Churchill smoking a cigar in the library, "I ripped it right out of his mouth and stamped it on the floor."

There were still those who had a kind word for him. Said author Elizabeth Longford: "Anyone who was lucky enough to serve under him when he was chairman of the Victoria & Albert Museum's Advisory Council experienced the charm and wisdom of a true public servant."

The Spencer son, Edward John, whom everyone called "Johnny," was born in 1924, a godson of Queen Mary and the Prince of Wales. An only child, he was close to his mother, a loving, sympathetic, outgoing woman who could hold her own in the company of scholars, despite her scant formal education. No son could have been more different from his father: Johnny was easygoing, friendly, gentle, obliging in contrast to his curt, cold father. And while the erudite Earl Spencer preferred books, his amiable son adored animals.

Educated at Eton and Sandhurst, Johnny joined the Royal Scots Grays in Europe in World War II, and his gallantry was mentioned in numerous dispatches. After the war, he spent three years in south Australia as an aide to the Governor General, then became equerry to King George VI.

Socially, he was *the* catch of the county, heir to an old title, a fabulous house, and an outstanding art collection.

As the Viscount Althorp, he socialized in the set of the young Royals, often dating Princess Margaret, and double-dating with Princess Elizabeth and her new handsome husband, the Duke of Edinburgh. Then, when King George VI died, Viscount Althorp was asked to continue as equerry when the Princess became Queen Elizabeth. Later, he would become her Master of the Household.

In that tight, elevated social circle, the Spencers and the Fermoys, of course, knew each other. Frances Fermoy had developed an early schoolgirl crush on the Queen's dashing equerry. Educated by the usual string of governesses, she had followed the aristocratic pattern of living with a French family in Paris to study French, and then with an Italian family in Florence to study Italian. Like her mother, Frances was an accomplished pianist. She was only seventeen when, back in England, she again met her Johnny, who was then thirty, at a ball. They fell in love, and he asked her to marry him.

Johnny was headed for a six-month royal tour of Australia, and the spirited, romantic Frances was determined that he should have her portrait with him. She persuaded an artist to paint a life-size head of her in imperishable red oxide, in a single day, while she posed with only a short break for lunch, listening to classical music that included the St. John's Passion. Frances and her mother escorted the portrait aboard the *Britannia* as she said goodbye to her Johnny. All this would later be paralleled in the life of her own daughter, Diana.

Viscount Althorp, whom an Australian newspaper referred to as "Lord Allsop," was both a fisherman and a photographer. The Queen asked him to take movies of the royal tour, which he later edited as a fund-raising film for charity. He also made the news by catching a 222-pound marlin at Sydney. But the main gossip on the tour was the frequency of his phone calls to his fiancée. The Queen finally granted her love-struck equerry permission to leave the tour early, at Malta, to head home and prepare for his wedding.

There are not many weddings scheduled at Westminster Abbey, usually no more than three a year. In general they are for Royals, or those who serve the Abbey. The Spencer-Fermoy wedding rated the Abbey because all the Royals would be attending, including Her Majesty, the Queen. There were 1700 guests in the purple-cushioned pews, and a verger at the Great West Door said he knew which women to admit by their perfume. He could pick up a scent at twenty yards, he said, "and I've only been wrong once today."

The groom waited ten minutes at the altar because the Queen was late, and the bride delayed her arrival so as not to arrive before the Queen. It was a lavish wedding in white, with the couple passing under the raised swords of the Royal Scots Grays. Afterward a reception for 900 was held at St. James's Palace. The only photographer permitted to record the event was from the American magazine *Life*.

But the honeymoon was soon over. Because the young couple came to live in a house on the Althorp estate, the conflict between father and son son was constant. It was years before the two men managed a balanced relationship—but without affection. This was not the son Earl Spencer had wanted. In the same way, but more gradually, the new bride came to realize that this was not the husband she had wanted. He had traded in his equerry uniforms for a course at the nearby Royal Agricultural College. Johnny wanted to be a gentleman farmer. It was not the farmer she minded—it was the man.

Nine months after their marriage, their first child, Sarah Lavinia, was born. The Queen Mother acted as godparent. With the death of old Lord Fermoy, his wife offered Park House to the young couple in 1957. The gift was welcome and opportune: Shortly afterward, a second daughter, Cynthia Jane, was born. The Duke of Kent was godfather.

Park House was a paradise for children. It had trees for climbing and sweeping lawns for riding and running, and eventually even a heated swimming pool.

Asked what kind of a farmer he wanted to be, the Viscount Althorp admitted he "didn't know." He had bought a 250-acre farm at nearby Ingoldsthorpe, and his bride had added to it with an adjoining farm and cattle, bought with her own money. But the passion had gone out of the marriage. Frances's husband seemed happier with his animals than with people. There was his disappointment, too, for there was still no male heir to carry on the family name. A son was born in 1959, but had died the same day.

Then, on July 1, 1961, the couple had another child, disappointingly a third daughter. They had been so certain it would be a boy that they hadn't even selected a girl's name. It was not until a week later, when the local registrar knocked on their door to record the birth, that they finally decided on the name: Diana Frances. The christening came two months later at a local church in Sandringham, a far cry from Westminster Abbey where her oldest sister had been christened. Nor was there to be a royal godparent for this daughter. A Sandhurst classmate of her father, a cousin whose half-brother was the former Lord Privy Seal, a woman who had been part-time Lady-in-Waiting to Princess Alexandra, and two neighbors constituted Diana's godparents.

The baby weighed 7 pounds 12 ounces at birth, and her proud father had called her "a perfectly magnificent physical specimen." Fittingly enough, her birth announcement appeared above the Personal Column, on the left side of the front page of *The Times* of London.

Diana Frances was born in the year the Queen toured India, the year John F. Kennedy was inaugurated as the 35th president of the United States, the year the Russians built the Berlin Wall. It was also the year *West Side Story* won the Academy Award, Australia won the Davis Cup, and one of the most popular songs was "Love Makes the World Go Round."

2

The British monarchy," said a member of Parliament, is a "gang of lazy, idle parasites, living on wealth created by other people." Responding to this, the then Prince of Wales (later Duke of Windsor) said, "Parasites, maybe, but idle—never!"

The Prince of Wales pointed out that he had traveled over 150,000 miles to 45 countries and colonies, laid enough cornerstones to build a city, planted enough memorial trees to fill a forest.

"I'm one of those people who doesn't like sitting and watching something else go on," said Prince Charles. "I don't like going to the races. I leap in with both feet, and I don't believe in having a totally honorary position. I mean, if people want me to become a patron and just be a figurehead, they've got another think coming."

Lady Antonia Fraser put it aptly: "The British monarchy has an extraordinary ability to bend without breaking." It is a monarchy that has been around for a thousand years.

Many in Britain today consider the monarchy archaic and amusing, something that belongs in a historical museum, yet regard it with deep affection. Those who are not amused decry the cost of royalty as prohibitive, insisting that the money its upkeep requires would be better spent on hospitals and nursing homes. (The cost of the monarchy, including the maintenance of the royal yacht and the Queen's Flight of planes, is equivalent to the cost of maintaining three London museums.) And then there are the British intellectuals, many of whom seem slightly embarrassed by the whole thing.

Still, if you ask almost anyone in Britain whether they had a party to celebrate the wedding of Prince Charles and Lady Diana, the answer is "Why, *of course* we had a party!"

Everybody, all Britain, celebrated. Church bells pealed, guns

RALPH G. MARTIN

boomed, it was one big holiday in every pub, and in most private homes. Beer flowed, champagne poured, people were singing, laughing, cheering. The merriment extended into the streets.

The reason is simple: In the United States, a president is elected for four years, occasionally reelected for another four, and then goes back into the woodwork of history. In Britain, the nation's flag is never flown at half-mast for a king or queen who dies, for the line of succession is always assured: "The King is dead, long live the Queen." The British people see their Royals born, grow up, go to school, get married, have children—they become part of their extended family. Thus the Royal Family conveys a great feeling of continuity.

If you go to the Throne Room at Buckingham Palace to attend an investiture, a granting of royal honors to notable people, you walk past the hallowed halls lined with the priceless paintings of history, past the royal guards dressed in boots and spurs and swords and medieval helmets, all as stiff as statues.

Inside, the relatives of the honorees are quietly waiting, the sound of Scottish music adding gaiety to the dignity. There is a jarring note, however, when a voice over the loudspeaker asks, "Has anybody lost a pearl earring?" And, more jarring, the music suddenly switches to songs from *Oklahoma!* and Cole Porter. And then you remember somebody saying, "The monarchy in Britain walks the tightrope between the mystique and the relevant."

But the mocking of the monarchy ends as the national anthem sounds and everybody stands at attention, and even the men in wheelchairs stiffen. Then in come the yeomen in their ancient uniforms, followed by the Queen looking radiant in a brightly colored dress. Moving in careful rhythm before her is a long line of men and women in formal clothes, some of them kneeling on stools as Her Majesty's sword flashes in the air, tapping them on shoulders if she is creating knighthoods. As she hands them their medals and honors, she has pertinent words for each of them, plus a smile—with very little prompting from her equerry. She has done her homework well. One hundred and thirty people are honored in slightly over an hour, without hurry or fuss. It is impressive. It has dignity and drama.

Then there is the day the Queen opens Parliament. Although it is drizzly, the weather discourages nobody. The crowds are still massive in front of the Palace, and along the route. Promptly at

22

eleven the Palace gates open and the state carriages made of gold and glass, led by jet-black horses, are driven by uniformed footmen out of another age. You can see the Queen with the crown on her head, with her husband and son and daughter-in-law.

A disappointed photographer yells, "But I didn't get a shot of Diana!"

The Queen's entrance into Parliament is another moment of magic, complete with ancient rituals, unbending traditions. And while the speech she reads is actually written for her by a government official, every member of Parliament knows that this Queen is not only their Queen, but also the Queen of Canada, the Queen of Australia, the Queen of seventeen different countries and the Head of State of nearly fifty more in the Commonwealth. The British Empire is dead, but the Commonwealth is alive and well, and this Queen is their only contact to it. And, on Christmas Day, when the Queen speaks to the Commonwealth, as controversial as they may sometimes seem to be, the words and thoughts are her own.

In the days when Queen Victoria's nine children and forty grandchildren ruled the courts of Europe, a British schoolboy's definition of an island was "a piece of land surrounded by the British Navy." Nine kings rode with Queen Victoria to celebrate her Jubilee. As the monarchies of Europe disappeared one by one, it was predicted that there would soon be only five kings left: the king of hearts, the king of spades, the king of clubs, the king of diamonds, and the King of England.

Nothing can stop the flow of history, but the British monarchy today seems more durable than ever.

The Tudor despotism of the sixteenth century brought order to Britain after the baronial wars. Constitutional monarchy in the seventeenth and eighteenth centuries helped end the religious struggle. British royalty in the nineteenth century served as a symbol of security and a focus of national loyalty.

And what does the monarchy mean today?

"The popularity of the monarchy seems now to have become one of the most stable features of English public life," wrote the *New Statesman.*

Through Edward II, all the kings of England were of pure German descent. George I had been brought over from the small German principality of Hanover to become Britain's king. His son, great-grandson, and great-great-grandson, all Georges, followed and married German wives. A brother of the fourth George, who also married a German wife, became the father of Queen Victoria, who likewise married a German, Prince Albert of Saxe-Coburg-Gotha. Edward VII, Victoria and Albert's son, changed the trend by marrying Alexandra, daughter of the King of Denmark; but his son, George V, went back to the German line for his queen.

George V was a simple man of principle—dedicated, selfless, highly religious. He was happiest with his horses, his stamps, and playing poker. His belief in monarchy was almost devout: "The existence of the Crown," he declared, "serves to disguise change and therefore to deprive it of the evil consequences of revolution." On his desk he had a plaque whose words he made all his sons memorize: "I shall pass through this world but once. Any good thing, therefore, that I can do, or any kindness that I can show a human being, let me do it now. Let me not defer nor neglect it for I shall not pass this way again."

To this George V added his own unique footnote, especially intended for his wayward son the Prince of Wales, that he should not make himself too accessible to people. The King quoted: "The monarchy must always retain an element of mystery . . ." Bagehot had observed, "we must not let in daylight upon magic."

His was not, however, a loving family. "My father was frightened of his mother," George V told a friend. "I was frightened by my father, and I'm damned well going to see to it that my children are frightened of me."

"My father doesn't like me," said the then Prince of Wales, who added sadly, "I'm not at all sure I particularly like *him!*" Asked about his mother's lack of affection, the Prince replied curtly, "Too German."

"She sat like this, stiff as a statue, never bent to anyone," recalled novelist Barbara Cartland, who was presented to Queen Mary as a debutante. And yet, the Dowager Lady Patricia Hambleden, Lady-in-Waiting to Queen Elizabeth the Queen Mother, recalled the story of the Princess Royal teaching Queen Mary how to dance the shimmy behind a screen: "King George came in, saw it, and exploded."

At the death of his father, the Prince of Wales became Edward

VIII, and soon went elsewhere for affection. When the government refused to accept an American divorcée as his Queen, Edward abdicated to marry "the woman I love."

"I knew Wallis very well," said Barbara Cartland. "I knew her husband Ernest Simpson since I was seventeen. She just didn't understand the nonconformist conscience of this country, and the colonies. I remember her telling the King, 'The rabble will never let you go.' "

Edward's brother, Albert, the Duke of York, a shy, stammering man, became King George VI.

"Dickie, this is absolutely terrible," he told his cousin Lord Louis Mountbatten. "I'm quite unprepared for it. David (as Edward was known to his family) has been trained for this all his life. I've never even seen a State Paper. I'm only a naval officer." To which Mountbatten promptly replied: "There is no finer training for a king."

If he was not an intellectual, George VI was an honorable, virtuous man of simple piety. It was said of him that he was so full of unresolved tensions that he never knew true calm. His father had been a fierce man, and it was terrible when his father yelled at him and he could not reply, except to stammer. When he and Elizabeth were children together at a Christmas party in London in 1905, given by the Countess of Leicester, the precocious, exuberant five-year-old Elizabeth felt sorry for the painfully shy boy of ten and gave him the crystallized cherries from her sugar cake.

His full name was Albert Frederick Arthur George, but she called him "Bertie." When he courted her, he had been slim, fit, and handsome, an excellent tennis player (he won the RAF doubles at Wimbledon), and a squadron leader in the Royal Naval Air Force. When he was with her, he was so relaxed he almost never stammered.

He courted her for two years before she agreed to his marriage proposal. The Queen Mother pooh-poohs that now. "The story that he had asked me two or three times amused me. Do you think I am the sort of person Bertie would have to ask twice?"

When his brother abdicated, Bertie admitted, "I broke down and sobbed like a child." There was even some talk that the stammering Duke of York might be bypassed and the throne offered to his younger brother, the dashing George, Duke of Kent. Elizabeth herself called the kingship "an intolerable honor."

There were those close to her who claimed she had shared her husband's shock at becoming king, that she had cried for a week. The cynics, who feel that every woman wants to be queen, say that if she did cry, she shed tears of joy. But there is no question that she later denounced the Duchess of Windsor as "that damned woman who killed my husband" because she felt that ascending the throne had shortened her husband's life.

"When I first met her as Duchess of York, she was a very quiet little thing, terribly shy," said Barbara Cartland. "She blossomed when she became Queen. Asked whether she was tired after the coronation, she said, 'No, these people gave me something.'"

It is one thing to be born and bred a Royal, to know that some day you will be king or queen; it is quite another thing for a commoner—however uncommon—to become one. Elizabeth Angela Marguerite Bowes-Lyon was born at the turn of the century, the youngest child in a family of nine, to the Earl and Countess of Strathmore, titled Scots of distinction. (Years later in Africa, a young indignant native pushed his way toward her and enumerated all the problems Africans were having with the English. She listened intently, then said, "I know exactly what you mean. We Scots also have had our problems with the English.")

Her young life was spent in the quiet country hunting and fishing, with horses, music, painting, and sewing.

It did not prepare her to be a Queen. Her ancestors had shed their blood for the kings of Scotland, but her father wanted none of his family involved with the royal court. But Elizabeth had a mind of her own. She was an extraordinarily pretty and vivacious young woman, and Bertie seemed so shy and quiet. When she finally accepted his proposal, King George V wrote in his diary, "Bertie is a lucky man."

She was Duchess of York for a dozen years before her husband became king. The consensus of their closest friends was that George VI could not have endured his role without her. She helped him practice proper breathing to minimize his stammer—it had caused long silences and obvious stage fright in his first radio broadcasts. When people came to her for help in royal decisions, she would always say, "First I must ask the King." He relied on her for much: her common sense, strong instinct, the smiling serenity of her courage. Complimented once on a speech, the King looked toward his wife and said lovingly, "She helps me."

Whether she ate hot dogs with President and Mrs. Roosevelt at Hyde Park, or danced a jubilant Scottish reel, or shook a thousand hands, somehow she maintained an easy smiling buoyancy, no matter how tired she was. Admiring the Queen, a southern U.S. Senator slapped the King on the back and said, "My, you're a great Queen-picker."

The King developed lung cancer, and began to use a tanning lotion for his face so the people would not sense his illness. But the more "burnt-out" he became, the more bubbly she was. She took whatever burden she could from him, increased her own schedule of engagements. Whenever he needed her, she cancelled everything to be with him.

When the Germans began their blitz of Britain in World War II, the public and press urged the Queen to take their two young daughters to the safety of Canada. Her reply sounded like a clarion: "The Princesses cannot go without me. I cannot go without the King. The King will never go."

The most heavily blitzed part of London was the East End, and the Queen went there often. Asked whether she felt it was appropriate to "wear her best dress" on her visits, she answered simply, "Of course. They would wear their best dresses if they were coming to see me." When an East End official said how honored they were to have her come, she stared at the smoldering ruins and cut him short: "The honor is purely mine." And when the Germans bombed part of Buckingham Palace, she said something the British never forgot: "I'm almost comforted we've been hit. It makes me feel I can look the blitzed East End in the face. They are so brave."

Winston Churchill called her "that most valiant woman," and Hitler said she was the most dangerous woman in Europe. She never had a finer compliment.

Through the deprivations of the postwar years and the death of the King from lung cancer in 1952, the Queen's extraordinary loyalty to the British nation never wavered.

She seldom cried. She learned how to stand still at a parade no matter how tired she was. She even learned how to ignore biting flies in the heat. When someone asked her how she could be so brave, she said quietly, "Not when I am alone."

People felt of Queen Elizabeth the Queen Mother that she was the least royal of the Royals. As Kenneth Harris put it, she was "the one who was most like 'us' . . . ." Unlike her relatives, the Queen Mother always talked about "my daughter" instead of "the Queen" and "my grandson" rather than "the Prince of Wales."

"The King is dead, long live the Queen!"

A Scottish fortune teller once told Elizabeth Bowes-Lyon that she would be a Queen, and the mother of a Queen. And now, indeed, her twenty-six-year-old daughter was Queen Elizabeth II.

Her father lying in state in Westminster Hall, the young monarch made a short speech to the British people, then excused herself, saying "My heart is too full"—and wept on her husband's shoulder.

Her mother wore black for a year, seldom spoke in public. Princess Marie Louise once complimented the Queen Mother on her composure, and she answered quietly, "Not in private." It was Sir Winston Churchill who persuaded her to come back to public life. She would be a widow longer than she had been a wife, "this great mother-figure and nanny to us all," but, as one of her senior staff said, "Not a day goes by without the King's name being mentioned."

The new Queen's beloved grandfather, George V, whom she called "Grandpapa England," had given her the nickname Lilibet because that was how she lisped her own name as a child. He had told her, too, that she must learn how to ride a horse: "The English people like riding and it would make you very unpopular if you could not do so."

When she was a girl, she and her grandfather had a game they played. At a specified time, the two of them would get binoculars and try to sight each other—he from Buckingham Palace and she from her window at 145 Piccadilly, home of the Duke and Duchess of York. And then they would wave.

She adored her Uncle David, the Prince of Wales, who always played games with her when he visited. When she saw the newspaper headlines during the abdication crisis, the ten-year-old Elizabeth asked, "Is Uncle David in trouble?" When she learned from a footman that he had indeed abdicated, and Papa was King, she rushed to tell her sister, Margaret.

"Does that mean that you will have to be the next Queen?" Margaret wanted to know.

"Yes. Someday."

"Poor you," said Margaret.

Her father, George VI, had predicted that when Lilibet became Queen, she "will be lonely forever."

Much of the freedom and some of the fun disappeared when Elizabeth's father became King. There was now always a detective and a policeman with her wherever she went. She now curtsied before her father instead of rushing to kiss him. She now referred to her parents as the King and the Queen, instead of Papa and Mummy. And now, more often than ever, she would ask her governess about her busy parents. "Do you think I shall see them tonight?"

Nevertheless, the King and Queen provided a home where every room was open to the children, where "Mummy" and "Papa" joined in pillow fights with the girls. It was a home of hugs and kisses and books to be read. Their mother had had such a lyrical childhood and insisted her daughters would too. Their father had had none of it and wanted them to have all of it.

Elizabeth was tutored in history, geography (particularly the Commonwealth countries), and her heritage. "I am partly English and partly Scottish." Then she paused and added, "But I think I am other mixtures too: Some of it is Hungarian." (Queen Mary's grandmother had been a Hungarian countess.)

Even at the age of ten, Elizabeth read books on horses and declared that the best thoroughbred was a cross between a Hungarian breed and an Arabian. She herself rode well by the age of six.

When told they were going to move to Buckingham Palace, the reluctant Elizabeth asked, "Do you mean forever?" Her sister, Margaret, four years younger, feisty and full of fun, was equally reluctant. Margaret was more of an extrovert than Elizabeth, and less solemn. She also had a gift for music and mimicry. "If you see somebody with a funny hat," Elizabeth told her once before a garden party, "you must not point at it and laugh." Occasionally Margaret might bite Elizabeth in a short fight and Elizabeth would complain, "Margaret always wants what I want." Generally though, the two sisters became close, giggling friends, members of the same Buckingham Palace Girl Guide pack that was made up of children of Court officials and employees. The Guide pack had the use of the thirty acres of the Palace gardens, with its own boating lake as their private playground.

Despite the difference in their ages, the two princesses were dressed almost identically throughout their childhoods, down to the color of their strap shoes. But the sisters could not have been more different.

Margaret was dressed once as an angel for a fancy dress party. "You don't look very angelic, Margaret," her mother told her. Margaret smiled mischievously. "That's all right, I'll be a Holy Terror."

Elizabeth always looked and acted like a little queen—disciplined, orderly, systematic. "Isn't it lucky," Margaret told her mother, "that Lilibet's the eldest?"

Lilibet agreed.

But her destiny still didn't seem to faze her. When Lajos Lederer was sculpting her she gave him an autographed photograph saying, "This is the first time I signed my name since I became heir to the throne."

Princess Elizabeth first met Prince Philip of Greece at the Royal Naval College at Dartmouth in July of 1939, when she was thirteen. The Royal Family had arrived there on a cruise aboard the yacht *Victoria and Albert*. New cadet Philip, aged eighteen, was assigned to look after the two princesses. King George VI, meanwhile, was spending the day reminiscing with his cousin, Lord Louis Mountbatten, Philip's uncle. The girls' governess recalled that Philip was offhand and bored. But he was quite handsome, "fair-haired . . . rather like a Viking, with a sharp face and piercing blue eyes." After ginger crackers and lemonade, he said, "Let's go to the tennis courts and have some real fun jumping the nets."

When the royal yacht finally steamed away, Dartmouth cadets rowed after it, but they all gave up the chase except for Philip, whom Elizabeth "watched . . . fondly through an enormous pair of binoculars."

Prince Philip of Greece in fact had no Greek blood. He was descended from the Danish Royal Family, who were sent all over Europe to become monarchs of different countries, from Russia to Rumania. Philip's grandfather was a king and his great-great-grandmother was a queen. He could boast more blue blood than Elizabeth, tracing his ancestry back to Charlemagne. His family had been exiled from the throne of Greece, then recalled, then exiled again on a British light cruiser. On the journey the infant Philip slept in an improvised cot made from orange crates.

He had been born, almost as simply, on a dining room table on the island of Corfu in 1921. He was a fat, belligerent baby with four much older sisters—all of whom married German princes. The exiled family lived for a while in Paris at the home of his mother's brother, George, second Marquess of Milford Haven, elder brother to the more celebrated Lord Louis Mountbatten. Uncle George, a kind and loving man, sent Philip to school at Cheam, in England.

Philip's father soon became a Monte Carlo playboy and his mother donned the flowing robes of the Christian Sisterhood of Martha and Mary. "My mother's life is her own business," Philip later said. As for his father, he said, "I don't think anybody thinks I had a father. Most people think that Dickie's (Lord Louis Mountbatten) my father . . ."

Lord Louis took his nephew in hand after his brother George died in 1938. Philip was by then in Scotland at Gordonstoun.

"The Mountbattens had this squalid little house on Chester Street," said Barbara Cartland. "Prince Philip came to live with them and stayed on the top floor—what we thought of before the war as the servant's bedroom. I remember when the charwoman went in to clean his room, she used to tell him, 'Put your long legs up on the bed because I've got to clean under the bed.'

"I would say he was very much on his own as a young man, brought up very liberal, nothing grand about it. And I know he was tremendously influenced by the extraordinary lives the Mountbattens led."

Following the family tradition of both grandfathers and both uncles, Philip joined the Navy and saw combat during World War II. His ship took part in the Sicily invasion, and he later fought in the war against Japan. His bravery was mentioned in dispatches.

Uncle Louis helped him become a British citizen, and gently prompted his marriage to Elizabeth.

"I mean, after all, if you spend ten minutes thinking about it—and a lot of these people spent a great deal more time thinking about it," Prince Philip was to muse later, "how many eligible young men living in this country were available?"

During the war, eighteen-year-old Elizabeth Alexandra Mary Windsor enlisted in the Auxiliary Territorial Service and learned to read a map, change a tire, strip an engine, drive in a convoy. On the Princess's night table throughout the war was a picture of Prince

Philip. He had visited at the Palace, gone to the theater with the family, come for Christmas. She had sent him socks she had knitted. They had corresponded.

"I suppose one thing led to another," Philip said. It was at Balmoral in 1946 when they first began talking seriously about marriage. Her father thought she was too young at twenty and needed time to think it over. He planned a prolonged trip for the Royal Family to South Africa. As a parting gift, Philip gave Elizabeth a recording of "People Will Say We're in Love." She reportedly played it continuously. By the time they returned, said Prince Philip, "It was sort of fixed up."

Philip won the King's favor at Balmoral by showing his frugality. He had come for the weekend without tweeds or formal clothes, except for a dinner jacket given him by Lord Mountbatten. Philip never even bothered with slippers or wore pajamas.

The wedding, on November 20, 1947, was held at Westminster Abbey. When King George VI made his son-in-law Duke of Edinburgh he said, "I wonder if he knows what he's taking on. One day Lilibet will be Queen and he will be Consort. And that's much harder than being a King."

On their honeymoon in Scotland, Philip brought along only two suitcases; his bride took fifteen, plus her pet corgi, Susan, and two hot-water bottles. Two of their best friends at the time, Eileen and Michael Parker, remember them as a loving, laughing couple who brought the usual bottle of gin when they came to dinner. And Philip delighted in making his own cheese soufflé. It was impossible to enjoy it in the Palace, he said, because "by the time it gets from the kitchen to the table, it goes flat."

Of the two, Elizabeth was the one more obviously in love. Less than a year after their wedding, part of the royal nursery at Buckingham Palace was transformed into a surgical ward and on November 14, 1948, Charles Philip Arthur George was born.

Prince Philip, who was playing squash with Michael Parker, raced upstairs when he got the news and had a huge bouquet of roses and carnations for his wife to see as soon as she woke from the anesthesia.

When Elizabeth looked at her son's fine long fingers—"quite unlike mine and certainly unlike his father's"—she noted, "it will be interesting to see what they become."

Charles & Diana

The year 1948 saw Gandhi assassinated. It was the year Queen Wilhelmina of the Netherlands abdicated in favor of her daughter, Juliana. Harry Truman was elected President of the United States, and a favorite American song was "All I Want for Christmas Is My Two Front Teeth."

And it was the year a future king of England was born.

33

3

Those who only slightly knew Diana Frances Spencer claimed that she was sweet, lovely, and liked children—but that she was "as thick as two short planks."

Those who knew her better said she was street-smart, had an amazing instinct about people, a refreshing honesty, and more common sense than a dozen academics.

Those who knew her best added that it takes an extraordinary young woman to emerge without real trauma from being an ordinary teenager in jeans to assuming the role of the future Queen of England. They agree she doesn't read many books, but how many Royals do? The favorite known reading matter of both the Queen and the Queen Mother—which the footman delivers on a silver platter—is *Sporting Life*.

Before she became a princess, Diana Spencer was discussing somebody with Stephen Barry, then valet to Prince Charles. "You know how many O levels (academic achievement tests in specific subjects) she has?" Diana asked in awe.

"How many?"

"Nine!" said Diana.

"And how many do you have?" asked Barry.

Diana hesitated. "Two."

"Don't worry," said Barry, "you've done more with your two than she has with her nine."

It is questionable whether she even had two.

Diana's stepmother confided to an intimate: "How can you have an intelligent conversation with someone who only had a single O level? It's a crashing bore!" But whether Diana had two or one or none means little to the British public.

In assessing Princess Diana's qualities, it is generally agreed that her sweetness derives from her paternal grandmother, Cynthia, Countess Spencer. She inherits her tall, blond loveliness—as well as her strong will—from her mother. Some of her love of music comes from her maternal grandmother, Ruth, Lady Fermoy. And her amiability, kindness, and easygoing nature come from her father.

Diana had the same governess as her mother—Gertrude Allen, whom she called Ally. Ally was a local institution in nearby West Norwalk, having taught coveys of young aristocrats to read and write. She was then white-haired, in her sixties, and lived several miles away in a small cottage. Ally was also responsible for teaching Diana to be neat, tidy, perfectly turned out and proper.

Most people agree that Diana was a delightful little girl, if sometimes on the prim side. When she was born, her older sisters Sarah and Jane treated her like a practice doll. And when they went away to school, she had the whole nursery wing to herself.

In time, too, Diana had her own live practice doll to diaper, feed, and bathe—a brother, Charles. "She has always loved babies," recalled Ally. "Babies and soft toys. She was a very sweet-natured little girl."

She could also be a tomboy. She missed her brother's christening because she had hurt her head in a fall. As soon as she was able, she had learned to slide down the stone steps of the house on a metal tray. And she could be devious. Told not to do something, she would neither cry nor be defiant or confrontational, but she would somehow still manage to do what she wanted. Nanny Janet Thompson recalled a case in point: She had scolded Diana for not eating the crusts of her tea sandwiches, and later was pleased when she no longer saw any crusts on the table. Thompson was not pleased, however, when she eventually found piles of crusts hidden under the ledge of the nursery table. The stubborn Diana had simply put them aside.

There are those who say that Diana's husband first saw her when she was in diapers, and he was twelve. She smiled at that. "A lot of nice things happened to me when I was in nappies." Diana's mother met Charles when he was also in diapers, and later watched over Charles at children's parties. In the same way, the Queen once placed her hand close to the ground and laughingly remarked about Diana, "I knew her when she was so high."

The closest neighbors of the Spencers at Park House were not the Royals, but Reverend Patrick Ashton and his family, who lived at the nearby rectory, and the Sandringham land agent Julian Loyd.

Their daughters, Penelope Ashton and Alexandra Loyd, were among Diana's closest friends.

Children like Diana were taught early to speak when spoken to, chew with their mouths closed, sit up straight, smile and shake hands when introduced, and disappear silently. Parents arrived shortly before bedtime to say goodnight. Her father, however, did say of the nursery: "This is a wonderful room for playing bears in. We used to play bears here on our hands and knees."

When her brother arrived, Diana would accompany her mother on walks with the baby in the pram. And, once a year, she would attend her grandmother's piano recital at her music festival at King's Lynn. The Queen Mother always came, too, and so got to know Diana a little better.

Whenever the Queen Mother came to Sandringham, Diana also got to see both her grandmothers, who were the Queen Mother's ladies-in-waiting. She seldom saw her grandfather, Lord Fermoy, who still feuded with his son. "My father hated people," Earl Spencer insisted.

In contrast, Diana's father loved people. He played on the local cricket team with Julian Loyd, worked with a local opera group, and set off a marvelous spectacle of rockets every Guy Fawkes Day. The Viscount Althorp was so conscientious about his many meetings and causes, some of which required four hours of driving each night, that Diana often asked, "When's Daddy coming home?"

His wife often asked the same question.

Frances Fermoy was restless. She felt that her husband spent more time with his committees and the animals on his farm than he did with her. In searching for things to do, she even became a volunteer bus driver for neighboring parishes. She was not impressed with the fact that her husband's grumpy father was seventy-five, and that Johnny would someday soon be the 8th Earl Spencer. She considered Althorp too bleak a place to live, and too remote. With her two older daughters now away at boarding school, she had time for more frequent trips to London. Young Diana's mother had grown into a sophisticated, stylish woman who liked concerts, theater, people, parties.

And she had fallen in love with another man.

His name was Peter Shand-Kydd, an Edinburgh University graduate, a Navy veteran, and forty-two. He was married to a lovely and talented artist, and had three children. He had inherited his father's wallpaper business, but had no interest in it. Instead, he took his family to Australia, starting a 500-acre sheep farm there. He brought his family back to Britain when the venture failed. The Shand-Kydds and the Spencers had met at a dinner party. Diana's mother was then thirty-one.

Restless and romantic as she was, Frances saw him as "a bit of a gypsy," and a charmer. According to the first Mrs. Shand-Kydd, her husband and Lady Spencer became lovers that spring in South Kensington.

Diana's mother now took a flat in Cadogan Place in London and told the press, "We are living apart now. It is very unfortunate. I don't know whether there will be a reconciliation or anything like that." Her husband described the separation as "a thunderbolt, a terrible shock. How many of those fourteen years were happy? I thought all of them, until the moment we parted. I was wrong. We hadn't fallen apart. We'd drifted apart."

A servant described the scene simply. "One day she was just not there anymore."

For the Spencers' two older daughters, it was an emotional trauma. They loved their gentle father as much as their sparkling mother. For six-year-old Diana and her younger brother, it was a fresh excitement. Their nanny took them on the train to join their mother in London. Diana went to a day school while her three-year-old brother went to kindergarten. On most weekends, they would head back again to Park House to see their father. But the original excitement soon grew into sad, lonely weekend treks of torn emotions.

The whole family was together at Park House for Christmas of 1967—their last Christmas together. "Johnny now insisted that Diana and Charles should be sent to school in King's Lynn, seven miles from Park House," said their mother, "and that they should henceforth stay at the house with him. He refused to let them return to London."

In this decision, Viscount Althorp had the full support of their family and friends. Even Lady Fermoy was bitter enough at her daughter's actions to side with Johnny. In that tight, aristocratic circle, there were certain things that one did not do, especially when one had four young children.

But Diana's mother disagreed, and sued for custody. British law generally favors the mother's custody. Unfortunately for her, Peter Shand-Kydd's wife had sued earlier for divorce, branding Diana's mother as an adulteress. Shand-Kydd lost custody of his three children, and Frances Roche Spencer lost even more.

Her own custody case then came up, in June of 1968, when she sued Viscount Althorp for divorce charging cruelty. He countersued, branding her an adulteress in the Shand-Kydd case. The court trial was prolonged, bitter, and highly publicized.

Diana was then almost seven years old, a student at Silfield School in King's Lynn where the emphasis was on good manners. "'Shut up' was a swear word." It was a large house with three adjacent wooden buildings for classrooms, and in fact didn't look like a school at all. Children came to the house only to eat at the low yellow tables, or to go to the bathroom. The discipline was old-fashioned and learning was by rote. Diana was in a class of fifteen boys and girls, all of whom wore red and yellow uniforms. Her close friend Alexandra Loyd was there as well.

Diana's father was careful to deliver the children on time (solemn little Charles went to a nursery section in the mornings), put their Wellington boots in the proper place, and be there punctually to pick them up. When he couldn't come, he sent his gardener, whom Diana called Smithy.

The girls were surely old enough to read and comprehend the newspaper headlines concerning their parents' divorce scandal, and to overhear others discussing it. Diana's grandmothers came often now to provide an emotional buffer, not just for the children but for their shocked father. "I was distressed, even though I got custody of the children," he said. "I never thought I'd marry again. I just wanted to bring up my children. It was very hard alone."

It was hard for Diana and her younger brother too. She grew closer to him, tried to mother him. She grew even more mischievous. "She was a bit of a nuisance then," said the butler, Ainsley Pendry, who used to chase her out of the kitchen, and pull her off the banister. Her favorite cat, Marmalade, died. Ally left. Ally recalled how Diana loved stories with happy endings, especially about kings and queens.

She spent more time alone in her nursery cutting and pasting and painting. She still rode her bicycle furiously down the long gravel path. But she fell off her pony and broke her arm. It took three months to heal and she never wanted to ride horses again.

Diana said afterward that she had "adored" her two years at Silfield. Headmistress Jean Lowe had been impressed by how well Diana knew how to read and how clearly she wrote. Lowe also observed that Diana dedicated all her school drawings to "Mummy and Daddy," but that she never talked about her mother at school.

The divorce became final in April of 1969, and Diana's mother married Peter Shand-Kydd within the month at a quiet civil service. They bought a house with a big garden at Itchenor on the coast of Sussex, and Diana and her brother started commuting again on weekends and some holidays. Diana liked it there because she could swim as much as she liked, and sail.

Her father also tried to give her more of his time. He took her to his farm to see a new calf. She had his love of animals, and she seemed to concentrate much of her affection on a tan and white guinea pig called Peanuts. She won first prize with it at the Fur and Feather Section of the Sandringham Fair. For her seventh birthday, her father surprised her with a camel named Bert that he had borrowed from the Dudley Zoo for the afternoon party. Twenty incredulous children took turns riding on the camel while its keeper walked it back and forth across the garden.

But she kept her mother's picture next to her bed. She was still "the kind of child who was always first to put a log on the fire or would go around the house in winter closing the shutters." She was always compulsively neat, making sure her brother put away his toys.

The staff noted that she laughed less often now and her quiet was deeper, her smile more quizzical. They nicknamed her The Duchess because she seemed to have developed a self-possessed grace, a private presence unusual in such a little girl. She now dressed her teddy bear in her brother's baby clothes, and no longer seemed interested in dolls. Swimming was a solitary pastime, and she seemed to swim more, becoming expert at it.

Diana's next school was Riddlesworth Hall, which also emphasized manners and respect. She was nine when she entered, gawky and growing fast. Her mother took her shopping at Harrods in London for the proper school uniform: gray skirt, gray knee-length socks, gray Harris tweed coat, a cherry headband.

Riddlesworth Hall was in Norfolk, only two hours away from her father's home, in the hedgeless fields and woodlands that she loved. Surrounding the school were woods of beech, rows of ripening corn, and the sharp smell of fresh air. Earl Spencer, who kept a full photographic record of his children, took her picture the day Diana went to Riddlesworth. With her shoulder-length blond hair, off the collar, she gave him a look of sunny cheerfulness mixed with a trace of teasing.

"That was a dreadful day," he said. "Dreadful losing her."

Riddlesworth was formal and traditional in its teaching methods. The school prospectus said, "The basis of a good education has always been the family . . . every child will have the opportunity to be good at something." . . . Headmistress Elizabeth Ridsdale—known to the 120 girls as Riddy—wanted her school to be a warm, friendly surrogate home. Diana needed that most of all.

Diana did relax more at Riddlesworth. It was the kind of school that used an old cowbell to wake up the girls at 7:30. After breakfast, the students made their beds, met for prayers, and fed their pets. There was a Pets Corner, and Diana brought along Peanuts. (Birds were no longer permitted because a macaw had made improper remarks.) Children learned multiplication tables by memorizing and chanting them aloud.

Headmistress Riddy admitted, "I can't remember her awfully well because she was a perfectly ordinary nice little girl." Diana, she said, "was extremely average . . . but she did try hard." Riddy taught the arts and crafts course, and again didn't recall Diana excelling in any of it but was impressed by "how awfully sweet she was with the little ones."

What made Diana less homesick was that some of her Silfield friends were also at Riddlesworth. Also, her mother and father alternated visiting on weekends, always with "tuck" boxes. Her father still has her first tuck list, written in a child's round, careful handwriting: "Big choc. cake, ginger biscuits, Twiglets."

Diana loved sweets. Children were rationed one piece of candy a day, and Diana gorged on her hoarded candy on Saturday and Sunday after lunch, during rest period. Her favorite candy was something called "cream egg."

Sunday meant sausages for breakfast and dressing up in her fancy best with hat and gloves. Diana hated the required heavy black walking shoes, however. Her favorite hymn at church, which she was allowed to select as a senior (and which she later selected for her wedding), was "I Vow to Thee My Country."

Her private time came during the Sunday afternoon walk past Goose Girl's Cottage on One Tree Hill. The place was so personal that some of the girls even gave names to their favorite climbing trees, and always carved their initials in the bark.

Diana was always faithful in writing to her parents at least once a week. Teachers liked her because she was neat, obedient, and always volunteered to help. She even won the Legatt Cup for helpfulness at the end of her first year.

Diana was eleven when her paternal grandmother, Cynthia, died in 1972. Countess Spencer was the grandmother whom Diana most closely resembled physically and in personality. Diana remembered her as the warm woman who showed her the fascinating huge attics at Althorp, filled with everything from old pictures to forgotten chamber pots. Diana went to her memorial service in London, and the Queen Mother was there as well. Diana's older sisters were sensitive enough to realize that their grandfather might now be lonelier than ever, and they started writing him letters. His answers, belying the rough frost of his reputation, were surprisingly charming and tender. What they learned was how much he had hated Latin, arithmetic, and French irregular verbs. "I also would have liked to have hanged, drawn, and quartered the writer of the Greek grammar."

The old earl died in 1975 but before he did, he and his son became largely reconciled. Much of the credit for that went to Raine, Countess Dartmouth, a dynamic woman of forty-five, and the wife of Johnny's old friend, Lord Dartmouth. Raine was the daughter of the celebrated author Barbara Cartland who had written some 360 books, mostly romantic novels with happy endings, but also everything else from cookbooks to biographies. A noted beauty of her time, Barbara Cartland had had a long-lasting romance with Lord Mountbatten after the death of his wife.

"I loved Dickie. I don't pretend I didn't, but we were far too old to be anything but very close and, if you like, romantic friends." His photographs were everywhere in her mansion. "Just before he was assassinated," said Cartland, "he told me 'What I want from you is a novel.' So I said, 'Well, that's all right, darling. You'll do the naval part, and I'll do the love.' We wrote five chapters before he was killed."

Raine was a public figure in her own right, who often made headlines campaigning on issues for the Greater London Council on everything from the cracked cups at the London airport to the banning of the film *Ulysses*. A television personality, a forceful speaker, she was also a woman of much humor and fun.

When Johnny brought Raine to meet his father, "she amused and provoked old Jack Spencer and he, in turn, was kinder to Johnny. It was as though she charmed them both," said a close friend.

Johnny and Raine were then collaborating on a book for the Greater London Council called *What Is Our Heritage?* She wrote the text, he took the photographs.

"She came to me," said Barbara Cartland, "and said, 'Mummy, I'm madly in love, just like one of your heroines.'" Barbara Cartland added, "What could I do? You've got to stand by your daughter."

"My fault is I fell madly in love with a man when I was forty-five," said Raine. "Most women turn to good work when they're over forty, but I'd done mine. I had eighteen years in local government and twenty-six in public life. I wanted some privacy. But since I'd been talking my head off for years, nobody could understand my keeping quiet.

"I've been more lucky than I deserve, and I suppose people resent it, to be married to two wonderful husbands and have four beautiful children of my own. When I met Johnny, his marriage had been over for years, and he was a very lonely and unhappy man.

"I'd been helping with his work, and later with his house opening. I never thought falling in love would happen but you know how these things happen gradually, until you discover you just can't live without the other person."

Diana's father added: "I had my chances with girls. I took out one or two girls, but in London, not at home. Somehow they didn't seem, well, suitable. Raine had brains and beauty, and she came to me as an older and wiser woman. She's much better now than when she was rushing about, getting half a page in *Who's Who*, long before she met me."

"The first bouquet Raine ever gave was to the Queen (now the Queen Mother)," said Barbara Cartland of her daughter. "And I don't know who was the shyest. Raine used to go to the children's parties with Princess Elizabeth and the other young Royals at Londonderry House."

Shortly after Johnny became the 8th Earl Spencer, he moved to the ancestral 8,488-acre estate of Althorp, and Raine was seen there much more often. A member of the household staff punned to the press, "It never Raines but it pours."

Diana was then fourteen and, following in the footsteps of her mother and two sisters, was a student at West Heath School near Sevenoaks in Kent. Her older sister, Sarah, had starred in the West

Heath school plays, excelled in everything from piano to lacrosse, passed six O levels, then was expelled at sixteen for drinking "because I was bored."

Sarah had been the true tomboy as a child, a redhead with a terrible temper. "I tended to break the furniture." She also rode her pony into the house so he could meet her grandmother.

Sister Jane was still at West Heath when Diana arrived. Quieter and more controlled than Sarah, Jane was captain of the lacrosse team and had passed eleven O levels.

Both older sisters were bitter about their potential new step-mother and gave Diana partisan accounts of everything that was happening. Diana's mother, meanwhile, had moved with her new husband to a plain whitewashed farmhouse at the end of a road-causeway overlooking Loch Caitlin on the island of Seil on the iso-lated west coast of Scotland. They had a sheep farm of a thousand acres, with Diana's mother acting as bookkeeper, and breeding her own very small Shetland ponies. She opened a gift shop a dozen miles away in the fishing village of Oban, and even talked of starting a toy factory. Diana came there on school holidays, and occasionally brought a friend. Everybody wore jeans and Diana went fishing, boating, searching for lobsters, and helped her mother at the gift shop.

Diana was beginning to look more and more like her mother. They both had the same blond beauty, the same lovely legs, the same way of flashing their eyes or pursing their lips to show impatience, the same smile. Both had been born in the same room of the same house, had walked the same wooded walks, played on some of the same lawn with some of the same toys. Her mother even could tell her about West Heath, because she too had gone there, and had been "captain of everything."

West Heath had been founded in 1865 as a religiously oriented school "to develop confidence and character." Its prospectus stressed "a general education to train the students to develop their own minds and tastes and realize their duties as citizens." Set in a lovely woodland of 32 acres with a great country house, it was the kind of place that named its dormitories after flowers. Its royal pride was Princess May of Teck, who had been a student there before becoming the Princess of Wales and later Queen Mary.

Principal Ruth Rudge indicated early to her students that she was more interested in letting them develop at their own speed, rather

43

than stretching them. Nor did she want her girls to get too attached to "a best friend," because, as she said, "they're bound to break up and have trauma."

One of Diana's close friends at West Heath was Carolyn Pride, who later became a roommate in London. Carolyn described Diana then as "someone with whom you could never be bored . . . a very companionable person. I loved her sense of humor. I loved her thoughtfulness and kindness." Another classmate, Diana Chamberlain McDonald, added, "She was the sort to help anybody who looked miserable or unhappy. She was always the first to offer a smile."

Principal Ruth Rudge recalled that Diana would visit an old woman who lived nearby, making her tea, and doing some of her shopping, but mainly supplying company and conversation. She also helped out at a center for handicapped children. She seemed to have an easy way with children. "She was a girl who noticed what needed to be done, then did it willingly and cheerfully," said Rudge.

Rudge pointed out quickly that Diana was not a goody-goody girl. She had her own share of minor infractions: talking when the lights were out, hiding extra chocolates, making other girls giggle by saying something at the worst possible time. Punishments involved polishing brass, weeding the garden, cleaning extra baths. "She wasn't good all the time and she wasn't bad all the time," said Rudge. "A perfectly ordinary girl." Rudge's most vivid memory of Diana was the way she dressed, often in bright red dungarees. "She had a sense of color. And she was meticulous about the way she looked."

She was neater than most, and cleaner. Each girl was scheduled to have three baths a week—Diana managed to take one every night, even if the lights were out. She washed her hair more often, too, as well as her clothes.

Surely her classmates were highly aware of the scandal of her parents' divorce, and the charges of adultery. Rudge made her office open to any girl with problems, but this was not something Diana would discuss with her or anyone else. What her classmates most remembered about Diana was how very private and very controlled she was. As one of them put it, "She did not wear her emotions on her sleeve."

As a former student, her sister Sarah could visit whenever she wanted, and she did. She and Diana would have tea or lunch together.

Jane did the same thing after she graduated. And when they talked about Raine, as they always did, they had a bitter phrase they repeated: "Raine, Raine, go away . . ."

Lord Dartmouth had sued Raine for divorce, charging Earl Spencer with adultery. The Court gave Dartmouth custody of the four children. Raine and Johnny were soon married in a quiet civil ceremony, without the presence of any of their children.

The new Countess Spencer quickly took charge of Althorp.

Althorp lies about 75 miles northwest of London in the heart of Northamptonshire. It is a treasure house of art, with one of the finest private collections in Europe. A 115-foot gallery upstairs contains ancestral portraits, many of them by family friend Sir Joshua Reynolds. On the ground floor the china cabinets have hundreds of pieces of rare porcelain. When Raine came, she brought a portrait of herself as well as one of her McCorquodale ancestors to add to the collection.

"When my father died," said Earl Spencer, "I was left with debts of two and a quarter million pounds. That meant something had to go to meet the punitive death duties. I hate selling anything that belongs to the family, but what am I supposed to do? It costs us 80,000 pounds a year to keep up Althorp House, and obviously not all of that comes from revenue from the visiting public. I'm afraid you must blame this country's tax laws, not me."

With her usual energy, the new Countess Spencer was determined to make Althorp the best restored house in England. The staff soon felt her iron hand. She fired many of them, including some old retainers. That embittered Sarah and Jane Spencer all the more. But much was done, and quickly. The plaster work was repainted, the curtains and carpets cleaned and restored, the furniture recovered and regilded—and, most important of all, the paintings were cleaned. "The cost of restoration has been immense," said Earl Spencer. "A pair of globes in the picture gallery cost 10,000 pounds to restore. The chairs cost 2,000 pounds each and there are two sets of 30 chairs to be done."

"They were all painted with Woolworth paint," said Countess Spencer. "That's why it cost so much, getting that muckage off." She looked at the carpets, now dazzling with color. "A hundred years of gravy have come off."

When Diana came to visit on a weekend or holiday, she showed

45

none of the anger of her sisters. She loved her father, and felt his wife deserved her respect. She treated people kindly as long as they treated her kindly. For her, it was that simple.

"I did have a rotten time at the start," Countess Spencer later admitted. "Sarah resented me, even my place at the head of the table, and gave orders to the servants over my head. Jane didn't speak to me for two years, even if we bumped in the passageway. It was bloody awful . . ."

Then she added, "I didn't break up their parents' marriage."

More sourly, she told an intimate that the only Spencer "with any gray matter at all" was her husband.

"I used to visit them often," said Barbara Cartland. "Diana was very quiet, very sweet, and terribly nice to my youngest grandson, who was then eleven. It's unusual for a girl of sixteen to be very nice to a boy of eleven. She used to play with him, take him to the cinema. She absolutely adores children, you see. I also used to bring a stack of my novels—I still write more than twenty a year. I'd bring them for my daughter, but Diana would simply seize them, sit in a corner, and start reading."

Diana liked Althorp: the impressive gate with its four large gold balls on the top; the long, long road to the house with the huge yews, some of them 300 years old, along the gently rolling lawn; the golden orange of the local stone of the stable. She enjoyed cycling all over the area to the nearby villages. When she wasn't riding her bike, Diana liked to chase around the vast grounds on a pale blue beach buggy. And she liked the local people—slow-speaking, shy, but friendly.

Showing a visitor some family pictures, Earl Spencer pointed to one with Diana and said, "And here she is dressed up in the curtains. She always loved dressing up."

The cook, Rose Ellis, recalled how Diana would come into the kitchen when she came home "and if she thought nobody was looking, she would scrape the pots with her finger and lick off the food enthusiastically."

Butler Albert Betts remembered her sweet tooth for chocolate cake with butter icing, lemon soufflé, "and a lot of raspberry and strawberry ice cream." He added that "she was always immaculate, washed and ironed her own jeans, did all her own chores . . . a self-reliant, loving, domesticated sort of child . . . the kind of girl who never forgot to send birthday cards on the right day."

Diana was intrigued by the Oak Room, where the first Earl Spencer was secretly married while a ball was going on downstairs. If she was impressed with all the portraits in the portrait gallery, she might have been interested to learn that one of her forgotten ancestors (the younger brother of the fourth Earl Spencer) was a Catholic priest, Father Ignatius, who had launched a Crusade for the conversion of England. Diana's ancestor might wind up being a saint. Father Brian D'Arcy of Dublin is researching evidence of Spencer's two reported miracles. Spencer went to Ireland in the last century asking the Irish to pray for the English to be converted to Catholicism. He died penniless in a ditch in Scotland.

Also unheralded was her father's brother, a private detective.

Despite these two mavericks, the Spencers were considered part of the real aristocracy of Great Britain because their titles existed before the Industrial Revolution. Harold Brooks-Baker of *Debrett's Peerage* noted, "There are only about 150 families that fall in this category." Nevertheless, about the Spencers specifically, he added, "There is nobody in the family of any great importance."

Little did young Diana know how this would change. Nor could she know as she herself roamed about Althorp's rooms that one day a guide would point to a tea set and tell the many tourists, "You might be interested to know that Lady Diana played with that Victorian tea set when she was a little girl and had dolls' tea parties."

Back at West Heath, Diana realized she would never be as good as Jane at lacrosse—even though she was good enough to make the team. She knew she would never be as good as her mother in tennis. (Her mother had starred in the junior Wimbledon in 1952.) Or be as good an actress as Sarah. But she was a better swimmer than any of them, winning several prizes, as well as the Diving Cup. "When she dived," a teacher remembered, "you never heard a splash." And she was good at a game called netball. "It was much easier for me to get the ball in the net," she said, "because I was so tall." She liked playing the piano, too. After hearing a piece played once, she could repeat it. "For someone who started late," said Principal Rudge, "she made phenomenal progress."

She was also a marvelous dancer, "mad keen" about it. To get out of certain physical activities, "Diana would paint eye-shadow on her legs, and pretend they were bruises," said a classmate. But she

47

would never miss a class in dancing. Best of all, she loved ballet, and twice won prizes for it. She went to London as often as she could to see ballet performances, and saw *Swan Lake* four times.

"I'm obsessed with ballet," she later said. "I always wanted to be a ballet dancer . . . but I just grew too tall."

She was not very good in French. Most of her peers had spent holidays in France with their parents. Diana had never been to France. Nor had she ever even been in an airplane.

Anorexia, "the slimmer's disease," was a growing school problem at the time. But not with Diana, who was always ready for a second helping and loved the baked beans served for breakfast. On her birthday during her last summer at school, she took two dozen friends to the field near Gracious Lane Bridge, where they all gorged on a brace of pheasants and a variety of cookies, candies, and potato chips. What wasn't eaten was thrown at one another.

Carolyn Pride remembered that Diana "wore braces for a short time," but "she was always as lovely as she is now." She didn't wear much jewelry. She had had her ears pierced and wore gold studs. She also had a silver bracelet with hearts, wore a gold Russian wedding ring on her little finger, and—her favorite—a chain around her neck with the letter D. That was a gift from her school friends, and she wore it on her engagement day.

In November of 1977, the Prince of Wales had been invited as a guest at a shooting party weekend at Althorp. He and Sarah had been dating, amid much newspaper speculation. Diana was home that weekend, and Sarah introduced her sixteen-year-old sister to Prince Charles in a ploughed field at Sandringham. The twenty-nine-year-old prince thought Sarah's sister "jolly," and Diana thought him "pretty amazing."

A newspaper publisher whose granddaughter was at school with Diana had donated a picture of the Prince of Wales in his Investiture robes. It hung on the wall of Diana's dorm and she surely looked at it more carefully after having met him.

But Diana had more immediate concerns. She had failed all her O levels the first time around, and now she was taking them again in December. Again, she failed them. Against the advice of her father, she decided not to finish at Heath, instead choosing to go to the

Institut Alpin Vidamanette at Château d'Oex near Gstaad, Switzerland, where Sarah had had such a good time.

Before she left, West Heath gave her the Miss Clarence Award for service to the school. As Ruth Rudge said, "We don't give this award every year. It's presented only to outstanding pupils."

"It was one of the most surprising things that had ever happened to me," said Diana.

A friend noticed that Diana had cut out and kept a newspaper clipping about academic failures who become gifted and successful in life.

4

T he small woman in widow's black was standing behind the long line of soldiers holding the hand of her three-year-old grandson, waiting for the arrival of the new Queen of Great Britain. Suddenly, she realized that at a certain time in the ceremony, the soldiers would simultaneously stamp their guns to the ground, and the noise might frighten the little boy. There was no time to warn him about this, so she thought, "When the time comes, I will hold his hand more tightly." And so she did. Afterward, she told her Lady-in-Waiting, Dowager Lady Patricia Hambleden, "I was very proud of Charles. His face reddened, but he did not cry."

Overnight the little boy who played with soldiers was Duke of Cornwall, Duke of Rothsay, Earl of Carick, Baron of Renfrew, Lord of the Isles, Great Steward of Scotland, heir to the throne. His parents had been in Kenya, in a lodge called Treetops, when his mother got the news that her father, George VI, ill with cancer, had died in his sleep. The King was dead, long live the Queen!

His grandmother had come to him that day, still sobbing, and he had tried to comfort her. "Don't cry, Granny . . ." She called him "my gentle little boy." All her life she would love him the more because his temperament so reminded her of her sensitive husband. All through his childhood he would stay with her for prolonged periods, sometimes six months at a time, while his parents were on royal tour. The Queen Mother became a central, loving part of his life, somebody he would always turn to, even in adulthood, whenever he had problems, whenever he was lonely, whenever he had a potential bride for inspection.

When Charles was born, the bells of Westminster Abbey pealed 5,000 times, the guns boomed 41 salutes, Trafalgar Square was floodlit in baby blue, the Navy gave every sailor an extra ration of rum, and the massive crowd outside the gates of Buckingham Palace sang "Go to Sleep My Baby."

The whole world soon knew that he weighed seven pounds six ounces at birth, was golden-haired, and "made a great deal of noise." They did not learn that he was being breast-fed by the Queen, who insisted upon this "un-royal" practice. The court circular referred to him as "the infant Prince," and the silk-and-lace gown he wore at his christening had been used by every royal baby for four generations.

By royal decree, a strait in the Antarctic was named after him, as well as an uncharted channel near the Elephant Islands.

Charles was a chatterbox of a child and one of his first words was "No." When he was one, a royal press release announced that he had six teeth.

The main woman in his young life was his nanny, Helen Lightbody, a no-nonsense nurse from Scotland who firmly believed that "Regular habits make happy babies." Before Charles was two, the nursery had a new addition, his sister Anne. And, as soon as they were within the age of reason, they had a governess, Katherine Peebles, who also came from Scotland, was also strict, but had more of a sense of humor. When their mother became Queen, they seldom saw her for more than an hour a day. Charles once asked her to read a story to him and she said wistfully, "I wish I could."

Buckingham Palace can hardly be considered a home. With some six hundred rooms, it's more of a museum heavy with history. The Queen's father had called the royal family "the firm," and her husband referred to Buckingham Palace as "the office," observing that they "lived over the shop." They did indeed live in some two dozen rooms on the second and third floors, serviced by about 200 footmen, pages, housemaids, basement maids, chefs, kitchen help, messengers, etc. There were six dining rooms, red carpets, mirrored doors, marble staircases, bronze balustrades, and approximately 300 clocks.

Like her mother (and her future daughter-in-law), Elizabeth II was neither an academic nor an intellectual. But she learned more constitutional law than most of her ministers, more about the Commonwealth than any of its leaders, more about the world than she ever wanted to know. She had been taught by tutors, but she had learned by living. Like her mother, she was at heart a country woman who preferred the outdoor life with horses and dogs. She would have loved being more with her children. She would have wanted her husband sharing her life at her side instead of now having to walk several steps behind her as dictated by royal protocol.

Duty was now the driving wind of her life. When her mother was Queen, her principle was: Never cancel an engagement. If you have a headache, take an aspirin. It would be the new Queen's motto, too.

Lunching with her mother at Clarence House, Her Majesty thought she might have another glass of wine. The Queen Mother looked at her with a twinkle and said, "Are you sure you should? Don't forget you have to reign all afternoon.''

She soon knew that she was always on stage, with somebody looking at her constantly. She soon knew that she must always be ready to show a lively interest in everything, ready with a kind word, ready with a smile, ready with an indulgence for a nervous host, ready with a bland answer for a provocative question, ready to pose for a picture, shake a hand, acknowledge a cheer. However boring her partner, she must be polite; however tired, she must stand up straight; however worried it must never show.

She liked to laugh, but now there was less to laugh about, and no time. Her daily work schedule left no seconds to spare. Surrounded by senior advisors, she was prompted, instructed, directed.

Her son finally got the full impact of who she had become just before her coronation, when he was four. He asked a man what he was doing, and the man replied, "I'm getting these things ready for the Queen.''

"The Queen?'' asked the little boy. "Who is that?''

"Why, your mother!''

There was one tradition that the new Queen abolished. Her children would not have to bow or curtsy to her, as she had been made to do as a child.

Prince Philip had his own firm ideas on raising children. When a footman hurried to close a door behind Charles, the Prince told the footman to leave the door alone, that his son was perfectly capable of closing it himself.

Prince Philip wanted his son to be "a man's man.'' He saw him always surrounded by women, and it worried him, especially since he was forced to travel so much on naval duty. (Charles's great sorrow was that his father had never been able to come to any of his first five birthday parties. "My father sent me notes," he said sadly.)

It was Prince Philip who chose the three pictures for his son's nursery: a harbor scene, another of minesweepers at sea, and a third showing a stretch of coast in the moonlight, with shadows of Englishmen answering a ship's call. He also bought his son a miniature cricket bat and what became the boy's favorite toy: a specially made little electric car in bright red, with firm instructions that it must not be driven indoors. He let Charles sit and watch him dress in his uniform, took him for a piggyback splash in the basement swimming pool, and played ball with him in the garden whenever time permitted. The strictness would come later, and so would the spanking, but Prince Philip was a concerned and loving father.

He felt no joy when he received news in Kenya that his wife was now Queen. "I never felt so sorry for anyone in all my life," said his equerry. "He looked as if you'd dropped half the world on him." The easy romance of his life was now over. His wife now belonged more to the country and the Commonwealth than she did to him. In public, he could never again call her "darling" or even "my wife." Their time together would be severely rationed. Only at Balmoral and Sandringham would he sit at the head of the table and make the daily decisions. Now he could advise her, and she would listen, but she would also need to listen to many others before making her own final decision.

"The consort's constitutional position is such that if he is going to do a job," said Prince Philip, "he has to create it. Unlike the sovereign, he has no job.

"I haven't any particular talents," he added, "and I haven't any particular ambitions." His problem wasn't one of frustration, he said, "but of trying to figure out an area in which I could be helpful."

There was little question how much his son needed him, idolized him, copied him. When little Charles walked, he held himself stiffly, with his father's habit of clasping his hands behind his back. He had his father's prominent ears, the same quick turn of the head, the same curiosity, wanting to know all the answers.

He was delighted when he was finally allowed to wear a kilt, like his father. But one day, the kilt was laid out for him along with a pair of underpants.

"I'm not going to put those on," he said, pointing to the underwear.

"Why ever not?"

"Because Papa doesn't wear pants under his kilt."

It was carefully pointed out to him that pants *are* worn under kilts by those taking part in strenuous Highland games or Scottish dances.

His father's rules were firm: Show more responsibility. Never run toward your mother, shouting. You must always remember your position and who you are. Once, as the Queen was piped aboard the royal yacht, officers and crew lined up to shake her hand. The young Prince had not seen her for 162 days and he too lined up to shake her hand. "No, not you, dear," the Queen was heard to say as she led him away to their private apartment. Charles learned a snappy salute, a firm handshake, and the importance of punctuality: "I have to see Granny at half past ten and not a minute before."

The sacrosanct times for the children were after breakfast and after tea, when their parents gave them their undivided time. There is the touching story of the young Queen Elizabeth persuading her Prime Minister to push back the time of their weekly Tuesday night conference so she could be with her children during their bath time. Both parents read books to them—*Babar* and Beatrix Potter. Prince Philip also helped them put together their model toys. "Princess Anne was very good at model-making," said their assistant nanny, Mabel Anderson, "but not Prince Charles—all fingers and thumbs, I'm afraid." (At five, Princess Anne was already a self-reliant young lady with her mother's blue eyes, fair hair, and strong willpower. "I can write," she declared. "I can sew. I can bathe myself.")

If Charles's father was an awesome god who could do anything, his mother was a ruler in charge of "heaps and heaps of soldiers." And the Palace was a place with long gray corridors where he could pedal his tricycle on the royal red carpet. He had his miniature guns, his miniature fishing gear, even his miniature bagpipes. Of course, he had his own pony. His was a protected, highly privileged childhood.

It was an adventure when his governess took him to Trafalgar Square Underground Station, let him buy his own ticket, hand it to a ticket-taker, go down on the escalator, and watch the trains go by. More typical were inspection tours of the *Britannia* which Mummy and Papa owned.

There was a danger in all this, the danger of becoming pompous and priggish. "What right have you to photograph me?" he once asked a servant girl. "Who *are you?*" A proper spanking in the proper place reminded him of his manners.

By his seventh birthday, his governess felt Charles's reading skills were good, his handwriting clear, his drawing imaginative, and that he had a keen ear for music. He thought then he might like to be a railroad engineer. For a birthday present, he got a copy of *Black Beauty* and a space suit. His aunt, Princess Margaret—who described herself whimsically as "Charley's Aunt"—characterized her nephew as "a sturdy little rip . . . a bang-bang-banger."

In a long article in the Sunday *Express* the editors wrote, "Now is the time to worry about a bride for Prince Charles." They noted that there were only nine monarchies left in Europe, and the only bridal possibilities were a princess in the Netherlands and another in Denmark, both slightly older than Prince Charles. There was equal pessimism about suitable potential brides among the "little patricians . . . whose blood is undiluted blue." The paper proposed the idea that a bride might come from the dominions.

Then: "Need the public decide so soon? . . What is better: to make up our minds while he is still a child? Or to wait, say twenty years, for another tragic royal crisis?"

The royal watchers were soon out in full force. When Charles was eight, they noted "the Prince's hair is even closer to his eyebrows than usual. Not one photograph of him has ever revealed his forehead." Queried about it, his barber sniffed, "We never discuss the heir's hair."

The burdens of his heritage now grew stronger. His father suggested that Charles should stand during his lessons, since he must learn to stand for prolonged periods without fatigue or fidgeting. He also insisted that when being introduced, his son should repeat the person's name to develop his memory. And, of course, punctuality continued to be drilled into him. Once when the young Prince was joining his parents for a public appearance, he was told to be in front of the staircase exactly one minute before they arrived. When he rushed over, he heard his father's voice from above: "Fifteen seconds late, old fellow."

All previous princes had been tutored at the Palace, but Prince Philip decided that his son should have more: "We want him to go to school with other boys of his generation, and to learn from other children, and to absorb from childhood the discipline imposed by education with others."

Hill School was a neighborhood day school for the sons of the very rich. It was in a drab red-brick building, set behind Harrods, in the Knightsbridge area, not far from Buckingham Palace. It overlooked a garden, and right around the corner was a plaque on a house saying that Lillie Langtry had lived there. Langtry was the famous actress and mistress of Prince Charles's great-grandfather, Edward VII.

The headmaster said, "Each boy takes his turn to ring the bells and captain the games teams. Every boy has to take part in the school play. Making everybody participate is aimed at stopping any boy feeling he's the best—or the worst—at anything."

Charles wore the school uniform—a cinnamon-colored blazer and cap with gray corduroy trousers. The other boys, including a grandson of Prime Minister Harold Macmillan, were instructed to call him by his Christian name. When word got out that Charles was a student, photographers and sightseers jammed the area. One of the newspapers wrote: "Stop crowding the Prince. Leave him alone. Give him the chance of growing up as a normal, natural schoolboy."

That, of course, would never happen.

"It's all very well to say they're treated the same as everybody else," said Prince Philip of his children. "But it's impossible. I think that what is possible, and in fact necessary, is that they should realize they're not anonymous."

Charles became expert at rope-climbing and soccer, "went through the field like a bomb." "He has terribly nice manners," said one of his classmates, "and always says, 'Please may I have the ball.'" He reportedly didn't like boxing, "because I don't want to hurt my friends." He was good in geography, mediocre in arithmetic.

His next school was Cheam, some 60 miles from London. Cheam was not only one of Britain's oldest preparatory schools—founded in 1646—but among the most expensive. "Cheam looks for the happy boy rather than the brilliant one," said the headmaster.

But the boys were hardly happy. Discipline was strict, and the cane was occasionally used across a boy's bottom. Years later, on a tour of Tasmania, Prince Charles met the headmaster's son and told him, "I remember your father well. He caned me once—no, twice."

He arrived a glum, tense nine-year-old boy who still at times sucked his thumb (his mother had been a nail-biter at his age). He had never before been so completely away from home. As a new boy, he was regarded as a "mealy-eye," and was forced to sleep in a dormitory with eight other boys. When the Queen saw his battered old bunk, with a hair mattress over wooden slats, she said, "You won't be able to jump up and down on *that!*"

In her Christmas Day talk to the people that year, the Queen said, "We want our son and daughter to grow up as normally as possible. We feel that public life is not a fair burden to place on growing children. I am sure all of you who are parents will understand."

But how could she hope for this when the boy was called into the school office to hear his mother say on BBC radio, "I intend to create my son Charles Prince of Wales today." "I remember being actually embarrassed," he said afterward. It was at that moment when his "awful, inexorable fate" truly dawned on him.

It became a schoolboy challenge to "tough up" the Prince.

Barber Cecil Cott was at Cheam and one day saw "a lad who was bigger and older than Charles holding his [royal] head under the water in the bath . . . Charles was shrieking away at the top of his lungs so I said, 'Why stand for that, youngster? Do the same to him!' At last Charles got this lad's head in the bath . . . tumbled this lad in . . . the only trouble is that Charles went in as well. There they were, both fully dressed, and up to their knees in it, soaked."

He was plump and shy and found it difficult to make friends. When he stepped on somebody's foot during a soccer game, the boy sneered, "Hey Fatty, get off my foot!" In class, he spoke in barely audible whispers, shifting his weight nervously from one foot to another when he answered a question. "I stopped and asked him once how he was getting along," said a Master at Cheam. "He blushed beetroot red, shuffled his feet, mumbled something inaudible, then shot off along the corridor." It also took him a long time to realize that some of the boys might be especially nice to him simply because of who he was.

Charles later admitted that he was truly homesick, and that he had sometimes cried. One of his nannies, Mabel Anderson, remembered, "He dreaded going away to school." His mother had a more philosophical comment: "I have two faces. One, my public face. Charles also has a public face, but he doesn't know it yet." He would soon learn to hide his private feelings.

His father had been a first-class athlete at Cheam, but Charles was hardly a star at sports, and was regarded as "hopeless at team games." He was worst at cricket, best at soccer. But when he was finally made captain of the soccer team in his final year, his team lost every match that season. Said the soccer coach, "Prince Charles seldom drove himself as hard as his ability and position demanded."

His father tried to supplement his sports training by teaching him how to sail, shoot, and play polo (first by using bicycles and a tennis ball) during his summer vacations. Charles said that, if his mother would let him, "I would like to be a sailor. My heart is set on the sea." Would he like to sail with his father? "No, not with Daddy; but I want to sail on ships like those he sailed on. I like small ships. I'm always frightened, but it's all right, really. It's so exciting."

Prince Philip took him duck shooting when he was ten, first giving him a spring-loaded gun that fired suction-tip bullets. A year later, his father bought him his own shotgun and he became "a ruddy good shot."

As for polo, Prince Philip taught his son the game almost as soon as he could sit on a horse. "Polo is a man's game," Charles told his younger sister firmly when she wanted to know why she couldn't play. The irony was that Princess Anne had inherited more of her father's athletic ability than Charles, also more of his drive and rebellious personality.

"There is a softness in Prince Charles that would have been nice in Princess Anne, and a toughness in her that would have been handy in him. Nature did it slightly wrong," said a family friend.

Prince Philip's concern for the heir's training eventually led him to enlist his oldest friend, blunt and boisterous James Robertson Justice, later Rector of Edinburgh University, to help mold his young son into more of a man. The bearded Justice had a castle in Scotland, and the three of them would go swimming in ice-cold lochs, eat over mountainside campfires. Justice, who was also a learned biologist and ornithologist, taught Prince Charles falconry and spearfishing.

His father even brought him back a baseball catcher's mitt from Chicago.

The Queen was more concerned about her son's academic record. The royal academic reputation was not good. Both the Queen's father and grandfather were near the bottom of their class when they first went to naval training college. She herself had been mediocre in mathematics, among other subjects. The Queen decided that Charles's French was not good enough, and she hired a tutor. There were days when he and his sister were ordered to speak nothing but French. As a result, he eventually won a school prize in it.

The cliché is that Prince Charles tried hard but was a dud at school. One of his former teachers, H. W. Gregor, refuted that. "I taught Prince Charles for four years at Cheam . . . [he] was good at all Arts subjects, such as English and Geography, and exceptionally good at History . . . His overall ability must have placed him not far below the potential scholars." He also praised the Prince's abilities as musician, singer, and actor, as well as his willingness to become involved in many school activities.

During a history lesson once, the class heard about some of the more disreputable monarchs of the past. A fellow student remarked to Charles that kings could be "pretty bad types."

"Oh, but they're different nowadays," Charles replied cheerfully.

In the decade following her accession to the throne, the Queen made state visits to Norway, Nigeria, Portugal, Sweden, France, Denmark, Canada, the United States, and the Netherlands. She had integrated herself into royal duties well enough so she felt she could again cope with motherhood as well.

Prince Andrew was the first baby born to a reigning queen in 103 years. The Queen was able to spend more time with him as an infant than she did with Charles or Anne in the first stressful years of her reign. Charles was then eleven.

To prove that the Queen's pregnancy with Andrew was not planned, Royal watchers pointed out that her tiring tour of the United States and Canada in 1959 coincided with the critical second and third months of her pregnancy. The Queen insisted on continuing her tour, despite warning, and only took along an extra seamstress to let out her clothes.

Prince Charles not only was excused from school to see his new brother, but also to attend the celebrated wedding of Princess Margaret at Westminster Abbey.

Charles was old enough to have read the earlier scandalous stories in the press about his aunt. She had first fallen in love with the slim, handsome Wing Commander Peter Townsend, who had been equerry to her father, then to her sister. He was sixteen years older, married, and the father of two sons. At first it was simply "a terrific crush," and then, after his divorce, it blossomed into a real romance.

Townsend later explained Margaret's qualities: "Behind the dazzling façade, the apparent self-assurance, you could find, if you looked for it, a rare softness and sincerity. She could make you bend double with laughing; she could also touch you deeply."

Always more sophisticated than her older sister, Margaret had her own set, mostly art and theater people, for whom she loved to sing and play the piano. She and Townsend had been thrown together for some nine years, during which she had gone from being an unsure teenager to a warm, lovable woman.

She needed the Queen's permission in order to marry before she was twenty-five. Her sister could not give that permission without the agreement of the Prime Minister. Sir Winston Churchill bluntly told the Queen it would be disastrous for her to give her consent before the coronation, and felt it best that Margaret wait until she was twenty-five. After that, she would still need the consent of Parliament and the Commonwealth, but not of the sovereign.

Townsend, in the meantime, was sent off to serve in Belgium. Both the Queen and Prince Philip sided emotionally with Margaret and Townsend.

The new Prime Minister, Anthony Eden, brought bad tidings: The Marquess of Salisbury, as Lord President of the Council and Leader of the House of Lords, said he would resign rather than permit the Princess, then third in line to the throne, to marry a divorced man. His opposition meant that Princess Margaret could not marry Townsend without renouncing her royal status, her right of accession to the throne. Her name would be stricken from the Civil List, which meant there would be no government income.

The final blow came from the *Times* editorializing that the Church and the Commonwealth could not countenance the marriage.

Townsend himself had a change of mind. "It was Peter who didn't want to," Princess Margaret said later. With the major part of his income going to his now ex-wife and the support of their sons, he felt he would not be able to provide the proper life for his Princess.

One morning she got a letter from Townsend saying he planned to marry a Belgian girl. "That evening I decided to marry Tony," she said. "Tony" was photographer Anthony Armstrong-Jones, a commoner. In their sophisticated circle, he was seen as a bohemian trendsetter. Princess Margaret said she felt "daring" being in his company; she said he introduced her to "a new world."

The Townsend scandal was of great importance to Prince Charles because it served as a warning of what he must not do. He must not, like his great-uncle David or his Aunt Margaret, ever consider marrying a divorced person.

Prince Charles had his own first date when he was thirteen. He put on a natty, single-breasted suit and took a girl, and two other young couples, to see *The Sound of Music*. By that time, he had made his first public speech at the fifteenth-century church of St. Peter and St. Paul, his text coming from St. Matthew about the three wise men. By that time too, his father had taught him to drive a car. He was still chubby, slightly short for his age, and very well behaved.

His mother was still not fully at ease as Queen. Her occasional nervousness and tension still showed when she chewed her lip, fiddled with a paper clip or her necklace, pulled at a glove. Her "Uncle Dickie" Mountbatten was still her constant counsel, urging that she must show herself as a person not a puppet, that royalty had to come more to terms with the masses and their government rather than being a warrant of its own power. She must let the breath of change blow away some of the Court cobwebs, he told her. The British people still wanted their pageantry. Again, it meant walking the fine line between the mystique and the relevant.

This Mountbatten would similarly drill into Prince Charles.

Prince Charles was gradually permitted to sit at his mother's right at certain official functions, learning things that only she could teach him. Public speculation now became intense about his next school. It was generally known that Her Majesty favored Eton, world-famous and near the royal residence at Windsor. "It would be disastrously unwise," said Lord Altrincham, himself an old Etonian. "Eton has become the snob school."

Prince Philip wanted his son to go to Gordonstoun, his old school, whose student body was a mix of fishermen's children as well as the sons of Britain's most noted families.

Prince Philip's wishes prevailed.

The seventeen-year-old Lord Rudolph Russell sent his sympathies: "My heart bleeds for Prince Charles," said the son of the Duke of Bedford who twice ran away from Gordonstoun. "My only recollections are of complete horror." A Sunday newspaper differed:

"Gordonstoun transcends both British class and national boundaries . . . these are precise reasons why it seems so suitable for an heir to the throne."

Gordonstoun sits on the Firth of Moray in northern Scotland, a ruggedly bleak place, 440 miles from London. It has been described as a cross between a Victorian orphanage and a Scottish commando camp. While it emphasizes physical fitness, its headmaster insists that its true purpose is "to build character."

The school motto is: "There is more in you." And they seemed determined to prove it. "You'll always be urged on to do what for you, personally, you think is impossible. If you're frightened of heights, you'll be encouraged to climb mountains," said Gordonstoun student Michael Fuchs. "If you're a good bat at cricket, you'll be made to bowl. If you're a natural at classics, you'll be put into science. And the first time you succeed in achieving what you thought was impossible, you will have laid the foundation of lifelong self-confidence."

"I hated every minute of my two years there," Lord Russell amplified. "You're always on the go. You get no leisure time at all during the day. You have to get up at seven and go for a mile run, whatever the weather, wearing just shorts and plimsoles and no vest. After that, you have to take a cold shower, make your bed, tidy your locker, and change, all by seven thirty. So you've got to run that mile like fury. Then you have to do the housework. This is the sweeping—sweeping out the dormitories, studies, and corridors of your house. But you have to make a rush for the broom cupboard, because there are not enough brooms to go round."

Then he told of the chore of waiting on a table of twenty-five boys. "By the time you sit down to your plate, some of the others have nearly finished. You have to gulp down your food so you are ready to clear away the dishes for the next course."

Another former student, Patrick Pelham-Jones, remembered that life there was dominated by bells. "There are bells for meals, lessons, and prayers, bells for bed. Bells for anything and everything."

Pelham-Jones also vividly described the commando course— jumping a ditch, running along narrow catwalks, heaving yourself bodily over an 8-foot wall, swinging Tarzan-style across a 10-foot drop at the end of a rope.

"If you fall from the rope, as I did on occasion," said Pelham-Jones, "you find yourself almost up to your neck in an obnoxious mixture of slime and mud, and are sent straightaway to Sick Bay for a big dose of castor oil to clear out any of the mixture you may have swallowed. Quite a few new boys lose their nerve and fall from the rope the first time they try to cross it. Charles didn't.

Charles slept in the Windmill Lodge with sixty-three other boys. It was a long, low building of stone and timber with a roof of green asbestos, the largest and newest house there. It got a coat of fresh paint when they knew he was coming. The bumpy gravel road from the west gate also had been cleaned and resurfaced.

Before his arrival in May 1962, a policeman questioned each new arrival, checking his name off a list. It was difficult after that to treat Charles as an ordinary new boy.

The young heir was often alone at Gordonstoun. He did know a couple of German princes and Lord Mountbatten's grandson, Norton Knatchbull. But usually he walked alone, carrying his schoolbooks in a shiny leather case, followed by his detective.

"I felt incredibly sorry for him," said one of his classmates, John Lamp.

"How can you treat a boy as an ordinary chap," added Pelham-Jones, "when his mother's portrait is on the coins you spend in the snack shop, on the stamps you use to mail your letters home, when a tall detective trails him wherever he goes? Boys who might otherwise chum up with him are frightened of doing so lest they be accused of 'sucking up.' "

"You see, loneliness is something that royal children always suffered from and always will," explained Lord Mountbatten. "Not much you can do about it, really. It's always the undesirable types who try to make up to you; the ones you really like tend to steer clear, in case they're accused of being snobs. Of course Charles didn't like the place at first. It's a tough school, and he doesn't like tough things when he first embarks on them. He's not the type to rush into something with an easy, short-lived enthusiasm; instead, he lives with it, comes to grips with it, and ends up doing very well at it."

At first, when the loneliness became unbearable, he went on weekends to visit his grandmother when she was fishing at Birkhall, not too far away. She had taught him how to fly-fish, a sport he has loved all of his life. But most of all, he would pour out all his problems, beg her to persuade his parents to take him away. She couldn't do that, she said, but she gave him all the comfort she could. "He is a very gentle boy with a very kind heart," she said of him, "which I think is the essence of everything." He was then only fourteen years old.

Things eased after the end of the first term. New boys wear navy blues until they prove themselves worthy of the school uniform of gray shorts and a light blue sweater. At that time, the new boy gets grabbed by his legs and arms, dumped into a bath filled with cold water, pushed down in total immersion. Prince Charles was no exception.

In terms of the press, Prince Philip was wise in favoring Gordonstoun over Eton for his son's teenage years. At Eton, photographers would wait en masse. But Gordonstoun was too remote. Still, whenever a royal story broke, the press pounced. The most memorable story concerning young Prince Charles was called the "cherry brandy incident." Though a ridiculous story, it was flashed around the world.

When he was almost fifteen, the Prince had earned his promotion to the Junior Training Plan at school which entitled him to greater leeway in selecting his outdoor activities. One of these was an expedition in June of 1963 aboard the school yacht *Pinta*, which landed at Stornoway on the Isle of Lewis in the outer Hebrides. Prince Charles, accompanied as always by his private detective, went ashore with four other boys to see a movie starring the buxom Jayne Mansfield, *It Happened in Athens.*

The detective went off to buy the tickets, and the boys went to the Crown Hotel to wait for him. Somebody spotted the Prince and crowds gathered and pointed. "I thought, 'I can't bear this anymore,'" said the Prince. In his search for privacy, the only place he could find was the bar. "Having never been into a bar before, the first thing I thought of doing was having a drink, of course. And being terrified, not knowing what to do, I named the first drink that came into my head, which happened to be cherry brandy, because I had drunk it before when it was cold, out shooting. Hardly had I taken a sip when the whole world exploded around my ears. I wanted to pack my bags and go to Siberia."

Serving alcoholic drinks to anyone under eighteen is forbidden in Britain. A free-lance journalist had seen the Prince with his cherry brandy and filed the story. The Palace at first denied, then retracted it. The papers had a field day, headlining BEND OVER, YOUR HIGHNESS. But instead of a caning, the Prince was taken off the Junior Training Plan. It would be years before he could smile about the incident. But it reminded him afresh of the publicity that would always surround him.

Some of the newspapers had coupled the story with other incidents: his skiing in the Cairngorms on a Sabbath, his killing of a stag ("Jolly good," said his father), which so antagonized wildlife associations. Even his near-Beatle haircut drew fire from the British Safety Council, which claimed it set a dangerous example in light of mounting industrial accidents caused by long hair getting caught in equipment.

The Sunday *Express* called the Prince "the most unfortunate boy in Britain," and the *Mirror* suggested the danger that he might become "a living tragedy." Both referred to the fact that although he might not become King until he was sixty, his life would be under constant scrutiny until then.

Prince Charles could compare notes with his peer, the sixteen-year-old heir to the Swedish throne, Prince Carl Gustaf. In Sweden, Prince Carl was treated as any ordinary citizen, even attending a co-ed public school. His freedom was almost complete—he even arrived at Gordonstoun without a detective.

Prince Carl was an Elvis Presley fan. Charles felt differently about music.

"I like music very much," Charles later told Kenneth Harris. "I like playing it and I like listening to it. The trouble is . . . if you don't practice you simply can't enjoy your own noise . . .

"I don't go out of my way to listen to pop sessions, but if I happen to catch it, I enjoy it. The Beatles sang splendid music, but I really prefer classical music, because I find the more I listen, the more I get out of them. Jazz I enjoy. But I'm no connoisseur. A piece by Berlioz from a choral work . . . *L'enfance du Christ* . . . I play it now, often. There's a certain passage in it which is so moving I'm reduced to tears every time.

"I love tunes and I love rhythm. Rhythm is deep in me—if I hear rhythmic music, I just want to get up and dance."

The severity of life at Gordonstoun was relieved by holidays occasionally, as when Charles and his sister went out one evening to the Garth Hunt Purney Club Ball at the White Hart Hotel in Windsor, where 150 youngsters danced the Twist, the Shake, the Hully-Gully, and the Drag. The Prince also requested that the five-piece band play the Charleston. One of the musicians described him as "fab . . . a real professional . . . a cool cat."

The Prince and Princess Anne gave their own pop music party at Windsor in the Crimson Drawing Room one year for a hundred young guests. It was their first hosted party. The battlements were floodlit, the huge red carpet taken up for dancing, a supper buffet laid out in an adjoining room. Charles provided his own selected music on a rented hi-fi rig. The criticism was not long in coming. Learning that champagne had been served, a British Temperance Society official described the event as "bloody awful."

The press continued to hover over Charles mercilessly. In 1964 *Stern* headlined: THE CONFESSIONS OF PRINCE CHARLES. This turned out to be an exercise book containing essays by Prince Charles which one of his Gordonstoun classmates had pinched and sold for pocket money. Scotland Yard sent detectives to get the book back, which they did. But the German paper had photocopies which it promptly published.

In one essay the sixteen-year-old Prince had noted that democracy meant "giving equal voting power to people having unequal ability to think." He also deplored the habit of voting "for a particular party, and not for the individuals." On censorship he wrote, "If the government were to take over the press, as Hitler did just before the Second World War, no one in the country would know what was really going on." His teacher's comment: "Quite well argued." In another essay on class consciousness, though, the teacher observed, "This makes no sense."

That same year Prince Charles passed five of his O levels, well above the national average. He had failed only in mathematics and physics, and later would scrape through the math.

"I failed my math exam three times," Prince Charles admitted. "I finally got it on the fourth attempt. I tried to learn German, but I regret to say I failed my exam at Gordonstoun. I didn't know enough vocabulary to pass it. I can just manage in French, but not well enough." A literature teacher who had taught both Charles and his father said, "Trying to teach Philip Wordsworth was pure loss. With his son it is worthwhile."

His father, however, had been the school's star athlete, captain of the cricket and hockey teams and won the silver medal for all-around prowess at running, jumping, swimming, sailing, and throw-

Charles & Diana

ing a javelin. Prince Charles preferred the pottery class. "His tea set was rather nice," said headmaster Robert Chew.

Charles relished acting. Undertaking to play the part of Macbeth, he seriously researched the role. His parents came to see him perform. The *Gordonstoun Record* review observed, "Prince Charles was at his very best in the quiet poetic soliloquies, the poetry of which he so beautifully brought out . . ."

When Charles was sixteen, his youngest brother, Edward, was born. The most studious and sensitive of the Queen's sons, Edward was to idolize his brother throughout his childhood.

In 1965 Prince Charles was excused from his classes long enough to attend the state funeral of Sir Winston Churchill. He had first met Churchill as a small boy at Buckingham Palace, when he asked the elder statesman to "pass the sausages, please." Through the years he had known him as "Uncle Winston," and had begged his mother to let him see "Uncle Winston getting his Garter." (Sir Winston was installed as a Knight of the Garter at St. George's Chapel in Windsor in 1954, with the young Charles in a white silk blouse watching all the pageantry pop-eyed from a stall to the left of the altar.)

Asked how his son was getting along at Gordonstoun, Prince Philip remarked, "Well, at least he hasn't run away yet."

But he often wanted to. Finally, he persuaded his parents to let him spend a term at another school before coming back for his final year at Gordonstoun.

During her tour in Australia, the Queen had promised to "send my eldest son to visit you, too, when he is older." After much discussion with the Australian Prime Minister, she and Prince Philip selected Timbertop, a division of the Geelong School. Called the Eton of Australia, it was set in the Australian hills, some 200 miles from Melbourne.

A French newspaper, *France Dimanche*, claimed that the Prince was being exiled there because he had fallen in love with a Scottish farmer's daughter.

Though eager to get away from Gordonstoun, "It was a very sad moment for me," said Charles, "leaving England, seeing one's father and sister standing on the tarmac waving goodbye." It was his first trip abroad anywhere without one of his parents.

Unlike the strict regimen of Gordonstoun, Timbertop offered a much freer routine with an emphasis on initiative and adventure. Prince Charles would have the responsibility of a young group, spending a part of his time overseeing such chores as wood-chopping, feeding the pigs, cleaning out fly-traps ("revolting"). Timbertop was a compound of nine huts, each with fifteen boys, supervised by one of the older students. Prince Charles shared a room with a sheep-farmer's son.

On weekends, all the boys disappeared into the bush with their tents and sleeping bags to fish, photograph birds, collect butterflies or orchids, or just walk and look. Supervision was minimal.

Prince Charles had never known such personal freedom. There were cross-country runs twice a week, and weekend hikes. After the first day of term, the press left him alone. What he liked best here were the long walks in the wild country, "being out on a mountain with the wind and the trees. The farthest I've been is 60 or 70 miles in three days, climbing about five peaks on the way," he said. "At the campsite, the cooking is done on an open fire in a trench." He reluctantly admitted his failure at sheep-shearing. "I made rather a mess of it, and left a somewhat shredded sheep."

There was also the test of weighing a python by letting it wrap itself around one, and subtracting that weight from one's own weight. The Prince remembered too plunging his hands "into a bowl of maggots to pick out something from the bottom."

Australians call Britons "Pommies" (short for pomegranates, because of their rosy cheeks). Their greatest term of endearment for a Brit is "Pommie bastard." When Prince Charles heard himself called that for the first time, he was absolutely delighted.

Charles would later regard his Timbertop time as "the most wonderful period of my life." More than anything else it enabled him to overcome his shyness.

Geelong sponsored an annual trip to Papua and New Guinea to tour the Christian missions. Prince Charles joined up. The plane stopped to refuel in Brisbane and there was a crowd waiting at the airport for a glimpse of him. "I looked out at the terrifying sea of faces waiting for me at the tarmac," he said, "and I was so scared I just couldn't move. I had to be virtually kicked out of the plane; and, as I walked towards the barriers, something clicked inside of me. All my shyness suddenly disappeared—and really, from that moment on, I don't think I ever felt nervous in public again."

He was met by a giggling gaggle of bare-breasted native girls at the airport. "The Prince marched past them with hands clasped behind his back, his eyes discreetly averted—except for a couple of glances."

What made Charles's stay at Timbertop special was the presence of Squadron Leader David Checketts and his family. Checketts was the thirty-five-year-old equerry to Prince Philip who came to set up a home away from home for Charles. It was much more than that. Never before in his life had Prince Charles ever had such a relaxed home life as he had on their farm on the occasional weekends and holidays. He made his own bed, helped himself to breakfast, acted as an older brother to the Checketts children, and indeed was there for the birth of a new Checketts child. Never again until his own marriage would he feel such a part of a warm, loving family. Checketts, an outspoken, rubbery-faced man, later became his own equerry, then his first private secretary, and always his friend.

"I went out there with a boy," said Checketts, "and returned with a man."

The Queen Mother arrived in Australia on tour in 1966 and the Prince spent some days with her. He told her to tell his parents that he wanted to spend another term there, and she could see by the change in his spirit how important it was to do so. His parents gave their permission.

Charles loved the fresh informality of the Australians, their lack of servility, their directness. "They were very, very good and marvelous people," he said. Looking back, he "absolutely adored it. I couldn't have enjoyed it more. The most wonderful experience I've ever had, I think."

Heading home, he joined his father and sister at Jamaica. "Gone is the fumbling lad who blushed when he was spoken to," said a *Daily Mirror* reporter. "In his place is a devil-may-care youngster with a wide, friendly grin. A swinger, in fact. Ask the girls."

When he returned to Gordonstoun for the new term, he arrived full of self-confidence, driving himself to the school gates, with six-year-old Andrew at his side (and his father in the rear, because he had only a temporary driving license). He had been elected "Helper" (or Head of the House) at Windmill Lodge, which meant he now had his own private room.

Charles was now eighteen. If his mother died, he would be King in his own right without any Regent. As a Counselor of State, he was one of six who would act for the Queen when she was abroad. They would have powers to assent to acts of Parliament, receive ambassadors, hold Privy Councils, and sign documents of state.

In the meantime, he broke his nose in a rugby game, played cello with the school orchestra in Edinburgh, and sang the part of the pirate king in the school production of *The Pirates of Penzance.* As part of the lyrics, the Prince sang, in perfect pitch:

But many a King on a first-class throne,
If he wants to call his Crown his own,
Must manage somehow to get through
More dirty work than ever I do.

He kept impeccable royal standards: no smoking or drinking. Even at a proper dance, he hesitated asking a girl for a date lest the publicity make her life too difficult.

Said an admirer: "He's far from meek, but he's the kindest, most considerate person I've ever met."

When Her Majesty arrived to open a new sports center at Gordonstoun, she kissed her son on the cheek in front of everyone, then asked the Headmaster to give the boys a long weekend off in the middle of the next term. There was much cheering.

The Prince passed his A levels in History and French, with distinction for a special optional paper. He was now eligible to enter a university. There was little question that he had hated his first years at Gordonstoun, but by now he could be more philosophical about it. "I did not enjoy school as much as I might have, but that is because I'm happier at home than anywhere else. But Gordonstoun developed my willpower and self-control, helped me discipline myself. It taught me to take challenges and initiatives, taught me a great deal about myself."

He was, however, glad to leave Gordonstoun. His father said, "There comes a time when you've had enough of it."

And now what would follow?

Prince Philip insisted that Charles's decision was primarily his own. "All the way through we've tried to explain to him what the situation is, what the possibilities are, and have tried to make him feel that he was just as much involved in the choice of his education as we were . . . It's not a question of being told what he is to do."

Well, not quite. He had a choice of going to a university or into one of the services. As his father put it, "he was keen to go to university."

To decide which one, Her Majesty the Queen had a small dinner party for the Prime Minister, the Archbishop of Canterbury, Lord Mountbatten, the Dean of Windsor, and Professor Sir Charles Wilson (the chairman of the Committee of University Vice Chancellors). It was Lord Mountbatten who said, "Trinity College like his grandfather; Dartmouth like his father and grandfather; and then to sea in the Royal Navy, ending up with a command of his own."

And that's the way it was.

Trinity was the biggest, the richest college in Cambridge University, with one of the highest academic standards. Founded by King Henry VIII in 1546, it had some 700 undergraduates, more than half from government-supported schools. Master of Trinity was Lord Richard Austen ("Rab") Butler, an elder statesman who had held numerous Cabinet posts, including that of Foreign Secretary. Butler expressed the hope that the Prince would "live in the college and take part in the life of the college."

Prince Charles agreed. He thought it would be "marvelous to have three years when you're not bound by anything, and not married, and haven't got any particular job."

The traditional Cambridge building consists of a series of staircases leading off each court. A dozen sets of rooms open onto each staircase, where all share the common bathroom. The Prince lived one flight up, to give him some privacy from public snooping, in a quiet corner of the college beside the river Cam. He had a small bedroom, a sitting room, a tiny kitchen, and a private telephone. All students had servants to clean shoes, make beds, tidy the rooms, and wake them in the morning. All wore gowns when dining in the Great Hall or walking the Cambridge streets after dark.

Charles was the only one of the 220 freshmen to arrive driving a red Mini-Metro with a crowd of a thousand waiting for him, including the Master of Trinity. Somebody yelled, "Good luck," and he answered, "I'll need it."

His response was prophetic because he ran into his usual social isolation. One of his few friends was Robert Woods, then in his third year, a noted oarsman and elder son of the Dean of Windsor. But for most other students it was the usual story: Nobody wanted to seem to be "sucking up" to the Prince.

The Master of the College had said earlier, "The important thing when he first arrives is to find young friends who will take him out. The danger is sitting in a room all alone and doing nothing. It's far better to go out to a pub with a friend, and have a drink." Butler added, "The nearer he can get to what the usual undergraduate does here, the happier we and his parents will be."

In the first week, the Prince was seen walking alone on the college grounds along the river, his head down. He started studying archeology and social anthropology and seemed to be working hard.

He sent his first refusal note to a young lady in Cambridge who had invited him to a party to celebrate the end of her nursing exams. "I sent Prince Charles an invitation because I thought he might be lonely," said Vivian Morgan. "I hope the note on the back of my invitation didn't put him off." The note: "With bottle, please."

To help him somewhat, Cambridge University's Footlights Club, the home of the best humorists, issued an edict banning jokes about the Prince of Wales because he was "too obvious a target." The edict read: "Prince Charles, hampered as he is by disadvantages of birth, will have enough to cope with in the coming months without bad jokes and worse manners from members."

In general the press agreed to leave him alone, and did. He actually went shopping in town, went to the local movies, joined an adult education class in pottery, played his cello in a public concert. These were the years of the "student protest" era, but Charles carefully chose new friends who were either polo players or members of an exclusive dining club called the Wapiti Society.

Living along his staircase was an economics student from Wales named Hywel Jones. A socialist who had read Karl Marx when he was fourteen, Jones opened the Prince's eyes to a view he had never heard before and almost got him politically activated. One evening Prince Charles knocked on Rab Butler's door to ask the Master of Trinity a question: Would it be all right for him to join the University Labor Club?

"Hell, no!" said Butler, carefully explaining the absolute need for the Prince to maintain political neutrality.

Prince Charles also told Butler that he wanted to switch his major from archeology to history.

"If you stick to archeology or anthropology, you might get a First," said Butler.

Prince Charles shook his head, and added his determination to study the British Constitution.

"Why?" asked Butler.

"Because I'm probably going to be King." Later he added, "I *feel* history. It fascinates me. I don't know whether it's me, or being born into what I was. I'm a romantic at heart, really."

The undergraduate newspaper *Varsity* asked the Prince to write an article for its anniversary issue. Among other things, he wrote that he found it hard "to accustom myself to the grinding note of an Urban District Council dust lorry's engine rising and falling in spasmodic energy at seven o'clock in the morning accompanied by the monotonous jovial dustman's refrain of 'Come All Ye Faithful' and the head-splitting clang of the dustbins." The singing garbage collector, Frank Clarke, was signed on by a national record company and became an instant celebrity. The garbage collectors agreed to postpone their pickup until nine.

Prince Charles used that core of an idea for a skit he wrote for a college satirical revue in which he sat in a garbage can, charging the press for interviews and songs. There were forty sketches in the revue called "Revulution," and Charles took part in fourteen of them, mimicking Lord Butler and impersonating the Duke of Wellington. The visiting press liked the line in which the Prince, under an um—brella, said "I lead a sheltered life." Even more they enjoyed the lascivious look in his eye as he escorted a young lady offstage saying, "I like to give myself heirs." In one skit, he forgot his lines and said, "What the hell comes next?"—and got the biggest laugh.

His mother once came to visit him in his Trinity rooms. She was wearing a bright green coat and matching hat and he met her at the bottom of the staircase, kissed her, and escorted her upstairs. They talked, had fried chicken, and she slipped away quietly.

"When he first came up, he was astonishingly naïve and old-fashioned about girls," said one of his Cambridge friends. "He really thought that girls who slept with their boyfriends weren't quite 'nice.'" He had taken girls to the theater, girls who thought he was "great fun." His father had told him to look people straight in the eye when he talked to them, and women particularly seemed to love it. "When he looked at me with those lovely blue eyes, I went all weak at the knees," said one woman, adding, "He has a lover's voice."

Prince Charles, however, was the first to admit that he was still very shy about "pulling in the birds." However, he added, "I think one has to conquer it."

At that time, though, it was Lucia Santa Cruz who had conquered him. A tall, dark, "quite ravishing" daughter of the Chilean Ambassador to London, Miss Cruz was helping Lord Butler research his memoirs, and she was soon researching Prince Charles. She was three years older than he, knew much more about life and love, and was willing to teach him.

There was no question of any serious romance, particularly since she was a Catholic, but there was also no question that it was a very warm relationship. Lord Butler helped the romance along by slipping Lucia the key to the Master's Lodge. He recalled that the Prince "asked if she might stay in our lodge for privacy, which request we were very glad to accede to." Butler added that he felt it his duty to let the Prince enjoy his final days of freedom.

5

The last Welsh Prince of Wales, Llewelyn ap Gruffydd, was killed in 1282 by the English invader Edward I. The invader also beheaded, disemboweled, and quartered Llewelyn's brother. Edward I then declared his infant son the first English Prince of Wales. Now, nearly 700 years later, Charles was about to be declared the twenty-first English Prince of Wales, but only the second to be invested at Caernarvon. Of the twenty previous Princes of Wales, thirteen became Kings, six died earlier, and one spent his life in exile.

A year before, when he was nineteen, Prince Charles was formally installed at Windsor Castle as a Knight of the Garter, joining such giants as Lord Mountbatten and Generals Alexander and Montgomery. The Order of the Garter is Britain's oldest chivalric order. Only the sovereign, the Prince of Wales, and twenty-four knights-companion can belong to it at any one time. In the ceremony, Her Majesty touched the sword to her son's shoulders, and buckled the dark blue satin garter below his left knee, pronouncing him a Knight of the Realm and a member of the Order of the Garter. The origin of this ritual was an incident in which Edward III picked up the garter of the Countess of Salisbury. When a courtier laughed, the King put the garter on his own leg saying, *"Honi soit qui mal y pense"*—Evil be to him who evil thinks. That motto has since been inscribed on the garter.

The investiture was scheduled for July of 1969, and Prince Charles had to take time out from his other studies to spend part of the summer taking a crash course at the University College of Wales in Aberystwyth to learn the Welsh language so he could make a speech in it. (Welsh is the everyday language in many rural villages, but only one out of every four Welshman can speak it.)

"It doesn't mean anything to me," twenty-four-year-old Cardiff mechanic Paul Jenkins said of the investiture. "Having an English Prince of Wales, it's daft." Asked whether he spoke Welsh, he answered, "Not a word. That's daft too."

Nevertheless, some 75 percent of the Welsh approved of the investiture. Only a minority called it "a cynical charade, a mean and contemptible maneuver."

Asked if he thought wearing a crown would make him feel like a different human being, Prince Charles said he hadn't worn a crown since his mother's coronation "and that one fell down over my head."

There were some friends who felt that if Charles truly had the choice, he might decline the crown. "I think he's too kind, too gentle," said one. "He's not soft for a boy or a man, but he's too soft for a king."

The student chairman of the University College Hall disagreed after getting to know Prince Charles. "I sense a genuine feeling of interest by the Prince in learning as much as he can about the people and the country whose name he'll bear. He is a master of etiquette and conducts himself with aplomb. He'll make a King."

Aberystwyth was an isolated, insular community dominated by students and Welsh nationalists. The nationalists even had their own pub, which only the boldest Englishman ever entered, and their own dormitory filled with placards proclaiming, "Let Monarchy die!" Female nationalists sang "We Shall Overcome" in Welsh. Recalling the execution of Charles I, some nationalists handed out leaflets saying, "Let the axe fall!"

Her Majesty was concerned "for my son's safety," but the Prime Minister assured her that he would be guarded round the clock by a hand-picked team. Still, what does a protecting team do when the Prince impulsively decides to talk to the protestors?

"I had slight butterflies as I walked up," he said, "but I just went to see what it was these people really were getting at . . . They were standing there, and they were, I thought, perfectly ordinary people and I thought, you know, one could talk to them as perfectly ordinary people.

"One somehow feels that because they're demonstrating and they've got placards that they're . . . a group apart somehow, and some sort of modern ghastly phenomenon. So I asked one chap who was holding a placard what it meant—because it was in Welsh . . . he just in fact hurled abuse at me and said, 'Go home, Charlie,' or something like that. So after I'd asked him some more questions, I gave up. There was no point."

At the Welsh college, he lived in Pancycelyn Hall, made his own bed, carried his own tray, and started getting handknit sweaters from the women in town. His detective slept in the room next door.

The Prince occasionally visited Sir Michael Duff, the Lord Lieutenant of Caernarvonshire, an old family friend.

"Would you like a drink, Sir?" asked Sir Michael.

"He blushed to the roots of his hair," said Sir Michael, "so I asked, 'Aren't you allowed to drink?' and he answered, 'No, it's not that. It's just that I'm not used to being called sir.'"

Again it was a lonely time for him. "I haven't made many friends."

The idea of a formal investiture was devised by Lloyd George in 1911 as a Welsh political ploy for Charles's great-uncle David, who became Edward VIII, and later Duke of Windsor. But David rebelled when he saw the costume he had to wear: white satin breeches with an ermine-edged mantle of purple velvet. He could only envision what his Navy classmates would say. His mother, Queen Mary, finally persuaded him, saying that his friends would understand that duty required him to do things that seemed "a little silly."

When asked about that, Prince Charles said, "Well, I don't really have the same sort of apprehension about it as the Duke of Windsor did. Perhaps one of the reasons is that I'm not as young as he was. He was only seventeen [Prince Charles was then twenty], and I think I felt very nervous and unsure of myself . . . I'm not going to dress up as he did. I look upon it as being a meaningful ceremony. I shall also be glad when it's over."

He would not wear the white satin knee breeches, white silk stockings, and the trailing purple mantle. His velvet cloak would be short enough to clear the ground so no trainbearers would be needed.

Prince Charles added that he did feel the ceremony was worth the money "to make it dignified, colorful, and worthy of Britain."

With all the threats by Welsh extremists, the Prince admitted, "It would be unnatural, I think, if one didn't feel any apprehension about it. But I think if one takes it as it comes, it will be much easier. I don't blame people demonstrating. They've never seen me before; they don't know what I'm like. I have hardly been to Wales, and you can't really expect people to be overzealous about having a so-called English prince to come amongst them . . . as long as I don't get covered with too much egg and tomato, I'll be all right."

But the worry went deeper than fear of ridicule. There were bombs and bomb threats. Ten sticks of explosives were found on a beach where the Prince often went to study. If they had exploded they would have killed anyone within 30 yards. In a security sweep, the police picked up nine members of a Welsh paramilitary group with plans to murder Charles "if necessary" to prevent his investiture. Meanwhile, four students staged a hunger strike protest, noting that Caernarvon Castle was a symbol of conquest built by Welsh slave labor. Members of the Welsh Language Society splashed paint over signs with English place names. Extremists tried to saw off the head of the seafront statue of the previous Prince of Wales, Edward, Duke of Windsor.

A time bomb earlier had shattered the Temple of Peace building where the investiture committee was scheduled to meet. Welsh-speaking Special Branch men had infiltrated the town and campus and before it was over, some 2500 policemen, including armed Scotland Yard officers in bulletproof vests, would join 2500 soldiers in and around Caernarvon.

The Prince readily recognized that the Welsh had some legitimate cause for discontent. For centuries, the government in London had deliberately repressed Welsh language and culture. Unemployment was high and the Welsh complained that nothing much was being done for them. One Welshman said, "Wales desperately needs an ambassador. If Charles can do for Wales what his father's done so well for England, he'll be a hero after all."

It didn't hurt Prince Charles at all for a specialist in Welsh heraldry and genealogy to inform his people that the Prince was descended from Llewelyn ap Gruffydd, the last native Prince of Wales.

"I'm told," said the Prince of Wales, "that I'm descended three times over from the original Welsh princes. My grandmother, Queen Elizabeth, is descended twice over through both sides. So I seem to have quite a lot of Welsh blood in me."

He became a hero when he spoke on the last day of the National Eisteddfod at Baerystwyth of the Urdd, a Welsh young people's organization. He wrote the speech himself, had it translated into Welsh, and spoke in Welsh after only six weeks of cramming.

"I've got a good ear and I can mimic, and I like doing it. It was damned hard—it's a hard language, very rich and very complex," he said. "But I enjoyed it."

He told his audience he would fight to keep their language alive.

He was articulate, opinionated, and amusing. And he was "matey." "I have found time to read Dafydd ap Gwilym [a vigorously amorous Welsh poet] in bed and now I know something about the neighboring girls of Llanbadarn."

The Welsh loved that remark. They loved his wit, and more than that, they loved his fluent Welsh. The biting wind of criticism had changed. The older Welsh women now called him "a real *nice boy*." "*Geuw geuw* [good gracious], why would anybody want to hurt the boy?"

Mayor of Caernarvon, Ifor Bowen Griffiths, was even more bubbly about it: "Charles has been the ace in our pack. When he stood up at that Eisteddfod and started to speak in Welsh he wasn't just a boy, he was a Prince. You could have put a suit of armor on him and sent him off to Agincourt."

Churchgoers throughout Wales now prayed for the safety of this prince against some mad extremist. A Welsh nationalist had been overheard planning to strap a hand grenade to his stomach and throw himself at the prince, using himself as a human bomb. But another known nationalist was heard to say, "If anybody lays a finger on that lad, they'll swing from the nearest tree."

The man in charge of the investiture ceremony was Prince Charles's uncle, Lord Snowdon, the former Antony Armstrong-Jones, himself a Welshman. The Queen had made her brother-in-law Constable of Caernarvon Castle.

Snowdon designed the spectacle as a television event. And so it was. It all seemed so anachronistic at a time when three young men were preparing to land on the moon. And yet, five hundred million people were glued to their television sets all over the world, mesmerized by this ancient fairytale pageantry. A thousand years of history was streamlined into sixty minutes to present a monarch for the Moon Age.

A nationalist summed it up: "This is a land where men cry. Understand that, and you are near to understanding the Welsh."

A youth threw an egg at the Queen's coach—and was almost lynched. There was some small, scattered booing but it was quickly quieted as the Queen's procession began, heralded by trumpets, preceded by yeomen of the guard, in their brilliant red tunics with encrusted gold braid, and gentlemen at arms with plumes flying like the ribbons of a maypole. Everywhere were brilliant banners. Then the crowd of thousands at the castle greeted their Queen with the

Welsh national anthem, which Princess Margaret sang in Welsh. And when the camera came in close on the face of the Queen as the crowd sang "God Save the Queen," there was something marvelously moving about the scene, with the eerie ruin of the castle as a backdrop.

It became even more moving when twenty-year-old Charles Philip Arthur George Windsor, tense and pale, made three separate bows before his mother, then knelt before her on a cushioned stool while she carefully placed the gold coronet on his head. With equal care, the Prince took the crown—encrusted with 75 diamonds, 12 rubies, trimmed with ermine and velvet—in his own hands to readjust it to a steadier position on his head. She also gave him a gold rod of office, a gold ring—an amethyst held by two Welsh dragons—a sword, and an ermine and velvet mantle. She quietly reminded him to keep the gold rod raised. In her proclamation she had called him, "Our most dear son Charles . . ."

As he knelt in front of her, he placed his hands between hers and repeated the ancient oath of homage, an act that went back to the earliest days of feudalism:

"I, Charles, Prince of Wales, do become your liege man of life and limb and of earthly worship, and faith and truth I will bear unto you to live and die against all manner of folks."

Mother and son then exchanged the kiss of fealty, and then Charles addressed the crowd and the world in impeccable Welsh, his voice warm, calm, strong:

"The demands on a Prince of Wales have altered, but I am determined to serve and to try as best I can to live up to those demands, whatever they might be in the rather uncertain future. One thing I am clear about, and it is that Wales needs to look forward without forsaking the traditions and aspects of her past."

As if to accent this, a formation of jet planes flew low over the castle.

When it was over, Prince Charles caught his father's eye and smiled. "Oh, Mr. Thomas," said Her Majesty to her Secretary of State, "it's been a wonderful day."

Everybody agreed that the ceremony had been an enormous accomplishment for the Prince. For a Britain that was supposed to be a broken-down, washed-up nineteenth-century industrial nation, this was more than royal soap opera. It was something stirring, dramatic, and elegant. As the Observer put it, "The monarchy is back in business, and much more professional, devoted, potent, and slick than we had ever supposed it could be. What is more, it seems plain that most citizens not only tolerate the Royal Family but actively want them."

That evening the Prince of Wales had a private party for a few of his closest friends aboard the *Britannia*, which had hovered in the harbor. The guest list did not include Patricia Nixon, who had come for the ceremony, nor the young Princess from Luxembourg, Marie-Astrid. But it did include Lucia Santa Cruz, who had spent a weekend with the Prince at Balmoral.

For the next four days, the Prince of Wales toured all over Wales as the people sang "God Bless the Prince of Wales" and yelled "Good old Charlie!" Welsh beauty queen Laurwena Davies said, "He's gorgeous . . . he's a smasher." One newspaper called him "The Pied Piper of Wales."

He was now much more than that.

On his return to Cambridge, the tone of his evening talks with Rab Butler became more serious, with a broader range. Butler, a huge, Buddha-like figure, would sit in his book-lined study, wrapped in wooly scarves, nibbling on ginger cake, telling the young prince about behind-the-scenes Parliamentary politics. "I'd tell him who was a bloody fool and who wasn't, and I'd explain things about the constitution to him, and tell him all about the part he'd have to play. The boy has great gifts, great gifts, even more so than his parents. The Queen is one of the most intelligent women in England, and brilliant at summing up people, but I don't think she's awfully interested in books. Prince Charles has a tremendous affinity for books. They really mean something to him."

Butler was the one who urged Charles to go into college theatricals, saying, "You're soon going to have to make public appearances, and it's essential for you to learn how to deliver throwaway lines." The Prince later admitted that these theatricals had taught him an accurate sense of timing for his public speaking.

"He gave my wife and me a dinner in his rooms once," said Butler, "and he did most of the cooking; and I must say it was very good."

With fellow students, though, friendships continued to be difficult. "He's a quiet, easygoing sort of chap, and superficially, he's easy to know. But deep down he's a very private person," said John

Molony, whose father was Attorney General for the Duchy of Cornwall. "I don't think anyone gets to know him really well—not that he's standoffish in any way, and he's certainly never pulls royal rank on anyone. In fact, it's a funny thing. Somehow he always behaved as if he were *our* social inferior, and not the other way around."

If somebody argued that what he had said was illogical or condescending, Prince Charles wouldn't bristle, he would simply ask them to explain what was wrong.

His loquacious Welsh friend, Hywel Jones, spent more time with him sitting about in their dressing gowns, drinking coffee, talking into the early hours. Looking back at those conversations, Prince Charles agreed that they did much to modify his natural conservatism.

"Charles was certainly extremely interested in political issues, although he rarely put forward his own views," said Jones. "But those he did express were surprisingly open-minded and flexible. His thinking is far less hidebound and stereotyped than I think most people would suspect. He's highly intelligent and worked very hard."

One of his tutors added that when Prince Charles first came to Cambridge, "we thought we could work up some courses for him. But five minutes after he arrived, it was perfectly obvious that he could take any course he wanted. He has a natural ability for working quickly and absorbing quickly, and writing about it fluently. He is frightfully well organized." The tutors' consensus was: "Solid, not brilliant, but intelligent. Capable of giving shape to an idea."

"Beneath the syrup of many public comments about royalty, the Prince emerges distinctly as somebody who could be the most intellectual king since James I, and the most cultured since George IV or Charles II," wrote the *Times* of London.

Asked what he thought of a university education, somebody quoted Prince Philip, who had said, "I'm one of those stupid bums who never went to university and a fat lot of harm it's done me." Prince Charles smiled and answered, "I'm one of those stupid bums who went to university. Well, I think it's helped me. You see, I really wanted to go . . ."

In a lighter vein, the Prince said in a television interview at the time, "I often feel that the whole fun of university life is breaking the rules—I'll probably get sacked when I get back.

"I think, for instance, the gate hours have been abolished. The gates were shut at six o'clock or whatever it was, six-fifteen, and you couldn't get in . . . but now I think they've done away with it altogether. Half the fun at Cambridge is to climb in at all hours of night, and it's a great challenge. It's been going on for years. And what does it matter, really?

"The guest hours have been lengthened. You can have a girl in your room until two o'clock in the morning instead of twelve o'clock. Well, I mean, that's all right."

There was another side of Prince Charles. On a train from Cambridge to London, it was so crowded that passengers were standing in the corridors. Charles saw an elderly lady standing outside his first-class compartment. He opened the door and invited her to take his seat. "Very kind of you, sir," she said, "but I only have a third-class ticket."

"Don't worry about that. I'll take your ticket and find a seat farther down the train."

Nor did she know who he was.

In a Cambridge college debate, the Prince showed how well he could think on his feet, attacking pollution, noting we had become "creatures of technology." His great-uncle, Lord Mountbatten, had come as a devil's advocate, taking the other position. But the Prince's side won.

Prince Charles won his college degree, with honors in history— the first college degree to be awarded an heir to the British throne. His tutor, Dennis Marrian, described it as "three years' hard slog," but Master of Trinity Lord Butler said it was rather remarkable that the Prince could get a good degree "considering all his other duties." Butler felt strongly that if the Queen had not called up her son for intermittent royal duty, he might well have graduated with high honors.

When he was twenty-one, Prince Charles celebrated his coming of age with a birthday party at Buckingham Palace for 400 guests. The black-tie buffet supper and discotheque dancing were enlivened by champagne, fireworks, and a concert by Yehudi Menuhin and his Festival Orchestra of thirty-two string players. Nobody was able to recall the last orchestral concert in the palace. The Prince selected the program himself. Menuhin said, "He has taken pains over each item. He has a tremendous passion for music."

Most of the older people left after the fireworks, but the party lasted until breakfast. The most popular dance number was "Everybody's Talking at Me," the theme of the film *Midnight Cowboy*.

Despite the fact that ladies were permitted to wear pantsuits, it was a very proper party with no drunks.

Beyond the fun and the frivolity, there was also seriousness. Like medieval knights and sovereigns of yore, the Prince of Wales went to the 900-year-old Chapel of St. John in the Tower of London on the morning of his twenty-first birthday to swear that he would "give and not count the cost" and "fight and not heed the knocks." He knelt in the candlelit chapel and prayed:

"Teach me, good Lord, to serve thee and your people as thou deservest . . . to labor and serve thee without asking for any reward save that of knowing that I am doing your will . . ."

His mother had said simply, "Prince Charles must be brought up to be a good man, because if he is not a good man, how can he possibly be a good king?"

6

Feminists insist that Diana Frances Spencer has set back the feminist movement at least twenty years.

They claim that the Princess of Wales, who became the model for millions, has a personal reputation of being too sweet, too neat, too obedient, too unwilling to fight authority.

The accusations are only partly true. She was, after all, a much-loved, well-mannered child of privileged parents. She was surely not as aggressive as her sister Sarah. But, as Prince Charles often said, "I was told that before you marry the daughter, you should first look at the mother." Diana had her mother's stubborn will and spirit. She knew what she wanted to do, and however more quietly, she did it. She was the one who decided not to graduate from West Heath, and she was the one who decided to go to finishing school in Switzerland.

The Swiss school turned out not to be a good choice. "When Lady Diana arrived," said the headmistress, "she was a lovely girl—but rather young for a sixteen-year-old." And her French teacher remembered Diana not for her French, which was poor, but for her self-imposed goals. "She was very idealistic about what she wanted for herself. She knew she wanted to work with children—and then wanted to get married and have children of her own."

The Institut was an elite school for European aristocrats, and all the girls were supposed to speak only French. Of the sixty pupils, only nine were English. One of them, Sophie Kimball, befriended Diana and the two broke the school rule and spoke English together. Diana took courses in dressmaking, cooking, and skiing. But without fluency in French, and with few friends, she was seriously homesick. After six weeks, she returned to England, telling her parents that she was through with school and wasn't interested in any debutante party to get socially launched. Her plans were now to settle in London and get a job.

Her mother had kept a house in London's Chelsea section after her divorce, and Diana moved in there. She learned to drive a car, took a cooking course, learning how to make everything from sauces to soufflés. She also signed up for dancing lessons with the idea that at some future time she might teach it. One of her Cordon Bleu classmates, Laura Grieg, a friend from West Heath, moved in with Diana in her mother's four-story house. Later, Sophie Kimball, her friend from Switzerland, also joined them.

Diana was now seventeen. Her sister Jane, twenty-one—after studying art in Florence—was working in London as an editorial assistant on *Vogue* magazine. Sister Sarah, after attending the Swiss school and then the Conservatoire School in Vienna, was also back in London and working for a real estate agency. Sarah was now most prominently mentioned in the press as Prince Charles's girlfriend.

The less flamboyant Jane was the first to marry, in April of 1978. Her husband was thirty-six-year-old Robert Fellowes, whom she had known since Sandringham days. His father had been one of the Queen's land agents, and now Robert was Her Majesty's assistant private secretary. Many of the Royals, including the Queen Mother, came to the wedding, and the reception that followed at St. James's Palace. The Queen gave the newlyweds a rent-free ("grace and favor") apartment at Kensington Palace, and Earl Spencer made available a house on the Althorp estate.

Diana's father seemed a truly happy man now. "We're still passionately in love," he said. "But sex isn't the overriding thing in marriage, is it? At our age—well, mine, though Raine won't mind growing old and being a grandmother, so she says—you either become very dependent on each other or you grow apart. We're very dependent." Then he added, "I've seen her without her makeup. I've even seen her with her hair dead straight in a gondola in Venice, in the rain. I liked her better that way. That doesn't stop her recurling it. She loves her clothes and jewelry, and I'm happy for her. I don't mind how she is, as long as we're together."

There was a general feeling among many that Earl Spencer's wife dominated him. His answer to that was, "People imply that I have very little to do with the running of Althorp, and my wife rules over everything. In fact, everything we have chosen for the house has been done together. She's an amazing person, but you've got to control her. When I'm cross, I'm very direct with her. I will shout, 'Now bloody well listen to me for a minute!' and she does. I sit her down and say, 'You're a tremendous person, Raine, and a very special person, but you've got to . . . limit your output.' And she says, 'I'm sorry, I love you.'

"She grumbles that I'm too soft and kind and nice with people," he continued, "that I'm too idle, I don't work hard enough. But I'm very strong, strong as steel underneath, so we do have our occasional rows. When I jump at her, she jumps back at me, but it doesn't worry me. She always comes round to my decision in the end.

"She's much better at dealing with problems and getting at the root of things than I am. In my little way, I think I can guide her, and keep her calm and steady . . . she'd do anything to help me."

She soon proved how true his words were.

In September of 1978, Earl Spencer collapsed in the courtyard at Althorp with a brain hemorrhage. He fell into a coma.

The doctors were generally pessimistic about the outcome. Raine took charge. Whenever doctors seemed to give up hope, she moved him to another hospital.

"I'm a survivor," she said, "and people forget that at their peril. Nobody destroys me, and nobody was going to destroy Johnny so long as I could sit by his bed—some of his family tried to stop me—and I willed my life force into him."

Her husband agreed. "Without Raine, I wouldn't be here . . . I'd be dead. Raine saved my life by sheer willpower. The doctors had me on the death list eight times, and they kept at her to order a coffin. They said I'd need a miracle to survive. Raine was my miracle. It's entirely due to her—her love for me, her determination not to let me go—that I'm still around. I couldn't talk to her, but I knew she was there, hour after hour, week after week, holding my hand and talking about our holidays and my photography—things she knew I liked.

"She used to shout at me sometimes, bless her, 'Can you hear me?' she'd yell.

"I wasn't afraid of dying. I'm not the sort of person who's afraid. I think at one very bad stage I had a choice of life and death and I knew that, at that moment, I didn't want to die. Anyway, Raine wouldn't have let me. She stops at nothing!"

"In a situation like that," Raine said later, "if you sit down and cry, you cry for yourself. The only thing I could do for him was to use my life and energy for his life.''

When he was at Brompton Hospital in South Kensington, Countess Spencer gave instructions that nobody, not even his children, should be admitted to his room. But when she left his bedside for a short while, the nurses let his three daughters know. They came in through a rear door to see their father, still in a coma.

The coma lasted for four months. When the doctors were most pessimistic, Raine heard of a German wonder drug, unlicensed in England, called Aslocillin. She contacted her friend Lord William Cavendish-Bentinck (later Duke of Portland), the head of a drug company. He checked and discovered ''a bit of luck,'' that his company had some of the drug in England and were about to start clinical tests. Raine herself collected the medicine at Victoria Station and persuaded her doctors to use it on her husband.

That afternoon she was with him playing a tape of *Madama Butterfly* when her husband suddenly opened his eyes ''and was back.''

''She was absolutely magnificent,'' said a friend about Raine after the ordeal. Even Earl Spencer's daughters agreed. ''The wicked stepmother'' had saved their father's life. Grudgingly, they now accepted her, although Sarah might still mock the way Raine called their father ''Johnikins, darling.'' And they found it difficult to believe when the butler, Ainslie Pendry, recounted how Raine had called in the local vicar, Reverend Malan, to bless all the rooms at Althorp to exorcise any ghosts that might have caused the Earl's illness.

The myth was that the Spencer children were grudgingly reconciled to their stepmother after she saved their father's life.

Raine denied it. ''I could have saved his life ten times over, and spent all my money doing it, and it wouldn't have changed anything in his children's attitude towards me.'' She was right.

Diana and her stepmother were always respectful of each other, even though Raine sometimes snidely referred to her as ''Pigeontoes.'' Diana came to visit often, but usually stayed outside the main house in one of the smaller buildings on the land. Fellowes traveled wherever the Queen went, so Jane was often alone now and welcomed Diana's company when she came to Althorp. Jane and Diana were rather alike, and closer to each other than to Sarah. They really confided in each other, and Diana was most excited when Jane told her she was pregnant.

Diana had signed up with several employment agencies for temporary work: Knightsbridge Nannies, for babysitting; Solve Your Problems, for housecleaning; and Lumley's, for making canapés at cocktail parties. She was soon doing part-time work for all of them and enjoying it. Her first real job was as a live-in babysitter in Hampshire for three months for the Whitakers. Major Jeremy Whitaker and his wife, Philippa, were old friends of her father.

"She was also a great help around the house," said Mrs. Whitaker. "If there were strawberries to pick, she would help. Or meals to be fixed. She didn't mind work at all. If there was a job to be done, she did it."

Diana wanted to train as a ballet teacher so she enrolled at the Vacani School of Dancing both as a student and a teacher.

The Royals, including Prince Charles, had been taught how to dance by Miss Vacani. Diana worked for her, teaching some two dozen two-year-olds how to dance to the tune of "Hickory-dickory-dock," and then taught some older children.

"She tried it for about a term, but she realized that you've got to be absolutely dedicated, and she had a rather full social life," said Miss Vacani. "But the ballet helped her posture."

When Diana's mother decided to sell her Chelsea house, Diana decided to find a flat of her own. Sarah found her one at 60 Coleherne Court in Chelsea, near Fulham Road on the edge of an area that housed some Saudi sheiks. This bohemian section was filled with small, lively restaurants and interesting shops, not far from Kensington Palace where Jane had an apartment. Sarah's flat was also close to Fulham Road.

Diana's new apartment was in a nondescript block of flats and was a spacious three rooms with high ceilings. It cost about 50,000 pounds, but Diana now had some money of her own from a fund left for her and her sisters by her American great-grandmother, Frances Work.

Her mother came from Scotland to help her decorate and they concentrated on traditional wallpaper and comfortable sofas. Diana even had two ready roommates, Sophie Kimball and Philippa Coaker.

Although Diana was now eighteen, she still looked younger than her years and wore jeans, baggy jumpers, and seldom any makeup. She neither smoked nor drank, nor took drugs.

At that time in Britain a slogan was coined to describe a certain type of young woman who loved jokes, didn't use big words, was sexually innocent, and regarded Sloane Square as the center of the modern world. They were called Sloane Rangers. Diana fit the description perfectly.

"One must not think too hard or it would disturb people," noted Ann Barr and Peter York, who popularized the term. "One must use understatements so as not to bore or whine. One must use the rights words in the right voice. Sloane Rangers love the past. All the good things have been going on for ages. That means old houses, old furniture, old clothes, old wine, old families, old money. What really matters to a Ranger are the people they know, where they live, family background, school, job." Other Ranger qualities were loyalty to friends, considering one's mother one's best friend, and the importance of virginity and marriage.

Diana and her roommates took their pleasure in an occasional glass of wine in the nearby bistros and shopping in the chic boutiques near Sloane Square, going to parties and country weekends.

Her roommates came and went. The new ones were nineteen-year-old Carolyn Pride, a West Heath schoolmate who was now studying singing and piano at the Royal College of Music. She was a keen horsewoman with a string of trophies. Then there was twenty-one-year-old Ann Bolton, secretary to an estate agent. She was the practical one. The extrovert was Virginia Pitman, a Yorkshire girl who had hitchhiked to Africa, took a trip up the Nile, and was now learning how to mend broken china.

Diana and her roommates not only exchanged clothes, but also records and magazines. Their favorite pop music groups were the Police, Neil Diamond, and Abba. They also shared the same hairdresser in South Kensington. Her roommates later persuaded Diana to have her legs waxed and her eyelashes dyed there, too.

"What all her friends loved most about her," said Teresa Mowbray, who knew Diana since childhood, "was her great sense of humor. She loved a joke, and had a tremendously hearty laugh that was really infectious."

"Mostly we all ate out, and just got our own snacks when we were at home," said Virginia Pitman. "If we had people at supper, I mainly cooked, though everybody helped, of course."

Diana was the one who invariably started washing up, almost before dinner was done.

Some of their favorite restaurants included a little French place nearby, the Poule au Pot, and an Italian restaurant called Topolino where the owner played his guitar in a sing-along. Their apartment had an upright piano which Diana used often, and their hallway was often a clutter of bicycles.

The girls had a strict rule concerning boyfriends: no poaching.

One of the young men who came around most often to see Diana was Simon Berry, several years her senior, an old Etonian and the son of prominent London wine dealers. When she made dinner at home, he said, "The meals were delicious, but plain. Eggs were one of her passions. There was nothing she liked better than to sit down to a plate of scrambled eggs. And she was so domesticated. She always seemed to be washing dishes or cleaning up, and she loved doing it."

Berry took her to dinner, the ballet, the Wimbledon tennis championships. And they were also part of a group of eighteen who spent a two-week holiday in 1979 at a chalet in the French Alps.

"One day she had a slight injury and stayed behind while the rest of us went skiing," Berry continued. "With eighteen people living in the chalet, we had dishes piled up in the sink, and there was clothing scattered everywhere. Diana washed up all the dirty dishes, swept the floor, and tidied it up to such an extent, the place was immaculate."

Diana then was still unsophisticated with a fresh, friendly, happy-go-lucky personality. "There was nothing hoity-toity about Diana," said Berry. "She had this wonderful gift of getting on well with everybody. You know, she has broken the hearts of dozens of young men. Chaps would meet Diana and fall instantly in love."

What the young men remembered most were her extraordinary blue eyes, really dramatic and sometimes appearing almost purple. And there was a wild country look about her. Sometimes she seemed unbelievably shy, the way she held her head down and blushed, "soft and vulnerable."

"She can look intensely serious one moment," said Teresa Mowbray, "then someone cracks even a mild joke and her face lights up in a beacon of laughter and joy."

"I was skiing down an icy slope," recalled Simon Berry, "and suddenly I heard the strident tones of Miss Piggy in my left ear, informing me, 'You're treading on thin ice, frog.' In the next instant, Diana went hurtling past me, with a big grin on her face. She's a great mimic."

Diana seemed slightly changed after the skiing trip in 1979. The family butler at Althorp, Ainsley Pendry, remembered, "Lady Diana got very angry because she wasn't allowed to use the stereo record system which was in the house. So she took up all the floorboards in the room and disconnected the wiring, so no one could use it."

The butler also remembered a high-spirited night when Diana had some friends in at Althorp for a small party. "Towards the end of the evening, after everyone had gotten a little merry, some of the boys grabbed Lady Diana and threw her in the pool. But instead of getting, out, Lady Diana threw off most of her clothes and swam around, laughing. The boys were applauding and enjoying every moment of it. Lady Diana's a lovely looking girl, and it was all innocent fun. Then she asked for her bikini, and put it on before she got out of the water." As an afterthought, the butler added, "Lady Diana's usually a very shy person, and she blushes very easily."

But he also recalled an earlier time when an older man had arrived at Althorp for a family visit. Diana had been swimming in the pool. She was just getting her robe on when the man complimented Diana on her tan. She smilingly opened her robe for his full view of her bikini, then calmly walked away, "leaving the old gent spluttering, 'If I was only fifty years younger!'"

Cook Rose Ellis remembered a conversation with Diana in the Spencer car: "I told her I was keeping newspaper cuttings about Lady Sarah, her sister, and her friendship with Prince Charles. Lady Diana replied jokingly that it was the nearest her sister would get to the Prince." Then, when the cook teased Diana about not having a steady boyfriend of her own yet, Diana laughed and said, "I'm saving myself for Prince Andrew."

Describing her then, a friend said, "It was as if her day-to-day existence only consumed a part of her that did not matter, as if her innermost heart were elsewhere."

For all her slightly added sophistication, she was still a teenager who liked bubble gum, Yorkie Bars, and still liked to gorge on a box of chocolates. "I don't know how she never gets fat," said Alexandra Loyd at the time. "Her complexion is amazing, considering what she eats."

She was still a romantic, her head filled with the plots of Barbara Cartland novels, and she now had the real-life example of her own mother who had remarried for love. Among her social peers, the question of career was always secondary to the choice of a husband.

Author Nancy Mitford once said, "The purpose of the aristocrat is most emphatically not to work for money." Certainly for Diana money was never the main reason for work. Her roommates paid their share of the rent, she had her great-grandmother's fund, and her parents were generous with her. Her mother bought her a car, and when she cracked it up, her father bought her another.

She could have found a job in some chic boutique, as most of her Sloane Ranger peers did. But what she really wanted was to work with children, something she had discussed with one of her classmates at West Heath, Sarah Robeson, as well as with several of her teachers.

For a time, she acted as babysitter for an American couple, Mary and Patrick Robinson. "This charming girl reported for duty," said Mrs. Robinson, "and she was so refined and well educated that we knew she must be somebody special. All I can say is that Lady Diana was wonderful with children." Mrs. Robinson soon learned how special Diana was when she phoned that she wouldn't be able to babysit that day because she "was being presented to the Queen."

Diana's big job was at the Young England Kindergarten. The school was housed in St. Saviour's Hall in Pimlico, a short bike ride away from her apartment. The old stone building had a big play area, a stage for plays, and access to a park. Diana's sister Jane had been a West Heath classmate of Kay Seth-Smith, one of the two young women who ran the school.

The school catered to children from two to five, and believed more in love than discipline. For a student body of seventy, it had a staff of ten. Diana was one of two training assistants.

"Diana first came only in the afternoons," said Kay, "but she got along very well with the children and the parents liked her. It's always very active around here, and she handled it well." She helped them mix their paints and sort out their glue pots and scissors, cut up their paper, cuddled them when they cried.

"Dealing with children requires your total involvement," said Kay. Diana was soon working with the older children in the mornings, too. Among her charges was the great-great-granddaughter of Sir Winston Churchill, and the great-grandson of Prime Minister Harold Macmillan. One mother called her "a pied piper with children."

At the same time, Diana was still taking dance lessons in the evening: Latin American dancing, jazz dancing, tap dancing. At Althorp a servant recalled how Diana would tap dance by herself for hours to records played on the phonograph.

Sarah finally married in May of 1980. Her mother had paid for the wedding, just as she had paid for Jane's. She also agreed to having Raine sit in the front of the church with Earl Spencer. Sarah was then twenty-five, and her groom was ex–Guards officer Neal McCorquodale, the twenty-eight-year-old son of a printing millionaire, a cousin of Raine.

Bridesmaid Diana caught the bridal bouquet.

After the wedding, she and Simon Berry were discussing what they wanted in life. "I would love to be a successful dancer," Diana said, then added with a playful glint, "or maybe Princess of Wales."

Diana seldom went to fashionable night clubs or cocktail parties, although she had all kinds of invitations on her mantelpiece. She was simply not very comfortable with highly sophisticated people. But one day she received an invitation she could not refuse.

It was from Sarah Armstrong-Jones, daughter of Princess Margaret, whom Diana's father had once dated. Lady Sarah was a good friend of Diana's and had also been a bridesmaid at Sarah Spencer's wedding. The invitation was to spend a few days aboard the royal yacht *Britannia* during Cowes Week. Sarah added a note: The Prince of Wales would be on board.

7

I f we were to believe everything printed about the Prince of Wales before his marriage, we might visualize a handsome daredevil who not only flew his own planes but jumped out of them, raced his Aston Martin at breakneck speeds, dove 50 feet under the ice in the Arctic, sailed in hurricane winds, took the Tarzan course in Marine training, skippered a minesweeper through North Atlantic gales, escaped from a submarine, played a slashing game of polo, and skied impossible downhill slopes. Then, when the sun set, he hopped in and out of bed with bevies of beauties from all over the world. In most of these activities he seemed a carbon copy of his father, Prince Philip.

The truth is that Prince Charles is nothing at all like his father. Prince Philip took up sports out of sheer pleasure, enjoying more than anything the sharp edge of competition and the challenge. The Prince of Wales has done most of these things mainly to prove to his father—and to himself—that he could do anything his father did, and perhaps more, and perhaps better.

The son surely did prove that he was the equal of his father in courage and skill, but he could never truly be like his father. There is a photo of Charles and his father on his desk in Kensington Palace, on which he has written, "I was not meant to follow in my father's footsteps."

Of his father, the Prince of Wales has said he was a strict disciplinarian, that he would frequently tell him to sit down and shut up. "It was very good for me. I think he has had quite a strong influence on me, particularly in my younger days. Now I am becoming more independent. I think I may be slightly late developing."

Prince Philip is an extrovert with a quick tongue and acid wit. Although the British press took pains not to report it, he traveled almost six months a year, and there were persistent rumors that he was enjoying women wherever he went. In the small circle around the Royals, there were even strong snickers about the historic royal tradition of producing children "on the wrong side of the blanket," one aristocratic lady smilingly noting that she had seen a young woman in London who looked remarkably like Princess Anne.

It must quickly be pointed out that there has never been any hard evidence surfacing about any of this. Prince Philip is a handsome man and it is not unlikely that a great many women have pushed themselves at him, as they have at his sons. But nobody among the Royals has a stronger sense of duty and responsibility than the Prince, and nobody would be more careful.

What must be noted is that it is traditional among aristocratic families in Britain for the partners to have a strong social and working relationship, but to sleep in separate bedrooms and live separate lives.

Prince Charles, unlike his father, is essentially a shy man, a loner, a very private person. As his close friend and advisor Sir Laurens van der Post put it, "He's following his own star." Give the Prince a choice and he'd quickly prefer a quiet week working on his farm in Cornwall rather than any hectic activity on a playing field. One of those who play polo with him—a game he does love—says that he will never be a truly strong player because he will not be hard enough on his horses. The Prince's answer is that "a horse is not a bicycle."

If we are to believe those who know him best, Charles was really a romantic who preferred seriously concentrating on one woman at a time. He admitted that he fell in love "very easily . . . I've been in love with all sorts of girls and I hope to fall in love with lots more." But whenever it became serious, whenever the press pounced on it, he became, according to his longtime valet, "very careful and very cautious."

Ever present in his mind was the stark example of his great-uncle, the former Prince of Wales who became King Edward VIII, then abdicated because Parliament would not countenance a divorced woman as his Queen.

Times had changed, but not that much. Prince Charles knew that he could not marry a woman who had slept with too many other men—some might be tempted to sell their stories to the press. A Prince of Wales could not marry a woman so bright and vivacious that she would soon get bored with the unending, grueling royal routine. A Prince of Wales could not marry a divorcée, or a woman of a different religion. "If I marry a Catholic, I'm dead. I've had it," the Prince said. A Prince of Wales could not marry a woman with strong political leanings. Indeed, before he could marry anyone, he knew he must have the approval of both the Queen and Parliament.

The abdication of his great-uncle always remained the raw royal nerve. Mountbatten said of the Duke of Windsor, "I love him very much. He was my greatest friend—he was best man at my wedding. He had the greatest possible charisma and charm, but I thought his laying down on his job and his abdicating was wrong. I told him so. The fascinating part is that he made a very good Prince of Wales, but not a good King."

"Having tried to learn from other people's mistakes—yes, in one's own family," Prince Charles said, "I hope I shall be able to make a reasonable decision and choice."

If Prince Charles was "shaken rigid" by "the Edward VIII situation," the royal concern was even deeper that the longer the Prince remained unmarried, there was always something dramatically unexpected that could destroy a romantic young man's sense of royal duty.

The myth was that Prince Charles, learning the lesson of his great-uncle David, the Duke of Windsor, had stayed clear of married women. His great-uncle had concentrated on such women for his love affairs because he considered them "safe," since the press never mentioned them. That turned out to be his fatal flaw. The press now had the Prince of Wales under a probing searchlight that never dimmed. Any amorous encounter between a married woman and Prince Charles would have meant a huge public scandal.

The fact was that his relationships with Dale, Lady Tryon, and Camilla Parker-Bowles had been much more intimate than most people suspected. They not only served to vet the bridal possibilities of his current women, but they provided soft shoulders for confidences and discussions. He came to them as he came to no one else. Among a close group, the feeling was strong that his relationship with these women was even more special than that.

Charles himself in 1969 put it this way: "This is awfully difficult because you've got to remember that when you marry in my position you are going to marry someone who perhaps one day is going to become Queen.

"You have got to choose somebody very carefully, I think, who could fulfill this particular role and it has got to be somebody pretty special.

"The one advantage about marrying a princess, for instance, or somebody from a royal family, is that they do know what happens.

"The only trouble is that I often feel I would like to marry somebody English. Or perhaps Welsh. Well, British anyway."

As it was, Prince Charles knew that any woman he dated, however innocently, was fair game for the press. Every new woman was turned into a picture, a headline, a potential princess. BACHELOR PRINCE CHARLES ENTERS MARRIAGE ZONE read one headline in 1973 when the Prince was twenty-five.

"The name of the game," wrote the London Daily Mirror, "is to find the lady who'll be the next Queen."

"His taste runs to the rosebuds of England rather than to the tiger lilies of the tropic south," a royal equerry reported to the press. Predominantly in favor were the tall, willowy blondes.

In the spring of 1972 one of the blooming rosebuds was Georgiana Russell, described by one reporter as "a smashing blonde bird in black slacks and a cream-colored shirt with the tails hanging out." Her brother Alexander had been a Cambridge classmate of Prince Charles.

The gossip columnists were exultant because she came from such an interesting mix of parents. Her father was Sir John Russell, Britain's Ambassador to Spain, and her mother was a former beauty queen who had been both Miss Greece and Miss Europe. Georgiana was a gifted linguist fluent in French, Greek, German, Russian, Italian, and Portuguese, a sprightly, miniskirted young lady who worked for Vogue magazine, lived in an elegant townhouse in Belgravia, and was described as "the living expression of all that is young and free in Britain today."

Regarded as "vivacious and talkative," Georgiana admitted to the press that she was the mystery girl with Prince Charles when he returned to London from Balmoral. But then she would say no more, adding, "If I say anything, I will get stink from my parents—I really will."

It was quickly noted that she was eighteen months older than the Prince, that they had been seeing each other recently on his leave from the Navy. They were also seen in his car en route to the polo games at Windsor. Her father refused to speculate. "She lives in London and we leave her private life to her." Sir John previously had been Ambassador to Brazil and Ethiopia, and the Queen and Prince Philip had been his house guests.

The press soon uncovered some of Miss Russell's earlier boy-friends, plus the fact that she liked to wear see-through dresses and the briefest beachwear while in Spain, where she was regarded as a "sexy swinger," known as "Gorgeous Georgia."

The consensus was that she was "an outstandingly attractive catch" and that "the engagement seemed imminent." However, there were two prime complications: Prince Charles was serving as a sublieu-tenant on the HMS *Norfolk*, a guided-missile destroyer, and his leaves were only intermittent. But the more serious problem was that Georgiana was a city girl. Things probably started to fall apart the weekend Prince Charles invited her to visit his fishing place at Craigowan, in the Scottish Highlands. "I think she thought the weekend would be a glamorous interlude," said his former valet. "Nothing of the kind. He was standing with his feet in the water all day while she was bored out of her mind." A member of the staff predicted she wouldn't last the weekend. He was right. She went home.

When Miss Russell married someone else, the Prince saw a photo of her and said, "Good God. Her hair is black. She's not a blonde at all!"

The Prince was then twenty-three, and had already sampled a variety of activities in the service. After having flown 170 hours on four aircraft, he entered the Royal Air Force as a flight lieutenant. "The Prince is going to have to earn his wings," said the group captain. In his intensive five-month course, called Exercise Golden Eagle, he was scheduled to qualify on a supersonic Phantom jet. Plane maintenance was more comprehensive, however. "After all," said the group captain, "it wouldn't do at all for us to lose him."

Prince Charles described his fascination with flying as "a mixture between fear and supreme enjoyment." Then he added, "I believe in living life dangerously . . . I believe in challenge and adventure . . . I like trying my hands at things and if people say do you want to have a go, I usually say yes."

He became the first heir to a throne to make a parachute jump: He jumped 1200 feet from an RAF plane into Studland Bay in Dorset. "You're the chap who pushes me out, I suppose," he said to the flight sergeant. "Oh no, sir, no, no," said the sergeant. "We just help." In the jump, the Prince found himself flipped over, his feet caught in the rigging over his head. "Fortunately, my feet weren't twisted around the lines and they came out very quickly. A rather hairy experience."

According to the London *Times*, there were "enough assault craft to have assaulted half of southern England" when the Prince hit the water. He was fished out within twenty seconds. Those who saw him said he was "laughing and grinning." "I'm stupid enough to like trying things," he said.

When he was presented with his pilot's wings, and the Royal salute was sounded, he and his father, who also had qualified as an RAF pilot, stood facing each other and saluting each other. Asked if he planned to follow the pattern of his father, he said, "I wasn't meant to follow in my father's footsteps, in any sense or in any way." He insisted that his father had never imposed any decision on him.

"His attitude was very simple," noted Prince Charles. "He told me what were the pros and cons of all the possibilities and attractions and told me what he thought was best. Then he left me to decide. I freely subjected myself to what he thought best because I had come to see how wise he was."

There was mutual agreement about his entry to the Royal Naval College. His father had entered the Royal Naval College at Dartmouth in 1939 and served through World War II, at one time commanding the frigate *Magpie*. His grandfather, King George VI, an earlier Dartmouth graduate, was also a naval officer.

His parents had taken him on a visit to Dartmouth years before. The Commandant mentioned the royal ties with Dartmouth and added, "I hope the tradition will continue."

Dartmouth had been the place where Prince Charles's mother and father met. His father had been an outstanding cadet at Dartmouth, following in the tradition of his uncle and namesake, Lord Mountbatten. Mountbatten, now Admiral of the Fleet, lived near Dartmouth on his vast estate, Broadlands.

Prince Charles spent considerable time with his great-uncle at Broadlands, mostly listening. They formed a tight bond that lasted throughout Mountbatten's lifetime. "Prince Charles was really the son that Lord Mountbatten never had," said novelist Barbara Cartland. "He always wanted a son, and he adored Prince Charles. He told me that Prince Charles was an exceptional young man, that he would be a very great King. And Prince Charles told me that he felt that Mountbatten was 'the most exciting, the most interesting, most intelligent person I've ever met in my life.' "

In the course of their wide-ranging conversations, Mountbatten offered Charles advice on just about everything. Royalty was the core of his life, and his great-nephew was the future King.

"Oh, I wish Uncle Dickie wouldn't try to persuade me to do something I really don't want to do because I hate to say no to him," Prince Charles confided to Mountbatten's private secretary, John Barratt.

"Well, that's the one thing you *must* do," Barratt told the Prince. "You must say no when you really don't want to do it."

"At one time, Lord Louis told me something I never forgot," said Barratt. "He said, 'I know I'm bossy and I know I'm pushy, but if you ever see me too bossy or too pushy with the young man, let me know.' He always referred to Prince Charles as 'the young man.' " Several times Barratt did remind him.

It was generally known in the royal circle that "the young man" did not have a warm father-son relationship with his own father. Not only was Prince Charles in awe of his father, but, some said, fearful of him. His father was tough and strict. When his father said, "Move your bloody arse," Charles moved quickly.

"I actually heard Prince Philip cursing his son in four-letter words," said a former Palace photographer, "while Prince Charles stared at the ground."

Prince Philip was now traveling more than ever before. Just as the Queen often went to her favorite uncle for a day of counsel and riding, Prince Charles now turned to Mountbatten whenever he needed a sympathetic ear and wise advice.

Prince Philip was grateful to his uncle for harboring him when Lord Louis's older brother died, for easing him into British citizenship, for giving him the honor of his name, for prompting his marriage with Princess Elizabeth, for being a constant advisor. But still he resented Mountbatten for supplanting him in his son's affections.

There was perhaps another reason for Prince Philip's concern over the growing intimate relationship between his son and Lord Mountbatten. Mountbatten had been a great hero in World War II, one of the giants. Noel Coward had even made a movie, *In Which We Serve*, demonstrating his courage during the sinking of the ship of which he was captain. He had regained all the lost honor of his own father, deposed as First Sea Lord during World War I because of his German ancestry—Lord Louis himself had become First Sea Lord. And at the end of the war he was in command of all forces in the Southeast Pacific, having the full glory of being the last Viceroy of India.

But there was a secret scar and it was deep. Lord Louis's wife, Edwina, was an extraordinary woman, a brilliant and beautiful heiress. They had two daughters, but their marriage had gone sour early. Lady Mountbatten took many lovers, including India's Prime Minister Nehru. There was a great scandal over her reported love affair with a black American singer. There were prolonged trips abroad with a single woman friend.

Mountbatten himself had admitted that he and his wife "spent all our married lives getting into other people's beds." Mountbatten was not as promiscuous as his wife, but his affairs were more prolonged. In the tight aristocratic circle, the strong and persistent rumors were that Lord Mountbatten was bisexual. In the twenties, when the prime criterion for social success was "to be amusing," this would not have been unlikely. What must be said, however, is that sex was simply not a driving part of his life.

Prince Philip was in Berlin when Prince Charles graduated from the Royal Naval College and the Queen too was unable to attend the exercises but Lord Mountbatten flew down especially to be there. Afterward, he and his great-nephew took a helicopter to Buckingham Palace to lunch with the Queen.

Prince Charles's next assignment was aboard a destroyer. "I am looking forward to it very much. I hope I won't be too seasick. I will have to stock up with seasick pills."

"At sea, you learn to live with people," his father had told him. In the long days at sea, in the exchange of reminiscences, a fellow officer said, "We learned a lot about the Prince, but nothing about the rest of the family." He learned the life of a seaman, "that peculiar knowledge which only winds and sea, dark night and mist can give." He also learned about missiles, computers, and 4.5-inch guns. He took time out to pass his test for underwater submarine escape. Someone noted that he was the first naval officer in several generations who knew for certain that one day he would be Admiral of the Fleet.

Lord Rab Butler once asked Prince Charles of his service in the Navy, "Isn't that a bit of a bore?"

"He turned to me with a look of surprise," said Butler, "and said, 'But it's my duty, it's my job.'"

But royal duties often interrupted his naval duty. There was a visit to the Prince of Wales Division in Germany, where as a new officer he had to sing a song and eat a raw leek; a private dinner party for his parents' silver wedding anniversary, which he hosted; a pheasant-shooting holiday in southern Spain on the 2000-acre estate of the 8th Duke of Wellington. He spent five days there and the press came in droves from all over Europe because the Duke had a marriageable daughter, Lady Jane Wellesley.

Prince Charles and Lady Jane had known each other as children from the Buckingham Palace birthday parties, and they now rediscovered each other as adults. She seemed to have it all: the bluest blood, elegance, beauty, brains. A small, bubbly young woman, she was one of his few dark-haired "birds." The long camera lens caught them playfully pulling each other's hair and throwing melons at each other. The Prince was also reportedly seen actually kissing and hugging her. There were so many reporters swarming over her father's estate that the Spanish Civil Guard had to be called in. For once, the Prince lost his cool, cursed the intruders, then apologized. His reaction only seemed to heighten the gossip about the seriousness of the affair.

The press was even more convinced when Lady Jane was seen going to church services with the Royal Family at Sandringham, and later attending a film premiere with the Queen Mother. Lady Jane was then working for a travel agency in Chelsea, and the press so besieged her office that her boss said, "Tell the press to go to hell. Get rid of them and don't come back at all if you can't." She had to call the police to force her way out, jumped into a taxi, and dissolved into tears. "It was as if she had been found guilty of some ghastly sexual crime or murder or robbery," said her mother.

A Paris paper reported that the Prince had worn a false black beard when he visited Lady Jane at her home. The paper quoted a sharp-eyed neighbor who had recognized him "and could not keep her tongue in her pocket."

"Poor little Lady Jane," a friend told reporter Ann Leslie. "She'd have been an admirable choice, admirable. I may be wrong, but I really think the press has ruined her chances; after all, the quickest way of killing a romance almost before it can get under way is to focus public attention on it like that. Do you know they had to arrange not to sit together [at Sandringham], stand together, dance together, or go out in the same car together, just in case someone from the outside spotted them and it added fuel to the flames. As a result they scarcely saw each other, even though they were in the same house."

A London newspaper even reported with finality that the royal engagement already had been discussed at a Wellington dinner. The Duchess phoned her daughter, "flabbergasted and very embarrassed," calling the article "pure fabrication and utter nonsense." Lady Jane told the press more politely, "You mustn't jump the gun. It might be all wishful thinking."

Lady Jane was described as the tweedy type. "She has a tremendous sense of humor without being flippant. A typical Wellington, snappy at times, but sociable."

"Jane can lark around with Charles like she did with her brothers and he can relax completely," said a mutual friend. "The two are very good chums," said a Palace spokesman. But "The romance . . . is just not on."

But a Sandringham estate worker made his own unofficial observation: "They seemed to squeeze hands and kiss an awful lot." The press also quoted an intimate friend of Lady Jane: "Jane was the first girl he fell deeply in love with."

British bookies rated Lady Jane as their "hot favorite." She herself tried to cool the heat: "I do know Prince Charles but so do a lot of other young girls." Bookies, however, recalled that Princess Anne, too, had persistently denied any rumors of her engagement to Captain Mark Phillips almost up to the time of their engagement.

The Prince could always escape the press by going off to sea again. Lady Jane, in the meantime, seemed to decide that she preferred the potential of a television career to a future of shaking countless hands and going to endless meetings. "I don't want another title—I've got one," she declared finally.

Charles later had his own public explanation: "A certain young lady was staying at Sandringham; a crowd of 10,000 appeared when we went to church. Such was the obvious conviction that what they had read was true that I almost felt I had better espouse myself at once so as not to disappoint too many people." As the crowd's laughter died away, the Prince added, "As you can see, I thought better of it."

Amplifying that later, he said, "I certainly won't get married until I've left the Navy. I couldn't cope with both. It would be much too difficult a problem, and I think it is very unfair on a woman to be continually left behind. I'd rather wait until I could supply as much company as possible, particularly in the first years of marriage."

Then he added, "I would never recommend getting married too young. You miss too much, you get tied down."

The Prince of Wales took time out of his naval tour for a sad duty. He joined the Queen in Paris, where they visited his very ill great-uncle, the Duke of Windsor.

The Duke had had a blood transfusion that morning to give him the added strength to be dressed and sitting in a chair to receive his niece. He insisted that all the tubes be detached from his body so he could receive the Queen with dignity. One intravenous tube could not be removed but he kept it covered. Although he now weighed only 96 pounds and found it difficult to talk, his mind and memory were alert, his manners impeccable. At the gate, a photographer recorded the Duchess in her curtsey to the Queen, making a valiant attempt at a pleasant smile.

Ten days later the Duke was dead. In an unprecedented gesture of conciliation, the Queen invited the Duchess to stay with her at Buckingham Palace until the funeral rites were completed. Prince Charles was to be her escort, and the Duchess later recalled that he had called her Aunt Wallis and said he hoped he would be as good a Prince of Wales as his Uncle David had been. Prince Charles burst into tears when he heard the bagpipe lament "Flowers of the Forest" at the funeral.

What was even more memorable to some at the funeral was the behavior of the Queen Mother. Many years before she had publicly expressed her hatred for "that woman." She had blamed the Duchess of Windsor for the abdication, blamed her for the shortened life of her husband, who was forced thereby to be king. Despite this, at the funeral, the Queen Mother could not have been more gracious to the widow, even holding her arm.

When he returned to sea, Prince Charles was the second gunnery officer aboard the frigate *Minerva* on a tour of the Bahamas. He still had his other royal duties, however. For the Royal Regiment of Wales in Germany, he compiled a German-English phrase book entitled

"A Guide to Chatting Up of Girls." And he was soon practicing what he preached.

There was the daughter of the Duke of Westminster—and her sister; the daughter of the Duke of Northumberland—and her sister; the daughter of the Duke of Rutland—and her cousin; the daughter of the Duke of Grafton; the daughter of the Earl of Westmoreland; the daughter of Lord Astor; and even the daughter of his father's private secretary.

"Every time I go out with a girl," he said glumly, "it gets into the papers." Then he turned more philosophical. "When one has seen a great deal of life, taken out a large number of girls, fallen in love every now and again, then one gets to know what it's all about.

"At the moment, I don't feel like being domestic," he added. "I personally feel that a good age for a man to get married is around thirty." But, he admitted, "sometimes you are lonely."

He had a firm idea of the kind of women he liked.

"I wouldn't have a woman libber as one of my friends. Those idiotic women who go around telling all other women to think the way they do—basically, I think, because they want to be men—are, to my mind, totally wrong. The vast majority of women I talk to, meet, and like are women who know they are women and have nothing to lose by being a woman. They are feminine, they like doing and thinking about feminine things, and they know they can cope with any man who comes along."

But for those called "Charlie's Angels" the coping often came hard.

If Prince Charles called a young lady for a date, she was expected to make her own way to the rendezvous. If it was to be a quiet supper at Buckingham Palace, she would arrive at the gate, like anyone else, be ushered into a waiting room by the footman, escorted by the Prince's valet to his third-floor apartment at the end of a long corridor. There was no possibility of privacy or secrecy. And the Palace was not the place for an overnight tryst.

If the Prince took the girl for a ride in his own Aston Martin, his detective would be sitting in the back seat. Wherever they went, the detective would wait in the car. If they were dining in a restaurant, the detective would be at the next table.

"It's inhibiting enough being in an intimate situation with the heir to the throne without constantly thinking that you're keeping somebody waiting nearby," said one of his earlier dates.

The press made things even worse. A headline in the London Observer News Service Bulletin blared: PRINCE SEEKS LOVABLE PROTESTANT VIRGIN. Speaking to a group of journalists, Prince Charles talked about his irritation when freedom of the press turned into license and sometimes "cheap, sensation writing." It stirred up "the less attractive aspects of human nature." But another time, he was whistling in the wind when he said, "It's got nothing to do with anybody else, who I might want to marry or anything like that."

"I dare say I could improve my image in some circles by growing my hair to a more fashionable length, being seen in the Playboy Club in more frequent intervals, squeezing myself into excruciatingly tight clothes," he told some magazine editors, adding that the tight clothes would give his "poor tailor" apoplexy.

"Life, I can assure you," he said with a small smile, "is tough at the top."

However, he added, "I am me, and I intend to go on being me."

The press often tried to act as matchmakers. One of their most celebrated attempts was with Princess Caroline of Monaco, the daughter of Princess Grace. The two were to meet for the first time at a charity ball in Monaco. It didn't matter that there would be some 600 other guests including Prince Philip and Henry Kissinger. The fact that they would be seated next to each other was enough to kindle the hot fires of the wire services. A police fight with photographers ended in a crash of shattered glass. Three Italian photographers were later found locked in the lavatory.

"We both knew everyone would try to make a romance of our meeting," Princess Caroline later said.

The two met at the table, chatted amiably for a few minutes, then turned to talk to other guests. Caroline told a friend she thought he was too much of a "square." Charles later confided, "It was a disaster. She's just a twenty-year-old girl [he was then twenty-eight]. What else can you expect from someone that young?"

All these denials still didn't stop one reporter from saying that the Prince was "swept off his feet," and that Princess Caroline had called him "the most handsome and attractive man I've ever met."

Prince Charles, however, summed it all up with a quip: "Before I arrived, the world had me engaged to Caroline. At our first meeting, the world had us married. And now the marriage is in trouble."

A similar incident had happened some years before, on a trip to

Washington, when he had met Tricia Nixon. One of the headlines read: A ROMANCE?

The Washington trip had been a frenetic forty-eight hours of split-second scheduling arranged by President Nixon. It was recorded that the twenty-four-year-old Tricia danced three times with the twenty-one-year-old Prince. She was quoted as saying he was "groovy" and "an excellent dancer," and "the house is going to seem empty without them." (His sister Anne had accompanied him on the trip.)

Less charitably, the Prince said later, "I didn't like it much when they started matching me up with their older daughter. Which one is she? Tricia, isn't that right? I found her artificial and plastic."

He was more impressed, however, with President Nixon. "I thought that twenty minutes, at the most, would be the length of our conversation. But to my amazed embarrassment, it lasted an hour and a half. I was fascinated by all the subjects Mr. Nixon covered." And it was amusing to the Prince afterward that their long talk was immortalized by hidden tape recorders.

He found other subjects even more fascinating. During a port call in Bermuda, after many months of sea duty, he admitted, "It was jolly difficult smuggling girls aboard without the men knowing."

He tried to be a proper sailor. He kept his cabin festooned with pictures of his family. When a visiting naval friend asked, "But where are the girls?" the Prince replied, "Well, get up onto my bunk and you'll find a bulkhead shaft running along at eye level. They're in there." And so they were, "six or seven photographs of the most gorgeous creatures you've ever seen."

When his ship pulled into Fiji, there was a photographer ready to snap a picture of him doing a native dance with a luscious young lady. On that same island, the Prince reportedly went for an early morning swim in the pool, without a swim suit. He was surprised by the daughter of his host, who dropped her own robe to join him. Queried about the day's activities, the Prince reportedly said, "Well, it beats the Changing of the Guard, doesn't it?"

In another port, the Prince was asked how he gets by when he visits countries where he can't speak the native tongue.

"The best way to learn French is to have a French mistress," he said.

It was big news when the Prince joined some of his crew going ashore to see a sex movie. "It's the first time," said the theater's owner, Mrs. Bessie Phear, "we've ever had any royal patronage."

It was even bigger news in Montreal, when the Prince was again on shore leave, and asked a young lady to dance. Her name was Vicki Sampson, twenty-six, a secretary at a radio station. She turned him down flat. "His hair was too short and greased back," she said. Clearly she did not believe the song about the previous Prince of Wales, written in 1928 by Herbert Farjean and Harold Scott, that ended with these lines:

I'm the luckiest of females.
For I've danced with the man who's danced with a girl
Who's danced with the Prince of Wales!

In retrospect, she added, "I could really *die* now!"

An American girl who did not say no was Laura Jo Watkins, a twenty-year-old voluptuous blonde, daughter of an American admiral. She met Charles at a cocktail party at an exclusive yacht club in San Diego, where his ship was berthed. Wearing a tight silver dress, the excited Laura Jo asked a reporter, "May I go up and talk to him, or do I have to be introduced?" The two were quickly constant companions.

The London *Daily Mirror* already had suggested that the Prince might find a bride in the United States that "would work wonders for the Anglo–American alliance." The *Mirror* added that royal princesses were in short supply, "but America is full of blue-blooded heiresses with assets not confined to their bank accounts."

The green-eyed Laura Jo had spent a year in college, some time abroad, and was then attending a business school to become a legal secretary. A reporter recalled the incredible coincidence in the fact that the previous Prince of Wales first met the woman he loved just two miles away in another hotel on this same Coronado Island.

After dancing for much of the evening with the Prince, Laura Jo told reporters, "I found him fascinating, especially when he loaded up a double hamburger with every kind of sauce on the table and ate it without spilling a drop."

The HMS *Jupiter* seemed to be swarming with women guests that evening, most of them gaping at the Prince. "I can't stand those ladies posturing around him like that," complained the captain. The crew, however, tagged him "The With-It Prince." Toni Marie Sousa, an American friend of one of the sailors, quoted him as saying, ''They feel he's going to make a change for England once he becomes king.''

Some photographers were stalking the HMS *Jupiter* when they spotted a young Navy lieutenant and approached him with the request to try to persuade Prince Charles to pose for them. ''You're wasting your time,'' the officer told them. ''He's very pompous and not a very likable chap, you know. He isn't very bright either, by the way. I'm quite sure he will not meet you so you'd better go away and save your time.''

The grumbling photographers walked away, not realizing that they had been talking to Prince Charles.

The United States Ambassador to the Court of St. James, Walter Annenberg, lived nearby on his 1000-acre estate in Palm Springs. The Prince was invited to spend the weekend, along with Governor Ronald Reagan and his wife, Nancy, and a large sprinkling of Hollywood stars. Their consensus was that Prince Charles was more handsome than his photographs.

Laura Jo Watkins, who was also present, agreed.

For the British, one of Laura Jo's liabilities was that she was Catholic. An Anglican priest publicly urged that the Church of England should endorse the right of the Prince to marry the woman of his choice regardless of her religion. ''Upholding human rights is a more important Christian concern than the status of the established church.''

Before the HMS *Jupiter* left port, the Prince invited Laura Jo to dinner. Later he wrote her that his visit had been ''memorable.'' Laura Jo told her mother, ''He made me feel at ease.'' Laura Jo's mother was quoted as saying, ''We are terribly flattered.''

When the ship sailed, Laura Jo told friends she did not expect to see the Prince again. But the two corresponded and several months later, Laura Jo received an invitation to attend the farewell party in London for Ambassador Annenberg. The invitation had come on Prince Charles's request. A reporter recorded, ''Her father paid the fare.''

When the Prince of Wales made his maiden speech in the House of Lords, Laura Jo was sitting in his reserved seat. She heard him say, ''I rise with some degree of fear and trembling.'' He was dressed in a conservative suit instead of the once-upon-a-time black velvet and pink satin. In keeping with tradition, though, he chose a noncontroversial topic for his first speech, warning of the danger of too much government interference in sports. Before speaking, he was seen to look up to the gallery where Laura Jo was sitting. The last heir to the throne to address the House of Lords was Charles's great-great-grandfather Albert, in 1884.

Laura Jo had a midnight drink with Charles at Kensington Palace. She called him "Sir," in a teasing American way, and the Prince found her fun. Nevertheless, when she came to Buckingham Palace for further evening visits, the valet let her in through the basement entrance. She soon let it be known that she was "fed up" with the basement entrance. She thought the Prince was "a great guy," but that his world was "unlikable for kids like us."

The press was surprised not to see her with the Prince when he played in a polo match, but he chided them, "You don't think I'd be such a bloody fool as to bring her here." She did, however, fly to Florida to see him when his ship docked there. And she flew to France as a surprise guest at a Deauville weekend party for the Prince. But that was it. She summed up their short affair: "They wouldn't let us alone. There were always protocol people and guards around."

For whatever reason a romance was over, the ending was seldom abrupt. The Prince was often away for prolonged periods on naval duty and an affair might simply drift into nothing.

A series of other "birds" followed Laura Jo. British actress Susan George was more fun and she knew it. She was older than Charles, sexy, sultry, and almost overripe physically. She was invited to candlelit suppers in his rooms at the Palace, but never to meet the family. Neither was Jane Ward, equally busty and blonde, an assistant manager of the Guard's Polo Club. Royals frowned on the fact that she was a divorcée. They were frequent companions until she revealed to the press, "We tease each other and often flirt." After that, she said, "Enough harm has been done already. I may never see him again."

The absolute rule for all the Prince's women was a discreet silence. Sabrina Guinness seemed an unlikely candidate for his affections. She came from the rich brewing family, but she had a Hollywood past. Besides, she was too thin for his taste. She was also a city girl who would never pass the "fishing test." She was, however, invited for a weekend at Balmoral. When she woke up, the morning papers were brought in. On the front page of one was a story that she had refused an offer of marriage from the Prince of Wales—something she would never do. Humiliated, she then had to go downstairs and face the Royal Family.

"When you reach my age of decrepitude," said Prince Charles when he was twenty-seven, "you look at a girl and wonder if you could marry her. Obviously there are people I've thought of in those lines. You are very lucky when you find a person attractive in a physical and mental sense. Many people fall in love with someone when in fact they are only infatuated. To me, marriage seems to be one of the biggest and most responsible steps in one's life.

"Creating a secure family unit in which to bring up children, to give them a happy, secure upbringing—that is what marriage is all about. Marriage is much more important than just falling in love."

He insisted the Royal Family put no pressure on him: "No, no, not at all. They never put pressure on me."

If this was true earlier, it was hardly the case later.

Patrick Montague-Smith, the former editor of *Debrett's Peerage*, noted: "Court circles feel that it's his life and he must do what he likes. But obviously it would be a good thing to marry because there would be a second heir eventually. If he is still a bachelor when he ascends the throne, it would be the first time since King George III in 1760."

The Prince's persistent answer to the persistent question was: "I still haven't found the right girl."

The twenty-one-year-old Princess Marie-Astrid of Luxembourg was considered the most attractive female among Europe's royalty. She was the daughter of the Grand Duke. Not only had "Asty" taken an intensive course in English at Cambridge, but she had posed for pictures with the Queen. She was also a keen tennis player, a qualified nurse, and drove her own Fiat.

There was one hitch: Prince Charles had never met her.

Still, a Luxembourg paper solemnly reported that the Prince had called Princess Astrid "my idea of a perfect woman," praising her modesty and purity. It even intimated that the two already had had several "discreet meetings."

A London paper headline read: CHARLES TO MARRY ASTRID—OFFICIAL. The subhead added: "Sons Will Be Protestants, Daughters Catholic."

Despite royal denials over this newest "romance," the British press unleashed a fresh torrent of criticism over the Catholic issue.

The Bill of Rights of 1689 established that the King of England also head the Church of England. The Act of Supplement of 1701, amending the Bill of Rights, bars him from marrying a Roman Catholic.

It all started when King Henry VIII got a special papal dispensation to marry his brother's widow, Catherine of Aragon, in the sixteenth century. But after eighteen years of marriage, Henry decided to have the marriage annulled so he could marry Anne Boleyn. The Pope refused to annul the marriage, so Henry separated England from the Catholic Church and established the Church of England with the King at its head.

"To start tampering with these constitutional instruments in order to suit the presumed desire or convenience of the heir apparent is a risky, dangerous business," editorialized the *Daily Express*. The paper brought up the question of whether children raised as Catholics could become heirs to the Crown. Asty, it insisted, would have to convert.

Public opinion polls in Britain showed that most citizens would not object to Charles choosing a Catholic for a wife, or a foreigner, or a divorcée for that matter. It was mainly in northern Ireland that religion appeared to be a burning issue.

Buckingham Palace meanwhile announced: "There is no truth at all in the report that there is to be an announcement of an engagement of the Prince of Wales to Princess Marie-Astrid of Luxembourg."

Nonetheless rumors multiplied that the Prince of Wales had gone to Austria to meet secretly with the Grand Duke and Duchess of Luxembourg, that the Archbishop of Canterbury had been in contact with the Pope on the possible problems, that the mayor of Luxembourg City was getting the Foreign Office red-carpet treatment, and that Princess Asty had shyly told a reporter, "Of course I know Prince Charles." After a thorough check of its records, the Palace finally retorted, "The only time he may have met her was at his investiture when she was fifteen."

None of the royal denials fazed the press. A columnist offered his "exclusive" report that a clandestine meeting took place at Laeken Palace, home of Marie-Astrid's uncle, King Baudouin of the Belgians. "At a secret lunch were Prince Philip, a representative of the Church of England, Cardinal Joseph Suenens, the Belgian Primate, King Baudouin, and Queen Fabiola—and Charles and Marie-Astrid." The only thing the Palace would admit was that Prince Charles did have lunch with the King and Queen of the Belgians.

"You English are romantic," said a Luxembourg official. "Just because it is your Jubilee Year, you all want a fairy-tale wedding.''

But it was not to be. The Palace announcement could not have been more flat or final: ''They are not getting engaged this Monday, next Monday, the Monday after, or any other Monday, Tuesday, Wednesday, or Thursday. They do not know each other and people who do not know each other do not get engaged.''

Shortly afterward, Charles went grouse shooting near Wembergill Moor. A group of middle-aged women watched him curiously as he prepared to leave. ''Which of you am I going to be engaged to tomorrow?'' he quipped.

Mothers all over the world, from Brooklyn to Quebec to Tonga, sent Prince Charles photographs of their darling daughters who would make perfect princesses because they were beautiful, brilliant, domestic, virginal—and, occasionally, rich. The Prince kept all these photographs in a large candy box and once a year would distribute them among the male members of his staff saying, ''And here is the pick of this year's crop.''

He had, indeed, become a kind of sex symbol. The Toronto *Star* referred to it as ''Charlie-mania.'' They reported ''blue-rinsed matrons nearly pushing Charlie's police escorts into glass-paneled walls . . . simpering women clerks dissolved into shrieking and quivering as soon as the bachelor heir to the throne touched their hands . . . one teenaged girl almost swooned as the Prince spoke to her.'' His charm was described as ''high voltage,'' though an occasional criticism was heard: ''Well, I think his ears stick out, and one wonders whether they've considered an operation.''

An author submitted his manuscript on a Prince Charles story and the Palace objected to a line saying that the Prince had a normal sex life. The line was eliminated. Another royal observer said that the Prince was no more a ladies' man than any other red-blooded Brit.

''Getting kissed by women,'' said Prince Charles, was ''one of the perks of the job.'' Body language expert Desmond Morris, however, blamed it on his friendly grin. ''If he scowled or showed alarm or just cultivated a blank expression, it wouldn't happen.''

The Prince later revealed that a bathing beauty who had rushed up to him on an Australian beach for a celebrated lingering kiss had turned out to be a part-time actress in pornographic movies set up by a photographer who wanted the picture.

In the United States women were even more aggressive. Phones were jammed wherever Charles stayed and women pleaded with security guards to let them have anything he had used—towel, sheets, anything.

"I don't know how the idea got about that I am amazingly successful with women," the Prince said. "My constant battle is to escape, and that is sometimes a very difficult thing."

The Prince barely mentioned his fascination for Farrah Fawcett-Majors, the television star of *Charlie's Angels*, when her press agent put her on a plane to London, then alerted photographers as she tried to throw herself into the Prince's arms. That she was currently married did not seem to matter.

Margaret Trudeau, newly separated from her husband Pierre, the Prime Minister of Canada, boasted to friends that she would make Prince Charles fall in love with her. She was then living in a small Paris hotel, smoking marijuana, working as a freelance photographer. She said she knew Charles was interested because "when he first met me in Ottawa, he deliberately peeked down my blouse. I rarely wear a bra, and since the buttons were undone, he told me I was pretty enough to be an actress. He didn't blush in the slightest." He had given her his private telephone number, but when she called, he was away in Scotland. By the time he did return the call, she was involved with King Hussein of Jordan.

In meeting actress Susan Hampshire, wearing a similarly revealing dress, the Prince said, "My father told me if I ever met a lady in a dress like yours, I must look her straight in the eyes. Otherwise, someone might take a photograph of me in what might appear to be a compromising attitude." The actress obligingly cupped her hands over her most exposed parts.

At a Hollywood dinner in Charles's honor, Dean Martin told him, "I would like to be a prince and meet a princess for a day so I could take her out for one evening and at the end of the evening, I would say to her 'Your palace or mine?'"

"With a sexy glint in his eyes," Prince Charles admitted to photographer Allen Warren that he had secret fantasies about Barbra Streisand and Lauren Bacall. When he met Streisand, he said he "never dared to look her straight in the eye for his hidden fantasies would have been hidden no more." He did, however, ask her to sing for him and she was overheard to say, "Oh I've never played *that* Palace!" And when he met Bacall, he revealed that "his nerves got the better of him." He finally managed to say, "I enjoyed your performance in *Mame*"—which was embarrassing because she wasn't in that movie.

Charles felt there was no real reason why he couldn't marry a commoner. "There's no essential reason why I shouldn't. I'd be perfectly free to." He warned, however, that his wife-to-be should have some knowledge of her future role—"some sense of it"—or she "wouldn't have a clue about whether she's going to like it. And if she didn't have a clue, it would be risky for her, wouldn't it?"

His royal peer, Carl Gustaf of Sweden, only two years older, had publicly declared, "Love is all that matters. The girl that I marry may be a secretary or a government official."

Prince Charles disagreed. "I think one's got to be aware of the fact that falling madly in love with someone is not necessarily the starting point to getting married. If I'm deciding on whom I want to live with for fifty years—well, that's the last decision in which I would want my head to be ruled entirely by my heart. It's really a very strong friendship. Love, I am sure, will grow out of that friendship. This falling in love at first sight is not the way royal marriages are made."

"You marry the women you mix with," observed Royal watcher Sally Moore, "and since Charles mixes with the nobs—the peerage and landed gentry—the girl on his arm at the altar is far more likely to be a titled lady."

Davina Sheffield, the granddaughter of Lord McGowan, was not a titled lady, but she came close. A luscious blonde debutante with an extraordinary smile, she was described by the press as "fun-loving." The Prince was known to have her picture next to his bed, and they were seen often enough for a columnist to speculate: "One can never be sure about these things, but I have reason to believe that in the luggage the Queen took with her to Polynesia last night was the announcement of Prince Charles's engagement to Davina Sheffield."

Davina indeed had passed the fishing test at Craigowan, and Prince Charles even took her to a polo match in a royal carriage. She lunched with the Queen at Windsor, visited with the Royal Family at Balmoral, and seemed to have the approval of the Queen

Mother. The Queen Mum met all of her grandson's favorites. While she was careful not to pass any verbal judgment on them, the Prince could always tell how she felt by the way she looked.

Charles took Davina to a cove he had discovered in the West Country while aboard one of his small ships. The place was backed by high cliffs and accessible only by sea. The nearest habitation was a tiny hamlet of twenty thatched cottages with a pub and a general store. A detective alerted the locals, and a fisherman waited to take the couple to the small private beach. The detective waited at a discreet distance from the shore until it was time to leave.

"No one in the village takes any notice of them," said the pub owner. Then he smiled in memory of another Royal. "I think Prince Charles's father told him about this place to begin with."

The consensus among intimates is that Prince Charles did propose to Davina, and asked her to take her time to think about it. She went off to Vietnam to work with orphans, but when she returned five weeks later, the royal romance was all over: An earlier lover had told in great detail of their romance. Another story revealed that she had been caught naked in a men's changing room during a surfing expedition near Devon.

Next came the lovely Fiona Watson, daughter of Lord Manton. She was the proud possessor of a superb figure, but the royal relationship ended when the press pointed out that Miss Watson had revealed every one of her dimensions in eleven pages of *Penthouse* magazine.

Summing up the public attitude toward all potential brides for the heir to the throne, someone said, "Fifty million Brits will be waiting to see if she slips on a banana skin."

The press was not always able to identify his lady friends. A reporter once indicated that the Prince of Wales was going on a nine-day safari to Kenya with a "mysterious blonde." En route home, after the safari, the Prince of Wales saw the reporter at the Nairobi airport. "Here's your mysterious blonde bird," he said, smiling, presenting him with a stuffed pigeon covered with a long wig of golden hair.

His closer friends now seemed to detect a certain wistfulness in Charles. "Every time I give a dinner party," he said, "more and more of my guests seem to be married."

In São Paulo, Brazil, he went to the Hippopotamus night club after a round of trade meetings. According to a local report, he was dancing the samba until three in the morning "with near hysterical abandon."

Asked afterward at a press conference about marriage prospects, he replied, "I see neither wedding bells nor coronation bells in the near future. The Queen will not abdicate and that gives me about thirty years. Besides, if I got married, I wouldn't be able to do the samba like I did the other night."

When Prince Charles left the military in 1977 he was twenty-nine and had served on a variety of ships and traveled over much of the world. He also had qualified as a helicopter pilot and a Royal Marine commando—which he called "a most horrifying expedition." His great pride was getting command of a 360-ton minesweeper, the HMS *Bronington*, with a crew of thirty-nine. As part of a NATO exercise, the men actually found a mine and blew it up.

In recapping his years with the Navy for a BBC radio broadcast, the Prince talked about his first tour of the red light area, "the marvelous runs ashore in different places," as well as learning how to make bread and butter pudding with brandy, the hours shut up in the engine rooms ("noisy, oily, smelly compartments . . . I hated that . . . I felt claustrophobic"). On the other hand, he said, there were also quiet times when "I used to have marvelous talks with the sailors and find out a lot about their lives."

He thought the discipline was important, "being made to do a certain thing you do not want to do." He liked the flying; he liked the command of a ship, although, he said, "I was pretty petrified most of the time because I knew that if anything happened it would be headlines all over the place." Above all, he liked the opportunity to meet so many people from all walks of life.

When asked why he was leaving the Navy, he replied simply, "There are other things to do."

8

All my life I've been learning, proving myself." As Chairman of the Silver Jubilee Appeal in 1977, Prince Charles now held his most important job since leaving the Navy. In this chairmanship, he was not a mere figurehead: He changed policy decisions, bypassed incompetent committee members, and resolved arguments.

He was proving himself a contemporary man in an anachronistic mold. After he wrote a television speech appealing to the country's young people, the seventeen-year-old nurse who was chairman of his Youth Involvement Committee spoke for her group. "I'm afraid, Sir, the speech is illogical and condescending."

His private secretary tried to intervene, but the Prince cut him short. "It's my damn speech and I'm going to have the final say." He listened patiently to the young woman, and revised his speech to incorporate her ideas.

The Jubilee Appeal raised some 16 million pounds (at that time about $30 million dollars), mostly for youth projects.

Jubilee Day dawned miserable-looking, and the Queen selected an outfit of bright pink. The Queen preferred bright colors so she could easily be seen in a crowd. It was a day of trumpets and pealing bells and spontaneous street parties all over the Commonwealth, and a magnificent procession of royal carriages from the Palace to St. Paul's Cathedral.

Afterward there had been so much talk and print about the "Glum Queen," that she pinched her cheeks and said in her own defense, "Look, I simply ache with smiling." A staff member added, "Have you ever tried smiling for twelve continuous miles?" Only in the privacy of her home could she laugh out loud.

Jubilee Day was a day of euphoria and much love. On this day their Queen, who had already survived seven Prime Ministers, and her husband and children walked through the city of London while the people applauded and cheered and marveled.

They were cheering her discipline and her grace, her decency and her dignity, her conscientiousness and her respectability. They were cheering everything she symbolized: national pride, unity, patriotism, continuity. The British people felt about the Queen as Sherlock Holmes did of Dr. Watson: "You are the one fixed point in a changing world."

One of the vast audience of television watchers on that day was Lady Diana Spencer. She was sixteen then, and later that year would meet Prince Charles. If she watched hard, she learned much.

The Silver Jubilee had a great impact on the Queen's son. Nobody marveled more at this outpouring of affection than Prince Charles, who well knew how hard his mother worked, how religious she was about her royal duty, how much she would have preferred being home in the country in an old skirt with her horses and dogs.

"The distinguishing characteristic of British people is their ability to laugh at themselves," the Prince said, "to analyze themselves, to anticipate events, to adapt themselves to changing circumstances." As a man fresh out of the service, he said that it was too easy to glorify war but the most important thing was to prevent war from happening. "The secret to peace in the world could be found in a better education."

The Royal Family, he noted, could best communicate with millions of people throughout the world by example and initiative, through sympathetic concern, and a desire to see human values and standards upheld in the face of all else. In the Navy Charles had learned the premium on honesty to gain respect. "A sailor will see through you every time unless you are genuine and honest with him."

When the Prince visited a youth club in South London, he was met by banners and demonstrators chanting "Stop police harassment," protesting a recent wave of arrests of young blacks in the area. Instead of ignoring them, the Prince moved in among them urging the police and pickets to meet and discuss the issue, saying, "I'm sure there is some truth on both sides." "Well, what about it?"

the Prince asked the police chief. "I would be only too pleased to see them, Your Highness." Blacks promptly hailed the Prince's action, and a policeman saw a parallel with the police oath he took to exercise duty "without envy, ill will, or favor."

Prince Charles was "the first member of the Royal Family to take an official interest in the Community Relations Commission. He had spent hours with them discussing problems of black youngsters in cities, and various projects to promote racial harmony. "It takes guts to be the first Royal to come and visit us here," observed the regional development officer.

Scottish Laborite M.P. William Winter Hamilton, who had once called Prince Charles "a young twerp," now apologized, saying, "I believe Charles to be a sensible, pleasant young man." Then came the Hamilton cut: "Who wouldn't be contented and pleasant with a guaranteed untaxed annual income of 105,000 pounds a year which is likely to be doubled or even quadrupled automatically within the next five years?"

There was some talk that the Prince might be offered a job as personal assistant to former Home Secretary Roy Jenkins in his new post as president of the European Commission. But that didn't happen. Instead he found himself back on the merry-go-round of appearances, openings, handshakes, parties, cornerstone ceremonies, and too much small talk.

In dining with the Prime Minister and a group of Labor ministers, the talk turned to the Prince's role in the "Royal firm." The Prince told of a Qantas airline hostess who had said to him, "What a rotten boring job you've got." Then the prince turned to the ministers and said, "You don't understand! She was *right!*"

Visiting with some Cambridge students afterward, he revealed, "My great problem is that I do not really know what my role in life is. At the moment, I do not have one, but somehow I must find one for myself."

In a session with a group of Canadian students, the Prince was asked, "How can you be a normal person?" The Prince was silent for a moment, then stretched his arms as if reaching for something that wasn't there, and said, "What do you think? . . ."

"Being a monarch in these egalitarian times," the Duke of Windsor had written, "can surely be one of the most confining, the most frustrating and, over the duller patches, the least stimulating jobs open to an educated, independent-minded person."

Prince Charles confided to an interviewer, "The older I get the more alone I become."

A Palace spokesman unofficially observed, "Prince Charles needs a pretty remarkable woman at his side when he takes Britain into the twenty-first century. Some lighthearted flibbertigibbet won't do. He knows this. So does the Queen Machine."

The "Queen Machine" was the term coined for senior members of the Queen's personal staff, the small royal group who skillfully sized up all the serious candidates brought home to the Palace by Prince Charles. As one of them put it, "It is the questions that *she* asks rather than the questions that are put to *her* that matter."

"The girl he's searching for," said an intimate, "is the one who does not want to be Queen, who will only do it out of love for him."

The fact was, however, that almost all of the "candidates" wanted to be Queen. No matter how difficult the job, the magnet was overpowering and few would have refused it. Even if they had wanted to, their mothers wouldn't have let them.

One of the essential qualifications set by the scrutinizing Queen Machine was that the girl's family must fit in with royal circles. And Prince Charles found one that did.

Lady Sarah Spencer seemed perfect. She was, after all, the god-daughter of the Queen Mother, and her grandmother was the Queen Mum's Lady-in-Waiting. Her father had been the Queen's Master of the Household, and the families had been friends and neighbors for many years.

An effervescent, highly independent redhead, Lady Sarah was then working for an estate agent, whose boss described her as "a super girl who works very hard at her job. She drives a pretty hard bargain when it comes to selling houses." Tall and willowy, she looked like a stunning model.

Reporters assigned as royal watchers noted that Prince Charles and Lady Sarah had been seen together at seven polo matches in seven weeks, that Lady Sarah had been invited to be a guest of the Queen in the royal box at Ascot. Reporters saw the affair accelerating when the Prince and Lady Sarah spent a skiing holiday together at Klosters in Switzerland.

"I think of him as the big brother I never had," Lady Sarah insisted. Pressed on this, she added, "What do you expect me to say?

I enjoy being with him. He has a great sense of humor; he makes me laugh." Of course, she said, she was "very fond of him."

They spent a ten-day holiday together in a chalet with the young Duke of Gloucester, who was not expected to be a strict chaperone.

To hovering reporters, she now had to add, "Please, don't make any big thing out of this. Look, I'm having a good time here. It really is great fun, but there's no great romance going on. There's no question of an engagement."

Returning to London, Lady Sarah suddenly found herself in a goldfish bowl, her story and face in every newspaper. She said that people, "mostly older women," would stop her in the street and ask "You Prince Charles's girlfriend, then?" and "When are you going to marry him, dear?"

Even some of her friends started treating her as if she was already royalty, and "one or two of them would actually curtsy to me."

She continued to minimize her relationship with the Prince, which the press accepted as standard procedure, but it was reported that a close friend had said, "She is crazy about the Prince. You should see her bedroom—the whole wall is covered with photographs of him." She also kept a scrapbook of every press clipping mentioning their relationship. (The press also reported that she was suffering from anorexia nervosa, and was in and out of hospitals, the Prince giving her his strongest support.)

Lady Sarah then did the unpardonable by breaking the silence expected of every young woman dating the Prince—before, during, or after. "I decided to clear the air and state exactly what my relationship with Prince Charles was."

"I'm a whirlwind sort of lady," she said, "as opposed to a person who goes in for slow, developing courtships. I can assure you if there was to be any engagement between Prince Charles and myself, it would have happened by now.

"I wouldn't marry anyone I didn't love—whether it was the dustman or the King of England. If he asked me, I would turn him down. I would only marry for love. I couldn't marry for anything else and, at the moment, love just hasn't happened."

Then she added quietly, "He doesn't want to marry anyway. He's not ready for marriage yet. There's no question of me being the future Queen of England. I don't think he's met her yet."

Prince Charles surely would have agreed with her just then.

Fortunately, this was the time for him to make his annual fishing trip to the rugged Vopnafjordur district of northeast Iceland where his friends, the Tryons, had a cottage. "It's heaven. It's so remote," said the Prince. "Just you and nature." The Hofsa River also had some of the finest salmon. Charles managed to spend seven seasons fishing with them in Iceland before the press discovered the fact.

Lady Tryon insists that even though she and Charles were nearby—when he was at Timbertop—she never met him until they were back in England. She met him, she said, through the man she later married, who was a longtime friend of Charles. Lord Tryon is a tall, thick-set banker, who looks slightly somber and forbidding but has his own dry wit. His father was Keeper of the Privy Purse, Treasurer to the Queen. Lord Tryon grew up with Charles, on the same social scene, at the same parties.

Besides their fishing place in Iceland, the Tryons owned 700 acres in Salisbury. The Prince counted Dale and Tony Tryon among his closest friends. They were among the few on whom he might drop in unexpectedly, whenever he felt lonely. The affectionate nickname Charles gave Dale was "Kanga" (short for kangaroo), because she came from Australia.

The striking thing about Lady Tryon is that she is incomparably prettier than any of her photographs. As owner of the highly successful Kanga boutique on Beauchamp Place in Knightsbridge, she travels the world in search of fabric for her dress designs. The only words this sparkling, energetic woman will say about Prince Charles are words in high praise of his concern for human beings.

"Dale's not a beauty," said a friend, "but she attracts men easily. Dustmen whistle at her, so do schoolboys. And she loves it." When the Prince toured Australia, Dale Tryon flew there to act as his official hostess, whenever needed. It caused some talk, although she insisted that her husband would have come, too, but he was ill. "The press could have made mincemeat of me then," she said, "but they were kind."

It caused more talk when she named her son Charles, with Prince Charles as godfather. In one of Lady Tryon's two huge leather-bound volumes of clippings, there is a cover of *Private Eye*, taken at the time of the christening. The snide caption beneath the picture of Charles, Lady Tryon, and the baby insinuated it was more of a family picture. Friends, however, insist the baby is the "spitting image" of Lord Tryon. "There was never anything to these stories," Lady

Tryon said some years later, and a member of the royal staff agreed. "The Prince is simply not the type of man to dally with married women, and most certainly not to married women who are married to his friends."

Royal discretion was a way of life. Discussing the publicity problems for any woman he dated, the Prince felt "it's worse for her than for me. I have layers of things to protect me."

There was one woman that even the press knew nothing about. She was a blonde receptionist in Montreal, working at the British Consulate, a tall Welsh girl originally from Cardiff. Her name was Janet Jenkins. He had taken her to a discotheque one night, dined with her another night at Chez La Mère Michel. He was then wearing a "full-set" (beard and mustache) and had come in with a naval helicopter squadron aboard the carrier *Hermes*. She recalled later that he had sent his beef back because the sauce had garlic—royalty never touches garlic. She also recalled how much fun they had before he flew to London the next morning.

Nobody seemed to know who Janet Jenkins was when she called the Prince at the Palace months later, using his private number. But the Prince invited her to Windsor for lunch—while the Queen was away. Janet was tall and pretty, but shy and unsure of herself. She watched him play polo from the sidelines, where nobody would notice her. The following year, Janet came for a fishing weekend at Craigowan. They saw each other again when he went back to Canada, but that was the end. As a farewell present, she gave him a sweater.

A royal spokesman said admiringly, "Charles is so skillful in covering up his private life. It is almost impossible for anyone—except for the Queen, Prince Philip, and his private detective—to know his exact whereabouts."

The Prince had a variety of places to which he could take women friends. Aside from all his royal residences, the homes of certain close friends, and a flat in London, he had a hideaway on St. Mary's in the Scilly Islands off the southwest tip of England. His small bungalow there was set on a half acre overlooking the sea, hidden by high walls. Several hundred yards away there was a big field where his helicopter landed.

An islander who would not give his name said, "I'm not going to reveal anything about the Prince's private guests, but I can say that mostly they are rather pretty." "There's agreement among royal aides that the Prince enjoys a private life such as no other member of the Royal Family has ever experienced before.

To maintain that privacy, he tried various tactics. In addition to the ability to mimic different British accents, he even tried such disguises as heavy spectacles and a cloth cap. He himself felt it was "quite pointless." "I just looked like me trying not to look like me."

There were some officials who felt that "his desperate search for secrecy may cripple his dream of married happiness and he may end up being a bachelor for many years to come."

He was concerned that too many women pushing themselves at him usually had some ulterior motive. "The nicest are those who won't come up and make themselves known."

On a twelve-day tour of the United States, he found Americans easier to know, quicker to respond, more informal. He liked that. At a civic dinner for 900 in Chicago, he was diplomatic enough not to mention that in the 1920s, Mayor William Hale "Big Bill" Thompson campaigned with two rats in a cage which he referred to as "the King and Queen of England." Instead, Prince Charles recalled that another Chicago mayor had suggested to his mother, the Queen, on her visit in 1959, that she come back one day "and bring the kids."

"Well," said the Prince, "the Queen's not here. She's in Canada. But I've come back as a rather elderly kid."

Listening to him, the perceptive columnist Ann Landers said, "He really *is* Prince Charming."

"He's so young and fresh, so funny and sexy," said twenty-five-year-old Chicago secretary Sandra Stone.

While touring the University of Chicago, he asked an attractive student, Pat Yuzada, what kind of graduate work she was doing in psychology.

"Human development."

"You're not developing badly yourself," he said, smiling.

He told a crowd that he hoped he was not a burden to his hosts and suspected that they "sometimes wondered what the hell they were going to do with me."

His walks were carefully orchestrated and controlled, but the Prince occasionally plunged into a crowd of squealing girls. A watching aide said, "This is madness." But he also walked over to some Irish demonstrators who had booed him and asked, "What's the beef?" He offered to shake hands with one of them but the young

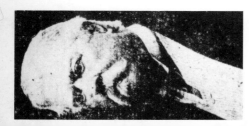

Princess Diana's American ancestor, millionaire Frank Work (1819–1911). Her American great-grandmother, Frances Burke Roche (1857–1947). Diana's parents, Earl Spencer and Frances Roche. *(Far left and left, Genealogical Publishing Co.; below, AP/Wide World Photos)*

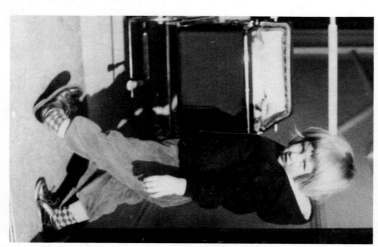

Diana was born into an aristocratic family with all the privileges. (*Below*) With her younger brother Charles. (*Right, AP/Wide World Photos*)

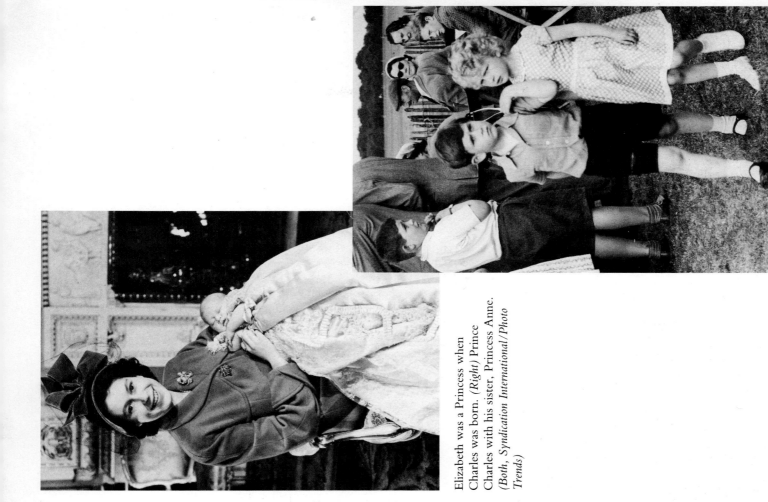

Elizabeth was a Princess when Charles was born. (*Right*) Prince Charles with his sister, Princess Anne. (*Both, Syndication International/Photo Trends*)

Diana grew up shy, often lonely. Her parents were divorced when she was six. (*Right, AP/Wide World Photos*)

Charles with his favorite Uncle Dickie (Lord Louis Mountbatten). He was a loner who loved adventure. (*Both, Syndication International/Photo Trends*)

Charles also loved the challenge
. . . (Both, Syndication
International/Photo Trends)

He had to prove himself to himself . . . and to his father. *(All photos, Syndication International/Photo Trends)*

Diana didn't know her destiny . . . but Charles knew his. (*Right, AP/Wide World Photos; below, Syndication International/Photo Trends*)

What the Prince of Wales didn't know was the future shape of his personal life. (*Syndication International/Photo Trends*)

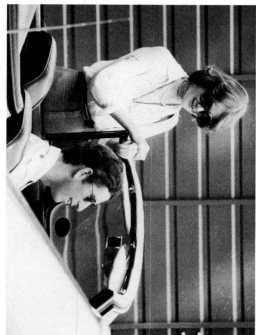

Dale, Lady Tryon (Kanga) and Camilla Parker-Bowles (*upper left and right*) were his two married friends to whom he brought his young women for approval. Laura Jo Watkins (*at right in center photo*), a California candidate, was not in the running. Neither was Lady Sarah Spencer (*below*), Diana's oldest sister. (*Upper left and right, Rex Features/RDR; center, The London Daily Mail/Special Features; below, Syndication International/Photo Trends*)

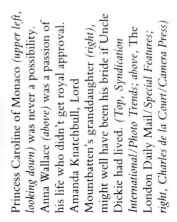

Princess Caroline of Monaco (*upper left, looking down*) was never a possibility. Anna Wallace (*above*) was a passion of his life who didn't get royal approval. Amanda Knatchbull, Lord Mountbatten's granddaughter (*right*), might well have been his bride if Uncle Dickie had lived. (*Top, Syndication International/Photo Trends; above, The London Daily Mail/Special Features; right, Charles de la Court/Camera Press*)

Mountbatten (*above with Charles and Prince Philip*) was killed by a terrorist bomb. At his funeral: Charles with the Queen Mother. Lady Diana (*opposite page*) was then just a young working woman in London. (*This page, both, Syndication International/Photo Trends*)

Diana's three flatmates: (*above, left to right*) Carolyn Pride, Virginia Pitman, and Ann Bolton. Diana then worked as an assistant in a kindergarten. Their courtship started slowly (*opposite page*) . . . but quickly blossomed. (*This page, above,* Daily Telegraph; *right, AP/Wide World Photos; opposite page, both, Syndication International/Photo Trends*)

It was called the wedding of the century, witnessed by some 750 million people all over the world. (*Syndication International/Photo Trends*)

man refused, calling him "a meaningless oddity." An observing police sergeant said of the Prince, "That kid's got a lot of guts, and I'm Irish myself."

There was a sadder, more romantic story that a Chicago columnist wrote about a woman who had called and said that the Prince had seen her in the crowd, walked over to her, said a few words, and kissed her. She wanted to see him again. She begged the columnist to take her as his guest to a civic dinner in the Prince's honor. She pleaded until he agreed to see her. She arrived in her evening gown, her hair smartly styled.

"I have seen many women who hang around backstage areas waiting for pop singers," said Bob Greene, "but this woman wasn't one of them . . . she wasn't crazy. She knew she was risking making a fool of herself. But a future king of England had picked her out of a crowd and kissed her—and she had to know, before he left the city, whether there really was something about her he was drawn to."

The columnist finally persuaded her that she had had her moment. "Real life doesn't work that way."

The Prince looked a bit peaked when he arrived in Atlanta, Georgia. That morning he already had flashed through St. Louis and Cleveland. But, inside the Georgia House Chamber, the Prince said with a smile, "I must admit I hadn't realized I'm the first Prince of Wales to visit Georgia. I hope it hasn't come as too much of a shock."

Said Jan Busbee, the pretty daughter of the Georgia governor: "I don't see why a southern girl shouldn't marry the Prince and become Queen of England."

Leaving Georgia, the Prince waved and said, "Bye, y'all." Then he grinned, adding, "I've always wanted to be able to say that."

In San Francisco, backstage at the opera, a singer, Patricia South, said she had waited for years to be able to tell him that they shared the same birthday. They then celebrated with a lingering kiss. Afterward Miss South said with a sigh, "He's so eligible and I'm so eligible."

He also kissed the cheerleaders during halftime at a football game, and, later, in Charleston, South Carolina reminded the citizens that their city was named after Britain's last King Charles.

At the end of his American trip, the Prince had a meeting with California Governor Jerry Brown. The talk ranged from solar energy and space programs to theology. The Prince was "impressed" with

American technology but expressed concern about dehumanizing factors. "He made the point of the importance of the individual in all this."

In praising American friendliness, Charles slyly asked for a "hand transplant" because of cuts caused by shaking hands with women with long fingernails. Referring to his mother's visit the previous year, he said, "I'm visiting the places which she missed—which is most of the United States."

A major turning point in the life of the Prince of Wales was his thirtieth birthday. He was no longer trying to be better than his father, or even to please him. He had reached the age and stage when he was trying to develop his own style, his own pace, his own goals. He knew what was expected of him, but this was his testing time. He wanted to make his job worthwhile. This was the time when he was more lonely than ever.

That's why, more than ever, he wanted to transform his birthday party into a giant ball at Buckingham Palace. He invited some 350 guests, including most of his former girlfriends. The invitation read: "Tiaras will not be worn."

To keep the mood informal, and slightly wild, he had three bands including a West Indian steel band to perform reggae, and his favorite pop group, the Three Degrees.

The reason he never drank much, he explained at the party, was that he was always terrified of being introduced to somebody—and burping. A drink he liked, though, was Bucks Fizz, a mixture of champagne, fresh orange juice, and a dash of grenadine. (Another fear he had at parties was being trapped by some bore. A slight rise of an eyebrow was a signal to an ever-watchful aide who came to the rescue with a "message.")

Among his gifts were a magnum of claret bottled in the year of his birth, 1948. He had complained that newspapers printed too little that was positive, and so the *Sunday Times* presented him with a column of good news including the item: "92% of first-class mail has been delivered on time."

Words came back to haunt him. The press jumped on Charles for his earlier statement saying he expected to be married by the time he was thirty, and pointed out that Prince Charles and the Duke of Windsor were probably the only examples in modern history of

Princes of Wales not marrying before thirty. "I regret having said that because now there is so much pressure on me to get married." He then smiled and said, "There's nothing wrong with *not* being married by the age of thirty. After all, many people nowadays do not marry at an early age."

Lady Olga Maitland was quoted as saying, "I'm beginning to think there is something wrong with the boy."

"Since you hear every rumor about every Royal," said a former member of the royal staff, "it is not surprising to hear that Prince Charles is gay. They whispered that because he took so long in getting married, and because the royal palace staffs—including his own—were filled with gays.

"It is, of course, ridiculous with Prince Charles. He's absolutely straight. He's a Scorpio, and highly sexed, and he loves his women. He still highly admires beautifully built women with their in-and-out dresses, sometimes more out than in. His highest form of flattery is a playful pat on a woman's rear. He does this constantly with his wife, but, if you watch carefully, you will see him do this occasionally with other women as well. But another trait of the Scorpio is loyalty. This is not a man who will wander from his wife. But he is not dead; he still likes to look and admire."

Despite his efforts at nonchalance, a London psychologist saw another side of him. After meeting the Prince, the psychologist described mannerisms that "are dead giveaways of a shy, reserved nature . . . little mannerisms like his habit of constantly pulling his mouth down at one corner when he speaks. . . . He also licks his lips a lot and strokes his nose when talking."

"Generally, though," Charles said, "people are still nervous on meeting me. I tend to have few, but very good friends."

He blamed that partially on himself. "I don't think I make friends all that easily. I'm still fairly shy. I think one has to conquer this."

He tried to fight his shyness with humor, so much so that he was tagged "The Clown Prince" and "Cheerful Charles." When he visited a farm and a horned sheep bolted between his legs, he said afterward, "I was worried about the horns. They almost ruined the dynasty." When he lunched with some Nepalese soldiers and ate curried snake meat, he said ruefully, "Boy, the things I do for England . . ." Visiting a college in Sussex, he told them, "I hope you infants are enjoying your infancy as much as we adults are enjoying our adultery."

"I would have been committed to an institution long ago," he said, "were it not for my ability to see the funny side of life."

He had acted in comic skits at Cambridge that he had written himself, and he now wrote light lines into all his prepared speeches. His favorite funny men on television were the raucous Goons, the team of Peter Sellers, Harry Secombe and Spike Milligan. They always broke him up into convulsed laughter.

There was a lot of laughter at the Palace, the Prince said.

"She's a very good mimic and laughs a lot," recalled observer editor Kenneth Harris about the Queen. "She obviously loves to laugh. She's quite different from what I expected." The impression she gave when he met her, he said, "is like her fantastic complexion, unclouded, light and bright, radiant, innocent, and natural." Even Socialist Cabinet Minister Richard Crossman had said of her, "She laughs with her whole face . . . she's really a very spontaneous person." A close friend had added, "Sometimes, when she and Margaret are together, they giggle like little girls."

Royal watchers noted that the Queen had "a gentle cackle or a loud laugh"; Prince Philip "boomed and roared"; Princess Anne "hoots"; Andrew "bellows in a shrill giggle"; and Prince Edward has a "shy chortle." Prince Charles's laugh was described as "a generous chuckle."

The Prince has some comic ham in him that surfaces quickly. Unexpectedly introduced at a vaudeville show, he hesitated, then went onstage and ad-libbed neatly for ten minutes. Once he did a double act with comedian Danny Kaye: The Prince told most of the jokes.

One of his favorite stories was on himself: "About three years ago I was elected as one of the world's best-dressed men. The following year I was elected as one of the world's worst-dressed men. At a tailors' dinner just after that, I decided to have my own back. I arrived wearing white tie and tails and an old tweed jacket over the top.

"The British are such a splendid race. They pretended I was normally dressed."

The author of the article in *Tailor & Cutter*, accusing the Prince of following "the cult of shabbiness," now grinned and said, "I surrender. The Prince has a great sense of humor."

In the course of a speech to Britain's Master Tailor's Benevolent Association, the Prince also revealed why he and his father often walk the same way, with their hands behind their backs. "It's not a genetic trait. It is because we both have the same tailor and he makes the sleeves so tight we can't get our hands in front."

The Prince startled another audience, at the Royal Thames Yacht Club in London, when he unveiled a bust of his father, the club's president. "I am not unaccustomed in any way to unveiling busts," he quipped.

He then added, "I now complete the process of helping my father to expose himself."

Prince Charles didn't relax the week of his thirtieth birthday or any week thereafter. His work reflected a mix of his independent leanings and the traditional needs imposed by his royal status. He placed wreaths at a war memorial, pinned medals on nurses at a children's hospital, gave a state banquet for the President of Portugal, turned on the Christmas lights in Regent Street, met with the International Council of World Colleges, worked with students for projects of world peace, attended a board meeting of a company making earth-moving equipment, continued his effort to learn more about the business world, and talked to the BBC Welsh Radio Service about fly-fishing, one of his loves.

In the two years since he left the Navy, the Prince had paid official visits to the Ivory Coast, Canada, Ghana, the United States, Venezuela, Brazil, Australia, Yugoslavia, and the NATO headquarters in Brussels. There were also private visits to France, Monaco, Germany, Spain, and Norway; holidays in Kenya, the Bahamas, Iceland, France, and Switzerland. An earlier Prince of Wales in 1875 traveled with a staff of thirty including three chefs and a bagpiper; Prince Charles flew in a Royal Air Force VC 10 with a staff of nine.

Any official travel was prepared months in advance down to the most specific details: who sits where and comes in when and eats what. Charles, like every traveling Royal, carried a full set of mourning clothes, as well as black-edged notepaper, in the event a sudden death in the family required him to return home.

People would sometimes ask him, "Wouldn't you like to have a life of your own? Wouldn't you like to be free?"

"Well, I have got a life of my own, and I like it," he said. "Perhaps I would like another life more, but this is the one I know. And free from what? Being free isn't doing what other people like to do, it's doing what *you* like to do.

"I'm not a rebel by temperament. I don't get a kick out of not doing what is expected of me, or of doing what is not expected of me."

Yet he did speak up when he felt it necessary. He protested the Catholic Church's refusal to approve the marriage of his cousin Prince Michael of Kent to Catholic Baroness Marie-Christine von Reibnitz of Austria. A Vatican official then accused him of "sheer impertinence."

When a polo match commentator wisecracked about the Royal Family, referring to Prince Charles as "Queen Elizabeth's little boy," the Prince climbed three flights of stairs to tell him to turn it off because "you're turning it into a barn dance."

No matter what he did or where he went, one question never abated: When will he pick a wife?

One of his strongest passions was for a sexy blonde young woman who was exactly his type. The daughter of a wealthy Scottish landowner, her name was Anna Wallace. He met her at a polo match, where he seemed to meet many of his girlfriends. She had a marvelous figure, a sparkling personality—and she loved hunting and fishing. The Queen Mother gave her approval, the Queen lunched with her at Windsor.

"He was head over heels in love with her, and I know he wanted to marry her," said a friend of hers.

Even the Prince's staff were rooting for her, all feeling that this modest young woman was not in love with her own publicity as so many were. Anna Wallace was one of the few to get a private tour of Buckingham Palace—with the exception of the Queen's quarters, which are always private unless one is invited.

"I know Anna very well," said another friend of hers. "She knew that she would never be acceptable to the Royal Family because of her past. She did have some previous love affairs. I know he asked her to marry him."

What Anna Wallace did, according to James Whitaker, was to call her former boss, the fabulously rich Iranian Homayoun Mazandi and ask him what she should do.

It was true the Royal Family, particularly the Queen, was not enamored of Anna Wallace, but for one of the few times in his life, Prince Charles was so besotted with this young woman that it seemed he would have defied them all, including the Queen, to marry her. Everyone noted how cheerful and contented the Prince seemed when he was with her. Then the Prince invited her to be his guest at the Queen Mother's eightieth birthday party, a gala event for 400 people that turned out to be the climax of the affair.

What Anna Wallace did not want to understand was that the Prince had a duty to circulate among his guests for most of the evening, leaving her alone at their table. Or perhaps she understood it all too well, seeing it as a small sign of her bleak future if she were to marry the Prince. She was a woman of some substance in her own right. There had been other men in her life and so she knew what her options were.

It was reported when Charles finally returned to their table, she was in a fury. Her nickname had been "Whiplash," and now he would feel the full force of it. "How dare you! I've never been treated so badly in my life." She went on in this manner, loud and clear, then stormed out.

The truth was that Anna Wallace did say all those things—but not to Prince Charles. There were some forty people within earshot, and she said what she felt in great anger and distress. But Prince Charles had never returned to the table from the ballroom. Finally, when Anna Wallace decided to leave, she broke down in tears and said, "I can't even find him to say goodbye!" Lady Tryon took her home.

The point is that it was not Anna Wallace who had turned down Prince Charles, it was Prince Charles and the Royal Family who had made the decision to break off their relationship. Because of her previous romances, the Royal powers had advised that she was simply not suitable. This news was devastating to the Prince; he was "more keen" on Anna than he had been on any other young woman.

A depressed Prince left the next morning for the royal yacht at Cowes, for what he thought would be some solitary windsurfing and some private thinking.

ady Diana probably never would have become Princess of Wales if Lord Louis Mountbatten had not been murdered.

The Prince had enjoyed countless women, most of whom proved unsuitable to be his Queen. He had been in and out of love, and often badly burned by it. He was now more than careful, he was extremely cautious. But it was obviously time to get married. He was past thirty and there was growing pressure from the public, the press, and the royal circle. The one man whose judgment on this matter he trusted more than anyone was Uncle Dickie.

Mountbatten always had regarded Charles as a surrogate son, just as the Prince regarded him as a surrogate father, and one of the most important influences on his life. At his funeral, the Prince said, "I adored him—and miss him so dreadfully now."

With his father away so much, traveling the world for almost half the year, the Prince made his second home at Broadlands with Uncle Dickie. In a way he was more relaxed there than he was anywhere.

"He did not have to go to a psychiatrist," said Anthony Holden, who knew him well, "because Lord Mountbatten helped him."

"You know the friendship between us is so odd," Mountbatten said. "We're separated by a half century in age and yet we can sit for hours in each other's company and we're never bored—we're very deep and affectionate friends. When we don't see each other, we still write to each other constantly. I remain young through him."

Mountbatten was the only man who could cheerfully tell Charles at a reception, "Don't spend your time chatting with your friends when you're here to work. Go and talk to some of those people who have never met you, and who have waited a long time for this occasion."

The two men greeted each other with a naval salute every time they met, and again when they parted. Their mutual respect was enormous. Mountbatten was not only a hero to his generation; he was Charles's hero. He was impatient with conventional methods, had the courage to make hard decisions with buoyant self-confidence, had a quick, incisive, imaginative mind. He could be obstinate, and sometimes had a harsh bark. He could act the democrat "but he was always royal underneath," even though he said, "Being royal's hell!"

What he told Charles, and everyone else, was that he was a slow starter, "rather un-bright," and became a success "because I worked twice as hard as the next bloke." He liked to quote G. K. Chesterton's Father Brown: "It isn't that they can't see the solution. It is that they can't see the problem." He tried to teach Charles to "see the problem," and was delighted when the Prince turned down some drafts of a speech Mountbatten wanted him to make, asked for his suggestions, then said, "Would you mind terribly if I didn't use them either?" and then wrote his own speech.

Mountbatten told everyone that Prince Charles had the same dedication and ability as the Queen—whom he called "Betty . . . my number one girlfriend." Asked whether he thought the Prince would make a good king, Mountbatten answered, "Well, if he isn't, I'll eat my hat—if I haven't a hat in heaven, I'll eat my halo!"

"I think he's the finest man I know today," Mountbatten added later. "I don't think I can fault him on anything. He is kind but he can be tough when it is necessary to be tough. He deserves a very good wife. I can tell you that he certainly won't fall for some light-weight secretary bird . . . People don't make it easy for him to marry anyone, do they? I mean, what chance has Charles to woo a girl? Girls like phone calls, telegrams, flowers, all that sort of thing. How on earth could Charles send a telegram to a girl? He can't even stop to joke with one without being married off next morning. And you can't marry a girl just like that, can you? You've got to get to know her. And that's not easy if you're a Royal, I can tell you.

"I'll make you this prophecy," he continued. "I believe the girl he finds will marry him for his own sake and will put up with having to be Queen."

The Prince respectfully called Mountbatten, "our male Queen

Victoria," and added, "I admire him, I think, almost more than anybody else. He's a very great person." Prince Charles had told his great-uncle, "I have no idea what we shall do without you when you finally decide to go."

When Uncle Dickie talked, "the young man" listened very attentively. Uncle Dickie now told Prince Charles, "Study the life and times of the Duke of Windsor. Don't imagine that because, like him, you have become a sort of royal pop idol, that the British people will always support you. They will back you only so long as you serve the country and do the job."

Listening to this, and viewing his own slightly chaotic romantic life, Prince Charles made his decision: He would let Uncle Dickie select his bride. He had said repeatedly, and he strongly believed it then, that his choice of a wife was "the last decision on which I would want my head to be ruled by my heart."

Mountbatten had felt personally responsible for pushing the marriage of his nephew Prince Philip to Princess Elizabeth, for whom he remained a lifetime advisor. Now, to place his stamp on the future King of England, he wanted Prince Charles to marry his grand-daughter, Lady Amanda Knatchbull.

Amanda was not simply The Girl Next Door. When Gordonstoun went co-ed, she was a fellow student of Prince Andrew, then went on to Kent University to get a hybrid degree that included specializations in anthropology, philosophy, and art history. She even studied Chinese at Peking University. Her ambition, she said, was to be a social worker—and she did eventually get such a job, at the Hammersmith and Fulham Borough Council. A teacher had said that she wanted to make up "for the privileges she was born to but which she feels she has not earned."

Charles and Amanda had known each other since they were children. Her brother Norton was one of his closest friends. They had gone to school together, went hunting, fishing, played polo together. Her father, Lord Brabourne, was a governor of Gordonstoun and United World Colleges, a pet project of Mountbatten's that also greatly interested Prince Charles. The Prince had joined the Brabournes on Caribbean vacations at Eleuthera. He had been at their home in Kent so often that the large, rambling, but cozy place seemed like another home to him. Amanda, nine years his junior, was not the sexy image of his dreams, but she was very bright, sensitive, attractive, and had a natural sweetness. Charles actually *had* proposed to her, several years before, at Mountbatten's suggestion, but she had asked for time to "think it over." More than most of his women friends, she had a highly specific idea of future royal responsibilities and was unsure she wanted to face them.

In an effort to persuade her, Lord Mountbatten took her with him to Africa to give her a greater taste of public life. Now he set the final scene. He had promised to escort Prince Charles on a prolonged grand tour of India, and Amanda would go with them. They would not only have all those days and nights together, but also the romantic setting of the moonlit Taj Mahal—where Lord Mountbatten had romanced his own wife.

"There's no question about all this," said Mountbatten's longtime private secretary, John Barratt. "Prince Charles had agreed to let his great-uncle select his bride. But Amanda used to wear those terrible old-fashioned clothes and I said to Lord Louis, 'How can any girl, dressed like this, expect to capture Prince Charles?' And so a sum of money was set aside for Amanda to go to Paris to shop for her wardrobe so that she would be absolutely dazzling in India.' "

And then tragedy struck. In August of 1979, an Irish Republican Army bomb was placed in a fishing boat, killing the vacationing Mountbatten instantly.

Mountbatten had said earlier, after receiving an IRA threat: "Who would want to kill an old man like me?"

The bomb that killed him, said the IRA, was designed "to tear out Britain's sentimental imperialistic heart."

"I think it's an awful thing to be sad at funerals," said Mountbatten. "I hope they won't cry; they must remember that all my life I enjoyed a joke, I've enjoyed the fun of life, and I'm only sorry I won't be there to see the fun of the funeral."

His epitaph?

He recalled what Admiral Sir James Somerville had said of him:

"Well, there's nobody I'd sooner be with in a tight corner than Dickie Mountbatten; and nobody would get me into one quicker."

Prince Philip was stolid during the funeral, but Prince Charles cried openly, and his eulogy was personal and moving.

"I remember after the funeral when they brought Lord Louis's

RALPH G. MARTIN

body back to Broadlands," John Barratt reminisced. "Prince Philip and Charles came and we had lunch. Charles couldn't eat and excused himself. Philip suddenly looked up and said, 'Where's Charles?' and I said, 'Well, he's gone down to the river.' Philip asked, 'Why?' And I said, 'I think he's been very emotionally moved and he wants to be alone with his emotions.' Philip said, 'Well, we'll be very late for our next appointment. We're supposed to leave soon.' And he told me to go find Charles. I found him along the river, his head bowed, obviously in anguish. I couldn't disturb him. I came back and told Philip that I couldn't find Charles. Philip was very irritated."

Even three months after the assassination, a Mountbatten neighbor, photographer Allen Warren, showed Charles a picture he had taken of Mountbatten. "Charles's eyes were full of tears."

If Charles had come to Broadlands to say a final goodbye to Uncle Dickie, it was also to set aside Mountbatten's marriage plans for him.

"I don't think the Prince would ever have gotten married, if it was up to him. He was a creature of habit, like most of us," said a good friend, "and he had a happy life. Woke up at a certain time. Everything prepared and ready the way he liked it. Excellent service. Exercise. Few problems. He always had a pretty girl in tow to think about, and be with. There were always trips to interesting places. The day was as crowded or loose as he had planned. Lots of waiting friends. Dinner parties. No waves to buck. He was a happy man. And he would have stayed that way if the family and the press didn't push him towards marriage. Of course, there was another factor: He did fall in love."

Lady Amanda Knatchbull decided to take a year-long tour around the world to do some more thinking. And by the time she came back, Prince Charles had found Lady Diana Spencer.

He had found her, and perhaps himself as well, on the *Britannia* in August of 1980, during Cowes Week. She had been to Cowdray Park in Sussex with Sarah Armstrong-Jones and some other guests to watch the Prince play polo in July, but at that time, he was still obsessed with Anna Wallace and they had hardly talked. But after Cowes, the Prince sent Lady Diana a dozen red roses and invited her for a weekend at Balmoral.

Was Diana surprised to receive a dozen red roses from the Prince soon after she got home? She didn't know it, but it was something he seldom sent to any young woman.

138

And just two months before she had been bridesmaid at her sister Sarah's wedding and she had caught the bridal bouquet.

Fifty miles west of Aberdeen, along the river Dee among the scented heather of Braemar, was the estate of Balmoral—17,000 acres of privacy where the Royal Family could be more family than royal.

The estate achieved royal status when its owner choked to death on a fish bone, and his successor quickly sold it to Queen Victoria. She tore down the original house and built a grandiose place of granite that she called her "dear paradise," a place large enough to house her staff of sixty. Today there are double that number.

Balmoral is a bizarre place, built in Scottish baronial style with pepper-pot towers, the eastern one filled with antlers and tartan chairs. The stone-floored entrance hall is usually littered with fishing rods, waterproof clothing, and Wellington boots. The rooms have tartan carpets and ancient gurgling plumbing; only the prize bedrooms have their own bathrooms.

Every year, for ten weeks starting in mid-August, the Royal Family brings tons of luggage and has a truly relaxed autumn holiday here. The men stalk deer, shoot grouse, or fly-fish for salmon; the women ride their horses, play charades, Scrabble, and other party games, picnic, or go for walks. Everybody wears their most casual clothes: for the women, sweaters and sensible shoes during the day (but long dresses in the evening) and for the men, tartan plus-fours or kilts (black-tie being reserved for formal meals).

More than anything else, the Queen regards Balmoral as her private hideaway. The same people are generally invited for the same weekend each year. Guests usually arrive on Thursday and stay until after lunch on Sunday. With the exception of the Prime Minister, these guests come from the Queen's closely knit circle of personal friends.

Meals are always on time, and the Queen arrives last. All female guests are given big, fancy breakfasts in bed, plus all the newspapers, but they are expected to spend the mornings in their rooms.

After dinner on Saturday evenings, the Queen usually shows a film—with the Pipe Major putting away his bagpipes and doubling as projectionist. Among the Saturday night guests there is always a member of the Scottish Church who stays the night so he can conduct services for the Royals the next morning.

There's a day when the local village people collect at a gathering to watch competitions in wrestling and other sports, and the Royals come too. A highlight of the Royal Family's holiday is the annual Ghillies' Ball featuring Scottish reels.

One of the rules at Balmoral is that no young Royal under twenty-one can drink alcohol. But one day the Queen was ill, and a young Royal—who shall be nameless—brought down to lunch an oversize medicine bottle filled with her favorite alcoholic beverage. The servant pretended not to notice.

In public, the Royals have no private life. Even in private, they have no private life—detectives and staff are always present. At Balmoral, though, the Queen will tell her detectives—who must obey her—"I'm going to walk alone in the moors." Then she and her dogs do go off alone, one of the few times she has true privacy.

It's easy to lose oneself in the winding walks at Balmoral, or along the lovely river Dee. Princess Elizabeth and Prince Philip did it when they were courting. And now Balmoral was the romantic rendezvous for Lady Diana and Prince Charles. What began at Cowes blossomed here.

Charles and Diana didn't know, however, that a pair of high-powered binoculars were trained on them, shattering the secrecy of their relationship. As they came in closer range, somehow Lady Diana caught the reflection of a telephoto lens in her small hand mirror. Prince Charles had always prepared all his young women for the inevitable publicity. But Diana neither ran nor panicked nor hid her face. She simply walked straight up the hill away from the river without turning her head back once. The photographer could only take a picture of the back of a tall young woman in a kerchief. She could have been anyone. The newspaper headline over the mysterious photograph said simply: THE NEW GIRL FOR CHARLES.

Meanwhile, at Balmoral, there was little question that Diana had the obvious approval of both the Queen and the Queen Mother. They had both known her for a long time. Diana's grandmother, Lady Fermoy, was absolutely delighted. Diana's sister Jane, who was then also in a small house at Balmoral with her baby, was similarly pleased. All of them, however, knew Prince Charles well enough not to get excited too quickly. There had been too many young women in his life in too quick succession.

Through their Palace contacts, the press soon discovered exactly who this "mystery" young woman was. By the time she came home to Coleherne Court, she found the press waiting. She was obviously embarrassed by the growing crowd of photographers and reporters waiting outside, but she still managed to preserve a gentle dignity.

"She would never duck out the back to avoid the photographers," said the Coleherne Court porter. "In the mornings she would come down early to the main hall, grab all the papers and sit there right on the floor, groaning and laughing as she went through them to see what they said about her.

"She was a wonderful girl. Such a nice manner she had . . . She was really super-cool and collected."

She had large grave eyes, a soft mouth, superbly cut thick blond hair, wore a natural polish on her nails, very little makeup, and almost no jewelry. She didn't look particularly trendy with her rolled-up sleeves, V-necked sweater, open-toed, low-heeled shoes, her skirt slightly longer than the current fashion.

The press, however, made a wrong assessment of her when they nicknamed her "Shy Di." That was another myth. In many ways, she was almost an innocent. She did blush easily, and it highlighted her vulnerability. But beneath the blush was a strong, determined will. If she had drifted through early life without knowing what she really wanted, she now knew.

At nineteen, Lady Diana Frances Spencer had a rather remarkable natural ability to adjust, to cope.

The press found her fresh, friendly, almost artless, but with a sense of polite humor. She was courteous enough to answer questions, but street-smart enough to remain discreet. "I will not say anything about Prince Charles," she told them determinedly. "No one has told me to keep quiet—it's my decision."

But when the photographers followed her to work at the Young England Kindergarten, their flashbulbs still popping, she put her foot down. "All of this fuss is disrupting my work with the children," she said firmly.

"I took my lead from Diana," said Vicky Wilson, who helps run the kindergarten. "She kept working, I think, because children require your total involvement. They need your total attention. I think she found this an amazing relief from other pressures."

One of her small pupils, James Dove, said of her, "She's a nice lady. She helps me with my drawings. I think she is very pretty, so is my mummy." Another little girl added, "We just call her Diana. I didn't know she was a Lady."

When a reporter reached Lady Diana, she was both noncommittal and sympathetic. "It's impossible for me to comment on it. I'm sorry. It must be a real bore for you."

The photographers promised to leave if she posed for a few pictures. What she did not know was that they had maneuvered her so that the strong sunlight behind her shone through her almost transparent skirt. The pictures were reprinted all over the world.

She was not amused. "I don't want to be remembered for not having a petticoat," she said. Prince Charles treated it more lightly. "I knew your legs were good," he told her, "but I didn't realize they were that spectacular. And did you really have to show them to everybody?"

She groaned when she saw one picture. "They look like Steinway piano legs."

If the British public smiled, they also sympathized. If there was a single word to explain Diana's almost instant appeal to both the press and the public it was "vulnerable."

She seemed so vulnerable that everybody wanted to reach out and protect her. She was everybody's sister, the girl next door, sweet, modest. What most people liked best of all was how easily she laughed. When a reporter asked her how she saw herself, she laughed and said, "No one's ever asked me that before. Well, I'm a normal person, hopefully, who loves life."

Astrologers were quickly corralled to predict their future: Charles was a Scorpio and Diana was a Cancer. His was a sign that indicates "an almost infamous passion." She, however, was slow to commit herself, but once she made up her mind would "unleash a torrent of passion." She also tended to rely on her instinct, on her ability to feel what was right.

Reporters zoomed in on anyone who knew her. "It is amazing, looking back, to think I used to give her advice about her boyfriend," said her hairdresser Vicki at Headlines. "She was so obviously in love and you know how girls talk to each other. We had a lot of friends in common. But of course I never knew who *he* was until the publicity began."

Because of the press, she now no longer cycled the two miles to work. Instead she drove her Mini-Metro, and reporters noted that she was a demon driver who always managed to get away when they tried to corner her. "She seems to be developing built-in wing mirrors to warn her when the camera was zooming up behind."

At this stage, an earlier favorite, Lady Jane Wellesley, older and more sophisticated than Diana, had become almost hysterical. Diana, not so shy, kept her cool, her nerve—and her goal.

She also continued taking care of the little American boy, Patrick Robinson, still took her ballet lessons, and waited for the frequent coded ring on the telephone indicating that the Prince was calling. He would never come to her apartment because television crews were waiting outside. But the Prince had been through all this many times before and had become an expert on maneuvers and deception.

They met on weekends, mostly in the homes of married friends such as the Parker-Bowleses. Camilla Parker-Bowles had vetoed Anna Wallace, but agreed that Diana was a winner, and told him so.

Diana knew better than anyone how serious Charles was about her when he took her to see the house he had bought for his future home. Highgrove House was about a mile from Tetbury in Gloucestershire in the Cotswolds. It had the advantage of being not far from London, and close to his polo-playing fields.

Highgrove was built about 1796 by a young lawyer named John Paul Paul. The Georgian structure was badly damaged by fire in 1893. Rebuilt and restored, it was a pleasant gray stone building facing northeast. Its former occupants had included James Roosevelt (the son of President Franklin Delano Roosevelt, a remote ancestral cousin of Princess Diana) and the son of Prime Minister Harold Macmillan.

Highgrove afforded great privacy. Set on 347 acres (almost the size of Hyde Park in London), it had a colonnaded porch, a magnificent entrance hall, a drawing room, a dining room, a study, a library, and a billiard room. Upstairs were four bedroom suites and a nursery wing. Five more bedrooms and two bathrooms were on the third floor. It was also a working farm with excellent stables, a stone fence, some splendid oaks, and a magnificent cedar. Though it could hardly be considered a bachelor's pad, it was more homey than Chevening, the stately 115-room country mansion on 3,000 acres in Kent that the Prince owned but refused to live in. The London *Daily Mail* promptly commented: "Such a house would be an ideal place for Prince Charles, who will be thirty-two in November, to start married life . . ." After seeing it, Lady Diana told friends, "It's perfect. I couldn't wish for a nicer house."

She went back there several times within the next month, usually with his valet, waiting for the Prince to come home from a hunt. The place was only partly furnished, not very comfortable, with three usable bedrooms. When the Prince returned, the two would have tea, then a simple early dinner of some egg dish on a card table in the sitting room. The Prince would then drive her back to London—with a policeman sitting in the back.

Public pressure for marriage increased: "Charles has been the World's Most Eligible Bachelor for too long. He's flitted from flower to Jane to Sarah to Leonora to Davina to Sabrina to Who's Left? Now he must take the final plunge into marriage to prove he's the man, and King, England expects."

Diana was still demurely correct with reporters. "You know I cannot say anything about the Prince or my feelings for him."

But everybody else could. "She looks just the sort of girl people would like Prince Charles to marry," said Barbara Griggs, an observer of Royals. "And if he announced his engagement tomorrow, it would certainly be greeted not merely with a huge sigh of relief that he's finally made up his mind, but delight that he's picked such an obvious winner."

The Prince was still, however, reluctant to make the final decision. He and Diana, completely unknown to the press, did sneak away to Birkhall for a visit. Birkhall, on the Balmoral estate, was the Queen Mother's home. She especially spent time there in the fall when she went fishing.

Birkhall is a large, white Queen Anne house, perched high among sloping lawns, white heather, blue and purple daisies, giant Himalayan lilies, many of them planted by the Queen Mother herself. Queen Victoria used the place for her poor relations. To get there, it's a short drive through the royal village of Balleter, where Diana bought toffees.

The Queen Mother was famous for her high tea at Birkhall. It included chocolate cake, a rich Highland fruit cake called Black Bun, and Earl Grey tea. Diana relaxed easily in one of the armchairs there, doing her needlepoint, waiting for her Prince to come home from a hunt, or from a game of polo.

The Queen Mother had taught him to fish and they would playfully argue about whether the "Hairy Mary" was a better salmon fly than the "Black Doctor." Together they would "hoot with laughter," over the woman in breast-high waders who, fishing in the Dee the same time they were, suddenly recognized the Queen Mother and automatically curtsied. Doing so, she slipped in the water and "was last seen floating towards Aberdeen."

The Queen Mum could have told Diana much during her needle-point sessions. She could have told her that the prime things you need to be a Queen besides curiosity and sincere concern are fortitude and patience. As Patron of London University, she had to smile 1500 times to 1500 students as she handed each a diploma. But then she would dance with them at their parties, and that she loved.

The Queen Mother better than anyone else in the Palace could have given Diana a course in public relations. She always knows exactly where the photographers are positioned, exactly where to stop to talk to someone to provide the cameramen with their best focus and best angle. And she is always ready to pose for still another picture. Photographers form her strongest fan club.

"She has a true genius for her job," an observer noted. "The Queen Mother is probably the biggest single reason why we still have a monarchy and so many nations do not."

At a party at St. James's Palace—where her two waddling corgis preceded her—she will look straight at people with her baby-blue eyes, listening to every word as if she were absolutely fascinated, never peering elsewhere to see who was more important. Always the most important person is the one to whom she is talking. If she could teach Diana a primary royal lesson, it was this.

Her stamina is legendary. She has requests for visits two years in advance. She is the patron of some three hundred organizations and charities, colonel-in-chief of eight British regiments, commandant-in-chief of all three women's services, and Warden of the Cinque Ports—and she takes all of it seriously. Yet, at the end of a long day of appointments, she can turn to her dear friend and private secretary, the elegant Sir Martin Gilliat, and ask, "Can we still make the last race at Cheltenham?" They usually can.

"At one time she had twenty horses in training," recalled Dick Francis, the celebrated novelist, who once was her jockey. "At her 100th racing win—she's had more than 300 now—we had a big party at the Savoy. I was no longer her jockey, but I was sitting at her table with some other jockeys. We were talking about horses and racing when Kenneth More, the actor, came over and asked the Queen Mother to dance."

"Go away," she told him, "I'm talking to my jockeys."

"But when I asked her to dance," added Francis, "she did dance with me. I think I was the first jockey ever to dance with her. She was absolutely unpretentious.

"One jockey broke his leg and came to the party in his cast, with crutches. And he asked her to dance. She looked at his leg, and he put away his crutches, and they danced. Then he went back to the hospital and went back to bed."

The Queen Mother had never been happy with Lord Mountbatten's influence on Prince Charles's marriage plans. She was concerned that his friendship with the Duchess of Windsor, his flirting with socialist ideas, his own scandalous marriage and bisexuality might have an effect on the future monarch.

The Queen Mother was so delighted with Diana, not simply because she was the granddaughter of a dear friend, but because she reminded her so much of her own young self, just as Charles reminded her of her late husband.

Many felt that Diana had much of the aura of the Queen Mother: "The same wide, grave eyes, the same sweetness of expression around the mouth, even when she is not smiling."

The Prince had said often that the key to marriage was shared interests, ideas held in common, plus a great deal of affection. He liked women who didn't smoke, who drank as little as he did, who loved the country, walks, fishing, who shared his love of laughter, who wanted the roots of home and family even more than he, who were, in a word, crazy about him.

The time spent at Birkhall surely helped to cement the Prince's decision. Yet his mother said, rather testily, "Even I don't know what's going on." And his father, who had kept clear of his love life, was overheard telling Prince Charles, "If you don't marry this girl, the press is going to jump all over you. You've got to make a decision."

"We were all rooting for Diana," said his valet.

Never before had there been such unanimity about any of his potential brides. Then why couldn't he make up his mind? Was it because this was a decision that had to last a lifetime? That there was a difference of thirteen years between them? Was it reluctance to give up his fun-loving freedom, his privacy? That he was fundamentally a loner? Or was it simply because she was so obviously in love with him, head-over-heels, passionately—and he wasn't?

At the end of October, the pair spent a weekend at the home of his friends Andrew and Camilla Parker-Bowles, whose home in Wiltshire was not too far from Highgrove. The Parker-Bowles house was the romantic rendezvous place for many of the Charles–Diana meetings, and Camilla was a fountainhead of advice and support. But Camilla, like Lady Tryon, would be cut off quickly soon after the engagement.

Charles had invited Diana to the Ludlow Races, where he jumped eighteen fences to finish second in an amateur riders' three-mile race, winning a prize of $631. Lady Diana said she had bet on the Prince at 10–1 odds. An observer recorded that she was "squealing with excitement as he came over the last fence."

The next day, he and Andrew were off on a fox hunt. Diana was in the driveway of the Parker-Bowleses' home when he returned, and ran to meet him. But when she saw a reporter, she quickly retreated indoors.

Speaking with propriety, Diana's mother told a representative of the press, "I believe her friendship with Prince Charles is nothing more than that. I see their friendship as a continuing thing. But I would not like to make any comment about a possible romance between them." More privately, to her friends, she worried about the impact of all the publicity on her daughter. "No one can stand up to this kind of pressure—it's impossible."

But Diana's mother was wrong. Diana was having a ball. She saw it as great fun and a great challenge to outwit the press, as she so often did now. The couple began to spend an increasing amount of time at Highgrove with a decorator, planning many changes. Pressed by an increasingly impatient press, one astrologer predicted, "Yes, there are definite signs of compatibility. Their horoscope points to more than a passing flirtation." Another added, "An old astrology book says that when a man's moon is in the same sign as a woman's Venus, they can fall in love with each other like a stroke of lightning."

Her impact on him soon became visible in small ways. In his dress, he was "a bit formal." She loosened up his wardrobe with colorful shirts, ties, sweaters, even loafers—something he had never worn before.

147

In the midst of this crescendo of speculation came the first whiff of scandal. The prelude was Princess Margaret's fiftieth birthday party, held at the Ritz Hotel in London. When Prince Charles was a boy and his parents were so often on royal tour, his Aunt Margo used to join forces with his grandmother to keep him bathed in affection. Margaret was another family example of what Uncle Dickie had warned him against. After the government had refused to let her marry a divorced man, she had married the "swinger" Antony Armstrong-Jones—and he never stopped swinging. Neither did she. They had two children, but their marriage quickly fell apart. Newspapers delightedly splashed the stories of their varied love affairs on the front pages.

The most recent of Princess Margaret's lovers was a young man exactly the age of Prince Charles. Roddy Llewellyn, an aspiring pop singer, was anathema to the Royal Family. Only the Queen Mother received him in her home. Now, for this birthday ball, Her Majesty firmly told her sister that she could not attend if Roddy were there. It would indicate that their informal union had Royal sanction. The compromise arrived at was that Roddy was allowed to come later in the evening, after the dinner.

By royal rules, the Queen's children were princes and princesses but Princess Margaret's children were commoners. Nevertheless her daughter, the delightful Sarah Armstrong-Jones, was the person most responsible for the romance between Diana and Prince Charles, since she was the one who had invited her to Cowes. In time she would not only be a bridesmaid at their wedding but a godmother to one of their children. But Princess Margaret was a striking example to Diana of everything that could go wrong under the royal roof, everything scandalous that she must guard against.

She soon got a taste of how a seemingly innocent event could blow up into a scandal.

After Princess Margaret's birthday ball, Prince Charles was scheduled for a tour of the West Country. He spent the night of November 5th on the royal train, parked on a siding at Holt in Wiltshire. Not long afterward, a story hit the front pages flatly claiming that Diana drove from London to meet her prince aboard the train.

According to the story, Diana passed through the protective police checkpoint and was escorted onto the train and spent most of the night with him. LOVE IN THE SIDINGS screamed one headline. The newspaper had checked the story with Diana first, and she had flatly denied it, but they had printed it anyway.

"Where do these stories start?" asked the Prince. "It's rubbish and it has put Lady Diana in such a bad light."

"I was *sooo* shocked!" said Diana. "I simply couldn't believe it. I've never been anywhere near the train, let alone in the middle of the night. I don't even know what it looks like."

In an unprecedented denial, Palace press secretary Michael Shea, speaking for Her Majesty, denounced the story as "totally false" and demanded a retraction. The paper refused, citing its sources as "impeccable." They later did call Lady Diana to apologize, "but that doesn't change people's minds about what they think when they read a story like that," she said. "The trouble is people believe what they read."

The press then intimated that perhaps the woman on the train with Charles that night was not Diana but Lady Tryon. Kanga laughed at that one. "Can you imagine me driving all night long to spend a few hours on a train?"

"I wish the bloody press would leave [Diana] alone," Prince Charles told his valet. "God save us from those bloody vultures," echoed his father. But the Queen was overheard to say, more quietly, "She will have to get used to that."

To reporter James Whitaker, Diana admitted, "I have cried three times during the last few months. But I promise not to do so again."

One of those times was when she was driving through London with photographers in such hot pursuit that she jumped out of her car crying, almost hysterical, and melted into the crowd. The photographers sent her a huge bouquet of flowers, apologizing for the distress they caused, adding, "Sorry . . . we love you . . ."

That week, Prince Charles took off for his long-scheduled tour of India—the one during which Uncle Dickie and Amanda Knatchbull had planned to change his future.

Diana later admitted that she had hoped to spend that weekend with him, "but we decided it was better not to get together because of all the fuss and bother it would have caused." But she did sneak away to see him off.

She had a special system of pickup arranged with Stephen Barry, then the Prince's valet. She would call him at a scheduled time and tell him to meet her at her sister's flat in Kensington Palace, or her grandmother's place in Eaton Square, or the home of a friend. She would then leave her car there and go out of a side door to his car. On this day, he took her to the Prince and the two went off in a state car driven by a detective.

"There was a big, dreary shed that looked like a bungalow," said Barry. "He couldn't kiss her properly in the shelter—there were too many people—so he just pecked her on the cheek. She was absolutely in tears. Then he walked out of the door to the plane outside. She sat alone until the plane took off. She didn't talk at all. She looked miserable. And then the chauffeur took her home. It was one of those dark, gray days."

Diana now found herself alone for three weeks to face the relentless press. Once again, she insisted that she had been home with her roommates on the night of the train incident, that she had been exhausted from the previous night's birthday party for Princess Margaret, and had gone to bed early.

The press seemed to be coming in for the kill, as they had with so many previous princely "birds." Her phone rang constantly with questions, even in the middle of the night. She was now not simply copy for the British papers, she had become a world story. The number of reporters and photographers outside her apartment had reached seventy. One photographer was even caught climbing through the lavatory window in Diana's school.

There was nothing she did or said that was too insignificant to mention. Not only was it reported that she drove a new red Mini-Metro, but also that it had twin silver side stripes and such extras as a tinted glass sun roof and radio cassette player.

Somebody even wrote a song about her: "Diana divine . . . my sweetheart sublime . . ."

Diana's mother was increasingly concerned. "Diana is totally defenseless. Freedom of the press means license to print the most hurtful things about her. As her mother, I mind very much." She finally wrote a letter to the editor of the *Times*:

. . . In recent weeks many articles have been labelled "exclusive quotes" when the plain truth is that my daughter had not spoken the words attributed to her. . . . May I ask the editors of Fleet Street, whether in the execution of their jobs, they consider it necessary or fair to harass my daughter daily, from dawn until well after dusk? . . .

Charles & Diana

Fleet Street editors convened with senior members of the Press Council for the first time in its twenty-seven years to discuss the subject. Sixty members of Parliament tabled a motion in the House of Commons "deploring the manner in which Lady Diana Spencer is treated by the media." They called upon "those responsible to have more concern for individual privacy."

It all added up to zero. The top reporters were assigned by individual newspapers as royal watchers with the sole responsibility of recording every newsworthy move by the "Royal Family"—meaning Diana.

She was forced to use a fire exit to escape reporters when they followed her into a Knightsbridge store. "The whole thing has got out of control," she said. "Everywhere I go, there is someone there. If I go to a restaurant, or just out shopping in the supermarket, they're trying to take photographs . . . There's always someone outside my door . . . I'm not so much bored as miserable . . . I'm sort of fed up, partly because it makes everyone else's life so bloody, particularly for the girls who share my flat. It's just not right at all."

What's more, she added, she didn't think the Royal Family "really know what's going on down here. At least we didn't talk about it when I was in Norfolk." They didn't talk about it because the Royals live with this kind of thing all their lives. "They've grown up with it, so they know what to do."

She did, however, escape the press for that famous weekend in Sandringham. She got a very fast driver "and we shot off in a puff of smoke. Then I had my new car delivered to somewhere else where I stayed the night, and then shot off to Norfolk. She had her own theory about the enormous surge of publicity. "I think it's because everything happens to the Royal Family in November. Princess Anne married and had a baby in November. It's the Queen and Prince Philip's anniversary. Then, of course, it's Charles's birthday, and everyone's dying for him to get married, and I was the one who was around this time."

Another reason for all this attention, she felt, was "because I haven't got a background. The background of leaping in and out of bed with people. I mean I haven't had a *chance* to have a background like that. I'm only nineteen." Then she added resignedly, "But people are longing to dig up something."

Caught by a reporter after visiting her grandmother, Lady Fermoy, Diana admitted she was "feeling the pressure. However, I'm still bearing up . . . I haven't been carried off yet." She felt sorry for the reporters, she said, "having to wait outside my flat in all weathers." She would not comment on Prince Charles. "I'm not going to say anything. Would you, if you were in my situation?" She did add, however, "I'm not going to go out this evening. I intend watching *Dallas* on television."

Some time later, she was found sitting alone on a park bench. She said it was because "I just wanted to be on my own for a few moments. I just wanted a good long think."

Couldn't she end all this speculation about the marriage? "I really don't know . . . I can't say. I just can't say anything."

She did have a comment about Charles's three-week tour in India: "One thing I don't want is a postcard from India saying, 'Wish you were here.'"

The importance of an engagement announcement to Diana was that it would immediately put her under the protection of the Royal Household. From then on, all public appearances, interviews, photographs would be monitored by the Palace. It would mean moving out of her apartment, giving up her job, severely restricting any possible press approaches.

One of the Royal Family's priorities for Prince Charles, according to Robert Lacey, was "to find a girl with no past." Lacey added, "There aren't that many nineteen-year-old virgins available."

To counteract the effects of the train incident, Diana's uncle, Lord Fermoy, was quoted as saying, "She, I can assure you, has never had a lover."

The myth was that Lord Fermoy was her favorite and that they were very close. The fact was otherwise. After she became Princess, he had repeatedly telephoned the Palace, but Diana notified her staff that she would not accept any of his calls. As she said then, "He never did anything for us when my mother left." When he committed suicide, though, she did go to his funeral.

The further fact was that Diana did at one time have a serious boyfriend for a short interval. He was handsome George Plumptre, who was six years older. He later wrote some garden books and married a fashion coordinator.

Barbara Cartland, Diana's step-grandmother, announced, "Prince Charles has got to have a pure young girl. I don't think Diana has had a boyfriend. That is marvelous in this day and age because you know what girls are like now—they have sexual affairs almost before they leave the cradle. It is frightening. The ideal for a perfect marriage must be a pure wife."

The headline of one newspaper article read: ROSE WITHOUT A THORN.

Emphasizing the Palace position, Press Secretary Michael Shea reported, "I am not going to deny this suggestion of an engagement." The Queen was reported to have said, "She is a delightful girl. Charles could not find a more perfect partner."

Pressed on his thirty-second birthday— "When are you going to tell us the good news, Your Highness?"—the Prince blushed slightly and answered, "You will have to wait and see."

Patrick Montague-Smith, former editor of *Debrett's Peerage*, who had spent his lifetime studying royalty, paid his tribute to Lady Diana: "She has dealt with a very difficult situation with great charm and dignity. She has coped with the attention of the world's press and television with the delicacy we have come to associate with members of the Royal Family. Such cool and aplomb is a rare quality in one so young." Later he added that she could assume any name she wished as Queen. "But the name Diana is as aristocratic as any, and was very popular in Georgian times."

Another compliment came from a *Daily Express* reporter: "Lady Diana is not quite as stunning as Davina Sheffield, not quite as sexy as Anna Wallace, not quite as clever as Lucia Santa Cruz. She is warm, reliable, quick-witted, open-hearted, cool, and very attractive. The most popular adjective used privately by my stony-hearted journalistic colleagues who have met her in the last few months is 'terrific.'"

However, an organization called The Anti-Marriage Association to Preserve British Bachelorhood sent Prince Charles a telegram: "Don't do it!"

Commenting on the Prince's indecisiveness, a gossip columnist broadcast that the Prince has "sowed all his wild oats" and was "now down to virgins."

Meanwhile, in India, the *Sunday Standard* suggested: "Why not wed one of our impoverished and beautiful princesses? Let him play polo. Let him rush over the muddy plains chasing our wild pigs. But let him also chase our princesses . . ."

The Prince was informed that Anna Wallace had married the youngest brother of Lord Hesketh. There was also a reported interview with Lady Diana, in which she had said: "I would like to marry soon. What woman doesn't want to marry eventually? I don't think nineteen is too young—it depends on the person . . ."

Asked if she expected to be married this time next year, she said, "Who knows?" Had Prince Charles proposed? "I can't say yes or no to that. I can't confirm or deny it."

The Prince, meanwhile, visited a movie set and was kissed by an Indian actress (kissing is taboo in movies in India). Asked about marriage, he said he was encouraged by the fact that if he became a Muslim he could have lots of wives. Whenever he made a mild joke like that, he scratched the end of his nose and passed his hand nervously through his hair. He also tended to twist the heavy gold signet ring on the little finger of his left hand.

There were more serious things to do and see on the trip. In his visit to a nursery for abandoned children, Mother Teresa of Calcutta showed him a day-old child found in a garbage can. He was visibly moved. There were tears in his eyes when he asked, "Who will adopt little Lella? What will happen to her?"

For almost fifteen hours a day, he saw everything from new industry to old maharajahs, and even squeezed in a game of polo. He crisscrossed the country, piloting his own plane, a Royal Andover, and he must have thought that he would become the first King of England who was not also Emperor of India.

His general mood was pensive, and he took time out for a mountain trek in the Himalayan foothills. A doctor went along carrying blood plasma in case of an emergency. As he climbed Mount Everest, he saw the vast whiteness turn to golden pink at sunset. His staff noted that he had been edgy when he started up, but when he came down there was a fresh calm in him, "as if some huge burden had been lifted from his shoulders."

Whatever it was, whatever decision he had resolved he kept it to himself.

Duty always had been the big word in his life. "I feel that royal duty, in a way, is slightly more inbred; it has to be," he said. "I mean, it has to be trained, in a way. You have a wider and more permanent duty, in the sense that you can't really relinquish it, you know, when you want to. Whereas I think you might be able to if you were an ordinary person. I would probably define it as being something you have to do, something you feel you ought to do, without particularly wanting to do it."

A royal marriage, he felt, was that kind of duty.

"There is such a thing as wanting to get married or the feeling that 'I've got to get married,' " said a noted London editor. "Winston Churchill's friends told him he better get married, so he did. He had had this prostitute, and his friends had warned him of disease and discovery. Well, with Prince Charles, it was a matter of duty and responsibility."

But it was getting to be more than that.

In the course of an evening, Prince Charles found himself with a friendly face, noted Fleet Street photographer Kent Gavin, whom he had known from many royal tours. Gavin asked him how things were, and the Prince blurted, "I'm missing Diana like you couldn't believe. We phone every night, and I've got letters she gave me . . ."

Another night, a week later, in the magic moonlight of the Taj Mahal, the monument to matrimonial love, the Prince was again with Gavin. "What love this man must have had for his wife," Charles said. "I know what that means now. I can understand it. One day I will bring her here . . ."

f he truly felt, as he did, that it was his royal duty to get married, if everybody, especially his parents, believed that Lady Diana was his perfect partner, if his feeling for this lovely young lady had grown from platonic to passionate, then why was Prince Charles still procrastinating?

The answer was to be found in a simple statement he once had made: "My marriage has to be forever."

Her Majesty had left a message when he returned from India that she wanted to see him the next morning. He knew why only too well. Instead, he got up at dawn to drive to Highgrove.

At Christmas ten days later, the family gathered in full at Windsor Castle. It was then that he told his parents that he was sure of his own feelings about Diana but not yet certain of hers.

It was hard to believe that he still doubted her love for him. This was a young lady who lugged her own luggage into her car and drove a hundred miles to some preselected rendezvous. This was a young lady who had gone through months of hellish publicity for his sake. If ever a love was obvious, it was hers.

What Charles probably meant was that he still wasn't absolutely certain that Diana knew what she was getting into. A *Washington Post* columnist wrote, "A woman so young, so inexperienced, so unworldly is not prepared to decide if she should be, for now and evermore, the Queen of England . . . After all, she's only a kid . . ."

Once committed she would have no exit. She would be trapped in the royal walls. The Palace might seem like a jail. Once engaged, the royal barriers would only admit to her circle those whose blood was blue enough; it was predicted Diana would quickly lose contact with her three roommates.

Carolyn Pride sadly agreed. "I know it won't be the same. We've known each other seven years, we went to school together, and I think she's a fabulous girl. But I think we won't see each other as often. In fact, I know we won't.''

None of them, obviously, recognized Diana's strong will. In the six months after her engagement, she called her friends often, met them for lunch and dinner, invited them to spend evenings with her at the Palace.

She would give up much to be a Princess, but not everything.

Of course, there were tremendous benefits to royal life. There would be cars and helicopters to take her from one place to another, several hundred servants waiting for her every whim. She would be able to shop for anything without care or concern. She could visit all of the wonders of the world, and people would curtsy. And one day, however far in the future, she would wake up in the morning and be able to say, ''I am the *Queen!*''

How could she say no to all this? But the Prince wanted to make absolutely sure that she truly knew what she was doing.

A London columnist summed up the consensus: ''He'd be a fool to pass it up. She's ideal.'' And someone else said, ''She has a history, but no past.''

''There cannot be another family so stiff with royal connections,'' said Peter Townend, former editor of *Burke's Peerage.* ''Listen to a few of these things . . .'' He then noted that King George, Queen Charlotte, and Queen Victoria were all godparents to Spencer girls, that the fifth Earl was Groom of the Stole to Edward VII when he was Prince of Wales, that the present Earl Spencer was godson of Queen Mary and the late Duke of Windsor, that the two grandmothers and four great-aunts of Lady Diana were all great friends of the Queen Mother and attended in the various positions of Lady of the Bedchamber, Woman of the Bedchamber, Extra Woman of the Bedchamber, Lady-in-Waiting, Extra-Lady-in-Waiting, and Mistress of the Robes.

What was genealogically interesting was that Diana and Charles were, through King Henry VIII, sixteenth cousins once removed, and seventh cousins once removed through William Cavendish, third Duke of Devonshire, a descendant of James I. Prince Charles was descended from every English royal family except the Stuarts; Diana made up for his lack by being descended from the Stuarts.

At the time of the engagement, the press dug deep into Diana's pedigreed heritage. James Whitaker quoted one acid comment by

Prince Charles: "I am getting fed up learning all about her past. I am beginning to think she is more Royal than I am."

It mattered much more to him that Diana was so young and fresh than someone older and more sophisticated.

"It's fortunate that Diana was so young when she married," said a member of the inner Royal circle. "If she'd been older, even if she'd been twenty-five years old, it might have been much more difficult for her to make the adjustment as Princess of Wales. So many functions can be so boring after a while, particularly large garden parties, or cocktail parties, where you must really be an actress, to pretend . . ."

Diana had said that she didn't even think about the difference in their ages. But she had once. Early in the courtship, she had discussed it with her friends, and had seemed concerned. The Prince himself had joked about his thinning hair. As time went by, as their relationship deepened, the thirteen years between them seemed to disappear. His age seemed to give her a greater sense of security; her youth, he said, made him feel younger.

If the age difference bothered Prince Charles, he would have been happy to read the dictum of a London University psychologist who noted that, "Girls frequently do follow the age pattern of the parents when they marry. If her mother had married young, it is very likely her daughter will. She will also tend to choose a man with roughly the same age difference because that is what she has become used to while growing up." Diana's mother was eighteen, her father thirty when they had married. What was ironic, of course, was that they were ultimately divorced.

Whatever he told his parents that Christmas at Windsor, there was one thing they both told him: There could be no more procrastination, the marriage issue must be decided soon.

A photographer had caught Lady Diana shopping in Knightsbridge, and asked, "How many stones are there in the ring you've just chosen?"

"Thousands," she said, giggling, and jumped into her car.

She spent most of Christmas with her father and family at Althorp, part of the time bedded down with the flu. She did, however, have an invitation from Her Majesty to visit at Sandringham shortly after the new year.

The press descended on Sandringham to see if an engagement announcement was forthcoming. Maintaining privacy is difficult at Sandringham because a public road separates the house from the stables, enabling the press to keep close watch without trespassing. Moreover, the 274-room house had four separate entrances.

The crowd of reporters and photographers brought out a rare testiness in the Queen, who told them, "Oh, I wish you would go away." Later again, she and Prince Charles drove up in a Land-Rover and the Queen sat stern-faced as her son and his Labrador, Henry, got out, walked over to the press and said, "A happy new year to you, but a particularly nasty one to your editors."

Diana's father had his own complaints about the press swarming over Althorp. "When they can't find anything out," he said sadly, "they just make it up." His speech was slightly slurred as a result of his brain hemorrhage and he added, "One German magazine said I was drunk all day. Why do they have to write lies? We can't protect ourselves. It's all right for the Palace—they've got their own police and press office. We've got no one."

Diana's mother got similar treatment in Scotland. She fended off all press questions with a standard answer: "The reason I am on close terms with my daughters is because they know things won't be repeated."

Another time, when she walked quickly away from photographers, they commented on her speed. "I've got good long legs like my daughter," she said.

Her daughter surely needed those long legs to race away from the press. She once caught a bus just as it was leaving, offered the conductor the fare but he just beamed at her. "Have this one on London Transport, Lady Di."

During the month of January, Diana still went to work in her kindergarten at Pimlico. After the press siege of Sandringham, Diana and Charles were more careful about their meetings. The best-kept secret was his hideaway house in the elegant area at Kensington Church Street. Only his closest friends knew of it. It was within walking distance from the Old Barracks in Kensington Palace, where Diana's sister Jane now had an apartment. The Prince's humor must have been tickled by the name of the pub nearest his place: "The Windsor Castle."

They were known to have met three times in two days. She met him for an early morning breakfast at Berkshire Downs to watch him exercise his racehorse, Alibar. To get there by seven, she had to start driving before six—a round trip of 150 miles.

Charles tried to tell her about all the tedium of royal life, but it was like telling a woman in love that there was dust on the shining moon. After one rendezvous at the home of his friends Andrew and Camilla Parker-Bowles near Chippenham, Diana told friends that Charles then seemed "strangely stifled," that he had talked about marriage in hypothetical terms: "If I were to ask you, do you think it would be possible?"

"I immediately felt the immense absurdity of the situation and couldn't help giggling," Diana said. "I still think the situation is absurd, but I just don't giggle anymore."

Two days later, she spent the weekend walking the grounds at Althorp. Her stepmother, Raine, told reporters, "She needs somewhere to think in peace. She is going to walk and be alone. She is very young, after all."

Lady Diana was next seen in the Knightsbridge shop of Janet Reger, specializing in filmy romantic underwear for trousseaus. Reporters and photographers even followed her into the shops. Finally she confronted one of them, Kent Gavin of the *Mirror*. "Why do you worry about what I buy? Do you want to know the color of my bloomers? Why are you so concerned about the fact that I look down so much? I look down because I'm tall."

Gavin tried to explain that he sympathized with her need for private time, but she had to face the fact that she was becoming the number one pinup of the world, and there could be no more purely private time whenever she stepped out.

The Prince was going to take his annual ski vacation at Klosters in Switzerland and asked her to join him. She refused, she said, because the press would make the "whole thing a circus" and "ruin his holiday." As it was, he skied with security guards, who carried automatic pistols while he wore a tiny radio transmitter in case he got lost.

She had planned a winter holiday of her own, joining her mother at her home in New South Wales. She intended to leave on February 6th. The Prince returned from Switzerland shortly before that and invited her to dine with him at Buckingham Palace. Before she went, Diana told her roommate Carolyn Pride, "I just know he is going to propose tonight . . . I just have the feeling that tonight is the big night.''

The Prince was a romantic and he set the scene with sensitivity and some drama. There were candles, flowers, the meal planned so there would be minimal interruptions from any servants. The couch was small so they had to sit close together while he explained their options and his plans.

Nobody else was there to witness the scene, but Diana's favorite romantic novelist, her step-grandmother Barbara Cartland, had described such a scene in lush prose in her novel *Bride to the King:*

There was tenderness in his voice which made her press her cheek against his shoulder. Then he said: ''Tonight, my darling, you are only a child, and not yet a woman, and that is why I want you to think that I am the Prince of your heart, just as you are the Queen of mine . . .''

''I love you,'' she whispered, as her head fell back on the soft pillows. She was a bride not of a king, but of the man whose heart was her heart, whose soul was her soul, and who would rule for ever a world which belonged only to them both. A world of love.

When Charles finally asked Diana to marry him, she answered ''promptly.'' ''Yes!''

He told her to think about it during her two weeks in Australia, consider more ''if it was all going to be too awful . . .''

But that night after his proposal, Diana was on a high. ''I guessed when I saw her face,'' said her sister Sarah. ''She was totally radiant—bouncing and bubbling.''

''I said, 'You're engaged,' and she whispered, 'Yes.' She told me they were getting married in the summer.''

''They are both over the moon,'' Sarah continued. ''He met Miss Right and she met Mr. Right. They just clicked. They're totally compatible. They have the same sense of humor. She is very giggly and he is giggly. She loves ballet and opera and sport in all forms. It's a relief that she will have the protection of Buckingham Palace at last.''

Sarah was right about Diana's radiance but not about the things she liked to do. Polo may be a passion with Charles, but it is not high on Diana's list, of favorites. She does love ballet and he loves music, but someone who knows them both very well insisted, "His enthusiasm for opera is largely fake—he doesn't know a lot about it. As for Diana, she hates going to the opera. But it's all part of the scene of classic royal nobility."

Diana could no longer keep the secret from her roommates.

"We started to squeal with excitement," said Virginia Pitman. "And then we started to cry." Carolyn Pride got the news through the door "while I was in the loo. No, it wasn't hard to keep the secret. We never dreamed of telling anyone. That's the way we were brought up." "It's like protecting your sister," said Ann Bolton. "We would simply never let Diana down."

Diana had also made a personal plea: "Keep your traps shut!" They all had a celebration breakfast the next morning, "a jolly meal." "It couldn't happen to anyone nicer," said Ann Bolton. When Diana told her father about it, he said, "You must only marry the man you love."

And she answered, "That is what I'm doing."

Diana soon left for Australia but the press never found her. Her mother flatly lied: "It is true my daughter is on holiday. It is true she is abroad. But she is not in Australia. She is not even in this part of the world." Her husband added, "You've got the wrong continent. Try the Caribbean."

She had ten marvelous days swimming, surfing, sleeping. Even the Prince found it difficult to penetrate her protective cordon by telephone.

"I said, it's the Prince of Wales speaking."
"How do I know it's the Prince of Wales?"
"You don't," he said, in a rage, "but I am."
Eventually he did get through.

Here's another myth: The press later made much of the fact that Lady Tryon—who had given her approval or disapproval to all of the Prince's previous young women—had flown to Australia to advise Diana on the pros and cons of a Royal future. The truth was that Kanga did indeed fly to Australia at that same time. "But I never saw Diana. I never even met her until after the engagement announcement."

Lady Diana was in fact the only one of his potential brides whom she had not met. The explanation? The Prince felt the increasing family pressure for a marriage. He finally had found a perfectly qualified young woman, too young to have had a romantic past, and he had fallen in love with her. He had made his own decision. Moreover, the royal powers had approved.

Diana returned to England incognito and was home for two days before the press rediscovered her. She informed her Prince that she had not changed her mind. He then formally asked her father for her hand in marriage. "I wonder what he would have done if I'd turned him down," mused Earl Spencer later. Discreetly, Lady Diana had a gynecological examination to confirm that she could bear children.

The Queen had brought up the question of an engagement ring to her son, and he left it to her. She called Garrards, the royal jewelers, and had a tray of rings sent to her. Diana later said she selected her ring, "the most expensive one." It was a large oval sapphire surrounded by fourteen diamonds, set in 18-carat white gold. A close family friend insists the Queen picked it.

"The ring was too big for her," said the friend, "and there was no time to alter it before the announcement. So if you notice the pictures at the time, she's often holding the ring to keep it in place."

"We had drinks with them at the Palace the night before the announcement," said Earl Spencer. "Diana is a giver, not a taker, and Charles is a very lucky chap to have her. Diana was looking radiant. She'll take it all in her stride. She's very practical and down-to-earth, and a very good housewife."

Countess Spencer was not impressed by the Palace apartment of the future King. It was basically Victorian, mahogany, and most ordinary. The bedroom was green, the sitting room blue, and the study dark brown. The Prince found it "comfortable." The only compliment the Countess could dredge up was that she found the elevator "clever."

The Archbishop of Canterbury was told the news early. Was he tempted to tell his wife?

"Slightly, over the breakfast table, but I resisted."

One of the first gifts Prince Charles gave to his future bride after their engagement was a pendant made of diamonds and emeralds in the design of the Prince of Wales feathers. It was a family heirloom that had belonged to Queen Mary. She put it on a velvet ribbon. The only other jewelry she had brought to the Palace after their engagement was a signet ring with the letter D on it.

At the Buckingham Palace investiture on the morning of February 24th, 1981, the Lord Chamberlain announced to those awaiting honors, "The Queen has asked me to let you know that an announcement is being made at this moment in the following terms: 'It is with the greatest pleasure that the Queen and the Duke of Edinburgh announce the betrothal of their beloved son, the Prince of Wales, to Lady Diana Spencer, daughter of the Earl Spencer and the Honorable Mrs. Shand-Kydd.'"

The word already had gone out in coded cablegram to key people in the Commonwealth. The Prime Minister and the Cabinet already knew. The Houses of Parliament cheered loudly at the news, and the crew of Prince Charles's minesweeper, HMS *Bronington*, fired a 21-gun salute. Mrs. Ronald Reagan was particularly delighted because she had ordered customized "Charles and Diana roses" from a British porcelain house for a scheduled visit of the Prince some months later.

The *Daily Express* headlined the news: ROYAL RAY OF SUNSHINE.

The stock market zoomed. People rushed to buy flags and photographs of the couple. Wedgwood announced "major plans" for commemorative crockery and glassware. Crowds collected outside Buckingham Palace, among them Diana's father, with his camera. "I wanted to photograph the photographers," he said. "I have photographed every important event in Diana's life and I wanted to record this one as well."

The Buckingham Palace staff knew all about it, hours earlier, because when they had come to work that morning they found the refrigerators all filled with champagne.

The unhappiest man in Britain was Member of Parliament Willie Hamilton, a royal critic who said, "We're in for six months of mush."

He was so right. But it was the kind of mush the world wanted.

Before the Prince paid his three dollars for the marriage certificate, he emphasized again to Diana how little life she would have of her own, that he would need all her support, her comfort. Basically, he was already on record as believing that the woman's role was mainly in the home—that's the way he had been brought up.

This would hardly deter Diana. She was, as Barbara Cartland said, "a feminine woman."

"Everybody's stunned by it," Cartland added. "It's really a joke because feminine women have been here since the beginning of time, and ruled the world very successfully. But you see, we'd lost the feminine women, got all these career women. Suddenly, this young girl, who doesn't pretend to be academic in any sort of way, has come in and defeated them all, just by being a woman. She doesn't try to be clever, just normal. Just like the Queen Mother. She is naturally interested in things, naturally fond of people, and absolutely *adores* children. And yet she's got a strong personality, vivacious but strong. Strength within herself. And magic. She's got magic."

Prince Charles already had a real sense of what he was. "I was very struck with something he once told me," said Anthony Holden. "He said, 'Whenever I go into a room, I am automatically the center of attraction. People's knees buckle and their conversation goes wild. That's fine. I'm used to that now. But I feel the need to prove myself *worthy* of being the center of attention, not just because of what my parents are, but because of what I'm *like*.'"

"I think that shows him to be a nice guy," added Holden, "not taking himself for granted at all."

While the Royal Family was "a firm" and monarchy was "a job," he still felt "you could not have a better one. You can do so much to help other people."

As for Diana, she would learn. "She'll be twenty soon," he said, "and I was about that age when I started. It's obviously difficult to start with, but you just have to take the plunge."

What he did tell her was, "You have to get through a certain amount of anxiety, or nervousness, or prejudice, or whatever, to start with, and it usually takes about twenty minutes or so before people are beginning to relax."

Diana herself now felt she was ripe to be Royal. "This is what I want," she said firmly.

There were prescribed formalities to be covered. Under the Royal Marriages Act of 1772, both the Queen and Parliament had to give their consent to the match. Within twenty-four hours, Prime Minister Thatcher traveled to the Palace to express the enthusiasm of the government. And Diana's mother added, "I greatly approve of my daughters marrying men they love." Diana herself said, "Oh, I never had any doubts about it." Her sister Jane, however, was overheard to say, "She doesn't know what she's letting herself in for."

Something of what Jane meant showed up in a German magazine with a cover picture faked to show Prince Charles with a baby in his arms and an inserted picture of Lady Diana. The caption read, "I want to give the Prince many pretty babies." Commenting on it, Lady Diana reportedly had her head bowed, her hands clenched when she answered, "I don't want to see this rubbish." Prince Charles was quoted as saying, "If you didn't laugh at some of these things, you'd go mad."

Maybe Diana did sense what was coming. When she left her apartment in Coleherne Court for the last time, she wrote a note to her roommates, giving them her phone number at Clarence House, and adding, "For God's sake, ring me up—I'm going to need you."

At the moment of the formal engagement announcement on February 24th, on the stroke of eleven, three policemen appeared on guard at the main door of Diana's apartment. More patrolled the nearby gardens.

Still to come was a formal document embossed with the Great Seal, promulgated at a meeting of the twenty-eight members of the Privy Council giving official royal and parliamentary consent to the match.

"Lady Di," as the press had called her, did consent to have her engagement ring photographed, but only after coyly tucking her fingertips into the palm of her hand. A close friend confided, "Di has bitten her nails for as long as I can remember."

"My nails are terrible," Diana told manicurist Rose Scott. "I've tried everything to stop biting them but nothing works. I suppose I'm too old to stop now."

A small flood of sympathetic suggestions promptly flooded in: Coat them with terrible-tasting gentian violet or aloe; wear false nails; have acupuncture treatments or hypnosis; "chew the petals of a wild rose." Psychiatrists claimed that one out of four people in the twenty-nine-year-old age group bites his nails.

London nail specialist Susan Hanford recommended semipermanent acrylic nails. "One lady broke a tooth biting one of them and it cost her 60 pounds to have it capped. She never did it again." "I can't get used to it," Diana said of the ring. "I even scratched my nose because it's so big—the ring, I mean."

Charles & Diana

Seeing the couple together, a spokesman for the British Footwear Manufacturers' Federation predicted that the new shoe style for women would be "flatties." Diana was just as tall as Charles (5'10"), and protocol decreed that she could not stand taller than the Prince of Wales.

Diana moved to a suite at Clarence House, and Prince Charles joined her and his grandmother for a celebration dinner, while the crowd outside chanted, "We want Di! We want Di!" Both came out, smiled, and waved.

A reporter reached Anna Wallace, the Prince's last love. "I think Lady Diana will make a very good Queen," she said. "She's very sort of dignified, discreet, and you know, all the things you ought to be." Her wry advice: "Be totally devoted to your husband."

I t was probably the best-kept royal secret of the twentieth century. Almost nobody knew.

After the engagement announcement, the whole world thought Diana was staying at Clarence House under the watchful eye of her grandmother, Lady Fermoy, and the Queen Mother. The whole world thought the two venerable ladies were giving their young charge a programmed period of preparation on royal protocol. The whole world thought Diana was being carefully sheltered until her marriage.

But the whole world was wrong!

All this time—for more than four months before the wedding—Diana was spending her nights with the Prince.

What had happened, and what nobody knew, was that the willful Diana had stayed at Clarence House only two nights, then moved to Buckingham Palace. Of course, one does not simply move into Buckingham Palace. Naturally, she had the support of the Prince, but it was the Queen's house. The Queen had to give permission; the Queen had to invite her. What was truly remarkable was that she did.

Consider the possible consequences. What if the press had found out what was happening? Here was a reportedly virginal young lady living on the same floor of the Palace as the Prince. Not only that: There was almost nobody else living on the floor. The Queen's two dressers, her maid, footmen, and the Prince's valet were tucked away in another wing. Princess Anne had her own suite, but was almost never there. Andrew had his own room, but he was in the Navy. And Edward was away at school. Those of the household staff who did live in the Palace lived on the floor above. The Queen and Prince Philip lived on the floor below. So Diana and Charles were without a chaperone, without any peering eyes, without any witnesses. For more than four months!

If the press had found out, there might have been a monumental scandal. Why would they take the chance?

The Prince must have made an emotional appeal to his mother. His father might have leered a little, but surely he was on his son's side. Her Majesty herself might well have remembered her own passionate love for her dashing fiancé before she was married. Besides, who would ever dare consider that anything improper could happen to the Royals behind the doors of Buckingham Palace?

It's easy to understand why Diana would want to move in. Clarence House was only a few minutes' slow walk to Buckingham Palace, but the distance seemed intolerable. With the world watching, she could hardly come and go at will. No matter how lovable they were, those two grannies couldn't compare with the man she wanted. She was overwhelmingly in love with her Prince. She wanted to be with him. As far as she was concerned, they *were* married. With an official announcement of the engagement, there was nothing except illness, death, or the end of the monarchy, that could have postponed their wedding.

Who would fault them? Who would truly care—as long as they were discreet?

It was almost too good to be true. Diana had moved into a small suite of rooms formerly occupied by the governess, in the nursery wing.

Her rooms were unpretentious, and included a sitting room. The furniture was cheerful, the flowers always fresh, and she had a television. One program she invariably watched was *Coronation Street*, a British soap opera. It was also a favorite of the Queen and the Queen Mother. The refrigerator was kept stocked with yogurt and other foods she liked.

A young Nursery Footman was assigned to attend her, but he complained to other staff that she never seemed to want anything. Whenever he asked, she would say, "No, I'll be all right."

"If the Queen was home when the Prince came back," said the Prince's valet, "he would tell Diana, 'Darling, I'm going to have lunch with Mummy.'" He would not invite her along because he and his mother would usually talk state business. The Queen was a loner, just like her son, just like Diana. In the evening, if Prince Philip was away, as he often was, she would dine alone on a tray in front of the television. "In all the months Diana stayed there, I don't ever remember her dining alone with the Queen. Or even lunch. I think she was a little afraid of her. I think one of the reasons Diana was so shy of her was that the two didn't have much to talk about. Diana didn't like horses and she didn't like dogs. But then we were all in awe of the Queen. It was an awesome thing for any of us to talk to her and nobody ever pretended to know what was going on in her head."

The valet would inform Diana as soon as the Prince returned from lunch with the Queen, and she would hurry to join him. All visitors to Prince Charles were first announced—except Diana. She would simply knock and walk in.

If any of the staff were within earshot, she would not call him "Charles" because it was too personal. Nor would she ever call him "Sir." He always called her "Diana." When the Prince had an appointment, he would tell his staff, "Keep an eye on Lady Diana for me, will you?" When he returned, his first question was, "Is Lady Diana all right?"

If the Prince was away on his daily working schedule, Diana often found herself alone in the afternoon. If she was tired of needlepoint or television or reading, she often went on solitary exploratory trips through the Palace with a Sony Walkman to provide music. As she often said, she didn't mind being alone.

But she did mind a lot of noise. The Palace staff was housed on the floor directly above her suite, just as the Queen was directly below. One night the staff had a somewhat rambunctious party. The next day, Lady Diana ordered earplugs to be delivered.

Nobody ever took her on an organized tour of the Palace to show her the various departments, to explain how the Palace worked, or what the household staff did. There was no planned program to teach her history, Royal style or ethics or manners. She simply picked up things by asking questions.

During her plentiful free time, she did a variety of things. Her mother had a London apartment on Warwick Square, and the two spent a lot of time together, mostly shopping for trousseau items. Reporters noted that Diana shopped at Harvey Nichols first, then Harrods. It was at Harrods that she bought the blue silk suit which she wore in her first official photograph with Prince Charles. She also bought jodphurs from Arte, lingerie from the White House on Bond Street, and shoes from Bertie's on South Molton Street.

Her mother was with her on South Molton Street when a modish young man rushed out of one of the shops and kissed her on the cheek—causing her to cover her face with her hands.

Everyone felt that the blue of her suit was lovely on her, but the outfit bunched terribly at the waist. When she saw herself in it, in the official photographs, it "threw her into the arms of her *Vogue* fashion consultants."

The fashion editors at *Vogue* really shaped the new Diana image. Diana's sister Jane had worked there as an editorial assistant before being married, and Jane, who was frequently at Diana's side, introduced *Vogue* to her Sloane Ranger sister in an effort to wean her from her Laura Ashley blouse-and-tweed-skirt image.

The *Vogue* editors were the ones who lightened her hair and darkened her eyelashes, persuaded her to slim down a bit, got her to stop slouching and be proud of her graceful height. They brought the best of British fashion to her and taught her what looked best on her and why. The shops, of course, were thrilled to lend Lady Diana anything she wanted after her engagement: The publicity was worth much, the future contact even more. But when Collingwood offered to lend her some jewelry she had admired, the Royal advisors said no. Royals were not permitted to accept contributions of commercial goods.

Diana bristled, retorting, "I'm not a Royal yet!"

The Prince's valet later recalled a photo of her in a magazine in which everything she wore, including jewelry, had been lent to her.

The duckling became a swan. *Vogue* editor Beatrix Miller earned her invitation to the wedding. Others—Anna Harvey, Grace Coddington, and beauty editor Felicity Clark—were all with her at the Palace just before the wedding to make certain that she really looked like Cinderella.

Few photographed as beautifully as Diana. Anthony Holden remembered when he was at the *Times* doing a layout on the Royals at Wimbledon. "We had a photographer shooting her for three hours, and she wasn't consciously posing—she was just watching the match. Well, we laid out about fifty photographs of her on the floor and we had to choose one for the front page. There wasn't one that we couldn't have used. She's just amazingly photogenic."

The General Trading Company had a royal warrant for "fancy goods," and Diana listed some 300 items she might want for wedding presents. They included fireplace bellows, two dozen champagne glasses, a dark green tablecloth, Royal Worcester china, a chicken fryer, two shocking pink lamps, two large beehive honey pots, a pair of Crown Staffordshire white cockatoos, a spice rack, six pairs of quilted table mats, a small George III mahogany three-tier what-not, two sun loungers with cushions, and a croquet set.

And no decanters, please.

Diana also spent a lot of time during her engagement period with Jane and her baby, who lived nearby in Kensington Palace. She occasionally would visit her other sister Sarah and her husband. The McCorquodales had a farm but kept an apartment in Chelsea, not far from Buckingham Palace. If Diana saw relatively little of Sarah compared to Jane, it might have been due to some residual sensitivity over Sarah's old romantic relationship with Charles.

On weekends, if the Prince was in town, Diana would accompany him to Windsor Castle where he played polo. She was there when he took an especially bad fall. And she was with him when his favorite horse, Alibar, collapsed under Charles on the walk back from a training canter. The Prince cradled the horse's head in his arms, his eyes wet with tears, and would not leave until a vet arrived and pronounced the horse dead.

"Lady Diana had tears streaming down her cheeks as she and Charles later walked away," a stable boy said. "They appeared to be comforting each other."

It was a tragedy they alone experienced and shared, and it brought them much closer together.

Another time, at a steeplechase, the Prince's horse tumbled at the eighteenth fence. Lady Diana was watching through binoculars in the company of the Queen Mother and Princess Margaret. As the horse stumbled, Diana half stood up and looked at where the Prince lay flat out in the mud. Then she sat down quickly and kept her eyes down as if too scared to look, and Princess Margaret moved to a seat beside her. But when the Prince stood up, the two women laughed in relief. Before the Prince moved off to change, Diana came down and put her arm around him. And the crowd applauded.

After one fall in a polo game, "his horse did a tango on his face . . . had he been kicked an inch higher, it would have been curtains." It left a scar on his left cheek. The Prince said, "My mother thinks I ought to have plastic surgery," but some felt that the scar was a point of pride with him. Friends noted that he courted physical danger because he was seldom challenged intellectually. He himself said, "I find that overcoming physical challenges and danger is incredibly helpful toward overcoming things normally—facing moral challenges." Diana hated to see any of these incidents. Nevertheless, although she would change many things in him, many habits, he would never abandon his polo-playing.

Her dislike of horses was nothing new. She recalled the time when her own pony, Romany, got into a panic, took a sudden sharp turn, throwing Diana out of the saddle. She was unconscious for a moment, then in great pain from a broken arm, and taken to the hospital.

Diana was too restless and too young to stay in the Palace's protective custody. Whenever she felt too cooped up, she took off in her little red car. But the difference was that now there was always a passenger. He was one of the Prince's detectives, Paul Officer. The first time he got in to join her, she said briskly, "It's all right. I can manage."

"Sorry," he told her, "we're part of your life now."

If she felt hungry at the Palace, she did what no Royal had ever done before—she went to the kitchen and helped herself. It was only when some of the staff embroidered things she said to them and passed the comments on to the press that she stopped her lone kitchen forays.

The press had a field day when Prince Charles took her to a Royal Opera House fund-raiser at Goldsmith's Hall. She arrived in a black strapless gown, so low-cut that even a BBC newscaster reported "audible, admiring gasps." The *Sun* noted that it provided more suspense than anything since the debate over who shot J.R. Said one observer: "I thought she was going to take a deep breath and fall out of it." On the *TV News at Ten*, there was a three-minute piece, complete with slow-motion reruns on Lady Diana's entrance to the hall. As the camera frame froze on Diana, revealing a dark spot on her left breast, the commentator authoritatively concluded, "It was definitely a shadow caused by the rose she was carrying." Prudence Glynn, former fashion editor for the London *Times*, was aghast, called it "a social gaffe . . . a fashion disaster . . ." She added, "In my view, it is very rash for royalty to be fashionable. Total anonymity is what you want for royal clothes." Fashion editor Jackie Modlinger of the *Daily Express* disagreed, saying, "Her sexy black taffeta dress made Prince Charles the envy of all the men . . . she is one of the best things that has happened to the fashion world for years . . ."

Diana's father agreed: "Jolly good for everyone, that. Made them sit up."

On a more practical note, reporter Jean Rook observed: "It takes courage, and a lot more, to uphold it. And sitting through an evening in that tight, boned bodice takes guts because, unless you stay upright and regal, the bones stick like fish knives into your midriff."

Perhaps this dress was her assertion of independence, an attempt to kill the "shy Di" concept once and for all, a slap at all the stuffy critics she disliked, a way of facing up to the challenging presence of Princess Grace of Monaco who was also at the fund-raiser.

Princess Grace's own fairy tale had ended long ago. She appeared almost matronly when Lady Diana curtsied to her. (Until she assumed the title of Princess officially, Diana would have to curtsy to thirty-eight categories of royal women in England senior to her including duchesses, marchionesses, countesses, and even the daughters of marquesses.)

A woman offered Lady Diana a single rose "to a lovely lady." Diana accepted it with the beguiling reserve which had become her trademark. The occasion was a dramatic debut. One columnist quipped that the royal couple would be known as "the King and Di." But when someone called her Di she answered quietly, "It's really Diana." "No one in her life ever called her Di," insisted her mother.

When she and Prince Charles got in their Rolls-Royce at the end of the evening, the Prince said something which gave Diana such a fit of giggles that she clutched her stomach. She looked radiant.

The two spent whatever time they could at Highgrove. "It's just like camping," Diana said of their visits there. "We've only got one room decorated downstairs, and the bedroom organized. Otherwise everything is being painted. There's nothing there yet—no curtains, carpets, or furniture—nothing."

Diana had specific suggestions and decided tastes. They soon also hired interior decorator Dudley Poplak who had a penchant for bright colors and catered to "a youngish market."

"I don't like the places I work in to look as if a decorator has ever been near them," said Poplak.

At the local village, an informant revealed that Lady Diana had popped in once to buy bubble gum.

There wasn't anything about her that wasn't news. Even though she was carefully shielded from the press now—she had the protection of two burly detectives who maneuvered her escape routes—there was at least one story a day about her printed in every London newspaper, and in many around the world as well.

She and Prince Charles did confront two television interviewers, after which Diana said, "I hope I coped all right."

She coped easily. She seemed a natural.

"If I may say," said the interviewer, "isn't it a tremendous change for someone of nineteen to make all of a sudden the transition?"

"It is," she replied, "but I've had a small run-up to it all in the last six months and next to Prince Charles, I can't go wrong. He's there with me."

In reply to a question, the Prince said of the age difference, "I shall be exhausted, I think!" He was, he said, "amazed that she's been brave enough to take me on."

Diana described herself as "an average cook," and then looked sidelong at Prince Charles and added, "You haven't tasted anything 'cause I won't let you."

Discussing the camera "poking at you from every quarter and recording every twitch you make," Prince Charles himself asked Diana, "Do you find after the last six months you're beginning to get used to it?"

"Just," she said, forcing a shy smile.

Did she have any particular interests? an interviewer wanted to know. How did she see her role as Princess of Wales?

She answered slowly, "A great challenge."

Then, more confidently, "Well, obviously it's children, but interests will broaden as the years go on. I'm twenty; I've got a good start."

He had been alone so much of his life, Prince Charles said. Then he looked at Diana. "It's marvelous to have a lot of support." For the first time in the interview, Diana took his hand and held it. "I'm glad," she said. "I like it."

Asked about being in love, Diana quickly answered, "Of course!" And Prince Charles seemed to blush when he said, "Whatever 'in love' means."

A photographer who had followed them everywhere, and caught them more than most, later smiled at the Prince's reply and said, "He knows what it means all right. He can't keep his hands off her."

"If you were to walk into a room in which you were alone with the Queen, the Duke of Edinburgh, and the Prince of Wales, would that make you a little nervous?" James Whitaker asked Diana. Diana seemed surprised. "No, why should it?"

She was, indeed, ripe to be a Royal.

As she looked at reruns of herself on television, she held her face in her hands and said, "Is that really *me*?" And then, "Did I really say *that*?"

What she had said, in response to a question about Prince Charles's support, was: "Marvelous. Oh, a tower of strength."

Prince Charles then had slapped his hand on the arm of his chair.

"Gracious!"

She had looked at him, smiling. "I had to say that 'cause you're sitting there."

Both laughed.

Diana did not yet fully understand that there was no need for embarrassment over her lack of formal dignity—it was her very naturalness that appealed to people, making her seem one of them.

Prince Charles had his own adjustment to make. Here he was, a young man in his thirties still living with his parents. His home had been a three-room suite with a surprisingly small sitting room with partly-faded blue curtains, a yellow sofa, two leather chairs, and some 300 servants. He always had said that "Marriage isn't an 'up' or 'down' issue. It's a side-by-side issue." He now had found his other side.

"I intend to work at it when I get married," he had said.

"She's the sort of person who will follow his lead, will stand by him and won't rebel," said a family friend. "She fits in perfectly with the old-fashioned conservative values of the Royal Family." Somebody else visualized her having the vitality and fun of a puppy.

What few saw then was the strong will of this young woman. The press wanted a sweet, shy bride and they made her one. The other side of her, the side her family and friends knew, her stubborn determination—that would become increasingly evident later.

As for the Prince, the consensus was clear: He had sown his wild oats. Once married, "he won't fool around. He's quite a religious chap."

They spent an early March weekend on the great Cheshire estate of Cholmondeley Castle, home of the Marquess and Marchioness of Cholmondeley, where the Prince went hunting. Lady Diana did not like blood sports, and the Prince had said prophetically of a previous fox hunt, "I'm going to enjoy it while I have the chance."

At Cholmondeley, the couple attended services at the family chapel. The Vicar of Bickerton that day in his prayer sought a blessing for all those about to be married. "And grant that they may live together in faithful love until their lives end."

12

The man who one day will be the King of England has said: "I would like to be remembered for trying to show there is a way of motivating people . . . that I have been concerned about their welfare and about their lives, about the things they feel strongly about or worry about. I would like to be remembered for taking a human interest in people in a world which tends to treat people like sheep or statistics."

This was a side of her Prince about which Diana knew little. This was the thinking Prince, the serious Prince, the philosophical Prince. This was the Prince who had said of the monarchy, "There isn't any power. There can be influence. The influence is in direct ratio to the respect people have for you." To get that respect, he refused to follow the accepted prescription for a Prince of Wales: "Wait, and stay out of trouble."

Although others helped him research, and even provided an occasional draft, the bulk of his speeches was his own—his own ideas, his own writing.

"Writing speeches is a major sweat," he admitted. "Actually sitting down and thinking is a major sweat, and worrying about whether you are going to say the right thing is another problem, of course, because everyone will jump on you."

Everyone jumped on him in 1979 when he told industry executives that they were just as responsible as their unions for the "bloody-mindedness in labor-management relations that [had] led to Britain's economic decline."

He believes in the importance of the human factor. He has warned of the dangers of today's "urbanized, advanced technological environment." He believes that Third World countries, as well as Britain, should develop labor-intensive, less depersonalized, and energy-saving "intermediate technologies" as alternatives to the "rural tradition existence of the past."

He cares about race. He is against injustice. Whatever he says about this, he knows he is vulnerable mainly because his mother is invulnerable since she is considered above criticism. His one mission, he insists, is to learn at first hand as much as possible about the people he will govern and the world he will help lead.

"I don't exactly travel around this country, or other parts of the world with my eyes tight shut or without listening to what experienced people have to say. Consequently, I think it is sometimes possible for me to see things from a broader point of view and thus to pinpoint the sort of issues which need to be raised and discussed."

A noted photographer, Allen Warren, who lives next door to the Mountbatten mansion at Broadlands recalled a party at which the Prince was present.

He found himself in a corner with the Prince, and the Prince asked, "What do you think is wrong with this country?"

The highly sophisticated photographer replied, "I think the country is made up of dull people doing dull things. Compared to the rest, Churchill was a freak."

A man alongside the Prince broke in angrily, "How can you call Churchill a *freak?*"

Prince Charles said quietly, "Let him go on. I know what Allen means."

The photographer marveled as he remembered this. "He really did know what I meant. And he was open-minded enough to listen."

The key word was: concern. There was more to it than the emotional appeal of a royal soap opera. "The great strength of the monarchy does not lie in the power it gives to the sovereign," a British commentator noted, "but in the power it denies to everyone else." In an informal and revealing television documentary on the Royal Family, the analyst observed: "While the Queen occupies the highest office of state, no one else can. While she is head of the law, no politician can take over the courts. While she is head of the services, no would-be dictator can turn the army against the people."

If monarchy was to be defined as a fairy tale with meaning, what kept it alive was that each monarch extended the reach of its meaning. Nobody knew this better than Prince Charles, and his bride-to-be would soon absorb it.

The new challenge was to gain the support of the young Brits, many of them under thirty, who felt indifference rather than ill will toward the monarchy. As one of them said, "You can kill the monarchy by a yawn as much as by a revolution."

A Cambridge student, Jonathan Holmes, wrote an open letter to Prince Charles: "How many Englishmen under twenty-five stand to attention when the anthem is played, or long for the great days of Empire? Your father's bluff common sense and your mother's gracious ordinariness are precisely the qualities needed to recapture the affection of our parents. That is precisely why they seem an irrelevancy to us. It is not that we dislike them, they simply do not seem to be important . . .

"If you are to be a King at all, you must be our King. I do not mean that you should agree with us, for we do not agree among ourselves. But if you showed clearly that you were preoccupied with our preoccupations, that you can dance to our music and sing to our tunes, you would do yourself and your office more good than would a hundred Garter ceremonies, or the dutiful launching of a thousand ships . . .

"We should like to have a King who is not afraid to speak out against hypocrisy and inhumanity, as your father has spoken out against stupidity and inefficiency . . .

"They will give you a smart blue uniform and a stiff upper lip. We would rather give you a girl, a grin, and a purpose in life. . . . Somehow you must find your voice and use it."

The feeling was deep in the British people that their monarchy was the keystone of the arch of their society. If the keystone went, the arch would collapse.

The Prince took time out to check on his duties as Duke of Cornwall. After all, this duchy provided him with an annual profit of more than 280,000 pounds in 1978. Prince Charles gave 50 percent to the Treasury as his voluntary equivalent of income tax.

It all began some six hundred years before when King Edward III set aside Cornish land for the sovereign's eldest son, the Black Prince. The duchy included 130,000 acres spread over Avon, Dorset, Cornwall, Devon, Somerset, Gloucestershire, Wiltshire, the Isles of Scilly, and city property in London. Among his tenants were farms, entire parishes, post offices, hotels, banks, shops, tin mines, oyster beds, and Dartmoor Prison.

The Prince was entitled to receive from the duchy in feudal dues a load of firewood, a gray cloak, 100 old shillings, a pound of pepper, a hunting bow, gilt spurs, a pound of herbs, a large salmon spear, a pair of falconer's gauntlets, and two greyhounds. He was also entitled to first claim on any whale or porpoise that washed ashore on his Cornish beaches, and he could insist on receiving 300 puffins a year from the people on his Isles of Scilly.

The traditional handover took place on a green beneath the stump of Launceston's Norman Castle. The language was ancient and ornate, and the Prince returned a receipt of a white rod. He also returned the greyhounds and put the rest in a museum "for the next time."

He had a personal interest in the threatened wildlife of the area, the research into a rare butterfly on duchy land, the conservation of the forests, the purchase of a farm he wanted to work himself.

On a typical day in Leicester he posed on stage at the YMCA with a man dressed as a horse, joined a barbershop chorus singing "When It's Sleepy Time Down South," asked a typist how she liked typing and a student chef how he liked making cookies. "Was it interesting?" he asked a woman in a sweater manufacturing plant who put a single stitch in every zipper. "Oh yes!" she insisted. "And how do you like your job?" he asked a man mixing smelly adhesive. "Lousy," replied the man.

He inquired about local layoffs, minority hiring, payroll taxes. He shook a great many hands and listened to a group of children singing "Tiddly Winkie Winkie Wink, Tiddly Winkie Woo."

At the end of one such day, his host said, "Thank God that's over!"

"It may be for you," answered the Prince of Wales tiredly, "but it's never over for me."

Prime Minister Gladstone in 1891 had clumsily suggested that Queen Victoria might abdicate in favor of her son, the Prince of Wales. The suggestion was ignored. No political leader has made any such suggestion to Queen Elizabeth. Everyone expects her to reign as long as her health permits. A newspaper poll conducted when she was fifty-five, however, indicated that 63 percent of the British public would like her to abdicate when she is sixty years old. It is likely that she will gradually give Prince Charles more and more of her duties. "Kingship is not a job but a status," editorialized the *Times*.

The Queen and her son both get their daily boxes of documents arriving by horse-drawn carriage, hers mostly in red leather, his in blue. They both get the same documents on foreign affairs, Cabinet papers, domestic reports, and even a rare request for a Royal pardon. The Prince makes his own comments in the margins. When Prime Minister Churchill went to see the young Queen Elizabeth, she mentioned her extreme interest in a message from the British Ambassador in Baghdad. Churchill found himself embarrassed because he had not read it.

Former Prime Minister Harold Wilson recalled a similar incident: "The Queen is the most professional head of state in the world. My most precious day was my Tuesday audience with her. At first I thought it was going to be fun to see a pretty woman and talk to her. But, my God, she put me through it if I hadn't done my homework." She does her homework and so does her son.

Rating the intellect of the Royals on a scale of one to ten, a close observer who has known the Royal Family for a long time gives Prince Charles a 6 or 7, Prince Philip 4½, and the rest, including the Queen, about a 3. In contrast, William Deedes, editor of the *Daily Telegraph*, says, "She's very bright, has a great deal of common sense, an enormous amount of experience, and she knows more about Constitutional Law than I do, and more about the Commonwealth.

"When I was at the Home Office," Deedes continued, "there was a deputy who dovetailed into the royal staff, helping arrange everything from parades to royal functions. In the same way the Queen has skeleton staffs in Canada and Australia, who blend in with her own staff whenever she arrives—because they know the territory, they know the problems. It is interesting that whenever the Queen goes to the United States, there is always a Canadian with her, since Canadians presumably know a little more about American ways.

"She once sat in on one of our editorial meetings and she made some excellent suggestions." Even among her few critics, the general judgment of the Queen is that she's canny and shrewd.

Her mind keeps keyed to her job. There is the story of the young man who had come to a funeral reception for a Royal friend. He had come early and the only two women there—dressed in black, "looking like two tiny black crows, each with a tall gin in her hand'"—were the Queen and the Queen Mother. The Queen later commented that the young man looked familiar. Yes, he said, he had been with her on her tour of India. The Queen sighed. "I can't help thinking," she said, "that things were better when we were there."

"The trouble is that people expect one to be a genius," said Prince Charles.

Later, he added: "Often you sit here and you think—what the hell can I do? The problem is *enormous*, and it's like banging your head against an immense brick wall: It never seems to have any effect. But it's very interesting if you bang your head against one bit of wall, eventually you will dislodge a bit of the brick, or you might knock one out, and at that point you are achieving something . . .

"I don't actually have a role to play. I have to create it. And there is no set book of rules, so to speak, as to what my job is in the scheme of things," he told Peter Osnos, then with the *Washington Post.* "I am the heir to the throne, full stop. That's all. I could do absolutely nothing if I wanted to. I could go and play polo all over the world, I suppose . . ."

The Prince has talked about his luck in being born wealthy and privileged. "I've often felt terribly strongly that you have an enormous obligation if you have everything you obviously need . . . received by accident of birth . . This business of wealth is a great problem, but if you have it, as I'm lucky enough to, then I believe there's a great deal you can do to try to improve circumstances for as many people as possible."

The Prince then discussed his Prince's Trust, aimed mainly at the alienated young of the inner cities. "I've built up a large number of contacts, people in all walks of life; those who deal with social work, probation, and aftercare for young offenders. Through a trust like mine, they see that there's an opportunity to get things done without too much red tape."

His father had told him: "Occasionally you've got to stick your neck out . . ." He also had said, "Listen to others. Check it out. Think about it, and then do what you think, but make up your own mind." Yet when he felt his son was wrong, his father had no qualms in telling him, "How can you possibly talk such nonsense? How can you be so idiotic?" And when the Prince screwed up his face and lamely tried to explain, Prince Philip would say, "Rubbish!" and walk away.

On the other hand, if Prince Philip had his own proposal, he would go to his son and say, "We think it might be an idea. What do you think?"

Prince Charles regards the Queen as "a marvelous person and a wonderful mother" who is "terribly sensible and wise." He is indeed much more like her than his father—particularly in her religious concept of duty, as Defender of the Faith.

"It's a great help to have a lot of people all doing the same thing," said the Prince, "because you can go and talk to them about it and about your own experiences and the amusing things that have happened, and you can learn a lot from each other."

It is closer to the truth, though, to say that the Royal Family seldom socialize among themselves, and almost never confront each other on their differences. Communication is mostly by memorandum, ladies-in-waiting, equerries, or private secretaries; and, occasionally, by telephone.

"There's a great network behind the scenes, mainly a verbal network," said an intimate. "If the Queen thinks that Princess Michael is getting too much publicity, wearing too many glamorous clothes, making a fool of herself, the Queen will tell her private secretary who'll tell the Princess's secretary. It's all roundabout, very little face-to-face. It would be too embarrassing. You couldn't very well say to the Queen, 'How dare you say that, Ma'am?' But everybody knows what's happening in all other royal households. Very, very discreet, very underplayed, very diplomatic, very, very civilized. Yes, and very English. They just don't call a spade a spade."

The one thing all Royals shared were two basic rules: Never miss an opportunity to relieve yourself; never miss a chance to sit down and rest your feet. It was similar to the two questions asked of all prospective ladies-in-waiting: "Can you hold your water and hold your tongue?"

A Royal trick that Prince Charles learned from the Queen was to rock slightly while standing—as if you're resisting a strong gale. It keeps the blood flowing and stops you from fainting.

A trick that Diana learned was to wear a mid-calf-length skirt when she's with Charles, because it enables her to stoop just slightly so as not to appear taller than him.

In the normal course of events, however close the Royal homes and castles—even when they live next door in Kensington Palace apartments—they seldom visit or dine together. In a large sense, it is like any other family. They mainly get together at weddings, funerals, holidays, and some ceremonials. There is the Christmas family holiday, the autumn holiday at Balmoral (where only invited relatives come for short periods), and the Easter holiday.

Every year, just before Easter, there's a small migration from Buckingham Palace to Windsor Castle; equerries and ladies-in-waiting leaving by chauffeur-driven car, housemaids in hired coaches, footmen by train, and vast amounts of luggage in trucks.

For the Queen, it's the start of a six-week holiday. It's also another reunion time for the family. Highlight is Easter Sunday breakfast time, after which they exchange small gifts—often pretty pieces of bone china wrapped in tissue paper. Holiday meals are held in the Queen's private dining room in the Queen's Tower, with its walls covered with gold damask and military paintings, its ceilings high and ornate, its picture windows overlooking the golf course. To serve them are two pages, four footmen, two under-butlers and the Yeoman of the Wine Cellar, all of whom discreetly leave between courses.

Then, every morning, marching up and down the castle's quadrangle, the regimental band plays. "One thing about this job," Prince Charles once said, "you do get your private orchestra most mornings."

"I didn't suddenly wake up in my pram one day and say 'Yippee!...'" recalled Prince Charles, discussing his own concept of royalty. "But I think it just dawns on you slowly that people are interested in one . . . and slowly you get the idea that you have a certain duty and responsibility. And I think it's better that way."

What can the Prince reply when Willie Hamilton complains about him in Parliament, "If two miners each earn 20 pounds a week, they will have to work fifty years before they will make, in a full working life, digging in the bowels of the earth, what we give this young twerp in a year."

And what does he say when a student hands him a paper which says, "The monarchy costs 800,000 pounds a year. How many houses can be built for that? Are you able to live at ease with yourself in comfort while so many other British people and human beings throughout the world are suffering?"

To all this the Prince replies, "The first function of any monarchy is the human concern for people." To this he adds, "The monarchy rests on popularity. Once you aren't popular, there's no point in staying around."

More than half the British people were ready to dump the monarchy in 1936, but now almost 90 percent want it to stay. For Prince Charles there was the challenge of change, "having the courage of your convictions when others about you seem to be losing theirs." Again, according to historian Walter Bagehot, the constitutional monarch has only three rights: "the right to be consulted, the right to encourage, the right to warn."

Here were some of the princely warnings and encouragements:

"I have not the slightest hesitation in making the observation that much of British management doesn't seem to understand the importance of the human factor . . . because the communications structure is inadequate . . .

"The more people understand about the background of immigrants who come to this country, the less apprehensive they would be about them . . .

"Many people fear the increasing dominance of technology and technical experts over all our lives . . . small is still beautiful . . .

"I don't think it would be a disaster if Britain withdrew from the Commonwealth and I am sure it could survive without Britain . . .

"How long we are to continue to live on this planet will depend to a large extent on how well the young people of different countries growing up today learn to understand and sympathize with each other . . .

"I believe in living life dangerously and I think a lot of others do too . . .

"I feel very strongly about the abuse of human rights in some countries . . .

"I wish some young people would use their energy and enthusiasm to help people rather than bashing each other . . .

"The more industrialized and artificial our lives become, the more standards tend to fall . . .

"I can make speeches until I am blue in the face, but I believe that's not really going to have much effect. It's the way you behave, the way you act, what things you do and how you do them and how you are seen to be doing them which is what ultimately is going to have an effect."

And . . . "If we don't change with the times, I am dead."

Despite all this, he continued to mock himself, and, occasionally, the monarchy. He once had called the monarchy, "the oldest profession in the world." In an earlier interview he had described himself as "a twit," and later said, "My profession is somewhat indefinable, and so I find myself holding forth on subjects about which I know too little for far too long."

He was much more revealing when he said, "I suffer from the constant battering that my conscience gets as to what I can try to do to help . . ."

He was a late starter in his concern for things. Brought up mostly by elderly females, he was lonely and a little lost, going through identity crises, almost desperate about finding his own role. He realized that upholding the monarchy was his duty until he died. His royal motto, after all, was "I serve."

"Prince Charles is doing everything right," said editor William Deedes. "He is learning an enormous amount. The Queen is helping him. When you compare him to his great-grandfather, and his shy grandfather and Edward VIII, you can see how far he has come, and how much he has learned and how much he is doing. He will be a good King."

"He really wants to know all about everything," explained Sir Laurens van der Post, who has known the Prince since he was a boy.

"He realized early that monarchy is no repeat performance, that each new monarch has to extend the reach of the monarchy. And that's what he's been doing so magnificently. But he's more complicated than most people think."

He helped the cause of human rights by royally snubbing Uganda dictator Idi Amin, refusing to shake hands with him. He helped the cause of British industry by persuading industrialists in Cleveland and Japan to build plants in Wales. He was so probing and persuasive in a long talk with Marshal Tito of Yugoslavia that Tito afterward cabled him, "I am impressed." He was pointed in his questions of Home Office Minister Leon Brittain asking about deaths in police custody. He made it clear he was not impressed with the answers. He met with leaders of the Common Market, NATO, attended meetings of the National Economic Development Council, board meetings of giant companies, contributed his own money for a project to help delinquents, orphans, and handicapped to give them challenging projects to help themselves.

"That guy works so hard you'd think he was running for office," said an American correspondent who traveled with him.

On an official trip to the United States—eleven cities in fourteen days—he lost fifteen pounds. And the least reported event was a tour of a plant near Los Angeles for recovering methane gas—a conservation idea he had long been interested in. It was part of his concern for vanishing world resources.

Another concern was architectural planning. "It would be a tragedy," Prince Charles told the Royal Institute of British Architects, "if the character and skyline of our capital city were to be further ruined and St. Paul's dwarfed by yet another giant glass stump better suited to downtown Chicago than the City of London."

The man credited with helping to shape Charles's sharp views on architecture was another older male mentor, Richard, Duke of Gloucester. Forty-five, married to a charming Danish girl, and the father of three young children, the Duke (who inherited his position when his older brother was killed in an air crash) was a practicing architect and good friend of the Prince.

Commenting on the public announcement that the British were lucky to have Prince Charles as their future King, Lord Mountbatten said, "It's not luck at all. It's a bloody miracle!"

13

She was sitting in the sun-filled summer house in the private park behind Buckingham Palace, talking about the upcoming wedding. She wore a gray and white matching loose skirt and blouse with ruffles, a bow, and rows of buttons. No, she didn't find it fun making up the guest list for the wedding—there were too many people she had to leave out. "It's been quite difficult—my side, anyway."

It was much more fun deciding what presents she wanted, and submitting lists to two London shops. She was already busy writing thank you notes. "There's so much coming in, it's very difficult to keep up with it all." Then her face glowed. "My list is completely empty. It's all come to us. It's marvelous."

She grinned. "But we have two houses to fill."

At last the most important details of the wedding were set. The date: July 29. ("Thank God!" said a representative of Moss Brothers, London's primary renter of formal wear. "If they got married during Ascot Week, we wouldn't have had a top hat in the place.") The place: St. Paul's Cathedral. Why St. Paul's instead of Westminster Abbey? Perhaps because her parents were married at the Abbey, and that hadn't turned out to be such a happy marriage. Or was the reason simply that St. Paul's could seat 2,500 guests to the Abbey's 2,000?

Bagehot had described a royal wedding as "a brilliant edition of a universal fact." Stuart Collier, a *Daily Mail* columnist, had calculated that the combined wedding-reception-honeymoon would cost almost a million pounds. *The Economist* magazine further estimated a world-wide television audience of some 750 million, and added, "If each gets only one pennyworth of enjoyment, that will more than defray the cost of the flummery . . ." And a housewife in the depressed East End of London said, "It's just what we wanted. A royal wedding will cheer everybody up . . . I think it's the best thing that could have happened."

"Personally, I prefer St. Paul's for this occasion simply because it's a longer route," said Cliff Morgan of the BBC. "From a television point of view, we have that lovely sweep up Ludgate Hill and round into the Cathedral."

Historians quickly pointed out the coincidence that the only other royal wedding in St. Paul's (actually the old St. Paul's, destroyed in the Great Fire) had been that of another Prince of Wales: Arthur Tudor, the elder brother of Henry VIII, married Catherine of Aragon there in 1489.

Confronting Diana at this time was a royal minefield of protocol. To help guide the bride-to-be, Oliver Everett was brought over from the British Embassy in Madrid. (Everett was the man whose quick thinking helped the Prince at a very critical moment. Two years before the Prince had collapsed after playing six chukkers of polo in 90-degree Florida heat. Everett hustled him away to their hotel, where Charles again collapsed. Everett applied cold towels and got him to a hospital. "Don't leave me, Oliver," the Prince had said. "I think I'm going to die.")

Diana had picked five bridesmaids, all younger than she. The oldest was seventeen-year-old Sarah Armstrong-Jones, daughter of Princess Margaret. Youngest was four-year-old Clementine Hambro, Diana's favorite pupil at her kindergarten and the great-granddaughter of Sir Winston Churchill. Two of the bridesmaids were goddaughters of Charles: thirteen-year-old India Hicks, Lord Mountbatten's granddaughter, whose father was interior designer David Hicks; and six-year-old Catherine Cameron, eldest daughter of Donald and Lockiel Cameron.

The last was the ten-year-old daughter of Prince Charles's racing trainer, Nick Gaselee. "It's been a big strain," said Gaselee. "She's had to keep it a secret at school for two weeks, and she was bursting to tell everyone."

Instead of a single best man, Prince Charles asked both his brothers, twenty-one-year-old Andrew and seventeen-year-old Edward, to share the job.

Andrew, known as "Randy Andy," was the handsome and boisterous charmer. "He and his brother are as different as chalk and cheese," said a friend of both. Andrew had taken the same educational route as Charles—Gordonstoun, Dartmouth, the Navy. Like his brother, he was also soon tagged by the press as "The Action Man"—flying helicopters and parachuting. Unlike Charles, however, he was much looser with women, and friends described him as being "as subtle as a hand grenade." He was the court jester, but he could be both tough and rude. In her early interviews, Lady Diana admitted that she originally had been invited to Sandringham to be paired off with Andrew.

Charles's youngest brother, Edward, regarded as the brightest of the three, didn't like being called a "goody-goody," but he had the reputation from an early age of being gentle, sensitive, and studious. He was called "Educated Edward" by those in awe of his nine O levels. Diana nicknamed him "Scooter," after a friendly Muppet character. He too had been to Gordonstoun and was slated for Cambridge. Like Charles, Edward was also intrigued with acting, and was originally shy with girls. Charles, in fact, was his idol.

Royal intimates, however, agreed that the relationship of Prince Charles with his younger brothers was more paternal than fraternal.

Lady Diana picked the same husband-and-wife fashion designer team who had made her daring strapless gown to design her wedding dress. David Emanuel was twenty-eight, his wife, Elizabeth, twenty-seven. "We want to make her look like a fairy princess," they said.

The Emanuels advertised themselves as bringing glamor back to evening clothes. Their evening gowns were generally intricately decorated, "blending the Pre-Raphaelite and Nell Gwynne styles." Their dress designs were described by the *Guardian* as "well past the borderline of the erotic."

Diana's hairdresser in South Kensington, twenty-five-year-old Kevin Shanley of the Headlines Hair and Beauty Salon, had created a style for her that looked like a soft wedge graduated to the nape of her neck. It was a layered cut, brushed off the face and touched up with "a little blonde highlighting." Women were besieging their hairdressers all over Britain for the "Di cut," as the London *Daily Mirror* launched a nationwide Lady Di look-alike contest.

Barkers' department store had sold out its stock of tea towels featuring the faces of the Prince and his Princess-to-be. Staffordshire

Potteries was rushing thousands of engagement mugs to Woolworth's. Wedgwood, Royal Doulton, and Royal Worcester were busy making commemorative figures, plates, and candy dishes. "This is like a breath of fresh air for us," said a Royal Worcester spokesman.

The Lord Chamberlain struggled against a swelling tide of wedding fever to prohibit the royal faces from appearing on T-shirts, although they were already etched on pencil sharpeners. Among the saucier souvenirs, considered in "bad taste" by the Palace, were bed sheets with the silhouettes of the royal couple. Buttons saying "Don't Do It, Di" were white on royal purple, and sold for 68 cents. A broker for Lloyds of London provided $22 million insurance against the possibility that the wedding would be postponed or cancelled.

Business also picked up at Althorp Hall. The Spencers had finished refurbishing the house for the paying public to visit. Besides a tea room in the stable block, Countess Spencer had installed a souvenir shop and a wine shop. For a fat fee, the Spencers also offered visitors three days of pheasant-shooting on their estate. The shooting party would stay on as guests of the Spencers, and dine with them. Bed and board would be 50 pounds extra. Novelist Barbara Cartland, the mother of Countess Spencer, organized a package which called for a grand finale lunch at Althorp with Diana's father and stepmother. It was billed as the Barbara Cartland Romantic Tour of England.

A spokesman for the Althorp estate said, "We don't get as many visitors as some of the larger homes, but we hope for a landslide now. The more the merrier."

Diana's mother, Mrs. Shand-Kydd, was also doing better business at her shop in Oban. "I am not just a newsagent, as people say. We sell everything here." The store, indeed, sold everything from baby buggies and go-carts to records and hula hoops. She would not, however, she said, sell tea towels with pictures of her daughter and Prince Charles. "I don't like them at all, they're awful."

An American reported overhearing this conversation with a Brit in a pub: "Don't you say nothing about Diana. She's a cracker. She's the greatest. Let's be honest about it. You ain't got anything like her, have you? I mean, you've got your hamburgers, hot dogs, but you haven't got anything like *her*. I mean, all you got is a White House, Mia Farrow, and hot dogs . . . ."

It was time for pictures and a farewell. The pictures were the official ones with Her Majesty. Diana, wearing a blue two-piece suit with a white sailor collar, looked at ease, making small jokes.

Two days later she was saying a tearful goodbye to her Prince, who was scheduled for a five-week tour of Australia, New Zealand, Venezuela, and Washington—a schedule made up prior to the engagement. She walked with him to the steps of the plane. He kissed her on both cheeks, patted her shoulder, trying to cheer her without success. She was visibly crying.

The Australian visit in particular was more than ceremonial. The Prince loved Australia and its people. It was one thing to be a wandering ambassador, but he now wanted a specific job. He made no secret that he wanted to be Governor General of Australia. The Queen was said to have approved it. Australian Prime Minister Malcolm Fraser even urged the Prince to buy a home in Australia.

In New Zealand, he found a national frenzy of Lady Diana fashion. Her photograph was everywhere. Six Lady Diana look-alikes suddenly descended on Prince Charles, within careful camera range. "Not bad," he told them, "but nothing like the real thing." At a dinner he confessed, "My fiancée is languishing 11,000 miles away while I'm pining here."

Still, his sense of humor did not disappear. In Sydney, he planted a tree with an impromptu comment: "Whenever I plant a tree, it's next to one that either my mother or father planted ten or twenty years ago. I've noticed the trees my mother plants tend to flourish, while the trees my father plants tend to wilt and die. And I can't think of any explanation for that, apart from the fact that trees must be snobs."

In Australia, the tone changed. Rumors of the Prince's possible appointment as Governor General seemed to disturb many Aussies. There were still the schoolgirls who fainted away at the sight of him, and elderly matrons fighting to touch him, but there were also signs calling him "a parasite," others saying "Charlie go home" and "Kings need workers, workers do not need kings."

"I am a normal, middle-of-the-road Australian nationalist," said Bill Hayden, leader of Australia's Labor opposition. "We have come a long way in a short time and we are now one of the greatest countries in the world, and I can see no reason why Prince Charles should take the position." Among other things, Hayden felt the job should be held by an Australian.

Former Labor Prime Minister Gough Whitlam was more blunt: "If the Queen's heir were to become Governor General, this would be taken as a sign that Australia is still subject to Britain."

What killed any remote hope of Charles getting the job was the publicity following some supposedly tapped telephone conversations between him and Diana. In them Charles had reportedly made disparaging remarks about the Australians in general, and Malcolm Fraser in particular.

According to reported excerpts from the tapes, the Prince had also voiced his anger at photographers who concentrated on his bald spot.

Diana was quoted as asking the Prince, "Are you behaving yourself?"

"Darling, you know as well as I do if I weren't behaving myself, the whole world would know in two minutes."

Diana was reported to have laughed and replied, "Where there is a will, there is a way. You and I managed, didn't we?"

The Queen called the tapes "checkbook journalism" and "utterly contemptible." They were finally declared to be fakes. Much of the damage, however—especially in Australia—had been done. Until further notice, Charles would now have to content himself with being the super-salesman of the British Commonwealth.

On his short visit to the United States, there were these comments from teenagers:

Did they think he was sexy?

"Yeeesss."

Should America have a Prince?

"Yeeesss."

Who?

"John Travolta."

When Charles accepted an honorary degree at the College of William and Mary, observers said he was working the crowds at Williamsburg "as if he were running for king." Everybody kept asking for Diana. In apologizing for her absence, he explained that if she came along now on all his tours and duties, "I think she would drop from sheer exhaustion before the wedding."

"There's just something nice about the continuity of royalty," said Virginia state librarian Steve Murden. "You don't have to worry about reelecting them all the time."

When the Prince asked a student, Sandy Smith, if she was supposed to be studying for exams, she answered, "Your Highness, I'm flunking German because of you."

There was some small discord. In a letter to the *Washington Post*, Jo Anne Sherman said she choked on her orange juice when she saw a photograph of Mrs. Lenore Annenberg, President Reagan's Chief of Protocol and wife of the former Ambassador to London, greeting the Prince with a deep curtsy. "Did we fight a war two hundred years ago over whether or not we should prostrate ourselves in the presence of British royalty?"

President Reagan hosted a cozy Saturday night dinner at the White House for Prince Charles. Among the thirty guests were Cary Grant, Audrey Hepburn, William F. Buckley, Jr., and Bobby Short, who stated "It was choreographed brilliantly." The dessert was Crown of Sorbet Prince of Wales—a mold of raspberry sherbet, white coconut ice cream, and blueberry sherbet.

The President and the Prince talked of horses and marriage. President Reagan commiserated with the Prince on his recent fall, saying, "Anyone who is going to ride, do things like steeplechase, polo, and so forth—there are going to be times when you and the horse part company." The Prince later added, "When you fall off, you get up. If you have a very bad fall, you are taken to the hospital. But it doesn't mean you have to stop doing what you are doing."

Of marriage, the President noted that there was a twelve-year difference between himself and Nancy. Marriage was "a very serious step," he added, "but your sense of humor will carry you through."

A British spokeswoman summed up the tour as "just a jolly jaunt before his marriage."

Lady Diana, meanwhile, was practicing her steps for the long walk up the aisle at St. Paul's. She used a long sheet as her train while moving around the ballroom of Buckingham Palace.

The processional route already had been decided upon. It would go along the Mall, Trafalgar Square, the Strand and Fleet Street and up Ludgate Hill—all lined by members of the army, navy and air force, plus an expected 1 million spectators. A group called Corporate Capers already had sold 700 places with window views in office buildings along the route. For $335, a person would have use of a pair of binoculars, a television set, and a hamper filled with lobster, steak, wedding cake, and champagne. In a more lasting tribute, Simon Adkins of Cornwall had tattooed the faces of Charles and Diana on his back—with room left over for their children. He said, "I can carry my devotion to the Royal Family with me for the rest of my life."

Finally the lovers were reunited. Prince Charles flew directly back to Scotland for a weekend at Balmoral, and Diana flew up to meet him. A dramatic headline told how her plane had been twice hit by lightning, but that she had calmly worked on a piece of embroidery during the flight.

Their wedding was now only twelve weeks away. The two fished together in the Dee for salmon. She didn't catch anything, but he caught two 12-pounders. They then picnicked in the fishing lodge near the river and were seen walking hand in hand.

In a large sense, they were already very much married. Despite the frenzy of preparations, they had evening privacy secluded in the Palace, the excitement of preparing their home at Highgrove, and this utter peace at Balmoral.

She and Charles had their first public walkabout at the opening of a memorial exhibition to Lord Mountbatten at his Hampshire home. A man in the crowd called out, "You're gorgeous . . . you're a cracker!" And twenty-eight-year-old Tony Clarke told her, "All the fellows at work think you're lovely." She smiled mischievously, put her finger to her lips, and said, "Better not let my other half hear that." The other half had received a smacking kiss from a middle-aged woman, Rita Brown, who said, "I can die happy now!"

In a letter to the editor of the *Times* in London, Major Ralph Rochester of Malt Field, Devon, wrote: "Sir, I have observed of late numerous girls who are taking pains to look like Lady Diana; but of the boys I have observed, none is making the least effort to look like the Prince of Wales. How should this be?"

They had a second walkabout in the Cotswold town of Tetbury, only a mile from Highgrove. The Prince had gone to open a new operating theater at the local hospital, and to meet their new neighbors. The occasion became somewhat chaotic as they were showered with flowers during the 90-minute visit.

They often arrived at Highgrove by helicopter with the Prince at the controls. Diana had become more decisive with her decorator about what she wanted in her home. "This young lady has a mind of her own," said one of her staff.

Someone said of Countess Spencer that there was a good and special woman inside "if you could see her." What was meant was that she covered herself with so many protective layers of clothes and makeup and personality that the real Raine was carefully submerged, truly visible to a very few.

One of the few was a big burly man, a 300-pound butler, Alan Fisher, one of the last of a breed. Born in Manchester, England, self-educated, he is a highly perceptive man of much wisdom and wit. "I am a Sagittarius," he will tell you, "which means I am on a perpetual high." He had worked for the Duke and Duchess of Windsor for six years and "she taught me everything I know—twice over. She had impeccable taste. They lived on a scale that far surpassed the Royal Family." He also worked for the Bing Crosbys in California. The celebrated singer tolerated Fisher as an unnecessary evil, "but Mrs. Crosby spoiled me." She even allowed him to wear his old sneakers with the striped pants and tailcoat of his butler's uniform—a habit he later continued with the Prince and Princess of Wales.

Raine called Fisher "Darling"—as she did most people. Fisher was working in the empty London home of "Jock" Whitney, former American Ambassador to Great Britain, when Raine called. It was an emergency, she said. Her husband, Earl Spencer, had been seriously ill, and couldn't dress himself. His daughter was getting married to the Prince of Wales, and they were going to the State Ball before the wedding. The Earl knew and liked Alan. Could Alan Darling please come and dress her husband. Alan Darling could and did.

It was a relationship that would soon have far-reaching ripples.

The countless details concerning the wedding were handled by others, but Diana did oversee the guest list of 2,500. The number seemed large, "but when you try to spread them out all over the world, it ends up with too few." A twenty-three-year-old Scotsman—Andrew Widdowson, who had been crippled in a rugby accident—received a surprise invitation. He was undergoing rehabilitation and planned to be a math teacher. Two years earlier, he had been Diana's date at a ball in Oban.

Another surprise was that Diana's famous step-grandmother and favorite author, Barbara Cartland, was not invited. The statement released by her lawyer was that she was eighty years old and weddings were for young people, so she was sending her son instead. The truth was that Cartland, who had more vitality than most people thirty years younger, had been originally invited, then disinvited. There were some who felt her celebrity might outshine that of the Royals. A public relations friend had advised her to release the statement she made. Somehow it seemed a shame that this woman whose novels were part of the romance of the bride's life could not see her plot come alive.

Others who received invitations included the kings of Belgium, Sweden, Norway, Rumania, Bulgaria, Greece, and Tonga, as well as their wives; Queen Margarethe of Denmark, Princess Grace of Monaco, the Crown Prince and Princess of Japan, Nancy Reagan, the retired headmaster of Cheam, two surviving Goons, more than 170 staff members of the various royal households, including cooks and charwomen, and Patrick and Mary Robinson, the American couple who had hired Diana as their babysitter.

Everything became increasingly official when Diana had her portrait painted for the National Portrait Gallery. The artist, Bryan Organ, previously had painted Prince Charles, looking anxious and lonely. He painted Diana sitting sideways on a chair, dressed in a black trouser suit with gold piping and a cream shirt open at the neck. The only jewelry she wore was a pair of tiny earrings and a plain silver ring. There is the hint of a smile on her lips. The gallery director called it "stunningly good." "What I think I saw is totally sacrosanct between the painter and the sitter," said the artist, but it wasn't about "flattery and deception."

Real flattery came from seventeen-year-old sixth form schoolboy Nick Hardy. He was part of the crowd one day as Charles and Diana headed for their helicopter. Leaning over the barrier and offering Lady Diana a daffodil, he then asked, "May I kiss the hand of my future Queen?"

She said yes, and blushed, "But you will never live this down." His classmates cheered.

Princess Anne was not in Diana's cheering section. She and her husband lived only eight miles from Highgrove. When a photographer wanted to take her picture, she refused angrily, saying, "I am *not* Diana Spencer! I never was a fairy-tale princess and I never will be."

More than that, there was a rift between brother and sister, and the rift soon became a gulf. They both had apartments on the same floor of Buckingham Palace, but rarely spoke or ate together. Prince Charles called her husband "Fog" because he was "thick and wet." Charles took special pleasure in competing against Mark Phillips in a camel race, and beating him.

Mutual friends insisted that Princess Anne was particularly incensed at how much Diana had pushed her even deeper into the royal shadows. All her life she had played second fiddle to the elder brother who was first in line for the throne. Now, nobody seemed to care that she was expecting her second child any day. And her son had *not* been chosen to be a page at the wedding.

Songwriter Nancy White wrote a ditty for Canadian radio, part of which said that Princess Anne may be a champ in the saddle, but she's never going to see her face on a stamp.

In contrast, Diana's face was everywhere. When the official British postage stamp appeared in honor of the wedding, it caused a small stir because it showed Prince Charles towering above Diana, even though they are the same height. The post office later admitted that Charles was standing on a box when the photo was taken.

Queen Mary had set the British tradition requiring British silk for royal occasions. Villagers in Dorset and Somerset had been busy harvesting mulberry trees in their counties all year. They needed twenty sacks a day to feed their silkworms to produce enough thread for a wedding dress. "We suspected there might be a royal wedding," said silk farm director Robert Gooden, "so we set out to produce an extra large crop of cocoons during last year's season."

The Emanuels were even busier than the silkworms. Their wedding dress design had to be the best-kept secret in Britain. "She's young and it has to suit her," said the Emanuels, who explained that they got their ideas mostly from watching movies.

They seemed an unlikely couple to be designing the royal wedding dress.

David Emanuel came from a family of eleven, the father a Welsh steelworker. His wife, Elizabeth, was the daughter of an American GI stationed in England during World War II. Her father, who had founded a chain of supermarkets, then became a Lloyds insurance man, backed Elizabeth and David when they set up a tiny dress salon on Brook Street, in London's fashionable Mayfair. They both had graduated from the Royal College of Art only a few years before.

Their clientele included many theater people as well as Princess Michael of Kent. The Emanuels now had the ultimate challenge of transforming a preppy Sloane Ranger, who was "not quite a dowd," into someone magical. As they worked, the blinds were always drawn. They brought in a safe, hoisted by a crane, to hide the bridal designs. For security, they burned all their scraps at the end of each day.

Diana's hairdresser had his own troubles during this frenzied period. "Everybody who asks for her style thinks they will look exactly like Lady Diana," said Kevin Shanley. "In fact, the hairstyle doesn't suit everybody. You need the right face." What of his hair-dressing plans for the wedding? "I can't say yet whether Lady Diana will be wanting a shampoo on the day." Her thick glossy hair nor-mally needed three shampoos a week, he said. "She has very good, strong, well-conditioned hair. But then most English hair is fairly healthy." As for the style, "I always advise going with what you know and like rather than trying something quite new for your wedding day." What Kevin knew, but didn't say then, was that he had little choice—her hair wasn't long enough for the classic royal chignon.

Wedding preparations were now coming to a climax. William Ma-thias, professor of music at the University College of North Wales, had completed the anthem commissioned for the wedding by Prince Charles. The short piece for chorus and organ would be the first music the young couple would hear at St. Paul's. The Bach Choir was also scheduled to sing, along with the thirty boys and eighteen men of the internationally renowned St. Paul's Choir.

"One of the reasons I particularly wanted to be married in St. Paul's is because, I think, musically speaking, it is such a magnificent setting, and the whole acoustics is so spectacular, with a 10- or 11-second after-sound, after-note," said the Prince.

He personally selected most of the music, all of it English, for the 70-minute service. The final hymn was a favorite of both Lord Mountbatten and Lady Diana, "I Vow to Thee, My Country."

"I've had a great deal of fun organizing the music with a great deal of help from the Director of the Royal College of Music . . . who I've known for some years. We've had a marvelous time getting together three orchestras that I'm patron of, and also, very exciting, Kiri te Kanawa, the Maori opera singer, is prepared to sing in the Cathedral. So I can't wait for the whole thing . . ."

In the Chatham dockyard, a short, stocky sailor, thirty-eight-year-old Chief Petty Officer David Avery, was busy creating a wedding cake for over a thousand guests—without a recipe. "It's in my head," he explained. "I first learned it twenty years ago and now I've added a few things and taken a few things out."

"It's a traditional rich fruitcake," he revealed, for which each raisin, cherry, sultana, currant, and piece of preserved fruit was individually inspected. It would weigh 168 pounds, stand 4½ feet high, contain about 50 pounds of marzipan, and an undisclosed amount of rum. In cake-baking, said the sailor, "the art is to cook the middle without burning the outside. A nice gentle heat, that's what you have to have." The 49 pounds of pure white royal icing would be made from egg whites, powdered sugar, lemon juice, and glycerine, and would be added at Buckingham Palace.

Another busy man was Major William Phelps of the Welsh Guards, whose job it was to make sure that the fairy princess had her glass coach. The same coach Queen Elizabeth had used at her wedding, it would be pulled by dapple-gray horses, driven by men in black top hats and red and gold livery. "We try to train the footmen to take the weight of the coach on their hands as they open the doors to stop the sway. It isn't easy." With large windows and special interior lighting, it gave crowds a virtually unrestricted view of any passengers inside.

There was strong concern in Scotland Yard on matters of security following the assassination attempts on President Reagan and Pope John Paul II—not to mention the unemployed British youth who fired six blank cartridges at the Queen at close range only a month earlier. (Unemployment in Britain had peaked at almost 2.5 million, more than 10 percent of the labor force. Joblessness had been rising at about 100,000 persons a month. Just weeks before, some 200,000 people had marched to Trafalgar Square demanding jobs.)

Part of the security concern also came from the tension caused by the hunger strike in Northern Ireland in which six Nationalist prisoners had starved themselves to death in the previous three months, as well as by the recent rioting in a number of cities.

The fact was that there could be no real security if the state carriages were used, as of course they must be. Along the route of the four royal carriages, there would be "a policeman every four steps as well as a soldier with a fixed bayonet every six paces." Sharpshooters were to be stationed on the roofs. Police already had checked everything from manholes to scaffolding poles, as well as every nook and cranny of St. Paul's.

Her Majesty, however, refused all suggestions of personal concealment. "It would be a victory for terrorism if we mothballed the state coaches and replaced them with limousines. The Queen won't hear of that," said a Police Federation spokesman. "The Queen feels that the public must be able to see her."

Weather permitting, she would ride in an open carriage.

It was part of the price to be paid.

The Queen wanted Diana to have a royal sample of things to come. She invited her to Windsor Castle for lunch with the President of Ghana, to Sandringham for dinner with King Khalid of Saudi Arabia. There were many other invitations, including one from the Young England Kindergarten, asking Diana to come to their end-of-term party.

"I ended up being battered and bruised," she said. "I had so many children crawling on top of me. I've got more bruises on my bottom than you'd think possible." But they presented her with a special collage they had made. "It was lovely," she said.

The royal mail already had jumped to some 25,000 letters a week. There were already 3,000 presents. What touched Diana particularly were all the things from children. "who've obviously spent hours of work on paintings, pictures, cards . . . " "There's a corridor stacked with it," said the Prince. "Forty sacks full of mail and presents we haven't started on yet. I mean, it's incredible . . . incredible kindness. I can't get over it."

The pressure was beginning to build up. Diana's new weight loss drove the dressmakers to distraction. To get rid of some of the tension, she had private dancing lessons at Buckingham Palace two mornings a week. Some ballet and tap, and then dancing to such music as "Top Hat, White Tie and Tails." It helped, but not enough.

She was watching Charles play in a polo match at Tidworth when suddenly all the photographers swung around to concentrate on her as she stood up unexpectedly, her cheeks heavily flushed. Lady Romsey put her arm around her to comfort her, and Diana simply burst into tears. She left with Lady Romsey, walking quickly to the back of the horses' enclosure. Prince Charles rushed to meet her there, put his arm around her, and led her to her car. She was driven home.

The wedding was only five days away.

The next day she was fine, watching another polo match, even inviting a small boy to sit on her lap. He happily obliged.

At a Buckingham Palace garden party for 2,000 disabled and handicapped persons, Lady Diana ignored the pouring rain. Dressed in a stunning red and white outfit with a saucy red boater hat, she and Charles zigzagged among the guests, many of them in wheelchairs, smiling and talking. Her comment on the rain was "Yuk!"—one of her favorite phrases. Then she said, "The weather can do what it likes today. But please, please, let it be nice on Wednesday."

She had another thought. "I shall sit down and sulk if it's like this in Gibraltar," one of the planned ports-of-call for the honeymoon. London bookmakers were offering 3-1 against rain on the big day.

A blind seventy-three-year-old lady asked if she could touch her engagement ring. Diana quickly took off her glove. "I mustn't lose it before Wednesday when I go to St. Paul's or they won't know who I am."

"Did you know we had a rehearsal at St. Paul's last night?" she asked someone. "I nearly fell, you know, tripped on some wires when I was walking down the aisle." Speaking again about the rehearsal, she told someone else, "Everybody was fighting. I got my heel stuck in some grating in the Cathedral and everyone was saying, 'Hurry up, Diana.' I said, 'I can't. I'm stuck.'" Then she added, "I don't know if I'll be able to remember what went on or if I'll just be in a haze."

One nervous young man, dumbstruck at facing her, finally blurted out, "Will you be watching the wedding?"

She giggled. "No, I'm in it."

It startled some people to learn that Lady Diana would not promise to "obey" her new husband. Even the feisty Princess Anne had not stricken that word from the wedding ceremony.

"Marriage is the kind of relationship where there should be two equal partners," the Dean of Westminster Abbey agreed, "and if there's going to be a dominant partner, it won't be settled by this oath.''

The Archbishop of Canterbury said the couple had laughed loudly when he told them that at least the word "obey" was better than the words it replaced from the marriage service of the Middle Ages—when the woman promised to be "bonny and buxom at bed and board."

The Archbishop also told them: "In marriage you are creating a new family. Children should be brought up in fear of the Lord. Sex is a good thing given by God . . ."

Other ministers offered other advice, in print: "Make love often," said Reverend Frank Cooke. "Seek to satisfy your partner's needs. Take time to make love."

"Learn to accept your partner as he or she is," advised David Watson, minister of St. Michael le Belfray in York.

"Find time for each other, for others, and for God," urged Methodist president Kenneth Greet.

There was something else Diana had decided. She would not follow the custom of walking one pace behind her husband. Nor would she call him "Sir" in public, according to tradition. As novelist Rebecca West observed about Diana: "She is genuine and not of a servile nature."

"It is unimaginable that she will stand or walk behind Prince Charles anywhere," said a Palace spokesman, "unless it simply happens to be practical for the purposes of a receiving line. Normally she will walk beside him.

"She will call him 'my husband' or 'the Prince of Wales' if she is talking to somebody else and by his Christian name or whatever she likes if she is talking to him." (It was reported that one of her pet nicknames for him was "Fishface.") Feminists who had been disappointed by many of Diana's values were heartened by this.

There was some concern about the Queen Mother, who was still recovering from a foot injury. She was, however, determined to attend the wedding and her spokesman said, "She is walking perfectly well."

Two nights before the wedding, the Queen gave a dinner party at Buckingham Palace for relatives and close friends. Diana's mother and father, and their respective spouses, attended. The festivities lasted until the early morning hours.

Diana had a portent of things to come. She put in a special request that she spend the last night before the wedding with her three former roommates. The Prince, after all, was having his stag night for twenty friends at White's, his most exclusive club. She wanted to spend her final night of freedom with her three old friends, giggling over the many female strategies they all had discussed together during her courtship. Some intimates insist that she even added the words, "Please . . . please . . ." to her request.

But the Royal answer was a firm no. A stag dinner was traditional; what she requested was not proper. What *was* proper was for her to have a quiet dinner with her mother, her grandmother, and the Queen Mother at Clarence House, and go to bed early.

Her other special request was to have at least one of her room-mates as a bridesmaid. They were, after all, her three closest friends and she had shared more with them than with anyone. Again, the answer was no. A Royal wedding was not a friendship party.

There was still one thing she could do, however, and that was to choose the seating arrangements in the Cathedral. She saw to it that her three friends had some of the best seats, close to the front, six rows in front of Nancy Reagan.

So on her last day as a single woman, Diana moved back to Clarence House. She had promised to go to bed early, but she did want to see at least the start of the fireworks display at Hyde Park. This spectacular display would reportedly rival the historic pyro-technics ordered by George II in 1749 to mark the Peace of Aix-la-Chapelle, for which Handel wrote his famed "Music for the Royal Fireworks." There would now be 500 military musicians playing mood music for the fireworks, abetted by the singing choir of Welsh Guards.

An estimated 12,000 rockets filled with more than two tons of explosives were scheduled to go off. At the finale an exploding replica of Buckingham Palace with huge sparkling likenesses of Charles and Diana would fill the sky.

Before that, Charles was due to light a bonfire, the first of a nationwide "chain of 101 beacons" stretching from one end of the country to the other. Not only was the fireworks display the biggest of its kind in Britain for over two hundred years, but it featured the biggest Catherine wheel in the world, its fire spreading over a diameter of 100 feet.

"I'm not supposed to see her the night before," said the Prince, "even by the light of the fireworks."

Diana said afterward that she had butterflies in her stomach. If she went to bed with butterflies in her stomach, and fireworks in her head, how could she sleep that night? Her bedroom at Clarence House was close to the Mall, where she would ride tomorrow in her carriage to the Cathedral. She could surely hear the booming of the cannon and the growing murmur of crowds along the route. How could she sleep? And if she did sleep, what did she dream?

She had just celebrated her twentieth birthday. And she had said, quietly, "I will just take it as it comes . . ."

14

What was in Diana's mind on her wedding day as she rode down the Mall in her glass coach, looking like Cinderella, on her way to marry a handsome Prince?

Only a year before she was a teenager in jeans serving beer in a place called Slim Jim's—part of an apprentice program in a cooking course. Now, more than 750 million people all over the world were watching her every move on television, with millions of women wanting to know absolutely everything about her—what she wore, how she fixed her hair, why she bit her fingernails.

What was she thinking as she sat in that coach with her brave father who insisted on walking her down the aisle despite the debilitating stroke that still left him feeling shaky? Her mother, grandmother, sisters were all keen as mustard—but she dearly loved this tall, dark, brooding, gentle man. Many felt that she was much like him. It hurt her especially therefore to read what he had told a reporter only a few days before: "I'm afraid I'll never see my daughter again, you know. No, I don't think I'll see her again . . ."

There were things she would not surrender as she entered this royal world, and he was one of them. Her children would know their grandfather.

The day had begun well before dawn for coachman Richard Boland. He was mucking out the stalls of Lady Penelope and Kestrel, the two mares that would pull the glass coach under his guidance. By the time the sun rose, there were two tons of sand spread along the two-mile procession route through the historic heart of London to St. Paul's. The police were already in place, scanning the route with closed-circuit television, soon to be joined by 2,228 officers and men of the British armed services. What the police were most afraid of was a lone man "with a gun and a grudge," like those who had tried to kill the Pope and President Reagan that year. Police were using everything from helicopters to sniffing dogs to assist them.

A twenty-five-year-old member of the Irish National Liberation Army had been jailed several months earlier for offenses that included a plot to bomb the royal wedding. Two Buckingham Palace footmen had been arrested two weeks before for possessing dynamite. The procession-watchers were urged to "adopt a bobby"—the one nearest them—and tell him immediately if they saw anything strange or suspicious. (It was later reported that there had been only a single arrest along the entire route that day—for pickpocketing.)

Diana reportedly was up at 6:30 on the morning of the wedding. From her window, she could see the tens of thousands of people on the nearby Mall. She turned on the television to watch the street scenes. Soon a large group including David and Elizabeth Emanuel and her sister Jane bustled around her. Among the other early arrivals were Kevin Shanley and his wife. He wore a T-shirt, and Diana teased him, "You'll need a tie today, Kevin."

She told him she'd had "an *enormous* breakfast," explaining, "I hope that stops my tummy rumbling at St. Paul's." She was exuberant, "on top of the world," but she told Jane that she hadn't slept too well. She smiled ruefully, "A bit difficult . . ."

Shanley came completely equipped with three hair dryers, ten combs, and ten hairbrushes. After blow-drying her hair, he complained again inwardly that it was too short for a classic chignon, but accepted the challenge of making it blend well with the jeweled tiara, a Spencer family heirloom. (A dazzling tiara worth almost $1 million and once belonging to Queen Mary was to be the Queen's personal gift to her new daughter-in-law.) He styled it much the same as he always had, the fringe falling to one side. He also put in rollers to keep her hair curled back from her face so the makeup artist could go to work.

The makeup artist was Barbara Daly, recommended by *Vogue* as one of the best in the business. She already had met Diana and picked the colors she would use, deciding to keep everything minimal and natural. She wanted to take advantage of the fact that "Lady Diana naturally blushes very prettily, and there's no point pretending that she doesn't." A usual Daly treatment took two hours. Diana's was done within 45 minutes.

The bride-to-be accepted one telephone call. From the way her eyes shone as she chatted, everyone knew who the caller was. But while talking, she removed the rollers. "I nearly had fifty fits," said Shanley, who had wanted them worn until the last moment. "They felt uncomfortable," said Diana apologetically.

The Emanuels went into high gear as the splendid wedding gown was revealed. Their secrecy had been absolute, and nobody but Diana had seen any sketches. There had been ten fittings for the dress, the final one for the tightly fitted boned bodice. "All brides lose weight," said David Emanuel. "I knew that it could only be a perfect fit if we did that last."

The Emanuels said hundreds of drawings had been made, but that they had submitted only three to Diana. As for the reported replicas "in case of accident," David Emanuel later admitted there had been no others. "We wanted to throw off the scent."

The "fairy tale" dress was made of bantam-weight crisp ivory silk taffeta and old lace. Elizabeth Emanuel, her mother, and an assistant sewed on every sequin and tiny pearl by hand. They also hand-embroidered the 25-foot train—the longest in English wedding history, so sweeping that it covered a great part of the red carpet in the Cathedral. The "old" was the lace that had belonged to Queen Mary; the "new" the home-grown silk; the "borrowed" her mother's diamond-drop earrings; and the "blue" a small bow stitched into the waistband. A tiny horseshoe of 18-karat gold and studded with diamonds was also sewn in for good luck. A wide frill edged the scooped neckline, and the loose, full sleeves were caught at the elbow with taffeta bows. A multilayered tulle crinoline propped up the diaphanous skirt. The ivory tulle veil glittered with thousands of hand-sewn sequins. (Diana sidestepped the tradition set by Queen Victoria of uncovering her face for the ride to the Cathedral. She also kept her veil on throughout the ceremony.) The bride's low-heeled shoes repeated the lace and embroidery of the dress.

When at last she put the gown on, David Emanuel sewed on a last stitch—simply as a personal superstition, for luck.

Despite all the secrecy surrounding the design, within hours after the wedding, polyester copies of Diana's dress were on sale in London for less than $1,000.

The Worshipful Company of Gardeners had the traditional privilege of presenting her with a bridal bouquet—which included gold Mountbatten roses. The bouquet also contained a shower of white orchids, gardenias, freesias, lilies of the valley, stephanotis, and some myrtle grown from a sprig that had been in the bouquet of another twenty-year-old bride, Queen Victoria—whose marriage was one of the happiest in the House of Windsor. The bouquet was later placed in Mountbatten's honor at Westminster Abbey's Tomb of the Unknown Soldier.

Astrologer Svetlana Godillo had warned that the last week in July was not a good choice for a wedding date "since Prince Charles *and* Lady Diana have strong Uranus transits." But Svetlana didn't have many readers in London. It turned out to be a sublime day—one in which fact surpassed fiction. "No Hollywood production could have matched what I saw today," said actor Richard Burton. It seemed to be everybody's wedding, and everybody wanted to know everything: the length of carpet at St. Paul's Cathedral (697 feet), how many brass buttons on the Prince's uniform (18), the size of the marriage bed (66 by 78 inches—with 1200 springs).

They learned that the Queen would pick up the cost of the wedding, but that the Department of Environment had spent $100,000 to decorate the ceremonial route and provide the red carpet for the Cathedral.

The four Oldenberg Grays that would pull the 1902 State Postillion Landau bearing the bride and bridegroom back to Buckingham Palace had been taking music lessons. "Any fool can make the horses go forward," explained head coachman Arthur Showell. "The great thing is getting them to stand still when the Household Cavalry goes clattering by."

The St. Paul's bellringers included a bank clerk, a train driver, a wholesale fruit market worker, and a doctor, and they had been practicing on Great Tom and Great Paul and the dozen big bells in the northwest tower. There would be a short peal of 30 minutes before the ceremony and a long peal lasting three hours and fifty minutes afterward.

Despite the uncertain weather, everything looked rosy for Britain. In the two months since the engagement had been announced, the *Financial Times* share index rose 100 points. Compared to the 10,000 people who watched the coronation of King George VI on television, there would now be an estimated 750 million people in 74 countries glued to their sets, the only Communist country included being Yugoslavia. It was the largest single-day event ever undertaken by the BBC, but in the United States, the coverage was even greater.

But *Boston Globe* editorial writer Otile McManus summed up the mood of millions by writing, "I don't care what anybody says. I'm going to bed early tonight. I'm going to set my alarm clock for the middle of the night. I'm going to get up in time for the royal wedding. I don't want to miss a word . . . I will toast Prince Charles with Rice Krispies and orange juice. I will wish them health, long life, and happiness. Just pass the Kleenex, please."

Peter Jennings, the ABC commentator, explained why American television was devoting more time to the Royal Wedding than it had to the space shuttle flight or the return of U.S. hostages from Iran. "It's the last of the great royal spectacles. It's got color, sweep, music, occasion, and it's a great romantic story. It captures the imagination."

"The royal scene is simply a presentation of ourselves behaving well," observed novelist Dame Rebecca West. "If anybody is being honored, it is the human race."

Not everyone was so unequivocal in their praise. Former Royal Life Guard Kenneth Greenwood, who had escorted Princess Elizabeth at her wedding in 1947, said: "Take away the monarchy from England and you've just got a banana republic." And British playwright John Osborne called the Royal Family "one gold filling in a mouthful of decay."

Nevertheless, for most Britons it was a day of symbolic union, drawing the country together. Only weeks before, there had been race riots in London. Now, black and white happily mingled in the same crowd, cheering and singing. If the Royals were dispensable human beings, they were indispensable embodiments of history. They had somehow married man and myth.

The wedding day was declared a national holiday, and the heart of London was closed to all public traffic. If the spirit somewhat resembled a Brazilian carnival, the scheduled efficiency was split-second British. The doors of St. Paul's Cathedral opened at 9:00 A.M. sharp and all 2,500 guests were advised to be in their seats by 9:30. At 10:14 a fleet of black Rolls-Royces left Buckingham Palace with nearly all of Europe's kings and queens. At 10:22, the Queen's procession of carriages—eight state landaus and divisions of Household Cavalry—left the Palace.

Aware that she was known to some as the Glum Queen, Her Majesty made a small joke that morning that she was practicing how to smile more often.

Asked what contingency plans there were in case of rain, the directing Lord Chamberlain said grimly, "If it rains, our plan is to get wet."

But now the sun came out through the haze. By tradition, the color of the Queen's gown may not be worn by any other female member of the Royal Family. Her dress this day was of aquamarine silk crepe de chine. Her husband wore the uniform of Admiral of the Fleet. Though it was untraditional, for security a detective with a gun posed as one of her footmen.

Fifteen minutes before her own departure, the Queen Mother tiptoed into Diana's room and said, "My dear, you look simply enchanting."

Someone described her as "a bride of nonpareil luminescence." Those around her marveled at her utter lack of nervousness and tension in these last minutes, her "happy-go-lucky" mood.

Everybody seemed to help carrying her enormous train as she took her father's arm and stepped into the glass coach. The train literally filled the coach. The contrast between the red leather interior and the white wedding gown was vivid. The Emanuels went ahead in a Rolls-Royce to be at the Cathedral when she arrived to make any last-minute adjustments on her gown before she marched in.

Just as she was settled in her coach seat with her father, Diana suddenly leaned forward and began singing the television ice cream commercial, "Just one Cornetto . . ." She was bubbling.

The two-mile ride from Clarence House to St. Paul's took twenty minutes, but for the British it lasted forever.

She was surely the one the crowds had come to see. They applauded the Queen, they cheered the Queen Mother in her fluffy hat of osprey feathers, they yelled their approval of Charles and Andrew in their bemedalled Navy uniforms, but they gave their greatest roar for Cinderella.

Eighteen-year-old Rosemary Harrison, who was one of the first to arrive at the Mall with her mother, having camped there for three nights, explained, "Before, the Royal Family were something your parents were interested in. But Lady Diana seems so natural and young. We were all a bit jealous, to be honest."

"I don't envy her, really I don't," said a salesgirl. "Her life won't be her own, will it? And she's so young to be taking it all on . . ."

For Diana, there were no negatives at that moment. It was such a joyous crowd, singing, cheering, waving, applauding, loving. Waves and waves of loving. Her father kept up the mood in the coach by making small jokes, pointing out funny signs and people in costumes. BRITAIN NEEDS CHARLIE AND DI read one sign. Another showed a huge photo of Diana with the words I HAD TO KISS A LOT OF FROGS.

Six Cambridge University students were wearing dinner jackets. They had come the night before, set up a formal table on the Mall with an elegant candlelit dinner of poached salmon and champagne. Other young people were still wet from splashing happily in the fountains at Trafalgar Square.

"It's a great day to be British," said seventy-two-year-old retired factory worker Geoffrey Tirson. His voice breaking slightly, he told how he was standing on that very same spot of grass the night Prince Charles was born, "and now, here he is, about to be married. I say God bless him and her and all of us."

Spontaneously people started singing "Rule, Britannia" and "God Save the Queen," many obviously in tears. Thousands of cameras were clicking constantly. Parents everywhere were thrusting their children into the air to get a better look at the proceedings and transistor radios were switched on to give the crowds an added dimension of what was happening elsewhere. Along the route, Diana saw all the hanging baskets of blue, pink, and white petunias, verbena, and phlox, and everywhere flags, bunting, banners, emblems of heraldry. A small group was loudly singing a new song, "Lady Di."

Since Diana had read everything about the wedding, she surely knew that some people had paid thousands of dollars for ringside windows near St. Paul's. Thirty Houston, Texas, socialites had paid $250,000 for a super-luxury wedding week which included rooms at the St. James Club and a Cordon Bleu lunch catered by Parisian chefs.

The climactic moment for the waiting crowds at St. Paul's, and for worldwide television, was the arrival of the glass coach, with the butterfly emerging from her chrysalis. It was the world's first look at the fabled dress.

A footman wearing scarlet and gold opened the coach door. Earl Spencer, slowly being helped, came out first. Then out came Diana, carefully holding the folds of her dress as she stepped onto the red carpet. Two of her bridesmaids were waiting to catch and spread out her train.

Perhaps in a petulant moment, Dame Rebecca West had said days earlier that Diana looked like a thatched cottage. At that instant on television, she might well have choked on her words. Diana looked like a dream.

In Lagos, Nigeria, a small group of British listened intently to the announcer describing the wedding dress. It was at a party given by Her Majesty's Acting High Commissioner. "They said it was taffeta," said a girl named Louise. She paused and asked, "What's taffeta?"

When they played the national anthem and the congregation stood to sing "God Save the Queen," a British diplomat at a party stood at awkward attention, a sherry glass in his hand, singing the words with shy defiance.

She climbed the twenty-four imposing granite steps to the west door of St. Paul's while the crowd roared. Women wept. There were shouts of "Good luck." A police sergeant did a bit of a jig. A dozen trumpets blared her arrival.

In an impish aside, Diana asked her bridesmaids, "Is he here yet?" Then, "Am I ready?" She asked the Emanuels, who were just inside the entrance to give the gown a final check before she made her grand entrance. They both said, "Oh, no," making frantic final adjustments to smooth the crumples.

"She was incredibly calm," said David Emanuel. "We were the ones who were nervous."

But afterward, she said, "I was so nervous I hardly knew what I was doing."

Her father's chauffeur had helped him up the steps. It would be a long three-and-a-half minute walk, down the aisle to the altar, longer for him than for her. He held her left arm in his crooked right arm, while the Cathedral clock struck eleven. She gave him a wide grin to boost his spirits. Then came the sound of the wedding processional, the sound of trumpets stationed around the Whispering Gallery playing Jeremiah Clarke's "Trumpet Voluntary," composed three centuries ago, backed up by the 7,080 pipes of the Cathedral organ.

Charles & Diana

Diana had laughed when Charles had picked the music earlier and said of it that you had to have something "stirring, dramatic, and noisy," because if you had something quiet, "you start hearing your ankles cricking, you know what I mean."

In her walk down the aisle Diana was graceful and serious, moving with a measured pace. For a flashing moment, she gave a broad, quick, spontaneous smile, then became serious again. Her immediate concern was for her father. He was holding on to her tightly to steady himself, taking most of the center of the aisle, and so Diana found herself walking more to the right, her long train brushing past the congregation chairs.

The two of them were preceded by eleven clergy wearing red, silver, and gold, followed by five bridesmaids and the two page boys—Mountbatten's grandson and Charles's godson.

Then the clergy parted, and there was her waiting Prince in full uniform as a Commander of the Royal Navy, wearing his blue sash as a Knight of the Garter. He grinned and moved toward her, whispering, "You look wonderful!"

"Wonderful for you!" she said.

The two now stood side by side in front of the high altar, their right hands clasped. With her left hand, she still held her father, to steady him. He would say of her afterward, gratefully, "She was a tower of strength."

Suddenly, without preamble, came the voices of the choir and a congregation singing the hymn, "Christ is made the sure foundation." The Prince had predicted that all the music would be so moving, "I shall, I think, spend half the time in tears." He did not. He had other things to think about now.

The lesson of the 70-minute ceremony, read by a close friend of Prince Charles, a Welsh Methodist, came from St. Paul's passage on love in the First Letter to the Corinthians: "Love never faileth . . . Love is patient; love is kind and envies no one." Poet Laureate Sir John Betjeman also had written a poem to celebrate the ceremony, and it began, "Let's all in love and friendship hither come . . ." The President of Zimbabwe, the Reverend Canaan Banana, also had written a verse which read in part, "It was worth living for the one most loving . . ."

What was so touching to the watching millions was how often Charles and Diana looked at each other, and held hands.

215

The "Glum Queen" again had forgotten about smiling, but she dissolved in laughter suddenly when the energetic choirmaster knocked off a lampshade with his baton.

Few noticed Lady Mary Coleman, Diana's godmother, continually looking everywhere—as much as she looked at the altar. She was checking the thousands of flowers throughout the Cathedral. It had been her responsibility to arrange them.

"Here is the stuff of which fairy tales are made," said the Archbishop of Canterbury in his sermon. "A marriage which really works is one which works for others . . . May the burdens we lay on them be matched by the love with which we support them . . ."

The service really began when the Dean of St. Paul's, the Very Reverend Alan Webster, intoned, "Dearly beloved, we are gathered here in the sight of God and in the face of this congregation to join this man and this woman in Holy Matrimony . . ."

It seemed as if the whole world was listening, as if this marriage was their marriage. The Archbishop later reminded people, "There is an ancient Christian tradition that every bride and groom on their wedding day are regarded as a royal couple . . ."

They were both obviously nervous. The Prince unconsciously rubbed his nose. Diana was grateful to have her face hidden by her veil.

"Diana Frances, wilt thou have this man to thy wedded husband, to live together according to God's law in the holy estate of matrimony? Wilt thou love him, comfort him, honour and keep him, in sickness and in health; and, forsaking all others, keep thee only unto him, so long as ye both shall live?"

"I will," she answered quietly, but firmly.

As Diana repeated the words of the ancient marriage vow, she seemed to be swaying ever so slightly in rhythm with the phrases. She gave the impression of being immersed in it, oblivious to all but Charles and the Archbishop.

Prince Charles's nervousness showed when he muffed one of his lines. Instead of saying, "all my worldly good with thee I share," he said "all thy goods with thee I share." Watching a repeat of the ceremony on television with other members of the Royal Family later, Princess Anne laughed and said, "He meant it. It wasn't a mistake at all!"

Diana's nervousness showed when she referred to her husband as "Philip Charles Arthur George" instead of "Charles Philip Arthur

George." Prince Andrew joked about it afterward: "She married my father . . ."

Finally it was done. "With this ring I thee wed . . ."

Then, "Those whom God hath joined together let no man put asunder . . ."

When the Archbishop of Canterbury declared, "I pronounce that they be man and wife together," the crowds outside Buckingham Palace, listening on their radios, stood up and cheered.

On a wooden platform above their heads, NBC-TV commentator Jane Pauley wondered what the shouting was all about. "What's happening? Has her blood turned blue or something?"

The royal wedding ring was made from the last bit of the same nugget of Welsh gold used for the wedding rings of the Queen, the Queen Mother, Princess Margaret, and Princess Anne. The nugget had been found in 1923 in the Clogau St. David's Mine in Gwynnet, North Wales.

They did not kiss then. But Joyce and Allan Andrews in Cyprus clearly heard the Prince whisper to his Princess, "Well done . . ."

When it was all over, the Royal Family assembled on the raised platform where the service had been held, chatting, joking, smiling. The Queen was beaming, the Queen Mother almost crying. Diana's father and mother were now arm in arm while their spouses were elsewhere. Her Majesty smiled broadly when the new Princess of Wales curtsied before her. Diana, Princess of Wales, was now the third most important royal lady in the land and would curtsy only to the Queen and Queen Mother—all others would curtsy to her.

Before they left the Cathedral, the couple signed wedding register No. 345 showing that "Charles P." ("Princeps," Latin for prince) had married "Diana Spencer, spinster." There was a touching intimacy in their signing because they left the group and walked alone to the register. It seemed symbolic, the two of them, setting out alone on their lives together.

As they left St. Paul's, the bride had a word of warning for her new husband: "Mind the steps . . ."

On the joyous return procession to Buckingham Palace, the Queen and the bride's father shared a carriage. Instead of getting in first, as was her royal prerogative, the Queen told the shaky Earl Spencer, "You go first, Johnny."

Diana had taken off her veil now, and the newlyweds rode together in an open carriage to the roar of the crowds. People along the route threw rice, confetti, and rose petals. There was a big banner alongside a church: LOVE FROM AMERICA. Another proclaimed: LOVE IS CHARLIE AND DI. The nearby Ritz Hotel had photographs of them on its front, nearly a full floor high. The *Times* of London had dedicated its entire front page to an unprecedented full-length picture of the couple, referring to this "day of romance in a gray world." At the Strand Palace Hotel, the management released a spray of red rose petals and 1,000 doves as the royal couple passed.

From the crowd there was another song, "Lady Di, Lady Di, Lady Di" (chick-a-boom, chick-a-boom-boom . . .). The pace of the carriages now slowed so the crowd could get a longer look.

At Buckingham Palace, a butler appeared outside the fence carrying a silver salver with two glasses and a bottle of champagne. Behind him came another man carrying a jeroboam of wine followed by two yeomen of the guard in their colorful uniforms. They marched toward the gate, poured the wine, drank a toast to the people, then turned and drank a toast to the Palace. The crowd roared.

When the newlyweds returned to Buckingham Palace, the crowds broke ranks, the whole Mall becoming a swaying human mosaic of people. Once the Royal Family were all inside the Palace, the crowd kept yelling for them to come out on the balcony. And, when the Prince and Princess came out onto the balcony, many in the crowd started singing "You'll Never Walk Alone." The yelling was particularly insistent for Cinderella. "We want Di, we want Di, we want Di."

It was unmistakably the face of Charles behind the curtained window of the balcony, peering out at the people. They could see Charles reaching for Diana's hand to lead her out to the balcony. She seemed slightly shy the first time they appeared, less so the second time. "Go ahead and wave," he told her, and she did. The third time, the crowd was chanting, "Kiss her, kiss her, kiss her." He kissed her on the hand. The crowd called them back a fourth time, and now they were yelling, "Kiss her *properly*."

Hired lipreaders, looking through binoculars, reported that the Prince said to her, "I'm not going in for that caper. They want us to kiss." But, utterly relaxed and exuberant now, she smiled and said, "Why ever not?" Prince Andrew reportedly also egged him on. Most of the family was on the balcony with them now, and the Prince took a quick look at Her Majesty to see if she objected. She didn't. He then turned to his bride and kissed her lingeringly on the mouth. The crowd went wild.

"Neither of us will ever forget the atmosphere," the Prince said of it later. "It was electric, almost unbelievable. I remember standing at my window trying to realize what it was like so that I might be able to tell my own children . . . It was something quite extraordinary . . . I was quite extraordinarily proud to be British."

Many had been cooling their champagne in the water around the so-called Wedding Cake, the Queen Victoria Memorial, and now corks were popping all over the place, people were singing the national anthem, kissing strangers, cheering, laughing.

"You can't explain to foreigners why we feel the way we do about the Royal Family," an architect said. "It's in-built, isn't it?" A British television commentator tried to describe the euphoria. "Just for a moment," he said, "the world seems a nicer, easier, and kinder place."

The wedding breakfast inside the Palace was mostly for family and close friends. Nancy Reagan went to a party given by the Prime Minister. There had been complaints about her regal convoy—twelve Secret Service men, six limousines, and a hairdresser—wherever she went, but she had been given high marks for her appearance, her style, and the fact that her bodyguards were female.

The 118 members of the Royal Family party dined on brill with lobster sauce, chicken breasts stuffed with lamb mousse, and strawberries and Cornish cream, all washed down with vintage Krug champagne. There were no less than sixteen wedding cakes; the Prince himself cut the enormous fruitcake with a sword. "If we'd known last year that he was going to get married," said the Navy chef, "we'd have baked it last year. The longer a cake matures, the more it relaxes."

At 4:20 P.M., on clockwork schedule, the royal couple got in their carriage in the inner quadrangle of the Palace. Attached to it were blue and silver heart-shaped balloons and a rough cardboard sign put on by Prince Charles's brothers that read JUST MARRIED. It had been printed, complete with hearts and arrows, with lipstick.

Their carriage drove them to Track 12 at Waterloo Station where the royal train was waiting, described by one observer as "the only clean train on British Rail."

The Prince was wearing a gray lounge suit, but his wife's outfit was bright with color: a tangerine suit and saucy tricorn hat with feathers. She had returned her mother's earrings, but she had borrowed her sister Sarah's pearl choker. Impulsively, just before boarding, Diana kissed Lord Maclean, the Lord Chamberlain, the sixty-four-year-old chief of the Maclean clan who had choreographed her perfect day. A few rose petals were still sticking to her dress.

Columnist Beverly Stephen thought that this surely "may have been the best week of Diana's life." But the Archbishop of Canterbury had described their wedding "not as the place of arrival, but the place where the adventure really begins."

The train left at 4:40, ten minutes late. Almost at that instant, the Central Electricity Generating Board reported a crisis. The demand for electricity suddenly jumped by 1800 megawatts, one of the largest increases in its history. It was as if everybody in Britain simultaneously decided either to go to the bathroom or make a pot of tea.

Elsewhere, celebrations had just started.

There were some 10,000 street parties throughout Britain that day and almost everybody indoors had a private party. On tiny Elizabeth Street, one of Diana's favorite shopping areas, the merchants organized an Elizabeth Street Fayre as a wedding celebration. The Duchess of Westminster opened the Fayre at noon, and Greek Princess Irene Galitzine awarded prizes for the best costumes on the theme of princes and princesses of the past, present, and future.

The Embassy Club on Old Bond Street had a Charles and Diana party; all the guests had to be persons named Charles or Diana. The Savoy concocted a special drink called Royal Lady: fill one-fourth of a tall pousse glass with gin, add one-fourth passion fruit juice, one-fourth Amaretto, and one-fourth of Diana's favorite liqueur, Royal Mint Chocolate. Finish with a splash of champagne and float a strawberry on top.

In the evening the Royals held their own party at Claridges. Guests included everyone from Nancy Reagan to Princess Grace. Prince Philip wore a boater with "Charles and Diana" written across the headband. The wedding tension over, the Royals were unroyally relaxed. The Queen was seen with her hands on her hips, not looking very regal. Dancing continued until four in the morning. Her Majesty

Charles & Diana

left earlier, but said she could have danced all night, and even did a little jig before she left.

Guests later described how Princess Margaret arranged a couple of chairs so that she could put her feet up and have "a good rest." The next morning at a Royal Naval ceremonial, Princess Anne apologized, "Please excuse me if I sound somewhat different today, but I am suffering from a hangover after a very enjoyable wedding."

15

T he honeymoon train was called Broadlands, in honor of Mountbatten—the locomotive was the same one used for Mountbatten's state funeral the year before. Broadlands was only a mile from Romsey, a small Hampshire village ninety miles from London. There, again, the whole town was waiting for them at the station, cheering, waving flags.

Lord and Lady Romsey had discreetly deserted Broadlands, and it had been closed to tourists for the week. Lord Romsey, who had inherited the estate, was Prince Charles's old school chum, Norton Knatchbull, brother of Amanda. Before its closing, there was a last surge of tourists paying their three dollars to see the honeymoon bedroom. Even more than that, they wanted to see the honeymoon bed. It was a magnificent canopied fourposter which the London *Sun* pictured on a full page with the blaring headline THIS IS THE BED.

Not only had the Mountbattens honeymooned in that bed, but so had Princess Elizabeth and Prince Philip.

The Portico Room had pink and blue curtains, was regally furnished with oil paintings, and had a splendid view of the parkland and the river Test.

Broadlands, a sixteenth-century Palladian mansion with huge Ionic columns, sits on a spread of 6,000 acres. It's comfortable and elegant, with a marble-floored anteroom, cluttered with fragments of classical sculpture. It's a house full of light coming from large windows overlooking a green park through which the Test flows quietly. It's a house where Mountbatten "played in private the wise uncle of a family." Prince Charles had written his great-uncle, "As you know only too well, to me it has become a second home in so many ways."

For the honeymoon six discreet servants oversaw the running of the sixty-room house. Five local youths who jumped over a wall were quickly apprehended by security guards and sent home. Since the boys' only crime was curiosity, there were no charges.

This finally was their time to be alone together: two days and three nights at Broadlands, plus another two weeks on the royal yacht.

Charles Smith, who had been Mountbatten's butler, recalled the time when Princess Elizabeth and Prince Philip had honeymooned there. They had had their dinner by candlelight at a small circular table in front of the log fire. It was most likely that Charles and Diana would have had the same.

There was an unconfirmed report that the Prince had his breakfast the next day on schedule, at 9 A.M. What was confirmed was the breakfast menu itself: sausages, bacon, eggs, kidney, and kedgeree (an Indian rice and fish dish).

It was also confirmed that they went walking hand in hand along the paths leading to the river Test. "They looked very happy," said Chief Superintendent Alan Lemish, head of the New Forest division. They also went fishing. The water bailiff, Bernard Aldrich, laid out their fly-fishing gear, including the favorite rod of Lord Mountbatten. The stream was noted for its trout and salmon. "If he catches a salmon, you'll hear about it," said Aldrich.

This had to be both a happy and sad time for the Prince. He had loved Mountbatten as he had loved no other man. The wreath he had sent to his great-uncle's funeral said simply: "From HGS to HGF"—From Honorary Grandson to Honorary Grandfather.

It was no surprise when the water bailiff reported that the Prince had gone fishing alone early the next evening. He had come here alone shortly after Uncle Dickie's funeral. He had much to remember. Mountbatten was buried close by in Romsey, in a twelfth-century abbey, his body facing the sea. He had specifically detailed his own funeral—who should carry his insignia, what hymns should be sung, even who should be invited to Westminster Abbey. "The only sad thing, Charles, is that I won't be there to enjoy it."

Diana fully understood her husband's feeling for Uncle Dickie. It was this kind of sensitivity that had helped pull them together.

There was a swimming pool on the estate, and they surely used it although they did not ride. Part of the second day was rainy, and a good time to spend in their room.

Before they left Broadlands, the newlyweds received a message

from a visitor at the gate, seven-year-old Marcus Cass, who wrote:
"Dear Prince Charles and Lady Diana. I came to Romsey to see you
but people kept pushing, so I wasn't able to see you. Mummy said
just cheer when other people cheer, so we did. I hope you are a
happy family."

Eastleigh Airport was only twenty minutes away, and waiting
for them was Prince Charles's old propellor-driven RAF Andover
of the Queen's Flight. He had flown it often, and now he took the
controls again en route to Gibraltar.

It had caused a diplomatic flap when Spain learned that the bridal
couple was going to board the royal yacht Britannia at Gibraltar.
Spain considered this a public slap since it claimed Gibraltar ever
since the British had seized it in 1704. In anger, King Juan Carlos
had decided not to attend the royal wedding—although he did send
a wedding gift of a bronze statue of a polo player and his pony.

Charles and Diana were in this tiny town that clung to a narrow
shelf on the west side of this famous rock for only 105 minutes, but
the 30,000 inhabitants gave them a reception that was rapturous and
frenzied. They traveled one and a half miles to the docks in the only
open car on the island, a brown Triumph Stag limousine that belonged to the Italian consul. Then a flotilla of some 400 small boats
escorted the Britannia out to sea while the band at the dock played
"Rule, Britannia." In the afterdeck of the royal yacht, the Prince and
Princess waved and waved, listening to the rumble of the 21-gun
salute.

Before leaving, they had entertained the Governor of Gibraltar
and other guests for drinks aboard ship. One of them, Lady Hassan,
said afterward, "They stood hand in hand . . . and kept looking into
each other's eyes while we chatted. It was beautiful to see two young
people so devoted. The Princess was very moved by the welcome
here. She kept peering out of the porthole and tears welled in her
eyes. She was overwhelmed by it all . . ."

She was soon much more relaxed.

Reporters and photographers from all over the world desperately
tried to trace their route, without success. They were pinpointed as
far away as Fiji. Actually they kept close to the Algerian coast for a
while, steering clear of populated areas, confining themselves to occasional shore trips at isolated tiny beaches. Then the Britannia sailed
along the coast of Tunisia, up to Sicily and the Straits of Messina,
to the Greek island of Ithaca.

It was more than a floating palace, it was a honeymoon hotel, but until recently it had lacked one honeymoon essential—a double bed. When Princess Anne honeymooned on the *Britannia*, she had her husband lash together two single beds. The forewarned Charles and Diana had a queen-sized double bed put on board before they left.

But their privacy was complete. The royal apartment was at the rear of the yacht; the crew's quarters were in front. A wide mahogany staircase led to their rooms. The royal apartment included a wine cellar, a 45-foot dining room which converted into a theater, a garage for their Rolls-Royce, a private galley, and offices and cabins for staff—these occupied the rear of all four decks. This time the staff was minimal—a private secretary, an equerry, a maid, two detectives, and a valet.

The Princess used the Queen's bedroom for her dressing room, and she and her husband spent much of their time in the glassed-in sitting room on the royal deck, or sunning on the veranda. They also went windsurfing together.

If Diana wanted to swim, they'd stop the yacht, lower the anchor, check the sea for safety. The Princess and her maid, Evelyn, would then swim at the back of the ship while the crew swam up front. Close by would be a lifeguard in a rubber boat.

The crew soon noticed that the Prince didn't swim at all. The sympathetic sailors, however, realized that he needed all the rest he could get. Diana was enough at ease with the crew to raid the freezer for ice cream in her bare bikini, giggling as she pointed in the direction of the royal bedroom, "It's him—he's asleep again."

The Prince had been a bachelor for a long time and, in many ways, was a creature of habit. For example, he always exercised every night, after brushing his teeth, shortly before going to bed. In remembering it, his valet said, "I must admit I did find that strange. One evening the Princess came out on deck, rather restless, and said to me, 'He's doing his exercises. I must leave him alone.' " Diana did her exercises in the morning, usually to a "workout" tape.

Everyone admitted that they had never seen the Prince so utterly relaxed in all the years they had known him. Besides sunning, the Prince liked to take an afternoon nap. That was usually the time when Diana went exploring. Part of her tour always included the kitchen, and she helped select the menu. Without warning one day, she appeared at the mess where some sailors were having a drink and singing songs around the piano. The music stopped and nobody said a word. "You could have heard a pin drop," said one of the sailors.

Diana not only insisted they continue but sat down herself and continued playing the song they had been singing, "What Shall We Do With the Drunken Sailor?" She next played "Greensleeves." Somebody offered her a can of beer, and she accepted, surprising everyone. Then the original pianist went back to the piano and started playing the Paul Anka hit song, "Diana." Everybody joined in, particularly at the line "Stay by me, Diana." By this time several petty officers arrived, suggesting that Diana leave. "I'm sorry I have to go," she told them. They cheered her, and one later said, "We were all tickled pink."

They were tickled even pinker when she wandered into their messroom just after shower time one afternoon when a few men still had only towels wrapped around their middles. When it was suggested that perhaps she should not be there then, she replied, "It's all right. I'm a married woman, aren't I?"

She and her maid were the only two women aboard, and when she walked around anywhere near the crew area in her bikini it caused some consternation. One of them said afterward, "There are 276 men on board *Britannia* and every one is in love with Princess Diana."

They sometimes saw the bride wandering on deck in her sheer cotton negligee and matching apricot dressing gown, early in the morning. Their consensus: "Prince Charles is a lucky man."

All over the Mediterranean, reporters and photographers were hiring planes and boats to check on tips as to where the royal couple were—and without success. Someone tagged it "the ghost ship," insisting that it had simply vanished. A Greek gunboat cooperated by warning a helicopter full of photographers to keep out of the area.

The *Britannia* had no set course and went wherever the honeymooners wanted. At the volcanic island of Santorini, with its craterlike cliffs, they went ashore to see an active volcanic cone. Before that they had picnicked off the northwest coast of Crete, at Cape Grabusa, enjoying a barbecue on a moonlit night. They moved through the Greek islands of the Dodecanese near Rhodes.

Otherwise, it was all very quiet and homey. Their suite was decorated in the style of an oak-paneled country house with handwoven rugs, bed covers of bright blue flower patterns, chintz curtains. They played cards, wrote hundreds of thank-you notes, watched a videotape of their wedding ceremony and giggled at their mistakes.

Occasionally they'd watch a film, such as *Chariots of Fire*, or listen to Diana's portable stereo—her favorites were Elton John, Supertramp, and the Beach Boys. Once they rescued a woman in a motor cruiser who was lost. She had bought the cruiser at a boat show because "she liked the interior fittings." The *Britannia* soon put her on her way.

Diana would visit the sailors in sick bay, and even brought drinks down to the stokers. Otherwise, she was persistently playful. Returning from some private time on a small beach, Prince Charles took a salute from officers at the head of the gangway, but Diana raced up with a bucket of water and poured it over her husband's head. He turned and chased her, both of them laughing.

Before they ever went ashore on any beach, two detectives would go first to scout the area. On one such beach party, Diana poured ice cubes on her sunbathing husband's stomach saying, "This will cool you down." And another chase started.

The ship's officers organized a barbecue on one island where they did all the cooking. A Royal Marine accordionist then came ashore. Someone handed out song sheets and everyone sang camp songs and sea chanties, with Diana's soprano joining them loud and clear.

The only formalities took place at Port Said when the royal couple entertained their only official visitors, Egyptian President Anwar al-Sadat and his wife, Jihan. The Prince had gone ashore to inspect a guard of honor, the governor of Port Said had put on a fireworks display, President Sadat added another award to Prince Charles's chest—this one Egypt's highest honor, the Order of the Republic, First Class—and gave Diana a gift of some jewelry.

More than all of this, the four of them found themselves in warm rapport. The Prince got on easily with Sadat, as he always did with older men. He was attentive, respectful, yet contributed his own comments. Sadat later revealed how surprised he was at Prince Charles's awareness of world problems, and his broad knowledge of Egyptian archeology. As for Diana, she and Jihan Sadat, a world leader in feminism, were soon exchanging confidences. In the sunset quiet, the Royal Marine Band supplied background music. In the course of a single day, a formal meeting had become an informal friendship. In fact, three days later, when the Prince and Princess flew back to

Britain from an Egyptian airfield, Sadat and his wife returned to the airport to say goodbye—and Diana kissed them both.

For three days afterward, Charles and Diana sailed out into the Red Sea for their last times of utter privacy. They went scuba diving, snorkeling, sunned themselves on a small sandy beach.

On the last night at sea, the crew put on a variety show of fourteen acts for the royal couple. Some of the jokes were pretty salty, and one large sailor even did an impersonation of the Princess during her kindergarten teaching days. Nobody laughed harder than Diana. The royal detectives and other royal staff sang a version of the song, "We Are Sailing," converted to "We Are Loafing." Diana's maid, in a bikini, held up cue cards with the new lyrics so everybody could join in. The Princess played the piano for another sing-along number. And when it was all over, Diana peered in on the mess where some were getting a final nightcap, and commented, giggling, "My God, you're all high as kites."

As they left the next morning for the airport, the crew lined up to salute them and give them three cheers. The Prince and Princess flew off to Scotland as the royal yacht headed for Australia to meet the Queen at the Commonwealth Conference.

But the honeymoon wasn't entirely over. Charles and Diana went directly to Balmoral for several more weeks of rest. Here they could get lost on 24,000 acres surrounded by the Grampian Mountains and the river Dee.

Before that, they agreed to a single photo session with the press in exchange for a promise of privacy while at Balmoral. The Prince wore a Royal Hunting Stewart kilt that had belonged to his grandfather, George VI. The Princess wore a brown tweed check suit with an open-neck cream blouse and a loose jacket. Both looked tanned, utterly relaxed, and very happy. Nobody had to tell them to hold hands. At one point, Charles even impulsively kissed his wife's hand.

Marriage was "marvelous," she said, and "highly recommended." The honeymoon had been "fabulous."

Had she made breakfast for her husband yet?

"I don't eat breakfast," she said laughing.

Were they going to go salmon fishing?

"The water's a bit too low for salmon."

Presented with a bouquet of roses, carnations, and heather, the Princess grinned and asked, "All on your expense accounts?"

They really were left alone after that. For the Prince, Balmoral was "the best place in the world." The nearby mountain of Lochnagar had prompted him to write a children's book for his brothers called *The Old Man of Lochnagar*. (Someone insisted he had given a copy to Diana when she was a small child.)

The two now took their long private walks on the heathered moors and in the course of the next few weeks had several visitors. Diana and Princess Margaret took time out to browse in a nearby village for antiques. Two of her former roommates, Carolyn Pride and Virginia Pitman, flew up to keep her company while Charles went stalking. There were still piles of thank-you notes to write. Sarah Armstrong-Jones arrived later to provide more company and conversation. Diana's sister Jane was there with her two-year-old daughter. Later, her grandmother, Lady Fermoy, arrived with the Queen Mother at nearby Birkhall. Her brother Charles and sister Sarah came as well.

One of the highlights for Diana was the Braemar Royal Highland Gathering with all kinds of games: children's sack races, hammer-throwing, tug-of-war. She particularly loved seeing the Highland dancing with the tossing of the caber—a young tree trunk. Everybody admired her Scottish plaid suit and her jaunty black tam o' shanter. She even joined in dancing the reels.

The Queen, however, was not amused when Diana giggled during the playing of the national anthem. She gave her a hard look. The fault belonged to Prince Charles, who had whispered in his bride's ear, "They're playing our song . . ."

Their last days of complete quiet at Balmoral were at Craigowan, the Prince's private place on the estate. He fished and shot grouse, she relaxed and remembered their courtship days and splendid wedding. They took more long walks together.

On a Sunday, they went to nearby Crathie Church. The sermon of the day was: "Go and bear fruit . . ."

16

What are we going to look forward to now?"

That question expressed a national mood. The royal wedding had touched a romantic nerve and the British were reluctant to see it over. A cartoon showed Prince Charles on the phone saying, "No, we don't want to put the show on the road."

But, of course, the show *would* go "on the road"—for the rest of their lives.

One of the gaudiest parts of the show at that moment was the wedding presents. More than 10,000 had arrived from all over the world, filling the private cinema at Buckingham Palace. Diana and Charles made a point of dropping in every day to examine the fresh loot. A retired Rear Admiral had the massive job, with a staff, of cataloguing and acknowledging everything. Diana was delighted with the whole scene. It was as if every day were Christmas.

The 350-pound King of Tonga, who had sat in an oversize chair at their wedding, sent a pair of saddles. Lord and Lady Tryon, whom Diana reportedly had gently eased out of their social circle, sent a painting of Vopnafjordur in Iceland, where Charles went annually for salmon fishing before he was married. A picnic basket came from Diana's aunt, Lady Anne Wake-Walker, and a tartan rug from Diana's seventy-eight-year-old great-uncle, the Honorable G. C. Spencer.

A boy who once dated Diana gave a large Royal Worcester bowl. West Heath School sent its former student a pair of silver salt cellars, and the Young England Kindergarten, where she had taught, presented the couple with a collage of the Hyde Park fireworks display. A bonbon dish arrived from Prince Charles's former nanny, Miss Helen Lightbody, who also added a silver vase and sugar tongs.

Their youngest bridesmaid, Clementine Hambro, gave two white terrycloth robes embroidered with their names. Princess Margaret's son, Viscount Linley, made them a dining room table at his woodcraft school.

Few of these private presents from family and friends were selected for display. What was shown at the exhibit at St. James's Palace was a tenth of the total: one thousand chosen gifts. The centerpiece was the wedding dress, and that was enough to bring a crowd of several hundred thousand people during the next two months, the line sometimes stretching for more than a mile, no matter how inclement the weather.

The display included a ribbon bag from a ninety-six-year-old blind woman; a painting by Raoul Dufy from President Mitterrand of France; a fresh potato shaped like a heart; a magnificent set of diamond and sapphire jewelry from the Crown Prince of Saudi Arabia; 300 uncut multicolored diamonds from King Khalid of Saudi Arabia; a glass wine cooler from the Automobile Association; four crates of table glass from the President of Italy; a set of garden chairs from the Queen and Prince of Denmark; a crocodile handbag from the government of Nigeria; and a ball-and-chain paperweight from the inmates of Dartmoor Prison. Mrs. Ronald Reagan brought a $75,000 Steuben glass bowl (which a Steuben spokesman said cost her $8,000, explaining, "We offer handsome discounts to the government").

Simpler gifts included Welsh wooden love spoons, a seven-foot-high thatched birdhouse, a waste basket, two Jersey cows, a bag of coffee beans, a negligee, and a popular book called *Happiness and How to Find It.*

The most expensive gifts were assembled in the Throne Room of St. James's Palace. The huge stone table from the King of Swaziland couldn't be shown because it was so heavy they thought it would break through the floor. A grand piano was displayed, along with a windsurfer, but a four-poster bed from Canada was considered too large. Most pets were refused and so was the gift of an American oil well.

Diana's personal gift to her Prince was a diamond-studded gold picture frame for his favorite snapshot of her. His favorite—the one he kept on his desk—was a picture of her, in a skimpy green bikini, that he had taken on the honeymoon yacht.

His real gift to her was the realization of her fairyland fantasy: a coach that didn't turn into a pumpkin, a royal honeymoon yacht sailing toward any whim they wanted. And as one practical Brit commented, "She won't have to carry any money anymore."

Unlike other Royals, the Prince of Wales did not get any money from Parliament—he was not on the government's Civil List of salaried personnel. His primary income came from the Duchy of Cornwall. It now added up to 550,445 pounds sterling a year, half of which he had voluntarily paid to the Exchequer. Now that he was married, he cut his contribution to a quarter.

Out of his income, the Prince had to pay the salaries of his personal staff, which included a private secretary, a deputy, an office manager, an equerry, and two valets. Diana now had a private secretary, a deputy, a maid, and three ladies-in-waiting. Charles also had to make contributions to the Queen toward the upkeep of his apartments at Buckingham Palace, Windsor, Sandringham, and Balmoral.

The newlyweds had to staff their own house at Highgrove with a cook, a housekeeper, three maids, a butler, and three footmen, some of whom also worked for them at Kensington Palace. If they had a large party, they borrowed staff, maids, and footmen from the Queen at Buckingham Palace and paid their wages for the night.

The Prince's biggest personal expense supported his passion—his horses. He kept ten polo ponies, four hunters, and a steeplechaser, but boarded them without charge at the Windsor Castle stables.

Besides horses, the Prince also maintained three cars—an Aston Martin, a Ford Granada, and Diana's Ford Escort. And there was the cost of their wardrobes—particularly Diana's, which created much controversy.

Among the rumors circulating was that they had bought a 21-room condominium in New York City's posh Trump Tower (untrue), and that Diana's former apartment at Coleherne Court in Kensington had been sold (true). Her three roommates moved elsewhere, but stayed together. Originally the apartment had been bought by Diana herself for 50,000 pounds. It sold for twice what she paid.

Diana was still on her fantasy high when she got her first shock from the real world. President Sadat of Egypt was assassinated. Prince Charles would go to the funeral. She wanted to accompany him, but the Royals refused. Egypt was declared "unsafe for foreign dignitaries." It didn't cheer Diana to know that for the trip Prince Charles was assigned seven added bodyguards.

If that shook up Diana, there was further worry concerning her first scheduled public tour with Charles, a three-day trip through Wales. Radical Welsh groups had threatened violence and an incendiary device was found in an army recruiting office in Pontypridd, where the royal couple was scheduled to visit. An extremist group had plastered the area with anti-royalist slogans. They were protesting, they said, because "of the steel and coal closure." Unemployment was particularly high in Wales.

A Buckingham Palace spokesman insisted earlier that the schedule of the Prince and the Princess that fall would not be "excessively heavy." Their short, tightly scheduled Welsh tour did not seem to bear this out, for they covered every county of Wales and almost every corner of it from the rugged north coast to the deeply depressed industrial valleys.

For Diana, the tour was more than daunting—it was sometimes frightening. Emerging from a car to see a pushing, packed crowd, all chanting her name, all wanting to touch her, "she can suddenly stop smiling," recorded an observer, "and look around with the purest terror in her eyes." "Welsh women love this air of vulnerability," wrote reporter Tom Davies, "and their dearest wish would be to take her home to administer many cups of tea, a mountain of well-meaning advice, and an aspirin to put her right."

Diana's vulnerability, along with her natural warmth and sensitivity, was a major reason that people felt she was "one of us."

Thoughtfully dressed in the green, red, and white colors of the Welsh flag, she even had learned some Welsh phrases including "*Diolch yn fawr,*" "Thank you very much." In their scheduled walkabouts, she seemed to search out the very young and the very old.

When Diana saw four-year-old Ruth Devonald dressed in a traditional Welsh costume, she went to her and said, "Look, I have a miniature version of you here," and pointed to a small doll someone had just given her. When a seven-year-old boy yelled out, "My dad says give us a kiss," she smiled and said, "Well then, you better have one." She kissed him and the crowds cheered. She approached an old soldier and complimented, "What nice shiny medals!" She then turned to his proud wife and asked, "Did you polish them for him?"

A mother lifted up her baby daughter announcing that her name was Diana Evans, and that she had been named after the Princess. One very old man in St. David's was so overcome by her presence that he burst into tears, controlled himself, then started crying again.

It was plain from the start that people wanted mostly to see Diana, not Charles. In every walkabout, she and Charles would separate, each walking on different sides of the street. The chant was always, "We want Diana." They would give him presents to give to her. His arms were soon full, and he told them, "I'm used to collecting things for her now, as you can see."

He was collecting things for himself, too. At a museum he admired a stainless steel lavatory with an ivory pull handle provided for the use of his great-great-grandmother, Queen Victoria, and he told the museum aide, "I collect old loos. If you are ever getting rid of any, I would like to buy one."

Commenting on that afterward, Virginia Wetherell, who runs a Victoriana shop in London's Highland Park, noted that antique loo prices have risen tenfold in ten years. "You are better off putting your money into toilets, so to speak, than into oil paintings or gold coins."

If he discussed his interest in loos with his wife, he might have remembered, when he bid farewell as skipper to the crew of HMS *Bronington*, being pushed around on deck in a wheelchair with a black polished lavatory seat and a toilet roll hung around his neck, in true Navy tradition. Then came a farewell from one of the sailors. "See you remember to keep your bowels open, sir."

As the people on his side of the street in any Welsh town would ask him to bring the Princess over to them, he would occasionally say, "Over here, darling."

He even mocked himself, indicating his wife and saying, "There's the person you've come to see." Indeed they had. When their Rolls-Royce approached an expectant village, the people yelled "There she is!" instead of "There they are!"

What was remarkable—aside from her occasional fear—was the ease with which Princess Diana mixed with people, bantered with them, naturally knew what to say. There is the standard royal tactical trick of initiating a conversation with a question such as, "Have you been waiting long?" Or, "Have you come far?" Diana, however, usually managed something more personal, even intimate, and sometimes funny.

But there were some negative incidents in Wales as well. A young woman broke through the police cordon to spray white paint on a royal limousine. A few shouted, "Go home, English princess." A couple tried to throw stink bombs in their direction.

But the masses loved this friendly young woman. They loved how she kept on walking among them, despite a torrential rain on the second day. She seemed to be at her peak of vivacity, leaning into the crowd, laughing, smilingly calling a small girl "a little chatterbox." On the other side of the street, the Prince was apologizing to those who wanted his wife. "I haven't got enough wives," he told them. "I've only got one and she's over there." He soon went over to her, slipped his arm around her. "Darling, don't walk about in the rain. You'll get so wet." For a while he walked alongside her, holding an umbrella over her, until a lady-in-waiting took over.

She was sodden, but insisted on finishing the walk.

"Over here, Diana, over here . . ." Then she spotted a sign: MY NAME IS DIANA TOO. That worked. She went over. An invalid woman nearby said, "You must be cold." Diana looked at her and said feelingly, "Not as cold as you, I should think."

But later, Diana was shivering, admitting to her lady-in-waiting, "My hands and feet are freezing." She didn't wear gloves because she knew the women wanted to see her rings.

They loved the way she rubbed one of her shoes on the back of her leg, just as they might. Twenty-five-year-old Mrs. Janet Lukie, expecting her first baby in May, listened to the Princess ask, "That morning sickness, isn't it dreadful? But they say after three months you're all right." Asked whether she wanted a boy or a girl, she giggled and burst out with the cliché, "I don't mind as long as it's healthy."

They kept giving her flowers. The bouquets filled the cars and still all the staff had their arms full. A high school band played a trumpet fanfare for them. A well-scrubbed children's choir sang a medley of nursery rhymes. Among the gifts they gave her were a black Welsh heifer called Sandra, a wooly black mountain sheep, a book of poems, a plastic hanger, and two armchairs.

They awarded the Princess the freedom of the City of Cardiff. She had to swear an oath that she would be obedient to the Lord Mayor and "obey his warrants, precepts, and commands." The only other woman so honored was Her Majesty the Queen.

There is a saying that if you put two Welshmen together you always get three points of view. But there seemed to be no quarrel about Diana. It was a national love affair.

"How proud I am to be Princess of such a wonderful place," she told them in her first public speech at Cardiff City Hall, "and of the

Welsh, who are very special to me." Accepting the loving freedom of their city, in careful Welsh she added, "I hope to come here again soon." She was very nervous and she spoke too fast.

A woman in Rhydyfelin summed up the Welsh feeling for Diana: "She's the flower in the royal forest."

Now, truly, she was the Princess of Wales.

There had been only eight previous princesses of Wales, none of them much interested in Wales itself. The first was Joan, the Fair Maid of Kent, described by an observer of the time as "the most beautiful woman in England." It was her garter that fell to the ball-room floor. King Edward kneeled to get it then gracefully said in French, "Evil to him who evil thinks." Thus began the Order of the Garter, Europe's most ancient order of chivalry. Widowed, with five children, Joan married the Prince of Wales known as Edward, the Black Prince.

The second Princess of Wales did not appear on the scene until a hundred years later, in 1470. She was Princess for only a year, when her Prince was killed in the Battle of Tewkesbury.

The third, Catherine of Aragon, married fifteen-year-old Arthur, the son of Henry VII, in 1501. Arthur died of the plague shortly after, and Catherine married his younger brother who later became King Henry VIII.

It took more than two hundred years to produce another Princess of Wales, Caroline of Ansbach, known as the "fat spouse" of Prince George, and "a she-devil." Her son Frederick, whom she openly detested and denounced, was the one who almost married Diana's ancestor, Lady Diana Spencer. Instead, his parents arranged a marriage with the unattractive and graceless Augusta of Saxe-Gotha.

The sixth Princess of Wales, Caroline of Brunswick-Wolfenbüttel, was so homely that the Prince of Wales, who first saw her only the night before their wedding, said to his friend, "Harris, I am not well, pray get me a glass of brandy."

The loveliest and most endearing Princess of Wales had been Alexandra of Denmark. Queen Victoria's son Albert Edward ("Bertie") had a scandalous history of many lovers, both before and after he married her in 1863. But Alexandra had said she would have married him "even if he was a cowboy." She was Princess of Wales for thirty-eight years before Bertie became King Edward VII. Diana's immediate predecessor as Princess of Wales (as well as her predecessor at West Heath) was Princess May of Teck. When her husband became George V in 1910 she took the name Queen Mary. She had a straight back, a beady eye, and great dignity—she was one of those women who "closed her eyes and thought of England" when she conceived children.

In this procession of princesses, there seemed to be no pattern, and few parallels. Diana would shape her own royal place. She would have expert help and guidance from the Prince of Wales who had a lifetime of training and a sense of history. "I believe we should be one step behind [what the public may want in the way of change]," he said, "rather than two steps forward." Nothing could go wrong, she would repeat, "as long as he is by my side."

Diana also had Oliver Everett to remind her of who was who and where to go next. If someone tried to monopolize her, he was the one who stepped in and steered her elsewhere. Also invaluable were her own three ladies-in-waiting, unpaid women of distinction who have a background of management and action. All of them were at least ten years older than she and two were married.

The three were supposed to be prepared for everything. They would take the flowers and gifts from her on tour, carry spare pantyhose and safety pins, and one of them would always stand guard outside when Diana visited the loo.

Diana selected them herself from a short list provided by the Palace. She wanted women who would be neither intrusive nor officious. And: "Did you notice," observed a Royal watcher, "that she never picks anybody on her staff who is *too* pretty?"

Anne Beckwith-Smith, who had studied history and art in Florence and Paris, helped organize exhibitions for the Arts Council in London and worked for Sotheby's in its English Picture Department. She was the only one scheduled for full-time work with the Princess. Helping to organize the Princess's public engagements were Mrs. Lavinia Baring, the thirty-year-old daughter of Sir Mark and Lady Baring who had worked at the Winston Churchill Memorial Trust; and Mrs. Hazel West, thirty-six, married to the Assistant Comptroller of the Lord Chamberlain's office. Educated in London and Paris, she had studied music and cooking.

Diana did not get much explicit guidance from the Queen. One of the most-repeated myths was that Diana dropped in on Her Majesty whenever she had a problem. She never dropped in. Basically, she was still somewhat afraid of her mother-in-law. If she smiled or giggled at a time when she shouldn't, a single withering queenly look would wipe away all mirth. In private, however, Diana showed her independent spirit at a royal dinner at Windsor when she impulsively went over to Charles, sat on his lap, and kissed him in the full presence of the family.

As they all would soon discover, she was a determined young woman. When she felt her police shadow, Paul Officer, was being overprotective—ordering her about as if she were his daughter—she had him transferred. Her new private detective was younger, and had a sense of humor. In the same way, she soon persuaded her husband to part company with some of his long-time staff—as well as some old friends. His valet left, saying privately, "You can't really blame her. She didn't want people around them who knew all about his other girlfriends. She wanted a fresh beginning."

The cast of characters in their lives was changing. His most important pre-marriage friendships were with Lord and Lady Tryon and Andrew and Camilla Parker-Bowles.

In his pre-marriage days, Prince Charles played his weekly polo near Windsor, came early and stayed late to "chat with the boys," and have a drink. "Not anymore," said one of his polo-playing friends. "Now it's in and out. He comes just before the game and leaves directly afterwards. Of course, we can understand it. He's newly married. Beyond that, we know she's not crazy about polo. It's a difficult game to get excited about if you're not actually playing, and I can see how it's boring to watch. But he's excited about it. She can get him to stop a lot of things, and she has—but I don't think she'll ever make him quit polo."

"I was with Prince Charles at a polo game," said a friend of his. "He asked me if I thought he was too thin, and I said, 'No, Your Highness, I don't think you're too thin.'

"Well, my wife thinks so,' he remarked."

Her insistence made him stop steeplechasing. There would be no more jumping over hurdles. It was too frightening for her. He had barely escaped serious injury several times.

In any discussion of steeplechasing, his eyes still get a glint. "If people could just understand the real thrill, the challenge of steeplechasing. It's part of the great British way of life, and none of the other sports I've done bears any comparison."

The difficulty was that, trim as he was, he would still need to lose more weight for ideal sustained riding. The constant danger was that one slight misjudgment and he'd be dumped on the grass, maybe under a horse's hoof. Since his international diary of scheduled events and tours was committed six months in advance, any serious injury would throw off an entire royal schedule.

A new difficulty was his worried wife. And so he not only announced that he was quitting steeplechasing, but proved it by selling his jumping horse, Good Prospect.

But the Prince now had a real reason to give way to his wife: She was pregnant.

17

She was already pregnant when they were touring Wales. Since the wedding, she had lost fourteen more pounds and there were many who felt she might have developed anorexia, especially since she now seemed to have little appetite. But she had boundless curiosity about babies, which explained many of her questions when they visited Llwynypia Hospital in the Rhondda Valley. She lingered at the bedside of new mothers and asked details about childbirth, spent an inordinate amount of time examining the new babies, and asked how much they cried and how much they ate. When they asked her when she planned to have a child, she just giggled. Prince Charles voiced his opinion that fathers should be allowed to be with their wives when the baby was born. After he had told this to a brand new mother, Mrs. Shirley Bowen, he turned to listening reporters and added, "I expect I'll get lots of letters about that."

Only a mile from Highgrove, the tiny town of Tetbury, a seventeenth-century market town (pop. 5000) whose property values had skyrocketed, went into high gear when the impending royal birth was confirmed.

The White Hart had only a dozen rooms. "I could have filled fifty at times since the Princess came," said the owner.

The villagers contributed money to replace the broken front gate at Highgrove with a handcrafted one of wrought iron as their wedding gift to the young couple. The gift was strictly local. Maris Cole, a primary school teacher, crafted it with her forty-one-year-old husband, Hector, who taught ironworking at a local secondary school.

After worrying about ornate designs, they decided that "something fairly simple would be okay."

Baker Michael Francis was ready to offer Diana his specialty of lardycake, a yeast bread laced with various fruits, raisins, nuts, and sugar. Grocer Colin Gray had stocked up on Patum Pepperium, "the gentleman's relish." Over at the Tack Shop, Sue Biggin already had a best seller in her three-dollar replica of Princess Diana's engagement ring.

Highgrove had a security problem. Two narrow public footpaths cut close to the main house, a perfect grazing ground for photographers and sightseers. The Prince petitioned that the paths be moved farther away. The house was also about a hundred yards from a main road. For privacy they installed wattle fences and big trees; for security, they had a police post in the farm buildings with television cameras scanning the area. The whole area was soon tagged the Royal Triangle because Princess Anne and her husband and Prince and Princess Michael of Kent all lived within a few miles of each other. Charles and Diana saw little of them. They were all "horsey" and Diana wasn't.

The newlyweds had their own special concept for a garden. They wanted it to be both fragrant and colorful. They found a sympathetic expert in an American, Lanning Roper (Harvard, Class of 1933). Roper had come to Britain with the American Navy in World War II, liked it so much that he stayed. Among other projects, he had advised the British National Trust about the gardens at Chartwell, the home of Winston Churchill. "Luckily," Roper commented, "the soil at Highgrove is alkaline and conducive to roses, lilacs, and flowering shrubs." Roper planned to retain the magnolia and wisteria at the rear of the house, as well as a large cedar tree.

Interior decorator Dudley Poplak, whom Charles and Diana had hired earlier, admitted that it was Diana's taste that primarily dictated the Highgrove style. When they first took it over, it looked like an attic of memorabilia brought from the basement of Buckingham Palace. There were all kinds of souvenirs of the Prince's various world tours, including a crocodile-covered coffee table. Diana, more than anyone, helped convert Highgrove into a comfortable home.

Poplak, also not a native Briton (he was from South Africa), delighted in the carved Irish marble fireplaces, the handsome moldings, and the impressive paneled doors. His largest problem was

241

knocking down walls to create a steel-walled inner room to protect the family from any terrorist attack. Windows also had to be refitted with bullet-proof glass.

Many of the wedding gifts fit in well with the couple's need to furnish the empty nine-bedroom house. A German firm offered a complete kitchen. Territorial soldiers presented them with an outdoor heated swimming pool. And, when Ray Cadman, director of the C. & C. Bedding Company in nearby Lye, heard that this royal couple did not believe in separate bedrooms, he offered them a king-sized bed, which was promptly accepted, with an added polite request for a brochure. The bed, said Cadman, was firm but not orthopedic.

During her engagement period, the *Sunday Times* observed that Diana had "defeated Fleet Street on her own terms." Fleet Street was back again with multiplied strength now. The public didn't simply want to know more about this young royal couple—they wanted to know *everything.*

The long-awaited major news was a simple announcement that seemed to stir the world. Cinderella was having a baby!

The Buckingham Palace statement issued on November 5th, 1981, was simple and straightforward. The royal baby was expected in June. The health of the Princess was excellent, it added, and "the baby will be second in line to the throne." There also seemed to be a special note of pleasure in the sentence, "The Queen was informed personally by the Prince and Princess."

"It's wonderful news," said a London pensioner, part of the crowd outside Buckingham Palace, waiting to cheer her. "They certainly didn't waste any time, did they?"

Princess Elizabeth gave birth to Charles exactly a year after her marriage. The Waleses' baby was expected to arrive eleven months after their marriage.

What was so extraordinary was the public reaction. You couldn't walk into a pub or a manor house without overhearing some comment on babies in general, and this royal baby in particular. Everybody seemed to have a piece of advice, a memory, a good wish, an excuse for another drink to make a toast.

Noted author and journalist Allen Andrews explained it this way: "The Royal Family is part of our family because we've lived with them all our lives. We've seen the Queen born, married, and become

Queen. Our relationship is deep, long and intimate. Their baby is our baby."

British bookmakers promptly offered 10-11 odds for a boy, evens on a girl, and 50-1 for twins.

Some medical researchers quickly volunteered that diet can help determine the baby's sex. To get a boy, they said, the diet should contain lots of salt, but no eggs, milk, pastry, or gassy mineral water. For a girl, plenty of eggs and meat—but without salt. They based this theory on the fact that the "Y" spermatozoa needed for chromosomes to produce boys did well in rich potassium solutions, whereas the "X" spermatozoa needed for girls did best on calcium and magnesium.

Analyzing the date of the baby's expected arrival, the press pinpointed its conception during the honeymoon at Balmoral. Step-grandmother Barbara Cartland exulted in the fact that it was a honeymoon baby. "The first baby should be conceived in the full bloom of romance," she said. "This baby will be a victory over the horrid modern practice of putting off a family until one or both partners' careers are established. It is a great mistake to delay a first child. It is interfering with nature and nature always knows best."

Then she added, "I hope it will be a son because it's what every English man and woman wants. In America, they seem to prefer girls."

Miss Cartland had a special recipe to help Diana enjoy a healthy pregnancy: plenty of vitamin E, which prevents miscarriage; bone meal, which stops tooth decay; vitamin B6 which stops morning sickness. Others had home remedies for morning sickness: a cup of tea, dry biscuits, and a bag of barley sugar sweets to suck on.

A member of Parliament anxiously announced a proposed change in the Law of Succession so that the eldest child of this royal couple would inherit the throne—no matter what its sex. Said Labor MP Michael English, "It is now a matter of some urgency."

On a calmer note, the Queen's own gynecologist-surgeon, Sir George Pinker, said he foresaw no problems, and that the family still had not yet decided whether the baby should be born at Buckingham Palace or in a hospital. St. Mary's Hospital was a ten-minute ride from the Palace. Diana told friends that she would like her children to be born as naturally as possible. The Prince again said he wanted to be there when it happened.

"Of course dad should be there to share the wonderful moment of his baby's birth," said Mrs. Catherine Moffat of Tayport, Fife. "After all, he enjoyed everything that led up to it, didn't he?" Mrs. Dawn Parsons of Tetbury, also expecting her child in June, said, "I feel ever so excited. I'm praying that we have our babies on the same day."

The computers were also kept busy. After researching royal ancestry, genealogists Lord Teviot and Hugh Peskett announced that the baby would be 58.8 percent British, the most British monarch since Queen Anne—and 4.69 percent American. David Williamson, senior editor of *Burke's Peerage*, added this footnote: "Both Princess Diana's grandfather and great-grandfather were twins. They were both on her mother's side of the family. And twins keep popping up in families with a history of them."

It was revealed that Princess Diana was pressuring the workmen to "hurry up" with the redecoration of the nursery at Highgrove. She had chosen the colors of gold and blue. The nursery was on the floor above their own bedroom, with a room for a nanny.

Something else that came out in the Royal wash was an unexpected visit to London the Princess had made from Balmoral, presumably to see all her wedding gifts. It was now admitted that she had come in primarily for a pregnancy test. Somebody else recalled that as early as last July, the subject was obviously on the Prince's mind because he stopped after a polo match to examine a baby in a pram and told the mother, "I can't wait to have babies myself."

Earl Spencer was properly partial: "It will be a very lucky baby to have Diana for a mother. She adores children and they adore her." Nobody predicted whether the Princess would collect the 25 pounds sterling the State granted to all new mothers.

The birth announcement only intensified the interest of frenetic photographers hiding in the bushes at Highgrove with telephoto lenses. One of the newspaper pictures showed the Princess with her arms around her husband's neck. Whenever Diana went to Tetbury, a posse of photographers trailed after her, clicking away. Sympathizers complained that the press was forcing Diana to stay indoors. In an editorial headline, "The Captive Princess," the *Times* of London declared, "It would be nice to think we are grown-up enough not to imprison a princess in a palace."

The Queen once again bent a tradition. She did something she had done only once before. When Charles first started school, she had called in the editors of the national press, radio, and television, and asked that they let this little boy alone at school, let him live as normal a life as possible. Now again she invited the editors to Buckingham Palace appealing to them to let Princess Diana have some privacy. As press secretary Michael Shea put it, she couldn't even go out and buy some candy without creating national headlines.

Brooding about this, one of the editors suggested that if the Princess really wanted some candy, she could always send a servant for it.

Her Majesty bristled. "That is the most pompous thing I've ever heard."

"The ridicule of that remark got all over Fleet Street," recalled another editor. "The Queen is very good at making an important statement in a light-handed way. That editor couldn't live it down. He was soon in drink, and soon out of a job."

The Queen was trying to quell a hurricane. Public interest in the Princess was so overwhelming that even the most decent editors found themselves bending to the force of it. They had to keep up with the screaming competition to survive. What most of them did do was to order photographers away from Highgrove—for a while. But if the Princess ventured anywhere into a public place, she was considered fair game, and the reportage was intense.

One of the perks the newlyweds were to have was an apartment in Kensington Palace, a seventeenth-century residence in one of London's most beautiful and centrally located parks (Prime Minister Disraeli described Kensington Gardens with its Serpentine Lake as London's "sublime sylvan solitude")—and only skipping distance for Diana from the Kensington High Street shopping area. Designed by Sir Christopher Wren, the palace is a harmonious, spacious spread of apartments in mellow red brick with white trim. Each apartment has its own graveled courtyard.

Once the home of William III, it was converted by George III into royal apartments. Victoria was born and made Queen here.

Of the twenty families now living at Kensington Palace, most are key Court officials and Royals, including Prince and Princess Michael of Kent and the Duke and Duchess of Gloucester. Princess Margaret occupies the north side ("the doll's house") and Princess Alexandra has an apartment "large enough for an overnight." Diana's sister Jane lives down the road in a house called "The Old Barracks."

The apartment selected for Charles and Diana featured three reception rooms, a dining room, a master bedroom suite, a nursery, and rooms for servants—on several floors.

Diana's dressing room at Kensington Palace has pastel green walls. It's a fresh, airy room, about 25 feet by 15 feet, featuring a white kidney-shaped dressing table, two high-backed chairs, a small wardrobe, an armchair, and landscape prints on the wall.

London is about a hundred miles from Highgrove. The royal couple now spent part of their time at their apartment in Kensington Palace because Tetbury had suddenly become a tourist center. At Highgrove, when Prince Charles went away on appointments, Diana often found herself alone except for staff people, and lacking companionship. But at Kensington Palace, she could see much of her sister Jane. The two always had been close, and they were now closer because they shared much more—motherhood.

Is it difficult to think of an apartment in a palace as "cozy"? Of course, it was more than an apartment. It had staff offices on the ground floor, staff bedrooms in the dormered attic. When you entered the foyer, you found antique furniture, fresh flowers, pastel green walls, pink carpeting, and a guest book whose first entry read, "Spencer (daddy)."

In renovating three floors for the Prince and Princess of Wales, decorator Dudley Poplak emphasized the comfortable rather than the chic, as he did at Highgrove. He left intact the distinctive Georgian staircase but put in a new marbled, mirrored bathroom, as well as a sitting room for the Princess and a second-floor study for the Prince. The good-sized study overlooks a quiet courtyard, the walls featuring pictures of his mother, grandmother, and Lord Mountbatten. On the tables are pictures of his wedding, on his desk a friendly litter of papers. The fireplace is flanked by two comfortable chairs.

Other rooms include two guest bedrooms, several bathrooms, a breakfast room alongside a music room, a nursery suite on the floor above their bedroom, a barbecue pit on the roof, and, in the nearby yard, a helicopter pad.

Harold Brooks-Baker, formerly of *Debrett's Peerage*, blamed the Russian Revolution partly on the fact that Nicholas II and Czarina Alexandra shared the same bedroom. "For hundreds, perhaps thousands of years," explained Brooks-Baker, "the really great families have had separate sleeping quarters for husbands and wives, also concubines and lovers. This is true for all aristocratic houses in the world.'' When a couple did share a bedroom for the night, they still hurried back to their original rooms before the servants came in because ''servants are sticklers for propriety.''

Diana not only had Jane for companionship at Kensington Palace, but also her good friend Sarah Armstrong-Jones. Though Sarah was three years younger, the two had much in common. Both went through the trauma of their parents' divorce, both had early ambitions to be ballet dancers, and neither was an academic (Sarah also had only a single O level).

Theoretically, Lady Sarah was tenth in line of royal succession, the most senior female Royal of her generation, but actually she was not a Royal at all. As her mother, Princess Margaret, said of both her children, ''They merely happen to have an aunt who is a Queen.'' Diana knew Sarah as a friend who liked to lounge in jeans, loved pizza and John Travolta, and enjoyed being known as a ''queenie-bopper.''

They often shopped together. Like Diana, she had her own Mini car. They would frequently scoot away and have lunch or go shopping. Sarah and Diana were much alike: They had the same zip and self-confidence and similar tastes. Since she was younger, Sarah did not intimidate Diana, as her sisters sometimes did—especially Sarah Spencer, who was a rebel and innovator just as Diana was.

In a strange way, despite the close-watching press, Diana found it easier to lose herself in London than in the isolation of Highgrove. Wearing a scarf over her head, a pair of oversize sunglasses, some unassuming clothes, she managed to sneak away for some off-the-rack shopping at Harvey Nichols, lunch with a former roommate at a small Beauchamp Place restaurant, spend an evening visiting the home of old friends, and even go to the ballet. Buckingham Palace is only a short drive from Kensington Palace and Diana frequently drove over to do her twenty laps in the Palace pool. Sometimes she was spotted, chased, and photographed, but she now had the strong buffer of Palace protection.

If the public couldn't see the live Diana, they could now see her likeness at Madame Tussaud's Wax Museum. ''It's quite good,'' said twelve-year-old Joanna Willey of London. ''But her hair is not quite right and she looks better from the side.'' The wax figure of Diana would later be updated because ''her smile is wider, her hair longer, and she has lost weight." A critic commented: "She looks terrible." The headline read: DI-ABOLICAL!

The question of her royal title was debated, the sticklers sticking with "Her Royal Highness." But even the former editor of *Debrett's*, Patrick Montague-Smith, who concentrated on such things, commented, "Everything has got more informal. I cannot see any objection to calling the new Princess of Wales 'Princess Diana.'"

After marriage, her proper title was "Her Royal Highness, the Princess of Wales," or "Diana, Princess of Wales," but she also could properly be called "Princess Charles." She would *not*, however, be officially called "Princess Diana."

Talking about the propriety of titles, Barbara Cartland revealed, "My son-in-law [Earl Spencer], who is now his father-in-law, always refers to him—when he talks to us about him—as Prince Charles."

Diana herself told a friend, "I hate all this heel-clicking and bowing and not being called plain Diana anymore."

Some traditions were ancient and unbreakable, as when a lady is presented to the Queen: Walking forward to within a few feet of Her Majesty, she bows as low as possible. The Queen then presents her hand to be kissed. The lady lifts the Queen's hand gracefully, then kisses the back of her own hand—never that of the Queen. To retire, she bows again and walks backward, keeping her face always toward the Queen until the exit door is reached.

One of the questions intermittently asked in Britain is: "What are Princesses of Wales supposed to be?"

A cynic suggests, "Brood mares."

But beyond producing royal heirs, they must be very visible. The public wants to see them, admire them, examine them, ooh and aah at them.

Diana made herself dramatically visible as she traveled in the same glass coach as for the wedding to the State Opening of Parliament by the Queen. It was the first time in more than seventy years that a Princess of Wales had attended the event.

This occasion is supposedly the Queen's day. It became immediately obvious, however, that all eyes were on the Princess, especially when she and Prince Charles and their retinue of pages entered the House of Lords to sit on one side of the Queen and Prince Philip while Princess Anne and her group sat on the other.

Diana wore a flowing white chiffon dress, with a satin bodice, rounded off with puffed sleeves stretching to the elbow. The whole outfit was, of course, topped off with a royal tiara. She was described as "a glamorous concoction almost beyond description, shimmering from head to toe." "She absolutely lit up the old place," said a member of Parliament.

She wore a pearl choker above a discreetly plunging neckline, and observers noted the Prince leaned over to her with occasional words of reassurance. The ceremony of pageantry was much rehearsed, but the seventy-four-year-old Lord Chancellor who came to collect the Queen's speech after its delivery found it difficult to rise from his knees. The Princess looked anguished for him, and Prince Philip was about to help when the Lord Chancellor, in a supreme effort, rose and gracefully backed away. Then the Queen, wearing the Imperial State Crown with the Black Prince's ruby glinting in the center, rose to leave. In the words of the official order, the Crown, Cap of Maintenance, and Sword of State proceeded under escort to the Royal Entrance. Her Majesty's judges proceeded through the Royal Gallery and the Gentlemen at Arms, and having handed in their axes, exited followed by the Yeomen of the Guard.

For Prince Charles it was old hat; for Princess Diana it was sheer magic.

In the carriage, Diana had sat next to Princess Anne. There was considerable press talk of daggers between them. It was probably true that Princess Anne felt a natural hurt at being so publicly shunted aside by this younger and far more beautiful woman who had so many of the natural graces that she did not.

Before Diana came along, Anne and her brother had much in common, including their love of horses and their wit. Diana's appearance not only changed this good relationship, but robbed Anne of any rightful limelight. And her pique may have been heightened because her father, Prince Philip, who is closest to Anne, had shown such a public liking for Diana. It was certainly true that Princess Diana and Princess Anne seldom saw each other. But the real reason was simply that the two women had little in common. Anne concentrated on horses and Diana preferred babies. Moreover, Charles and his brother-in-law, Mark, had even less in common.

Anne's style is light, self-mocking. Even her worst critics have never called her "pompous." She's a strong young woman, lithe and fit and well-balanced, qualities that have helped make her a champion international rider, the only Royal to have represented Britain in the Olympics. Her home and farm in the Cotswolds is hardly stately, but it overlooks a spectacular valley and lake. It's a casual country house with large dogs and horses and books and scattered toys.

Years before, when a photographer insisted on clicking away, Princess Anne spit out four-letter obscenities precisely timed to the clicks of his motorized camera. On a trip to Kenya with Charles back in 1971, he had amused reporters with accounts of how "the camels belch and burp and make a frightful noise," but she absolutely refused to talk to them or pose for them. On their trip together to Washington, she made similarly caustic comments on the quantity of cameras. Princess Anne had a reputation for tantrums. "When I appear in public," she said, "people expect me to neigh, grind my teeth, paw the ground, and swish my tail—none of which is easy."

There are those who have said that Nature made a switch with Charles and Anne, that he should have had more of her toughness and aggressiveness. Even when he was four and she was two, she was the one who waved at the crowds while he huddled in his seat. She later said that she would have liked to have been a truck driver in a different time "because I think you could run your own life that way." And how did she feel about being passed over in the royal succession? She said it varied between irritation and being "very grateful."

Reporters who said she was her father's daughter were right. She had his trigger temper, his aggressive opinions, and the same sharp quality of mind. One reporter tagged her "the wild one," but her aunt, Princess Margaret, defended her. "Anne's much more positive than I was, so I think she'll be all right. She's much tougher, too."

She absorbed herself in horses, like her mother and grand-mother—with whom she was not close. She became an expert show jumper. In 1973, she married the handsome Lieutenant Mark Phillips of the Queen's Dragoon Guards, and the Queen bought them a farm and home in Gatcombe Park in Gloucestershire.

Royal insiders intimated that even Her Majesty was beginning to resent the growing and overwhelming publicity for Diana. Even back at Balmoral, at the annual Braemar Highland Games, there was "decent enough applause" when the Queen came out of her car, but the "cheers became deafening" when Diana stepped out. Those closer to the Queen insisted that Her Majesty was delighted by the shift in press focus, since it took some of the pressure off her, and provided her with a little more quiet and privacy.

There was little question that the new Princess of Wales loved her role. She felt like an actress on stage, physically absorbing the waves of love from the audience after a fine performance. And there was little question that the Princess's performance *was* absolutely fine, that "she had not put a foot wrong," that she was a winner.

Her duties, however curtailed now that she was pregnant, were never-ending. A concert at Blenheim Palace, then dinner with the Duke and Duchess of Marlborough. (One of the floating and groundless rumors was that Diana and Charles would soon move into Marlborough House in London.) There was an annual Remembrance Day for the dead of two world wars at Royal Albert Hall. But even in the midst of that solemnity, the military bands played a tribute of light music for the expectant mother, with somebody singing the song "Congratulations."

At a lunch for the couple at the Guildhall in London, the Lord Mayor told the 600 prominent guests the great news about the baby. People stood up and cheered, yelling, "Jolly good show!" and "Bravo, Sir!"

The bride blushed. She must have been amused by the proliferation of ostrich feathers among the ladies—copying what she had worn in Wales. (The Prince's coat of arms features three ostrich feathers.)

The Prince made a short speech about the success of the recent tour in Wales—"entirely due to the effect my dear wife had on everybody." But when he tried to help his "dear wife" with her coat after lunch, she took a swift, swerving step to her right and said, "No, thank you," indicating that she did not yet want to be fussed over.

In York they rode in an open carriage and then did a walkabout and were showered with flowers, soft toys, and baby clothes. Seven thousand children cheered them on a visit to the City Stadium and Diana watched her husband acting like a schoolboy himself, riding the different trains at the National Railway Museum. The Prince then piloted a helicopter to take them to Chesterfield to open a shopping precinct. More toys, more flowers, more baby clothes awaited them.

They planted some flowering cherry trees in Hyde Park. The

Princess planted two to commemorate the royal wedding, and one in honor of her future baby. The Prince planted three more, in a special area, in honor of his great-uncle, Lord Mountbatten. Diana giggled as Prince Charles encircled her with his arms to help her lift the silver spade. Then when six-year-old Stephen Roberts presented her with a bouquet, she asked, "Have you taken the day off from school?" And when he nodded, she added, "How naughty," and smiled.

Some 150 organizations had asked the Princess to be their patron, and she chose five: the Malcolm Sargent Cancer Fund for Children, the Pre-School Playgroups Association, the Royal School for the Blind, a community center in the East End of London called the Albany, and the Welsh National Opera.

When it was time to switch on the Christmas lights on Regent Street she was ready to go solo in public. She stepped onto a Regent Street balcony in a midnight-blue velvet suit trimmed with silver piping and made a short speech expressing her delight.

She was so pleased and proud to have an infant within her that she was soon wearing tentlike maternity clothes—long before it was necessary.

On doctor's advice, she missed a trip with the Prince to Bristol, a concert in aid of the Multiple Sclerosis Society, and she canceled a trip to Devon, in the Duchy of Cornwall. To his disappointed tenants, the Prince said, "You all have wives, you know what it is like." A friend remarked, "Poor Diana. She doesn't just suffer from morning sickness—it's an all-day job with her." Even Diana admitted publicly, "Some days I feel terrible."

On a walkabout in Chesterfield, she had told bakery worker Mrs. Dorothy McLeish, "No one told me I would feel like I did." Mrs. McLeish, the mother of three, assured Diana she would "feel worse before it's all over." To her anxiously inquiring lady-in-waiting, however, Diana insisted, "I feel fine."

One day she helicoptered to Althorp to lunch with her father and stepmother. Before her marriage, her father had been quoted in the press as saying, "If only my little girl wasn't marrying Prince Charles . . . like everyone else, I'll only see her on the telly now . . .

"But honestly, what do I get out of it?" Earl Spencer asked, referring to the marriage. "You'll say the glory, but is glory the word? You make the point that the average family wouldn't know what hit 'em if their daughter married the future King, and I can see that. But some of my family go back to the Saxons, so that sort of thing is not a bit new to me and I can't feel it like maybe you would. I'm happy for my girl because she's got the man she adores."

When Diana lunched with them, she found things going well. In this royal wedding year, paying visitors to Althorp had doubled (about 400 visitors a day) and rooms were still available for "appropriate" functions. Her stepmother still greeted guests at the door, enjoyed a drink with them sometimes, and occasionally ate with them as part of her "first-class" service. She also had helped launch the British Tourist Board's guide to stately homes. The top seller at the Althorp gift shop was a nickel silver wedding medallion for $3.50. The wine shop was booming, with her father in charge. Bottles bear the Althorp crest and are marked, "Selected by Earl Spencer." Ordinary white and red table wines were priced at $5 a bottle, sherries at $7, and others considerably more.

Some of the press had accused of Spencers of "cashing in" on the marriage, and even charging photographers for the privilege of taking pictures on the estate. A recent item in the press concerned the Spencer gamekeeper, who had reportedly threatened a trespassing family with an axe handle. "We are being vilified by lies," said Countess Spencer. Then she added, "I have never been quite so unhappy in my life."

More serious concern, however, was expressed about the sale of art treasures from the great Althorp collection. Lord Spencer had handed over to the government two Van Dyck portraits in lieu of tax payments, and had sold several other items, including some ancestral silver. A leading silver authority, Arthur Grimwade, described the Althorp collection "as one of the greatest surviving groups of English ancestral silver."

If his speech was still slurred, Earl Spencer's mind was perfectly sound. Diana and her father had their usual delightful time together, chattering about a dozen things. Raine knew well enough when to listen. In front of guests, her husband could tell her as he once had, "Don't interrupt us when we're talking, it's rude. Run away and do your hair." When she replied archly that she had done her hair, he replied, "Then go and do your toes."

After her marriage, Diana remained close to her brother, Charles. He was seventeen, served as co-editor of the fortnightly *Eton Chronicle*, and had starred in the school production of *Henry IV*.

"He's a very sensible young man with a proper regard for his family's history," said his father. "He goes up to Oxford to read history in October, when he finishes at Eton. He got three A levels, grade one, which is more than I can say. He has no specific ambitions as yet."

There was a Rolls-Royce waiting after lunch to take Princess Diana to nearby Northampton to open the new post office. If there were a private time of special pride, perhaps this was it. Local girl makes good.

At the post office, she sent a telegram of congratulations to the Queen and Prince Philip on their thirty-fourth wedding anniversary. She also saw her old postman, Frank Barringer, who had delivered mail to Althorp for eighteen years, and made a short speech to a rapturous crowd.

She loved all of it. Her husband was concerned about her doing too many things, and the press speculated that she might be finding the goldfish-bowl life too dull, but at this point they were both wrong. She found it fun. She was touched when a woman gave her a hand-knitted baby jacket. "How old does the baby have to be before it can wear it?" Diana asked quietly. Or even a bar of baby soap. "That will be very useful," she said appreciatively.

Diana was well enough to be with the Prince at Sandringham on his thirty-third birthday on November 14th. When he went pheasant shooting, she joined him, listening to music on her Sony Walkman. Then they celebrated with a small dinner party.

18

Butler Alan Fisher got another emergency call from his friend, Countess Spencer. The Princess of Wales was coming for the weekend and she and her husband had unchangeable plans to be elsewhere for two days. Could Alan please come and care for her stepdaughter at Althorp while they were away?

In the course of their two days together, Fisher was less than mildly impressed with the young Princess—until she turned on the charm. "She could look at you with those blue eyes of hers and you just melted. She had a way, too, of sometimes taking your one hand in her two hands, in a remarkable intimate gesture that absolutely captured you."

During dinner once, the Princess asked him if he liked working in the country.

No, he replied, he did not.

"But you're here?" she said.

"Only because the Countess is my friend."

"Yes," she said appreciatively, "I know that."

Another friend said of the Countess: "Her little-girl charm is often called into service to camouflage a sharp mind and determination."

She was accused of making Althorp look "gaudy as a summer pudding."

Fisher soon got still another emergency call from Raine. This time, "the Prince has proposed himself and Diana for this weekend. The awkward thing is that we're also having the party for tenants this weekend to give them pieces of the wedding cake. Our young new butler can never cope with it all. Alan Darling, please help me."

Again, Alan Darling did.

Fisher suggested that Earl Spencer take much of Althorp's private treasure trove for use on the occasion of his daughter and son-in-law's visit. Spencer was aghast. Everything was so priceless. "If you can't use it now, when will you ever use it?" asked Fisher. "What are you saving it for?" Raine agreed. "Do what you want, Alan."

"I like to rise to a challenge like that," said Fisher, smiling.

Fisher used all of Althorp's elegant trappings, plus several dining rooms. Prince Charles had lived with such splendor all of his life. But Princess Diana, who was bred in this house, had never seen all these hidden treasures and kept turning over plates to see where they came from.

A Fisher touch was the use of the milkmaid's cottage, a couple of miles from the main house. He had the deserted place furnished and decorated as a surprise private picnic place for the Prince and his Princess. They were charmed.

On their way back to the main house, Prince Charles said to the Princess, "Wouldn't it be fun if we stole Alan away from Raine." Diana repeated this to Fisher as he helped her take off her boots. They offered him the butler's job at Highgrove. "With all due respect, Sir, I could never work in the country, for anyone." They then offered him the same job at Kensington Palace, not knowing that he had been interviewed twice for that job, and turned down. He became more than a butler—he became a confidant, a friend.

Charles was not a watcher, he was a doer. When he conceived a project, he wanted to see it happen. It explained why he didn't like to watch races—as his mother and grandmother did. He wanted to ride the horses himself. One of the books in his study, within easy reach, was entitled Adventures in High Endeavor.

He once had said, "I tend to lead a sort of idiotic existence . . . trying to get involved in too many things and dashing about. And this is going to be my problem, trying to sort of control myself, and, you know, work out something so that we can have a proper family life. It isn't easy, there's so much to be done, you know."

Those who saw him now, intimately, were amazed at how relaxed he was. The nervous little tic on his cheekbone seemed to have disappeared and he no longer kept turning his signet ring. Instead of a prematurely middle-aged man wearing subdued clothes, he now seemed more lively, more spruced-up, more casual. It was hardly likely now that he would "crumble and cry" in a confrontation with his father, as he once did. He was as busy as he always was, but obviously much happier.

"God willing, the 63rd Sovereign of all England . . ." He was fully conscious of that, just as he was fully conscious that he must never act on his feelings, must always express his views with caution, regard passionate convictions as undesirable, never show any disagreement with any other religion, interminably try to be all things to all men because "the nominal ruler of all fails in his function the instant he ceases to be a servant of all."

King George V kept a great distance from his people. George VI would have been happier as a country squire busy with his stamp collection, farms, horses. Edward VIII as Prince of Wales did have the caring and the common touch, but not the sense of responsibility. If somebody told Prince Charles that he could not be King, that they were abandoning the monarchy, he would likely feel it was a mistake, but he would probably continue to do what he has been doing. That's because he does care, he does have concern for the people and the world, and peace.

As patron of 147 societies, honorary colonel-in-chief of ten regiments, officer in three others, head of the Duchy of Cornwall, he must make himself endlessly available to his callers and conferences. In the course of it, he's had to develop a style of his own to suit the complexities of what is basically an undefined job.

"He really *doesn't* put on different faces to suit different occasions," said the late Lord Harlech, who knew him well. "He's remarkably unchanging."

Part of his style involves using his sense of humor to resolve difficult situations. At a highly heated conference on industry and environment, when the mood was quite ugly, Prince Charles broke the tension by saying, "As the bishop said to the actress, 'This thing is bigger than both of us . . .'"

"Crowds in London are very odd," said Prince Charles. "They just stand and stare . . . Sometimes you have to work very hard at putting them at their ease . . . When I visit a Youth Club or something like that, after twenty minutes—when it's time to leave—people start relaxing. They discover you're reasonably human. They relax just when it's time to go, which is maddening because you go on to the next place and you've got to start all over again!"

"All right, I'm pretty square," he once said, "but I couldn't care less. I cannot understand that one year you think one way and another year you think something else. I think there are so many things in life which are eternal, and so many things which are truths."

His style was to be what he was: not in the least condescending, a superb listener, beautifully mannered, respectful toward the elderly, asking probing questions to satisfy an enormous curiosity. He has absolutely none of what friends call "his father's breezy bloody-mindedness." Instead he operates on the persistent sense of "feeling I have to justify myself, my existence." His goal in life, he has said, is "to prove myself useful."

"No one should go around feeling sorry for him," said his old Cambridge friend Hywel Jones. "Sympathetic, maybe, but not sorry. . . He's a tough cookie."

"Wales gets steamed up privately over some issues," said one of his close friends. "But he has to keep his trap shut in public because if he said what he really thinks there would be no end of a stink."

As far as unchanging minds and eternal truths are concerned, the Prince admitted that if he wasn't destined to become Defender of the Faith of the Church of England, he might wish to belong to a religion which somehow combined the moral code of Christianity with the Buddhist respect for nature. When he first heard a Buddhist abbot in a temple in Kyoto, he felt that he had "come home" at last. Elsewhere, he said, "Perhaps by going to a Hindu temple I can help in some way to bring people together."

"There is so much bigotry about, it's appalling," he said. "Fear, ignorance, whatever the reasons behind racism, it's a tragedy. Because in the end, we've all got to get along together or what's the future going to be?"

In a visit to Bristol, the Prince found the flags of Bangladesh, Pakistan, and the West Indies all flying together to greet him. Shortly before, the different groups were in violent conflict. The Prince's arrival somehow had lessened the stress and changed the scene.

He made them smile even more when he apologized for his wife's absence saying, "I am sure you all appreciate the reasons. I am told after three months things are inclined to get better." As the laughter mounted, he added, "I am quite prepared to accept full responsibility."

It also took a tough cookie to tell British businessmen they could learn a lesson in hard work from Third World people. Talking of the Asians ousted by Idi Amin from Uganda, the Prince said, "Many of them came here without a bean. And they end up as millionaires. They know what the customers want and they seek them out. They keep their shops open day and night. Surely we should look to their example."

He intended to provide more jobs for local people by improving derelict areas and building new workshops and studios for small firms, employing four or five workers. He also planned a long-term project on anaerobic digestion—the process of turning organic matter into gas.

"I'm damned determined to try hard. I want to be with the people. I can't stand cities. I am a countryman, a country bumpkin. I would have been a farmer."

To enable himself to carry out his strenuous work schedule, Prince Charles keeps fit. "I have done the Hislop exercises [imitation jockey crouches] religiously," he said, "and I'm very keen on bicycling. For instance, on Wednesday, I managed to get down to Windsor for an hour and bicycled around the park for forty minutes out of the saddle." He was also proud of the fact that he did eleven miles around the steep country lanes in fifty minutes. As for skiing, he did the Weissfluhjoch-Kublis Run in just forty minutes before finishing second in the all-day Parsenn Marathon. "You see I have this awful thing of wanting to do things well," he said.

What he felt most strongly about was conquering fear. "You see, I had lost my nerve for riding when I was about fourteen. So my ambition was to go hunting. My sister is such a good judge that she bought me the perfect horse about five years ago, and I got my confidence back. I wish people could realize what a wonderful all-round riding school hunting is."

But the Prince was not able to persuade his wife about either riding or hunting. She despised blood sports. Nothing bothered her so much as the rumor that she had shot a stag on a deer stalk with her husband. She persistently let him know of her disapproval and it gradually took root.

So increasingly obvious was the Prince's growing passion for his

Princess that there were few things he would not do to please her. Some marital advice for the Prince came from Michael Palin of the noted *Monty Python* group of satirists: "Try to remember that married life is a bit of give-and-take, so: (1) cut down on the parachute jumping and the tank driving and the state visits to Fiji and spend more time with the washing up; (2) don't just throw your Admiral of the Fleet's uniform down on the floor as soon as you come in— put it straight in the washing basket; (3) don't fight over who has which bathroom—take twenty-five each; (4) leave the horses *outside* when you have company; (5) remember, times are hard in Britain, so try to economize on servants—for instance, one man could pull off both boots.

"But whatever you do, never spare the compliments. When you come home late from a hard evening at your Ruling Classes, to find her looking tired and cross and careworn after two hours spent scrubbing your polo socks, tell her she looks like a Queen."

Prince Charles liked to give Diana small surprise gifts. One of them was a personal mascot for the front of her car, a frog she called Kermit. (When a frog hopped over his shoe as he was planting one of his many commemorative trees, Charles delighted the audience by saying, "Somebody kiss it and it will turn into a Prince.") In turn, Diana's car mascot to Charles was a replica of a polo pony, a sign of the realization that this was the one sport he would never give up.

Talking about babies in an interview over the BBC, Prince Charles called for more screening of pregnant women to try to prevent babies from being born with disabilities.

On a weekend at Highgrove, they relaxed again. The pressure of the press was not as great as it had been, possibly because of the Queen's appeal. The Princess even felt it possible to drop in more often at a sweet shop in nearby Tetbury. The proprietor was impressed with how casual and un-posh she was, how informally dressed, "just like any one of us." He even recalled exactly what she had bought: some fudge, a packet of Revels, some strawberry Chewits, and Roses chocolates.

Highgrove was looking more like a real home, the hall done in a cheerful pink, the drawing room in attractive green with fringed curtains, the wood floors fully polished, a row of young sycamores screening the road. The town rumor was that Princess Anne had seen the house, rejected it for herself, then called her brother.

Diana was not well enough to attend a diplomatic reception at Buckingham Palace, but she recovered in time to attend a Royal Opera House ballet performance of *Romeo and Juliet.* Her sisters and their husbands joined them, as did Prince Andrew and Viscount Linley, son of Princess Margaret and Lord Snowdon.

Charles and Andrew were growing more and more unlike. It wasn't simply that Charles was a dozen years older. It was more that Andrew Albert Edward Christian, the Queen's second son, showed an arrogance and occasional rudeness that Charles never did. As one of his peers put it, "He's a bit of a show-off. Put it this way—he doesn't often let you forget who he is, or that the Queen is his mother."

Prince Andrew had just turned twenty-one. He was more like his father, just as Charles was more his mother's son. By the time Andrew arrived at Gordonstoun, it had turned co-ed, and that's where he created his lively reputation. He was taller than Charles (a six-footer) and more handsome. Charles referred to him as "the one with the Robert Redford looks." He didn't drink, smoke, or get into drugs, but freely admitted, "My only vice is women."

He went more for looks than for lineage and seemed to concentrate on voluptuous models. He even brought one home to mother. The young model seemed stymied for conversation, then smiled and asked, "How much did Your Majesty make out of racing this year?" After a shattering silence, the Queen looked expressively at her son and stalked out of the room.

He loved jazz, cars, fast sports, practical jokes, sailing, hamburgers, and acting. It was Andrew who had suggested inviting Lady Diana Spencer to a New Year's Eve party at Sandringham—before she got to know Charles—and danced the Scottish dance with her where everybody exchanges kisses at midnight.

Despite the size of Andrew's harem, he freely admitted, "I don't think I've ever been in love with anyone." The girl with him at the time added, "Except yourself."

"Andrew is very, very Royal," said a sailor who had been friends of both princes. "A mummy's boy. Not like Charlie. Charlie was great." Even Andrew admitted that his brother "is far better than me."

Andrew and his first cousin, Viscount Linley, had known each other from boyhood, even though Linley was two years younger. Linley needed all the support he could get. His parents' divorce had hit him the hardest. He said flatly that his father was the greatest influence in his life.

A handsome young man with blue eyes, the Queen's only nephew was a talented and creative craftsman in furniture-making who had left the royal nest a year before, with the support of his father, Lord Snowdon, to take a two-year woodcraft course in Dorset. He has also won some awards for his photography.

Totally unlike his mother, Princess Margaret, in temperament, Linley was basically shy, sensitive, and hated the public spotlight. He also found it difficult to adjust to his mother's young new companion, Roddy Llewellyn. He was much more at ease with his father's second wife, Lucy Lindsay-Hogg. Noted photographer Lord Snowdon had remarried, but still kept close to the Royals, and especially Charles and Diana.

Diana liked both Prince Andrew and Viscount Linley. They were of her age, and she felt free and easy with them, whereas Charles felt more than a little paternal toward both of them. All of them went backstage at Covent Garden to meet the ballet company after viewing a performance together.

Shortly afterward, Diana and Charles dined at the House of Commons with Speaker George Thomas and some of the senior political leaders. Diana found herself sitting next to the leader of the Liberal Party, David Steel.

"They must have sat me beside you because I'm so young."

Steel was charmed, saw the statement as a compliment to his youthfulness, and attentively concentrated on her for the rest of the dinner. Afterward he reached for his cigar, but when he remembered that the Princess was pregnant he hastily apologized.

Diana hated smoking, but she promptly picked up the cigar, put one end into Steel's mouth, and struck a match to light it for him, saying with a grin, "Don't worry at all!"

That's high style, or, as some say, a class act.

Another class act on her part was to brave a heavy snowfall to keep a date with some 330 children at St. Mary's Church of England Primary School in Tetbury. They wanted to sing some Christmas carols to her at the morning assembly. It was an appointment a pregnant woman could easily have cancelled on a miserable day, but she seldom disappointed children, especially now.

The weather worsened in Britain before Christmas, but there was a preliminary Royal Family get-together weekend at Balmoral just before the holiday. Royal watchers suggested that this was a *Dallas* meeting, with Prince Philip in charge assessing royal performances of the previous year. Prince Philip had been among the busiest Royals: 11 overseas trips and 303 engagements.

Despite his occasional rudeness and rough remarks, Prince Philip was generally regarded as a Prince with the strength of a King. Many compared him favorably to "Albert the Admirable," the Prince Consort of Queen Victoria. Technically, Prince Philip never had been made Prince Consort—for which there seems to be no ready Palace explanation. Certainly no Royal has worked harder, or with more dedication. "I am quite used to an eighteen-hour day," he once said. This includes painting for pleasure in a simple, unsophisticated style "that shows promise." And when a wrist injury stopped him from playing polo, he became an amateur coachman—carriage races with four horses, regarded as "fairly hazardous." "It can be a little nasty when you turn over with four horses."

A clear-eyed man with great energy and controlled restlessness, Prince Philip speaks with authority and intelligence on a variety of subjects, balanced by a sense of humor. He told Kenneth Harris that every time he steps out in public, "I put my foot into it." Summing up the Prince, Harris said, "He's inquisitive and curious about people. He has a great sense of responsibility and duty. He's a thoughtful man, and I like him."

He does believe, however, in exercising his authority. At any Royal Family dinner, the men wear evening clothes, including a special jacket called the Windsor jacket—beautifully elegant, royal blue, with special buttons. All the royal males wear this jacket—but only if and when they get approval from Prince Philip. After he married Princess Margaret, Antony Armstrong-Jones had to sit at such dinners in an ordinary jacket for several years. Prince Philip finally told him, "Oh well, I suppose you better go get a Windsor jacket."

While the Queen did not believe in family confrontations, her husband had no such qualms. And when the Prince criticized, everyone listened attentively. Away from the throne, he was the master of his family. Nobody questioned this, least of all the Queen.

The Queen was characteristically punctual, but there was one time she was inexplicably late. Prince Philip was waiting for her in a Land Rover, anxious to get to a polo match in which he was playing. Despite the fact that somebody else was in the car, Prince Philip was openly angry with her when she arrived. He then drove at such speed that the Queen, in front with him, made nervous clucking noises at intervals. The Prince then said if she made any more such noises, he would stop the vehicle and let her get out and walk. She stopped the noises.

When they arrived at their destination, the Prince hurried off without waiting for her. The other passenger, a Royal intimate, asked the Queen, "Why did you let him talk to you like that? After all, you're the Queen."

She looked at him, then said quietly, "Because I knew that he would have stopped the car and I would have had to get out and walk."

Nevertheless, to the Queen, Prince Philip is a breath of fresh air—her real contact with the outside world. When he tells her what he thinks, what he's heard, what he knows, she listens. She also listens to others before making decisions, and even the Prince would think twice before ever contradicting the advice of Her Majesty's private secretary. But she knows his great sense of responsibility and duty, and his great concern for her. At any function, the Prince always has an eye out for his wife. If he ever sees her tire, he pulls her aside somewhere for a short rest. This may be a marriage of separate bedrooms, but it's a good working partnership.

The Prince had the role of Chairman of the Board that December weekend, getting the family business out of the way before the holidays, because the royal Christmas is always a time of fun and games—five days of it.

Weeks before, the Royals and their staff had scoured the stores and catalogues for their Christmas presents. For many years, the Queen did her shopping at Harrods, having the store to herself an hour before it opened. Now, because of security, she selected from catalogues, or had assortments of possible gifts sent to her at the Palace.

Presents range from clocks to cutlery, from doormats to jewelry. Servants and staff specify exactly what they want, within a set price range, depending on their service; each receives that gift directly from the hand of the Queen.

Family gifts are exchanged at teatime on Christmas Eve, a Danish tradition started by the Danish Queen Alexandra. This year another

Danish woman was present, the Duchess of Gloucester. All presents were piled onto an 80-foot trestle table in the Red Drawing Room, alongside a large Christmas tree cut from the Windsor State Park. The room, with its red silk wall coverings, had been stripped of all other furniture, the rugs rolled up to reveal a clear wood floor. The family had joined in trimming the tree, sorting the presents into proper piles coded by colored tapes for each person. Prince Philip handed them to each of the twenty-nine assembled Royals. This is strictly a private party, no servants, the doors closed, but their cheerful noise can be heard all through the halls.

The parents and grandparents still fill stockings with goodies for the children to open on Christmas morning, and Prince Charles always stuffed funny things into old socks for his parents.

Christmas morning is a private time, each family in its own rooms in its own private tower. The Queen's Tower is for her immediate family; the Queen Mother uses the Lancaster Tower, and the Gloucesters and Kents have their own respective towers.

They meet again for church services at St. George's Chapel in the castle, and then lunch in the State Drawing Room. That, too, is totally private. Only the chef makes a brief appearance to carve the turkey—which comes from one of the royal farms. The four-course lunch usually includes Scottish salmon and plum pudding made from a recipe that goes back for generations. All the Royals wear party hats and have noisemakers. Lunch usually ends in plenty of time for everybody to watch the Queen's pre-recorded Christmas Day speech on television. Then there's a toast to the "birthday girls," the two Royals born on Christmas Day, eighty-year-old Princess Alice, Dowager Duchess of Gloucester, and forty-five-year-old Princess Alexandra, wife of the Honorable Angus Ogilvy.

After watching movies in a private screening room or a variety of programs on numerous television sets, or playing board games, everyone eats a cold buffet in the Oak Room, the children are put to bed, and The Game begins.

The Game is Charades, and the Royals love it.

"They have great trunks of dressing-up clothes left in the hall outside by the footman," said a guest who was there one year. "Capes and hats and dresses and anything you can think of. They come back and portray a character and you're supposed to guess who it is. They're demoniacal about it, all of them. They adore it. Princess Margaret is best at it. I think she's the family's top talent. She's also a deadly accurate mimic. They're all great mimics—the Queen, Charles, Anne, even Diana. But Margaret can also sing and play her own accompaniment. She once did a devastating impression of Sophie Tucker's Red Hot Momma."

"I laughed so loud," said another guest, "until the tears ran down my cheeks. I never imagined it would be such fun. At one stage we played a grown-up game of hide-and-seek. When I crawled under the heavy cloth covering a table, I found the Queen already concealed there. Both of us had tremendous difficulty trying to stop giggling and giving our hiding place away."

The Queen's sense of humor rarely surfaces in public, but there was the time when a television personality, Michael Aspel, asked her what she thought of the reptile house at Regents Park Zoo. "An ideal place for an assignation, I should think," she replied with a twinkle.

Charles and Diana once did their own fancy-dress dance, she dressed in an old man's baggy suit and hobnailed boots, leaning on two walking sticks, with a doddering shuffle, and he costumed as a widow with a tattered cardigan and weather-beaten headscarf.

What was noticed this Christmas was the way Charles and Diana were constantly holding hands, touching each other, looking at each other.

For the rest of the holiday, there was riding, hunting, golf, badminton, or just lounging, whatever one wanted. Then they all dispersed for home and met again on New Year's holiday at Sandringham.

It almost turned into a tragedy when Diana slipped on the stairway and fell partway down before she caught herself. They put her to bed, called a local doctor, concerned not only about her but about the baby. Her gynecologist confirmed that fortunately her baby had not been injured.

It was an odd, eventful way to start a new year, in which she would become a mother and turn twenty-one. Even stranger to her, surely, was the fact that less than half a mile away, such a short time ago, she was a young nobody living at Park House—where she had been born—full of romantic dreams and small expectations. Now she was, incredibly, the wife of a future King and perhaps the mother of another yet unborn King.

19

And how would you like to have cameras pointed at your tummy all the time?" the pregnant Princess plaintively asked the editor at a small dinner party.

What could he say?

He knew what had happened. The doctor had ordered Diana to take a holiday and so she and Prince Charles had gone off to Eleuthera. To avoid publicity, they had quietly booked a commercial flight as Mr. and Mrs. Hardy. (A citizen afterward complained because they had not honored some other English novelist, such as Charles Dickens or Somerset Maugham.) In any event, just before going, the Prince had publicly thanked the British press for giving him and his wife a publicity breather. "I am very glad to see the old spirit of fair play still does twitch here and there in Fleet Street."

Not for long, though. Photographers from two British newspapers caught the pregnant Princess in a very scant, very revealing bikini to prove that she really was five months pregnant.

To get the prized picture of the Princess, James Whitaker and photographer Kenny Lennox equipped themselves with jungle gear and binoculars, and started crawling through the land opposite the royal beach (Lord Brabourne's property) shortly before sunrise.

"We crawled, carrying a lens the size of a bloody howitzer for an hour and a half," said Whitaker. "By 7:50 A.M. we were in position, a half mile across the water from the beach. Finally Diana appeared at 11:20. When she turned up in a bikini, it was too good to be true. We also knew we'd be in trouble."

Photographer Lennox started taking pictures.

"Diana was rubbing suntan oil on the Prince's back. Sensational! I kept saying to Kenny, 'I've never done anything so intrusive in my life.' But it was a journalistic high. I've never had such a buzz."

"Chasing Royals is like a drug, an addiction," a reporter confessed.

The Queen was not amused. Her press secretary, Michael Shea, called it "the worst sort of taste." The House of Commons passed a bipartisan motion criticizing the papers. The British Press Council called for an investigation. In rebuttal, one of the papers editorialized, "We are sorry the Palace did not like our pictures but we do think Princess Di still looks terrific."

Another press executive, who asked not to be named, added, "They are showpiece personalities. If they can be shown getting married, they can be shown picking their noses or scratching their bums."

Nor did it end there. Back in Britain, one of the royal beaters on a pheasant hunt at Sandringham later reported to the press the first public spat between the Prince and Princess. "We couldn't believe our ears," he said. "The Princess had gone along on the shooting party just to be with her husband, and he was shouting at her to take part in the shoot. She shouted back, 'You know I didn't want to come in the first place!' " The public shouting match lasted several minutes and "the Princess gave as good as she got. She wouldn't harm a living thing if it was up to her."

By lunchtime, the couple was again described as "lovey-dovey." But then someone overheard the Prince saying, "Marriage is restricting."

For the third time that year, Diana got a new bodyguard. The first had been "too bossy," the second "too jumpy." The new man had apparently won her confidence when he comforted her the day the Prince's horse had collapsed and died.

"How can anyone call her coy?" declared one of the Prince's polo-playing friends. "How can people believe all that sugary stuff about her? She hires and fires with the best of them, and is very demanding."

"She's a tremendous fighter," said her former roommate Virginia Pitman. "She is tougher than she looks." "She has strength and character," added Hugh Montgomery-Massinberd, former editor of Burke's Peerage.

Diana now hired a nanny, thirty-nine-year-old Barbara Barnes, formerly with Lady Anne Tennant, Lady-in-Waiting to Princess Margaret. Lady Anne had a son and teenage twin daughters. (In the strange ways of the small aristocratic circle, Lady Anne reportedly was engaged to Earl Spencer before he met and married Diana's mother. Now here was Lady Anne providing a nanny for her former fiancé's grandchild.) "The children absolutely adore her," said Lady Anne about Miss Barnes. "She is exceptionally firm, with a great sense of humor. She even sang at our wedding. She has a very nice voice."

"I don't see any different problems in bringing up a royal baby," said nanny Barnes, the daughter of a forestry worker. "I treat all children as individuals."

No, she said, she had not gone to any nanny's college. Would she now wear a nanny's uniform? "Good grief, no."

Diana let slip the expected date of her first child's birth. During a visit to a medical center in Leeds, the Princess had chatted with seventy-four-year-old Edwin Wilson. It would suit him fine, he said, if her baby were born on his seventy-fifth birthday, June 10th.

"Oh, no," she said with a laugh. "It's due on my birthday [July 1st]." The Prince looked very surprised when she mentioned the exact date.

Speculation about the baby's sex was heightened when it was reported that Prince Charles had already been told the baby's sex after it was revealed in an ultrasound scan, but that Diana did not want to know. Some papers stated flatly that the baby was a boy. Diana's gynecologist, Dr. George Pinker, scotched this rumor, saying, "You don't employ scanning to sex a baby. It's done to monitor its growth." In the meanwhile, Diana was reported to be buying equal quantities of blue and pink for the layette.

Princess Diana finally suggested her own preference to Mrs. Sylvia Broomfield, part of the crowd at a community center in southeast London. As the Princess arrived to open the center, Mrs. Broomfield asked, "Is it a boy or a girl?" As Diana walked away, she shrugged and said, "It's a boy—I hope." She had told the same thing earlier to fourteen-year-old David Rowland. And when Mrs. Doreen Markland asked her how she and her husband were preparing for the birth, "She said Prince Charles was sitting at home reading books about pregnancy and telling her what she should do, and she didn't like it."

Had she changed her mind from the time she worked in the Pimlico kindergarten? At that time she had applied sticking plaster to her grazed elbows and bruised knees, moaning, "Please, God, may I only have daughters. Little boys are so rough."

Maybe Prince Charles had changed his mind, too. On an official visit to a Marks and Spencer store, he gave a four-year-old girl an impulsive quick hug, saying, "I wouldn't mind a little girl like this myself."

Diana's reaction to a woman with five-month-old twins was: "I couldn't cope with a brace." Their mother, Mrs. Patricia Woodgate, told her that "you don't really learn about children until you actually have them."

Diana had tickled the toes of one baby and said, "Oh the joys of things to come." Another time she said, "Men don't understand a woman's determination to have a baby."

Diana had not yet publicly announced whether she would have the baby in a hospital or at Buckingham Palace. The Queen had given birth to all four of her children at the Palace. Dr. Pinker and four members of his team could be at the Palace anytime within a half hour. Dr. Pinker himself—a kindly, firm-minded Scot—had booked a room in the Lindo Wing of St. Mary's Hospital, just in case.

Nursery furniture was already arriving at Highgrove. Most of it came from a corner shop on Golders Green Road in London called Welcome to the World. The owners, Eleanor and Laurence Cresner, had offered the furniture as a gift as soon as they heard the announcement of the pregnancy. "But we never thought they'd take us up on the offer," said Mr. Cresner. "We're rather out in back of beyond here and we're such a small company. So when a man from the Palace actually *phoned*—I nearly dropped the receiver!"

The *pièce de résistance* for the new royal baby was a frilly canopied four-poster bed made of golden pine. It was covered in gingham and white cotton, printed with tiny rosebuds, and had padded protectors tied to the sides so that the baby wouldn't harm its head. The nursery décor was pink and blue. "The cot sheets are machine washable," said Mrs. Cresner, who then giggled, "but she won't be too worried about that!"

"Of all the wall toys, we never thought she'd choose the frog," said Mrs. Cresner. "When her baby looks out of its bed, its eyes will meet those of an extremely large grinning frog hanging on the wall—a 'fabric wall sculpture.'"

Decorator Dudley Poplak, who came to the shop to select the various nursery items, told the owners that his royal clients were just like any other young married couple. "You know, they've got to watch their pennies."

The Prince, meanwhile, was poking fun at his expectant fatherhood. In a speech he said, "I was talking to an Irish racegoer recently and he said to me, 'I am delighted to hear, Sir, that you have proved yourself at stud.'"

The worst of the morning sickness was now mostly a bad memory, and the Princess was again in high gear on scheduled tours with the Prince.

For his part, Prince Charles had gone off to South Wales to visit the farmers hard-hit by some of the most destructive blizzards in recent history.

Aside from ceremonial visits, the Prince had taken the initiative to stimulate a job creation scheme in Liverpool and Birmingham—and more than fifty other projects were under consideration. Working quietly through his own charity, the Prince's Trust—established in 1976 to make funds available to people under twenty-five for self-help ventures—Prince Charles had helped organize projects to provide 200 jobs.

Prince Charles raised 16 million pounds in the Queen's Silver Jubilee Appeal of 1977. In launching Youth Business Initiative, as part of the Prince's Trust, the Prince helped 750 young unemployed people to start their own businesses within two years: a computer shop in Halifax, Desperate Dan's Cafe in Liverpool, a factory for fitted bedroom furniture in South Wales, a scones bakery in Glasgow.

"When you visit these areas as I do," said the Prince of Wales after a tour of city slums, "you begin to wonder how it is possible that people are able to live in such inhuman conditions."

In any serious statements he made, the Prince had to hedge and qualify so that he never sharply indicated any political leanings. He had learned that the genius of the Royal Family was its genius for consensus.

Yet, he said smilingly, he felt it part of his duty to "stir things up, to provoke discussion." He attacked terrorists as "arrogant subhuman extremists" with narrow-minded and intolerant ideologies. He attacked all the money wasted on bureaucracy and applauded the profit-sharing movement within large companies. Once again, he cheered the concept that "small is beautiful." And he talked of the urgent need to inspire the individual, "those who are looking for other ways of doing things."

One of his favorite stories concerned the time he toured a York-shire coal mine with Joe Gormley, the chairman of the miners' union. Gormley called him "Charlie," then added, "What the hell, we're all in the same game. If we don't succeed together, we won't succeed at all."

Diana kept close to her family as her pregnancy progressed. Her brother Charles often visited her on school holidays and the two were sometimes seen lunching in London restaurants. She increasingly spent time with her sister Jane talking about their babies. Sarah also visited more often now, and any lingering coolness between them was gone. Her mother had gone to Australia for two months following a gall bladder operation, but was now fully recovered and increased her visits to London from her Scottish farm. She and Diana delighted in their shopping expeditions.

Intimate friends now noted a growing personality resemblance between mother and daughter. Frances Shand-Kydd was bright, sharp, forceful, and charming. She was also an extrovert. "I have been told that I am honest to a degree," she said, "which some people might say isn't good. I suppose I have learned to become a politician."

So had her daughter Diana. She was similarly charming, more determined than forceful, equally sharp in her instincts, and was described as "bright-ish."

Asked a question about Diana that she didn't want to answer, Mrs. Shand-Kydd had a pleasant way of smiling and saying, "That's my secret." But she could also say, "I'm always proud to be my daughter's mother."

Yet it was another myth that Diana was close to her mother, closer perhaps than to anyone else. The lack of her mother's love—when she most needed it—has made her suspicious of the sincerity of anyone's affection. Diana was six when her mother suddenly left home and divorced Earl Spencer. Two years later, her mother sued for custody of her children, while being attacked for adultery by the wife of her lover. Diana's grandmother, Lady Fermoy, incensed still at what her daughter had done, testified in court that the children should remain with their father, not their mother.

All these sensational national headlines left an indelible scar on this little girl. She never forgot nor forgave. Her mother was simply not there when she needed her love most. It is true that Diana did visit her mother in Scotland, and in Australia before her engagement to the Prince. And her mother did come to London to help her shop for wedding clothes. But the hard fact is that there is still a distance between mother and daughter. Mrs. Shand-Kydd had dinner at Kensington Palace with her daughter only once in two years.

"When children marry, there should be a gap and you are maternally redundant," Diana's mother said. "If they want to ask your opinion, then that's nice. I don't have any feelings toward interfering in something that is their life. You should bring up your children to be independent. They should be self-sufficient and take responsibility for their own lives."

Her daughter's celebrity had rubbed off on her. She told of being recognized, a woman asking "if I were me."

"'Yes I am me,' I said. That usually produces a silence because they can't think of anything to say next."

Mrs. Shand-Kydd also told a story that happened in her gift shop in Oban. She was serving a woman who didn't know who she was and the woman kept gushing on about Diana. Finally she turned to Mrs. Shand-Kydd and asked, "Don't you think she is wonderful?"

"I thought for a moment," Mrs. Shand-Kydd recalled, "and said, 'It's a bit difficult for me to say.'" The woman leaned over and patted Mrs. Shand-Kydd's hand and said, "Quite right, my dear. As a shop assistant, you shouldn't give opinions. And one thing is for certain, she didn't come out of a home like you and I did." Mrs. Shand-Kydd enjoyed that very much.

Diana's mother had her own concerns.

"Supposing I were caught speeding. The press would sensationalize it—PRINCESS DIANA'S MOTHER ON CRIMINAL CHARGE." She smiled. "I am a lot more careful about my driving than perhaps I used to be."

Diana has her mother's same practical sense, her same steely resolve, the same sense of humor. At a millinery shop, the fitter told her, "You have a big head."

"Yes," she replied, "but there isn't much in it."

Prince Charles now had a different look—his clothes were more casual and colorful, often selected by his wife. Diana bought Charles a pair of designer jeans. They went from Kensington Palace to Highgrove to Buckingham Palace to Balmoral to Windsor Castle, packed and repacked. But he never wore them. They finally disappeared. He also wore his hair longer. Diana brought in her own hairdresser, Kevin Shanley, to do his hair.

Shanley had gone with them to Wales to give Diana a shampoo and blow-dry each morning and a comb-out before evening engagements. He also trimmed her hair once a fortnight. She would tell him, "Go on, Kevin, make it a bit lighter this time; you know my husband prefers blondes." (Her hair had been blond into her mid-teens but turned a mousy light brown as she got older. Shanley lightened it with blond streaks every three months or so.)

Britain now seemed filled with Diana clones. They wore Diana wigs, Diana's ruffled neck blouses, Diana's corduroy knickers, Diana's low-heeled pumps, Diana's string ties, Diana's Fair Isle sweaters, Diana's wide-brimmed straw hats and copies of Diana's engagement ring. Right after Diana was photographed wearing a sweater from the Inca Peruvian Shop, the store reported it sold 500 sweaters of the same design within three days.

Gone was Diana's freewheeling girlhood when she wore sloppy sweaters and inexpensive separates. "She now feels she can't wear the same thing twice," exclaimed her new designer, David Sassoon, who puts her down as "Miss Buckingham" in his appointment book.

Sassoon and his partner, Belinda Bellville, specialized in dazzling evening gowns such as the red diamanté-sprinkled net gown Diana wore to the premiere of a James Bond film. They also made her some outfits in green for the Welsh tour. A blouse they had designed brought them to her attention; she wore the blouse posing for a royal wedding postage stamp. (A Crown Agents spokesman for the Commonwealth countries announced a new series of stamps to be issued on Diana's birthday, two of which would feature her alone.)

Diana still often drove to the Vogue House underground car park and sneaked up the back staircase unnoticed. There the editors had assembled some of what they considered the best of British fashion "to help her," said Felicity Clark, "because, like any kid, she didn't know where to go. Also, she didn't have the time."

The Vogue editor was wrong on both counts. Diana did have the time. She loved shopping. And "she did know where to go." Fashion was a passion with her. She had devoured fashion magazines for years and had instinctive good taste.

It was true, however, that Diana seldom wore hats and didn't know much about them. When she first started wearing them, her hatmaker, John Boyd, had to draw arrows telling her which brim to turn up or down.

Boyd understood that Royals usually wear their brims turned up so the people can see their faces, but he believed that Diana still should wear some hats "down over her face to get the line correct," which she has done. He also believes that young people should be given freedom to experiment with their hats, even if they make mistakes.

Diana's mother had been a client of Boyd's and she brought her daughter to him just after her engagement announcement.

"I'd like that hat to go away in," Diana told him, pointing to one that was just being finished. There was no question, no discussion.

Before she went to Wales, she dropped in on Boyd, spotted a salmon-colored tricorn hat with ostrich feathers. "That's it. Don't alter it."

"She knows what she likes," said Boyd firmly. "When it comes to fashion, she knows exactly what she wants," echoed other fashion observers.

Boyd described the way Diana would rush into his Knightsbridge shop. "Diana is so amusing. She wants to look everywhere. She always asks to go to the workroom but I tell her we don't allow young ladies in there." He also pinched her once and told her she was too thin. "I'm not thin—I'm slim. And that's the way my husband likes me."

In designing hats for her maternity clothes, Boyd explained, "They should be small, simple, and follow the lines of the dress."

In addition to Boyd, *Vogue's* senior fashion editor, Anna Harvey, became a key advisor. She picked the best of off-the-rack warehouse designs, and brought them to Kensington Palace for Diana's inspection and selection. Boyd too would now more often bring his hats to her.

"I wouldn't be surprised if she didn't pay for a *lot* of her clothes," declared a knowing woman's magazine editor. "When she does pay for them, she often pays cash, so there's no billing to the Royal Palace accountants. Of course, she doesn't pay the cash, her lady-in-waiting does. Otherwise it goes to Prince Charles's accountants. Even when she does pay for it, I'm certain she gets a deep discount.

Having her as a client is the greatest publicity any designer or any shop can have. Even so, she does spend a lot of money. But let's face it, the Prince is loaded. And she's going to be a Queen.

"I'll tell you a secret. I do know that she has worn some American clothes, although she doesn't like it to be generally known. She's supposed to buy British."

Prince Charles brought his wife to still another royal home, his hideaway cottage on the Isles of Scilly, near Land's End. They had three days of rest from press and people. A speedboat took them on an evening run among the uninhabited islands and rocky islets, and they used a Land Rover to see the exotic plants of Abbey Gardens or wander along the docks. Special Branch police with sniffer dogs had scoured the islands for security, divers had checked the docks for explosives, medical teams were stationed nearby for any emergency.

This was to be the pattern of their lives: short hops to their luxury retreats surrounded with the ever constant threat of danger.

Other perks for Diana involved meeting film celebrities—such stars as Elizabeth Taylor, who was starring in *The Little Foxes*. Neither would report their conversation afterward, but the Princess inadvertently arrived just as Miss Taylor was trying to mimic her. Diana burst out laughing and Taylor was sheepish indeed.

In photographs taken of them together, Princess Diana seemed the sex symbol, Taylor on the dowdy side. Dr. Glenn Wilson, a reported expert in body language, now described Diana as a gracious lady with a naughty, vivacious streak. "She seems to have gained confidence. Sexy signals are shown for the first time."

Observers noted that Diana often flung herself at Charles in public, kissing him at the races, at polo matches, at the opera when the lights went down. The British had been indoctrinated to expect their Royals to be so reserved that their masklike faces never seem to crack. There had been considerable adverse comment when President Carter and his wife, on a visit to Britain, were seen publicly holding hands. But with Diana and Charles, the public was delighted.

Diana became engaged, married, and pregnant within a swirling nine-month kaleidoscope, and despite her great success with the British public, occasional criticism was still evident. If she wore a mink coat, the Animal Activists group loudly protested that she was abetting the cause of cruelty to animals. If she bought a birthday card for her friend Sarah Armstrong-Jones, the shop proprietor promptly reported, "It looked a bit saucy to me." If she lost weight during her morning sickness period, there was a public hue and cry that she was suffering from anorexia. Even her wedding gown was damned by one fashion writer as looking like "crumpled Kleenex." When she didn't feel well at a dinner party and left suddenly, there were those who complained she had been rude, and that the Queen was annoyed. A former schoolmate described her life as one of walking a tightrope in a circus act.

Mocking Diana's activity, a pregnant career woman complained: "Diana is the one working woman who's being rewarded for what every other working woman gets penalized for. She may continue working but I'll bet if she has any more morning sickness, she won't have to make any appearances before noon. And I'll bet if she gets tired along the way, she'll be able to cancel anything without fear of losing her job or ruining employment opportunities for other women."

"You can't do anything right," Diana complained to an editor at a party. "If I go to Harrods and come out with a box of something, the waiting photographers want to know what I bought. And if I tell them, then they print that I spent two thousand pounds. And if I *don't* tell them they'll print that I spent two thousand pounds on clothes. And if I come out without anything, they'll print that I went to Harrods for a half hour and didn't buy a thing. You just can't win."

She said this with more sadness than bitterness.

Palace protocol was hardly fun for Diana. In a note to a friend, she had described the formal dinners there as "yuk!" The ever-waiting public made her increasingly wary about going out, and there was always the unspoken knowledge that she and her husband were terrorist targets.

It was a great weight to bear for a young woman who preferred to be carefree and happy. But her mother had warned, "I do really think that when you marry, you marry your husband's profession."

Despite all this tension, a staff member commented, "She is so nice, I just can't believe it. I just pray she stays this way and doesn't let her position or the pressure of her job make her sour."

According to a poll, Diana had replaced even Prince Charles as the most popular member of the Royal Family. The more important

277

point was that she had matured almost precipitously. She could take it all, a friend commented, "as long as the Prince is charming."

He was more than charming. His pride in her was enormous. Before she stepped out of her car, in her daring black strapless gown, the Prince had warned waiting photographers, "Wait till you get an eyeful of this!" One of the things he still did was to slip small gifts under her pillow—perfume, jewelry, or Star Bars (a peanut butter concoction—the Princess's favorite candy). He also left romantic notes.

The thing he praised her most for, and in which she excelled more than any current Royal—except the Queen Mother—was her way with people. While she disliked the pretentious pomposity and the dullness of formal dinners, she loved the informality of the walk-about.

While the Queen had inaugurated the walkabout, she herself had a natural reserve and restraint. The Queen rarely shook hands, almost always wore gloves, spoke more to small groups than to individuals. Not Diana. She plunged among people with an obvious interest and relish. She held infants, kissed children, confided intimate secrets to motherly women, reached deep into a crowd to shake an old man's hand and crack a thin joke.

With the crowds now always edging toward Diana, the Prince once told her with a big grin, "Stop stealing the show."

Her tension showed most when she talked in public. Her early speeches were usually short, read hurriedly from index cards. You could see her physically sigh with relief when she was finished. Gradually, very gradually, she began to speak more slowly, with more expression. But she still hated it.

What she did learn fast were the royal tricks: how to shake hands with hundreds of people without hurting her own hands; the wisdom of visiting the ladies' room before dinner meetings—which are often interminable; and the best remedy for stifling inappropriate giggles (bite down on the inside of your lip).

The critics were always in waiting to watch and carp. During a visit to a Sony factory in Wales, Diana wore protective glasses. Someone gave her a book on childcare, a cassette player, and a baseball cap with the name SONY on it. She wore the baseball cap during the tour. A critic complained that the cap indicated her commercial endorsement of the company.

In the weeks before the baby's birth, she went to a christening, played darts at a youth center, went to a movie premiere, met a punk pop group, visited a pensioners' bingo session, and watched her husband play polo.

Without anger, she told photographer Tim Graham, "You and your friends rather spoil the game for me."

Summer is a busy time for the Royals. The Queen's official birthday celebration, with its famed Trooping the Color, takes place on June 12th. Two days later, the Order of the Garter Service is held at St. George's Chapel, Windsor. Then comes Royal Ascot week. This June, President Reagan and his wife were guests at Windsor Castle. Princess Diana met them, but did not attend a banquet in their honor. Instead, she had met the wives and children of the Welsh Guards First Battalion—who had suffered heavy casualties that day in the Falklands.

Prince Andrew was in the Falklands serving as a helicopter pilot on the HMS *Invincible*. For this historic interval at least, he was no longer "Randy Andy" to the press but "Hero Andy." His worst experience, he said afterward, was "seeing the *Atlantic Conveyor* hit, seeing the bits and pieces splashing into the water a quarter of a mile away."

Part of his job was to lure the Argentine Exocet missiles away from the Task Force, make them swerve toward the helicopter instead of toward a ship. He was hovering when another Exocet smashed into the destroyer HMS *Sheffield*, turning it into a blazing bomb.

Another part of his job was to search for survivors. His biggest worry was being hit by mistake by a defense missile firing back at the Argentines. "It really makes the hair stand up on the back of your neck. It was an experience, but I would not say I would not have missed it. If I had the choice, I would not want to go through it again."

Prince Charles and Princess Diana had moved back to their apartment in Kensington Palace, to be close to the hospital. It was fitting that one of their last trips during this pregnancy was to Broadlands to visit Lord and Lady Romsey.

RALPH G. MARTIN

Broadlands had been part of their beginning such a short time before, and it was a good place to complete a memory circle. Then, as now, Diana and Charles could stroll along the river without words, holding hands, thinking their merging thoughts. Then, as now, the flowers, the trees, the weather, everything was at its peak for them.

What was new was their expectancy, their excitement over the coming birth.

20

n Father's Day in June of 1982 the Prince of Wales had to fly to France for a meeting with President Mitterrand, but he sped home four hours later. Carefully adjusting her seat belt, Diana picked him up in her black Ford Escort and brought him back to their Kensington Palace apartment. He was supposed to play polo that day but canceled it.

Just before dawn the next morning, Diana nudged her husband awake with the news that her labor had begun. Accompanied only by their detective, they drove the ten minutes through deserted London, arriving at St. Mary's Hospital at 5:10 A.M.

Everything was ready, everybody was waiting.

St. Mary's is an unpretentious structure near the Paddington freight yards, but it is one of the top teaching hospitals in Britain, the hospital where Alexander Fleming discovered penicillin. And it was the place where the Queen's surgeon-gynecologist, Dr. George Pinker, had supervised the delivery of seven royal babies: the three children of the Duke and Duchess of Gloucester, the two of Prince and Princess Michael of Kent, and the two of Princess Anne.

The Lindo Wing is a red-brick building on a side street, South Wharf Road. The Queen Mother had dedicated the wing in 1937, and it still had a Spartan look. The maternity section on the fifth floor accommodates only eleven patients. Even Princess Diana's room was only twelve feet by twelve feet, with no private bathroom. It had a standard metal frame bed, a somewhat shabby armchair, a small teak wardrobe and dressing table, a telephone, television set, some extra chairs, and a bed table. The rate for the royal room was later disclosed as being $218 a day.

Not very plush for a Princess. But the doctors wanted these rooms stripped for action. Dr. Pinker would not wear white gown or mask:

His concept of a natural birth was that it should approximate home delivery as much as possible. He usually wore a plastic apron and rubber boots. And he agreed with the Prince that the father should be present. "I think it helps the mother. I also believe it strengthens family bonds."

Diana and Charles knew all this. They had been briefed in great detail by nurse Betty Parsons who had had thirty years of experience with more than 16,000 expectant mothers. She described natural childbirth as "huff and puff" and felt than any mother has the absolute right to decide whether or not she needs an epidural anesthetic any-time during labor. She also made sure Prince Charles understood how tired his wife would be in the first weeks after childbirth.

Dr. Pinker was well prepared for emergencies. He had available an incubator, an intravenous drip, and other sophisticated equipment if he noted any change in the Princess's condition during delivery.

What pleased Pinker most was that Diana had gone into labor spontaneously, and at term—two good signs.

Much had changed in the Royals' attitudes toward childbirth through the centuries. Queen Victoria was never described as preg-nant—she was "ill and indisposed." She herself described her preg-nancy as "that miserable lump" and stayed in seclusion until the "lump" was born. "What made me so miserable," she wrote her daughter in 1858, "was to have the first two years of my married life utterly spoiled by this occupation. I could enjoy nothing." And when her daughter was expecting her own first child—the future Kaiser Wilhelm II—the Queen called the news "horrid. What you say of the pride of giving life to an immortal soul is very fine, dear, but I cannot enter into that: I think much more of our being like a cow or a dog at such moments when our poor nature becomes so animal and unesthetic."

When Princess Elizabeth was pregnant with Charles, she was said to be in an "interesting condition." All photographs of that "con-dition" were prohibited. To Diana, though, her pregnancy was a public pride, and she relished the attention.

In their characteristic unstuffy way, it is quite probable that the Prince and Princess were both amused by the BBC satirical program, Not the Nine O'Clock News, which reported that Diana was suing a contraceptive manufacturer because its product didn't work.

The Prince had made his own saucy jokes on the subject to as-sorted audiences. He also had observed, "I am the father, and I suppose I started this whole business. So I intend to be there when everything happens.''

And now he was, holding her hand while she waited for her contractions.

As on the calendar, for the royal couple it was surely the longest day of the year.

The word went out early that Diana had been admitted and a crowd collected in front of the hospital, waiting in the rain, singing, cheering, listening for bulletins on their portable radios.

Although not unusual for a first child, the labor lasted almost thirteen hours. Pinker was assisted by a midwife, Sister Delphine Stevens, a no-nonsense nurse from Wales. Also present in the room was the anesthesiologist, constantly scanning his machines and, later, the royal pediatrician.

Charles sat at the head of the bed to stay out of the way. He was the first Prince of Wales ever to be present at his child's birth. (Prince Albert, the Prince Consort to Queen Victoria, was in attendance for all of his wife's confinements.)

For generations, the tradition was for the Home Secretary to witness royal births. The tradition dated back to the "warming-pan" plot of 1688 at a time of political turmoil, when a substitute baby was reportedly placed in the bed of the wife of James II. After that the Home Secretary was supposed to be present at every royal birth "in the succession" to make sure the royal baby "wasn't a fake."

When the Queen Mother was the Duchess of York, giving birth to Princess Elizabeth, she had said of this intruder, "If there has to be a gentleman waiting outside my bedroom door, I hope it's someone we know."

In an earlier generation, when the Home Secretary congratulated Queen Victoria on the birth of "a very fine boy," she quickly corrected him. "A very fine Prince!"

It was George VI who decided to abolish this royal tradition as "unnecessary."

Both outside the hospital and outside Buckingham Palace, the crowds kept increasing. They seemed to be coming from everywhere. People heard the news at home and took a train to London. Or they took a coffee break at work and never came back. Nobody seemed to notice the rain. A group arrived at St. Mary's with an enormous card of congratulations, signed by hundreds of people, and gave it to the guard to pass on to the Princess. A number of people brought champagne. Others had sandwiches, prepared for a long stay. People talked to each other as if they were neighbors instead of strangers, or even as if they were simply part of a large family. Some of the younger ones burst into cheers or sudden song. The older people watched everything as if they were sharing a warm secret. "I think we need a lift," declared Mrs. Eleanor Gruml. "I think it's such a happy thing to have babies and with all the bad news we've been having." Mary Finn agreed enthusiastically. "I think Lady Di is the best of the lot. She likes to meet working-class people."

Diana had wanted—and had prepared for—a natural birth, taking breathing and relaxation exercises. But toward the end her labor pains grew to such intensity that Dr. Pinker decided she should have an epidural anesthetic, a spinal block administered by an intravenous drip. This increased the chance that forceps might be needed and made her doctor all the happier at the decision to have the baby born in a hospital instead of the Palace.

Describing the birth afterward, Dr. Pinker answered the question of whether it was natural: "Yes, it was . . . well, almost. Just at the end the Princess did have a bit of pain relief, but I'm afraid I can't go into details."

Both parents heard their first-born cry "lustily." Procedure at St. Mary's gives the baby to its mother before the umbilical cord is cut and breast-feeding starts as soon as possible. The new royal tradition includes breast-feeding, and this was also Diana's wish. The infant was then washed, weighed (7 pounds, $1\frac{1}{2}$ ounces), wrapped in a towel, tagged "Baby Wales," and handed to its mother.

At Buckingham Palace, the official notice, framed in highly polished wood, pretyped and presigned by four doctors, and attached to the outer gate, proclaimed: "Her Royal Highness the Princess of Wales was safely delivered of a son at 9:03 P.M. today. Her Royal Highness and her child are both doing well."

On the gate outside the hospital entrance, a cruder, hand-printed sign read simply: IT'S A BOY!

The cheers of the crowd outside the hospital, now numbering over 500 in the cold drizzling rain, drowned out the noise of nearby traffic and drilling. "We want Charlie . . . ," they chanted. In front of Buckingham Palace, the crowd was much larger, people coming from everywhere, as if it were a national holiday again, as if it were their own baby.

The Queen had scheduled a trip to the Royal Air Force in Cambridgeshire that day. However, she had had a special radio link set up on her plane to hear the news instantly. Prince Charles called her first, then Earl Spencer, who was waiting in London.

"I've spoken to Charles," Diana's father reported to the hovering reporters, "and he's absolutely over the moon. Diana is very well and so is the baby. I think it's a very lucky baby to have a mother like Diana. I'm so proud of her. It's a very historic occasion. It's been a worrying day." Then he grinned broadly and added, "Now I'm going to have a beer."

Prince Philip, at a dinner in Cambridge, toasted his new grandson with a brandy. The Queen Mother received the news from Prince Charles at Clarence House.

Princess Margaret was attending a musical, *Song and Dance*. Directly after the performance, the star of the show announced the news and the whole audience rose to its feet and applauded. Princess Anne was in New Mexico at the time. Asked for her reactions, she replied, "That's my business!" Then she added, "too much fuss" was being made about the birth.

It was the first day of the tennis matches at Wimbledon, and Diana's mother had come down for it. When Mrs. Shand-Kydd heard of the baby's birth, she promptly notified her mother, Lady Fermoy, who was at a dinner party.

Prince Edward was in Gordonstoun, studying for exams, and Prince Andrew was still at sea off the Falkland Islands. The British troops had recaptured Stanley, the capital of the Falklands, only the week before, and the papers had headlined nothing else. Now, suddenly, the war was all but forgotten. Even the historic Wimbledon matches became a back-page item.

This new baby, now second in line of succession to the throne, would be known as "His Royal Highness." He might one day be the forty-second monarch since the Norman Conquest, the sixth in direct descent from Queen Victoria, the thirty-third in line from William the Conqueror.

Meanwhile, in Parliament, the bill was still pending to declare any first child of a Prince of Wales, whether male or female, heir to the throne. Sweden already had passed a similar law of royal succession so that the King's daughter could succeed by primogeniture without being superseded by her younger brother.

The Lutine Bell at Lloyds, which usually rang only for news of insurance disasters, would ring for this happy event. There would also be a 41-gun salute in Hyde Park by the Royal Horse Artillery and the Honorable Artillery Company at the Tower of London. And the bells would ring and ring at Westminster Abbey and St. Paul's.

Even the staid London *Times* rhapsodized, "In its small person all our tribal history." The newly hired royal nanny reported that she felt both parents had wanted a boy. *Debrett's Peerage* preened itself because it had predicted the sex correctly. Betting on the baby's sex even had exceeded the wagering with bookmakers on the question of "who shot J.R." of television's *Dallas*.

Prince Charles emerged two hours after the birth to a crowd greater and happier than ever. The throngs sang "For He's a Jolly Good Fellow" and the stirring "Britannia."

"Obviously I'm relieved, delighted . . . I think it's marvelous," he told them.

"Is he like his dad?" somebody yelled.

"No, he is lucky enough not to be," said the Prince, grinning.

"Does the baby have hair?"

"It's blond, sort of fairish."

"Have you picked a name yet?"

"We have a few names in mind. You'll have to ask my wife about that. There's a bit of an argument about it."

"Nice going. Give us another one, Charlie."

He laughed. "Bloody hell! Give us a chance!"

"How do you feel?"

He hesitated. "It's rather a grown-up thing, I find, rather a shock to my system." Another quick shock came from a firmly planted kiss on the cheek by a teenage girl who broke through the crowd.

As he left, Charles asked the revelers to keep it quiet since patients inside the hospital were trying to rest.

It was an impossible request. This crowd behaved as if it was New Year's Eve.

Princess Diana's room faced the quiet back of the building and she heard none of the noise. The report was that she had "an enormous appetite." She had done a good day's work. Her son, they said, seemed to be feeding well, too.

The Queen arrived the next morning at the hospital, responding to a cheer with a brief wave and a hint of a smile. The Prince greeted her with a kiss on each cheek. Diana's mother and sister Jane had

Their honeymoon was on a royal yacht in the Mediterranean. Their home was at Highgrove (*below*) near London. Diana was now part of the royal world at the State Opening of Parliament (*opposite page, above*) . . . and could kiss a Queen. (*Right, Villard/DeKeerle/SIPA/Special Features; below and opposite page, above, Syndication International/Photo Trends; opposite page, below, D. Halstead/Gamma-Liaison*)

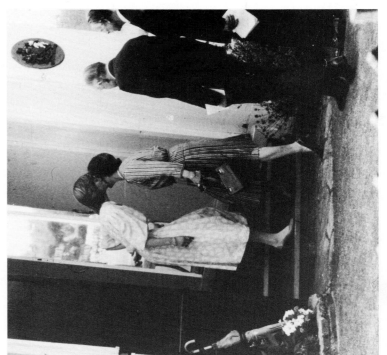

The people loved them. He was their future King, and she was their superstar. (*Tim Graham/S*

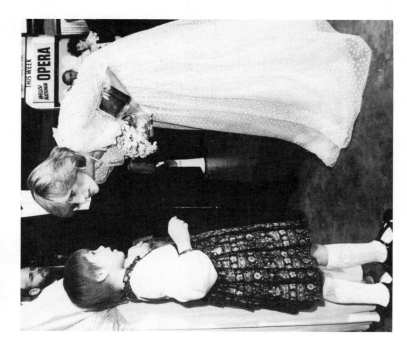

Diana enjoyed children . . . and listened when they talked. (Both, Syndication International/Photo Trends)

Princess Grace (*above*) and Elizabeth Taylor (*opposite page, above*) were both charmed by her. She had her own look and her own style . . . (*Above, Syndication International/Photo Trends; right, Rex Features/RDR; opposite page, above: AP/Wide World Photos*)

. . . and a sense of informality and fun.

Soon pregnant, Diana still kept up with her royal duties. (*This page, both, Syndication International/Photo Trends*)

(*Opposite page*) At the christening of their son William: (*above, top row, left to right*) the Duke of Edinburgh, Princess Alexandra, King Constantine, Lady Susan Hussey, Prince Charles, Lord Romsey, the Duchess of Westminster, Earl Spencer, Mrs. Shand-Kydd, Ruth Lady Fermoy, Sir Laurens van der Post, Prince Edward; (*bottom row, left to right*) Princess Anne, Queen Elizabeth II, Prince William, Princess Diana, Queen Elizabeth the Queen Mother. (*Both, Syndication International/Photo Trends*)

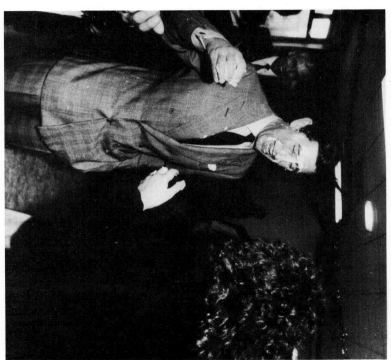

The Prince of Wales was everybody's target . . . and so was the Princess . . . but they weathered it well. (*This page and opposite, Syndication International/Photo Trends*)

She had flair and he had curiosity . . . and their marriage was generally happy. (*This page, both, Syndication International/Photo Trends; opposite page, Tim Graham/Sygma*)

Going against royal protocal, their older son William (*below*) tried to stand while his parents sat. Their second son, Harry (*right*), came quickly. (*Right, Snowdon/Camera Press; below, Tim Graham/Sygma*)

At Harry's christening: *(top row, left to right)* Lady Sarah Armstrong-Jones, Bryan Organ, Gerald Ward, Prince Andrew, the Duke of Edinburgh, Earl Spencer, Lady Vestey, Mrs. William Bartholomew; *(bottom row, left to right)* Lady Fermoy, Queen Elizabeth the Queen Mother, Queen Elizabeth II, Prince William, Princess Diana, Prince Henry, Prince Charles, Mrs. Shand-Kydd. *(Snowdon/Camera Press)*

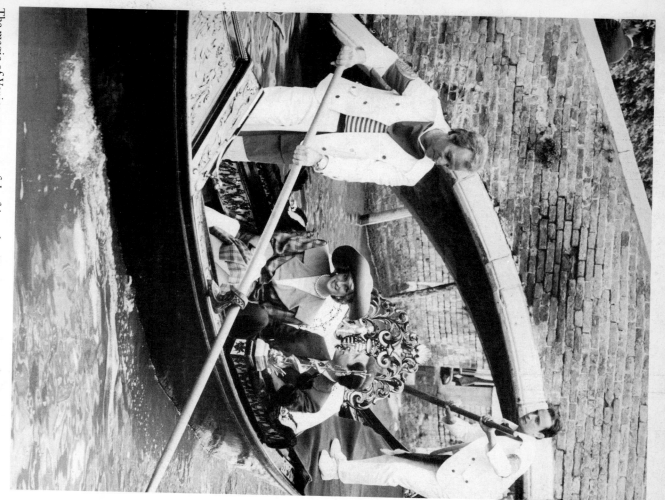

The magic of Venice was a part of the fairy tale. (*Syndication International/Photo Trends*)

been earlier visitors. Mrs. Shand-Kydd gave the first report of the day about her daughter: "She is looking radiant, absolutely radiant. My grandson is everything his father said last night—a lovely baby."

Diana's father was even more definitive. "He is the most beautiful baby I have ever seen."

The Prince of Wales took a realistic tack. "He is in excellent form, thank goodness, looking a bit more human this morning."

All the family visits were relatively short, so as not to tire the new mother.

There was no public discussion of circumcision. Five days after Prince Charles was born, he was circumcised by Dr. Jacob Snowman, a world authority on the circumcision ritual. Many Britons believe that all males born into the royal family have been circumcised by Jewish *mohels*, men trained to perform the ancient ritual of removing the foreskin. There is no actual record that this has been done, except for Prince Charles.

Exactly twenty hours and fifty-seven minutes after giving birth, the Princess of Wales walked out of the hospital, holding her baby, her husband beaming. The baby was so tightly swaddled in a white shawl that only part of his face was visible to the crowds waiting in the rain. On cue, the sun came out as they stood on the steps.

Wearing a loose-fitting green polka-dot dress, Diana looked weary, but was smiling warmly as she let her husband carry the baby to the car. Dozens of police held the crowds back. Charles gingerly handed the baby to her as she got into their chauffeured blue station wagon. The baby was fast asleep.

Before leaving the hospital, the two had said goodbye to the hospital staff, and Diana had asked them, "Will you be here next time?" She then turned to her husband and smiled, "I'm only joking, dear."

Normal practice involves a hospital stay from forty-eight hours to ten days and some doctors questioned Diana's early departure. Another medical opinion held that being at home reduces the incidence and severity of postpartum depression, and also reduces the risk of infection from hospital organisms. But the decision to leave was Diana's: "I am ready to go home." Dr. Pinker agreed. "Medically I can say I am not against anybody going out of the hospital early. She is in very good health and this will not cause any problems."

It was, of course, easy to understand why she wanted to go home.

At the hospital, however considerate the treatment, she was a patient in a small, stark room. At Kensington Palace, she was a Princess with a staff eager to meet her every whim.

As the couple got into the station wagon, somebody in the crowd yelled, again asking for the baby's name. "You'll have to wait," replied the Prince.

Patrick Montague-Smith, former editor of *Debrett's*, noted that there were "about two dozen boys' names they could choose from." He added that it would not be unusual for the child to get from three to five names. Bookmaker William Hill said the odds were even on George and 5-1 against William.

The reason the smart money was going for George was that the Prince had repeatedly defended his great-great-great-great-grandfather, George III, as "a great person who was interested in people," and had insisted that "my ancestor got a raw deal in history." He admitted that George III was "a bit of a prig, and extremely self-righteous," and added that he was not mad, but sick. Despite the fact that George III presided over the loss of the American colonies, Prince Charles admired him because he had "an incredible capacity for hard work and conscientious devotion to duty . . . a great sense of humor . . . I think he was a most wonderful man . . . a really great human being. He was also a great patron of the arts and a great patron of scientific development in the eighteenth century."

George was also the name of the Queen Mother's husband, and everyone knew how much the Prince adored her and would do to please her.

There had been six kings named George, eight named Edward, eight named Henry, four named William, two named James, two named Charles, and a smattering of others. A historian pointed out that the monarchy in the ninth century even had an Egbert. There seemed little question that the royal couple might go contemporary: The odds against Elvis were 1000-1.

Edward was quickly ruled out because of the immediate negative connection with Edward VIII, who had abdicated. Prince Charles was involved with the raising of Henry VIII's sunken flagship, and had made repeated dives to examine it. The last time there, he had mentioned suggestions that he might name his child, if a boy, Henry Charles.

The Prince publicly indicated that he and his wife had had a disagreement about the name. "It seems clear that William was

Diana's choice," said royal genealogist Harold Brooks-Baker, who regarded William as the least likely of fully "accepted" names. The Brooks-Baker view was that Diana "is a woman of decision and strong will, who is likely to have her way on all matters on which she feels strongly."

The history of England's four King Williams was varied. Back in 1027, William the Conqueror was also known as William the Bastard. His third son—the red-haired, unpopular William Rufus—became William II. William III had been a Dutch prince, the former Prince William of Orange, who became king by marrying Queen Mary II. He vanquished the Irish Catholics in the Battle of the Boyne in 1690. Diana's ancestor, the Earl of Sunderland, was one of his indispensable advisors.

The last King William reigned from 1830 to 1837, just before Victoria. He was "a jovial man" who gargled with two gallons of water every morning and wore "huge galoshes to guard against chills."

It is unlikely that any of this history had much to do with the selection of the new baby's name. Asked why the name was picked, Prince Charles said, "Well, we like the name William and it's a name that does not exist among close members of the family." Visiting a military hospital, Prince Charles told a wounded veteran of the Falklands war, "It's a very nice name."

Member of Parliament William Hamilton, the constant royal critic, caused some weak smiles when he said, "William is a very aristocratic name. I'm sure they had me in mind when they chose it." As to the baby's future, however, he predicted that it was "going to be one long story of nausea, deference, and Land of Hope and Glory rubbish for many years."

Almost nobody else seemed to think so. Even France's Communist paper *L'Humanité* wrote, "God save the next little King."

William Arthur Philip Louis was not, of course, scheduled to be the next King, but the next heir.

"We knew that both Charles and Diana were very keen on Arthur," noted Robert Lacey. "Diana thought the name of the king at the time of Camelot would have been very romantic." Arthur was also one of the names of both Prince Charles and his grandfather, George VI. That, too, pleased the Queen Mother. Philip, of course, was the name of the Prince's father. And Louis was chosen in honor of his favorite great-uncle, Lord Mountbatten.

The new Prince's nursery at Kensington Palace reportedly featured a cast-iron crib that the Windsors had used for the past century. All the Welcome to the World nursery furniture had been returned because news of the shop's contribution had leaked out and the Court was firm that there must be no commercial exploitation of any gift.

Mail and gifts had poured in from all over the world, with an emphasis on small, hand-knitted garments.

There was a congratulatory message from Diana's very distant cousin President Ronald Reagan, who wished the baby "health, happiness, wisdom, and love."

As for Prince William's American connection on his father's side, respected British genealogist Sir Anthony Wagner has established that the Queen is George Washington's sixth cousin twice removed, through their joint descent from a Virginian colonel, Augustine Warner. This would make Prince William one of Washington's closest living relatives.

During the early weeks, before Barbara Barnes took over, Anne Wallace, who cared for both of Princess Anne's babies, was in attendance. Dr. Pinker popped in regularly, as did pediatrician Dr. David Harvey and head of the royal medical household, Dr. John Batten. Both Charles and Diana were determined to do as much with the baby as possible including feeding, bathing, diaper-changing, and most of all entertaining the baby. Nanny Barnes reported, "I am there to help the Princess, not to take over."

When the Prince was late for a factory dedication in South London, he apologized, "I had one or two things to contend with—which, I may say, I am delighted to contend with." Asked whether this involved changing diapers, the reply was, "You'll have to put your own interpretation on it."

Diana had some of her own childhood toys in glass-fronted cupboards in the Kensington nursery, but it was filled mostly with selections from some of the 2,000 gifts that had newly arrived. Astrologers, busy predicting the baby's future, noted that he shared his mother's birth sign, Cancer, traditionally associated with home-loving, sensitive people; he was also expected to share his mother's good looks and zest for life, would talk early, be adventurous, and be unlikely to take part in blood sports. He was a Monday's child, fair of face. How could anyone complain about any of that, especially his mother?

On Diana's twenty-first birthday, which was almost an anticlimax, she had a small dinner with some old friends and roommates. She received about 2,000 birthday cards, including some from the Inner London Pre-School Playgroups Association, of which she was a patron. They were hand-delivered by thirty small children. Other children came with homemade cards and flowers, and in the rain sang "Happy Birthday" outside her door, but Diana didn't even know they were there—nobody had told her—and the children sadly went away without an audience.

Her mother had come from Scotland to see her and her ten-day-old grandson, who was toasted with champagne on the plane. Such a toast in Britain is called "wetting the baby's head." William had his head wet all over Britain. Diana's father and stepmother also arrived to wish her a happy birthday.

The Prince said he gave his wife some flowers and a hug, but he also gave her a necklace of diamonds and cultured pearls with a sparkling heart at its center, a custom-built Mini car, a sporty runabout, painted apple green, with a convertible foldaway roof and enough space for a folding cot and a nanny. There was a rumor that he had also bought an antique canopy bed that once belonged to Diane of Poitiers, the favorite mistress of King Henry II of France.

They scheduled the baby's christening to synchronize with the Queen Mother's eighty-second birthday. The six godparents they picked were an interesting mix. The press noted that the group was heavily weighted toward Prince Charles's side, but, in reality, it was well balanced.

Princess Alexandra represented the immediate Royal Family and yet was probably as sympathetic to Diana as she was to Charles. At forty-five, she was easily one of the most popular of the Royals, a woman of unstuffy charm and classic beauty, regal in presence but highly accessible.

When she was Diana's age, she was also known as a marvelous dancer, a gay conversationalist who loved to laugh, adored children, had a craving for sweets, and was a ballet addict. Her favorite jazz piece was "Ain't Misbehavin'." The second child of the Duke and Duchess of Kent, she was five when her father was killed in World War II. The first British princess to go to a girls' boarding school,

Alexandra married the Honorable Angus Ogilvy, second son of the Earl of Airlie.

Much of the public wrongly assumes that all Royals are rich. Princess Alexandra, first cousin to the Queen, and then fifteenth in line of succession to the throne, had no money of her own. Neither did Angus Ogilvy, since his older brother inherited both the family title and the family fortune. Ogilvy, with a background of Eton and Royal Scots Greys, took "a clutch of directorships in the City," London's Wall Street. He was also a director of Sotheby's, the noted auction firm.

Since Alexandra was drafted into official engagements and tours, representing the Crown, she had a royal allowance to help pay for staff and expenses. The couple's children, now teenagers, will not inherit any titles. Ogilvy refused an earldom because, he said, "I don't see why I should get a peerage just because I married a princess."

Alexandra and Diana got along very well indeed. She was not only the Royal Family's own favorite, but she was one of Diana's. She and her husband lived in a house at Windsor, leased from the Crown. Of their two children, young James showed an early flair for business enterprise. Their eighteen-year-old daughter, Marina, was a Royal dropout with a mind of her own. A "personality" girl with thick curly hair, she had her mother's bewitching smile. Marina had volunteered to work with natives in Central America. She definitely didn't want handouts from her parents."

Lady Susan Hussey, the Queen's senior lady-in-waiting, was reported as the Prince's choice for godmother to William, but she was surely more Diana's. It was Lady Susan, more than the Queen, more than the Queen Mother, possibly even more than her own grandmother, Lady Fermoy, who helped Diana the most in crossing the difficult bridge that separates aristocracy from royalty. Lady Susan was Diana's confidante, advisor, and friend in the months between the engagement and the wedding, when Diana lived in the old nursery rooms on the third floor of Buckingham Palace while Charles lived in another wing on the same floor. An aristocrat herself (she is the daughter of Earl Waldegrave), Lady Susan had done what Diana did—left the aristocratic nest to get an apartment in Chelsea, then a job as a secretary. Married to Marmaduke Hussey, the vice chairman of the *Times*, she described herself as "a perfectly ordinary housewife"—which she certainly wasn't. She was Woman of the Bedchamber since 1960. At forty-five, she had a daughter almost Diana's age.

Former King Constantine of Greece was clearly Charles's choice as a godfather, although he and Diana had a kissing-cousin relationship. The tall, slim Constantine was a cousin of Prince Philip; his wife, the former Princess Anne-Marie of Denmark, was a cousin of the Queen. Known to intimates as Tino, Constantine was twenty-seven when he became king and ruled for only four years before he was overthrown by a military coup that sent him into exile in England.

Ten years older than Charles, Tino was a close friend who shared his love for skiing, horses, and hunting. (He once even won a gold Olympic medal for yachting.) Like Charles, Tino also had studied history at Cambridge. He still had the distant hope that the Greeks one day might call him back to rule his homeland.

Charles always had sought the friendship and counsel of older men. After the murder of Lord Mountbatten, the seventy-eight-year-old Sir Laurens van der Post became his intellectual and spiritual mentor. A gentle, self-effacing man, Sir Laurens had a remarkable and fascinating background: The author of twenty books ranging from travel to fiction to philosophy, he was an Afrikaaner who still owned a farm in his native South Africa and wrote intensely against racism. He was also a friend and disciple of the late Carl Gustav Jung, the distinguished Swiss psychiatrist, about whom van der Post had produced several films for the BBC.

But where he captured the British imagination most—and Prince Charles was no exception—was in his explorations in the wilderness. When van der Post took Charles into the bush for three weeks during an official visit to Ghana in 1977, the Prince—according to van der Post—"had in effect a religious experience. He was put in touch with an area within himself which he didn't know was there and he will never forget again . . . suddenly this great hunger which he'd been unconscious of all his life suddenly flared up, and he changed."

Van der Post was a frequent visitor at the various royal homes, had even danced Scottish reels with the Queen Mother until three in the morning. Talking about the wilderness in his penthouse in Chelsea (he also had a small cottage in Sussex), van der Post had the look of a guru: long graying hair, penetrating eyes, a long, sensitive face. Van der Post would not talk about what he and Prince Charles have said and done together, but he would say, "I've known him since he was a boy, and he's always been a loner, a many-sided man, more complicated than most people think. He's been digging deep inside himself ever since Cambridge, maybe even before that. He has a great many friends from whom he selects different things that fill out the truth of himself."

Another of the six godparents was Norton Knatchbull, Lord Romsey. A grandson of Lord Mountbatten, he and Charles were at Gordonstoun together, but they had known each other since earlier boyhood. His sister, Amanda, was the girl Mountbatten had wanted Charles to marry. Knatchbull was now married to Penelope Eastwood, a tall, slender blonde Charles had once dated. Charles was not only best man at their wedding, but godfather to their first child; Diana was godmother to their second child.

Last of the chosen godparents was the Duchess of Westminster, hardly the least when it came to wealth. Nineteen-year-old Natalia Phillips was a secretary at *Vogue* magazine when she went to a ball at Blenheim Palace. There she met Gerald Cavendish Grosvenor, then Earl Grosvenor, who had a bachelor pad in Belgravia. They married, and shortly after he inherited the title of the sixth Duke of Westminster upon his father's death. Along with the title came 300 acres in London's posh Belgravia and Mayfair, a 1,000-acre sheep farm in Wagga Wagga, Australia, and assorted properties all over the world, making him the richest man in Britain.

Called Tally by Diana, the Duchess of Westminster shared with her a shy mischievousness.

Aside from the six godparents, the royal christening was restricted to sixty guests, mostly family. It was held in the splendor of the many-mirrored blue, gold, and white Music Room of Buckingham Palace. It was a distinctive room with fine bow windows, the same room where Prince Charles, and most of the Royals, had been christened. Baby William wore the same christening robe of white silk and Honiton lace originally worn by the first child of Queen Victoria. Princess Margaret declined to interrupt her Italian vacation to attend the christening. One of her aides explained, "The christening of your nephew's child isn't the most important occasion of the year." If the real reason was that she was piqued because she was not chosen as a godparent, she was in good company: neither were Charles's siblings or Diana's.

The ceremony was brief. The silver gilt lily font, which British monarchs have used for their christenings since 1841, was brought to Buckingham Palace from the Tower of London for the occasion. It was garlanded with apricot roses and white freesias from the royal gardens. Baptismal water was flown in from the river Jordan. The font was flanked by two tall white candles on brass stands.

When the Archbishop of Canterbury, in his pale gold robe, poured some of the water over William's head, the baby gave three little squeaks. Medieval Britons believed that such cries signaled that the Devil had left the body. Diana blushed after each squeal. The Archbishop urged the parents and godparents "to bring up this child to fight against evil and follow Christ."

The Choristers of the Chapels Royal, in their scarlet cassocks, sang two hymns during the 25-minute ritual, and Prince Charles used a royal handkerchief to wipe the royal dribbles from his royal son's chin.

As soon as the service was over, the guests posed for the official photograph, and then William opened his lungs and asserted himself. Diana looked flustered, blushed scarlet, tried rocking him without effect. Princess Anne, mother of two, made some clucking noises without impact. Prince Charles hovered uncertainly. Prince Philip kept deep in the background. The Queen commented that her new grandson had a good pair of lungs and would make a good speechmaker.

Diana saved the situation by sticking the tip of her little finger in the baby's mouth. That did it. As he sucked on it, he relaxed and seemed to calm quickly. But as soon as she pulled out her finger, the yelling started again. The Queen offered her regal finger. William rejected it. The Queen Mother offered hers. No ma'am. His father stroked his cheek. No, he wanted his mother's finger and only his mother's finger.

Prince Charles went over to the photographers at Prince William's christening and asked them if they had everything they wanted. "No, we need a picture of the Queen Mother with the baby."

"No problem," said the Prince and hurried off to the Queen Mother to set up the picture.

"The Queen Mother said she would be delighted," recalled the photographer. "She put down her gin and tonic, held the baby, and that was the picture."

When the aging Queen Victoria was photographed holding her

grandchild, there was concern that she might drop the infant, and so a servant hid under her voluminous skirts, actually supporting the baby with her hands and unseen by the photographer. With the Queen Mother's vigor, there was now no such worry.

When that scene ended and the nanny took William away, the guests all settled down to a champagne lunch in the state dining room. By tradition, the christening cake was the top tier that had been saved from their wedding cake. Charles and Diana had some pieces sent to men from the Welsh Guards and parachute regiments who had been wounded in the Falklands.

All the guests crowded in to congratulate them. Charles managed to corner his wife afterward, smiling at her and teasing, "Hello! Who are you?"

There was considerable speculation in the national press as to what motherhood would mean to Diana's future image and impact on the public. The wedding was a fertility rite, the newspapers said, and the new Princess embodied rebirth, "a renewal of the blood for the monarchy and, symbolically, for Britain as a whole."

More pointedly, a spokesman for Britain's Family Planning Association, organized to help increase the country's flagging birthrate, said, "She could be to us what the electricity power blackout was to New York in 1965. The Princess's popularity and publicity over the royal birth could encourage a lot of others to have babies early."

Even the *Times* of London solemnly reported that Princess Diana's buttonless tweed coat left "plenty of room for expansion." Diana and Charles did indeed want more children, however "angry and noisy" they became.

It was properly noted that Prince William would come of age in the year 2000, making him a young man of the twenty-first century. The *New York Times* summed up some of the mood in an editorial, part of which read: "The possibility of perfection is, in a way, what a royal birth is all about . . . The Prince and Princess of Wales's first child is not only a new link in an old and cherished chain but new magic for a nation's imagination."

In the horoscope of Prince William was this enigmatic note: "But before he marries—as a young man—he will design something— something that will be of immense benefit to humanity."

It also predicted that he would have two sisters as well as a brother and be crowned King around the year 2025.

21

I f Charles was "His Royal Highness" to the outside world, Diana ruled the roost inside the home. She now knew exactly what she wanted. One day her son would be King, but for as long as possible, she wanted him to be a normal little boy, getting all her available love and as much time with his father as possible—and privacy, privacy, privacy.

She knew how much she was asking. But the story that stayed stark in her mind was that of her mother-in-law, Queen Elizabeth, returning from a six-month world tour, being greeted by her first-born, five-year-old Charles, who stepped forward solemnly, shook her hand, then quickly retreated to hold the hand of his grandmother. This must never happen to her and her son.

Her Majesty herself never forgot this when people tried to press her into abdication so that Charles could become King. If there was a single reason to stay on as Queen—besides tradition and duty—it was to give her son and daughter-in-law a chance to be loving parents, to have the family life she had never had.

If you looked now at Diana's face, much seemed changed: Her eyes seemed deeper, more concerned, less carefree. The public now saw little of her, even less of her child. She had refused several invitations to parties given by close friends. She had stayed away from all official engagements. The one event she attended, because of the Royal Family's personal involvement through Prince Andrew, was the Service of Remembrance for the Falkland dead. But she returned promptly after the service to breast-feed her baby.

Nanny Barnes believed firmly in "fresh air and common sense," and so did Diana. The pram they used in Kensington Gardens was an impressive black-hooded one presented to the Royal Family in 1926 for Princess Elizabeth. It was later used for Princess Margaret,

Prince Charles, Princess Anne, Prince Andrew, and Prince Edward.
The thrifty Royals seldom throw anything away, and William
surely used the ivory rattle given to the Queen Mother when she
was born, and a bunting first worn by his great-grandmother Queen
Mary. But if he wore some of the clothes once used by his father,
he also wore Italian silk romper suits, T-shirts with Pierre Cardin
labels, smocked nightdresses from Spain, layette items especially
designed by Yves Saint Laurent (from Princess Grace), as well as
ordinary denim overalls. Many, of course, were gifts.

Despite the fact that the noisy High Street shopping area is only
a few minutes' walk away, Kensington Palace retains a surprisingly
rural air with secluded cobbled courtyards and secret walled gardens.
The Dutch Garden, closed to the public, has thousands of tulips
surrounding a large rectangular pool, a perfect place to sail toy boats.
Diana could look out of her window, as she once did, and say,
"Oh, look, Kanga is visiting Princess Michael . . ." Prince and Princess Michael, who also lived in a Kensington Palace apartment, seldom saw Charles and Diana. Prince Michael was a Director of Standard
Telephone and Cables. The Queen had never invited them to a Balmoral weekend.

Prince Michael was a full-bearded young man who had renounced
his rights to the throne under the 1772 Royal Marriages Act when
he married a divorced Roman Catholic, Baroness Marie-Christine
von Reibnitz. Lord Mountbatten had helped arrange that marriage.
The Baroness was a six-foot-tall woman who carried herself like a
Viking and seemed to wear her diamond tiara as often as possible.
Prince Charles called her a "Rent-a-Princess," Lord Snowdon tagged
her "Princess Pushy," and Snowdon's son, David Linley, reported
that he would give his worst enemy a Christmas present of dinner
with Princess Michael of Kent. It did not help her image when the
press revealed that she was not Austrian at all, but the daughter of
a German Nazi officer. "I had no idea," Princess Michael insisted.

Princess Michael wrote Mountbatten that Prince Charles told her
she was bringing the family into disrepute "with my grand behavior." Then she added how badly she needed Mountbatten's support,
particularly at family dinners "because the knives were out." Nor
did Princess Michael endear herself to the Queen when she complained about the bedroom assigned to her at Windsor. The Queen
responded quietly, "I can't understand that. I went around and checked
all the rooms myself. I think you've got everything you require . . ."

Diana meanwhile was busy getting back into physical trim, dancing to music from Diana Ross's album *Work That Body*, and playing tennis with her private detectives. When the press did see her, they carefully noted her sharp weight loss. Rumors again circulated that she was suffering from anorexia. They noted that her sister Sarah once had it, going from 112 to 82 pounds. A Palace spokesman denounced the rumors as "appalling."

It didn't stop there. One newspaper reported that Diana had bought almost two hundred dresses and suits during her first year of marriage, that her clothing bill often topped $2,550 a week, her gowns costing an average of $1,700 each, cocktail dresses $468, casual wear $350, with matching shoes, hat, and handbag for each outfit. And though a poll had voted her the best-dressed woman in Britain, the newspaper called her "a right royal shopperholic."

One of the most repeated myths of all is the one about Charles and Diana constantly quarreling over the cost of her clothes. "In all my time there," said the ever-present butler, "they never, ever once even *discussed* the cost of her clothes." Typical of many aristocrats, Diana was indeed "tight" about money.

So cost-conscious was the Queen that she sent back a dress to the original designer some ten years later with the request that he replace a panel which had a bad stain on it. Fortunately he had stored some of the fabric and could do it. It was not an expensive dress to begin with.

That fall of 1982 when Diana and Charles had flown with William to Balmoral for the annual family holiday, the press was again critical because they had flown together in the same plane—something the Royal Family is not supposed to do. What made it worse for some critics was the fact that the Prince piloted the plane himself.

"A fatal crash . . . would have meant the wiping out of two steps in the line of succession," an editorial emphasized. "The Queen and the Prince of Wales never fly together for this reason . . . Should not sauce for the goose be sauce for the gosling?" But then it added that the monarchy was protected because the Prince had brothers. "In the first years, it is proper that the child should be with his parents often, whether on the ground or in the air. The decision on these occasions should be respected as one for the parents themselves."

At Balmoral, the Prince went on his daily stalking hunt. The weather was abominable, with rain almost constant. A Balmoral estate worker told a reporter that there had been an open "royal tiff" between Charles and Diana because Diana was bored with being "cooped up" and wanted to get back to London. A newspaper translated this into "a blazing row" with the headline: RAIN-SOAKED PRINCESS BLOWS HER TOP. The story's impact multiplied when the paper reported that Diana and her son had come home without Prince Charles.

A watchful reporter also observed the fact that the Princess arrived ten minutes *after* the Queen—something that is just not done—at Royal Albert Hall for the Festival of Remembrance for Britain's war dead.

"She seemed quite flustered, not her usual cool, collected self. She looked grumpy and wasn't at all happy at being spotted." The story was that she and Charles had had an argument, and she had decided not to come at all, later changing her mind.

To add to all this negative pressure, Diana's mother was quoted in the newspapers about her divorce from Earl Spencer, intimating that he had been unfair to her in the custody arrangements for the children. Earl Spencer promptly retaliated, saying it was "cheap and hurtful" for her to comment publicly on their divorce. "It can only hurt Diana," he said.

Diana's mother also had been quoted as saying to an Australian friend that she wished Charles would devote as much time to his wife as he did to his horses.

The papers played up a reported increase in the sale of paintings from Althorp, an estimated two hundred sold from the total of over seven hundred. Though Earl Spencer denied the statistic, he did admit selling a few important paintings. "I hate selling anything that belongs to the family, but what am I supposed to do?" He had already reached the point of renting out rooms at Althorp for private parties, and now began offering the public, for a fee, a musical evening at Althorp accompanied by a candlelit dinner. The press mocked that in a Gilbert & Sullivan parody and it did not make good reading at Buckingham Palace.

Commercial exploitation of Charles and Diana was rampant. A paper-doll and cut-out book showed the couple and their son in underwear. A television puppet series depicted Prince William as a screaming brat. To cap it all, columnist Nigel Dempster accused the

Charles & Diana

Princess of Wales of becoming "a spoiled and bossy little monster" who was making Prince Charles miserable.

"Suddenly getting this enormous power, having people curtsy and bow and do everything she wants, she has become a fiend. She has become a little monster.

"Charles is desperately unhappy. He knows first of all he can never divorce her. Charles is very unhappy because Fleet Street forced him into this marriage."

Buckingham Palace dismissed all this as "rubbish."

What had happened? And why? Where was the truth in all this "rubbish"?

The basic truth was that news of the Royals sells newspapers.

By withdrawing from public life and public view to be with her infant child, Diana had forced the press to concoct stories about her to feed an appetite they had helped create.

To begin with, she was not anorexic. She had been a plumpish teenager, concerned about her weight. She was even more concerned about the weight she put on during her pregnancy, knowing that her husband preferred slim blondes.

Diana had admitted at a lunch for Duchy of Cornwall tenants that she was "watching my weight." But there were those who saw her put away a good meal with a healthy appetite.

What was probably true was that she did suffer a sort of post-partum depression, not uncommon among young mothers, which results in anxiety and weight loss.

What was probably equally true was that the cumulative pressure of negative reports had pushed her to the edge. It explained why she uncharacteristically covered her face and shouted "No!" when pho-tographers tried to snap her picture going into Kensington Palace.

All this is easily understandable.

As for being called a "shopperholic," for her, shopping was a great pleasure of life, and why not? The public loved to see her looking like a princess. The amounts were probably exaggerated, since she surely got discounts, loans, and even gifts of clothes. But even if she didn't, this was the woman who had single-handedly converted a dying British fashion industry into a multimillion-dollar international fashion center. Britain was now exporting its fashions all over the world, and the credit belonged to her alone.

The "tiff" at Balmoral? Of course it probably happened. She

loathed blood sports and here was her husband shooting deer every day. It was difficult to blame him because this was something he had been born and bred to do, something he had been doing all his life, part of his historic tradition. On the other hand, as a member of the royal household said, "Who can blame Diana? It's been terrible weather and she's been left to mope around." Her husband was not only an obvious target but the nearest available one.

As for her being late on Remembrance Day, she was not a paragon of punctuality. She was often late. So is the Queen Mother. This was a trait she would learn to change, especially when the Queen was present.

Surely none of this was monumental. She would eventually learn to adjust her habits and thicken her skin. Prince Philip and Princess Anne could describe the press with four-letter words. The Queen could freeze impertinence with a sharp look, or ridicule an editor and drive him to disgrace with a light remark properly aimed. Even the mild-mannered Prince Charles was now on occasion quite capable of demonstrating the royal chill. Now that she was one of them, Diana would have to learn how to survive.

The *Evening Standard* editorialized wisely: "It is inhuman and inhumane to expect her to stand up to the kind of mega-star pressure to which she is being subjected. As a matter of common humanity, press and Palace should take a new and urgent look at how that pressure might be eased."

What was absolutely false was the rumor that Prince Charles was "desperately unhappy." He had never been happier in his life. Nothing could be more natural than occasional spats with his wife. They had a thirteen-year difference in age, a difference in outlook, a difference in responsibility, a difference in training, a difference in taste. They were both bright enough, and in love enough, to bridge most of these differences. But flare-ups were to be expected. Nobody could question the physical feeling they had for each other. It was visible and tangible. They were invariably seen holding hands, constantly looking at each other with open admiration and affection. Prince Charles was a family man, and now he had his own family. He was a home-loving man, and now he had his own home.

If it were true, as several papers put it, that the Prince had sought medical advice for his wife, it was probably more because of her growing nervous tension than her weight loss.

Whatever the trouble or tension of this period, it disappeared and

Diana was soon in sparkling form again. She reunited with her old roommates to rejoice in the wedding of her friend Carolyn Pride to a disco manager and heir to a brewery fortune, William Bartholomew. At the opening of an extension for the Royal School for the Blind, she had advice for another bride-to-be: "Married life is wonderful, so don't worry." Visiting a children's playgroup, she told the mothers: "By the way, I am feeling *very* well." At a welcoming ceremony for Queen Beatrix of the Netherlands, the press got a good look at her and decided she did look healthy after all.

Her son was healthy too, she said. "William is enormous. He weighs sixteen pounds now and he's growing up very fast. He has started spitting. It's amazing the things they pick up at his age. I can't wait until William starts walking."

As a patron of the National Association of Pre-School Playgroups, she attended a session with mothers at a new playgroup. "Charles seems to want to share in the work," she told them. "He wants to bathe him all the time." She looked radiant, full of vitality, and she insisted once again, "I'm so happy and I feel so well." She even blew bubbles with a plastic straw for a three-year-old.

On a two-day visit to North Wales with Prince Charles, she dedicated a memorial to 226 men who died 48 years ago in one of Britain's worst mining disasters. She also rode a narrow-gauge railway, watched a staged inshore rescue, launched a new lifeboat named *The Princess of Wales* and headed straight for two-year-old William Evans holding a placard that read: MY NAME IS WILLIAM.

She also contradicted Princess Michael of Kent, who had said that Prince William had tufts of red hair. "William is blond. He has *masses* of blond hair." A Palace spokesman trying to breach the differing opinions by the two Royal women compromised with this description: "It's sort of blond with red glints. It depends on the light."

Describing the mood of the household during a weekend at Highgrove, a visitor reported effusively, "It's such a happy young household. The Prince often wanders around in jeans and an open-necked shirt which he would never have done at Buckingham Palace. There was always lots of laughter, but now with a baby it's even better. I have never seen a man change so much in his habits as the Prince has recently. Charles and Diana just sit and talk about babies the whole time."

303

With Princess Diana back again in gear, some of the intense press focus now was pointed at other Royals, Princess Anne and her husband canceled plans to visit Africa together and flew off in separate directions, causing rumors to multiply that their marriage was not doing well. Prince Andrew spiced up the front pages by going off for a fling with soft-porn actress Koo Stark on the Caribbean island of Mustique, where Princess Margaret earlier scandalized Britain by having a romantic tryst with young pop star Roddy Llewellyn while still married to Lord Snowdon. A new book revealed titillating details about Her Majesty's personal quirks: The Queen always traveled with her hot-water bottle, her monogrammed electric kettle, and a special white-kid lavatory seat. It also added that she liked jigsaw puzzles and deep pink long-stemmed carnations.

Prince Philip caused his own small flap by berating the people of the Solomon Islands for having too many babies. And Diana got a plea from Liverpool gynecologist Harold Francis, urging her to limit her family to two children. Francis predicted a "copycat boom of babies" following the birth of William.

"Princess Diana has to realize that she is a trendsetter and whatever she does, a lot of young brides will emulate."

Diana instead gave a royal seal of approval to natural childbirth methods by being guest of honor at a fashion show to raise money for Birthright, an organization researching problems of premature babies. Dr. George Pinker was on the council.

Prince Charles made his own medical contribution, offering to donate his heart, kidneys, and liver for transplant if he was killed in an accident. Doctors openly hoped that others would emulate him.

The Prince now took off alone for a short trip to Montezuma, New Mexico, to attend the dedication ceremony for the newest campus of the United World Colleges, whose 102 students represented 46 countries. The students were outnumbered by the celebrities, who included everybody from Cary Grant to Abigail ("Dear Abby") Van Buren to Merv Griffin. "If you are going to wage war against war," said Griffin, quoting Gandhi, "you better start with the children."

Charles took over as international president of the Colleges from his great-uncle, Lord Mountbatten. Its goal was to foster world peace. "The whole idea is to have people from different faiths and backgrounds and cultures being able to work together . . . to build up this awareness . . . to understand the other religions' points of view. It makes for tolerance. If we learn from other people and their faiths, we will have a much more reasonable understanding of the nature of our existence."

The Prince amplified this in discussing the Commonwealth. "One central problem about life lies in ignorance and prejudice. Most of us are prejudiced about something or other, and many of us are also ignorant about a great deal . . you cannot judge a country like a Third World country through Western eyes . . . One of the great advantages in having the Commonwealth is in the links it helps to foster between developing countries and the developed . . .

"People keep telling me that the most successful marriages are the ones where you have to make an effort, that you cannot expect the whole thing to be lovely, rosy, and successful unless you work at it. Exactly the same can be said of the Commonwealth."

Some were soon throwing his words about marriage back at him. "It is not enough to love his bride—as he so clearly does. It is also necessary to sustain her . . . wives are simply not left to their own devices . . . her desires . . . her desires are quite as important as his." Those were words from someone in the *Daily Mail.*

Columnist Nigel Dempster gave his private report of a dinner Diana had with her husband and "all his polo pals."

"She got up in the middle, threw her napkin down and said, 'I've never been so bored in all my life.' "

Did the world prefer the scenario of *Romeo and Juliet?* One night, that's just what they got. A packed audience for a variety show fund-raiser at the Royal Opera House on Christmas Gala night. Suddenly, a young man appeared onstage in the costume of Romeo. It was Prince Charles. The spotlight then switched dramatically to the royal box, and there was Juliet. Only it was Princess Diana. The audience gasped. While they still stared, unbelieving, Diana threw down a rope for her Romeo to climb. The Prince produced a ladder instead. The audience now broke into loud laughter.

"Speak to me," the Romeo-Prince implored his Juliet-Princess.

Diana replied with the words from the television ice-cream commercial she had sung at the start of her carriage trip to their wedding: "Just one Cornetto." Some people were laughing so hard that tears were streaming down their faces.

Prince Charles then raced up the ladder, bent down on one knee to kiss his wife, then publicly embraced her while the audience went wild, everyone standing, laughing, cheering.

Nobody enjoyed it more than the Prince and Princess.

At the family Christmas reunion at Windsor Castle in 1982, six-month-old William had his picture taken in his mother's arms. Another photo session took place in their Kensington Palace home. Prince William was plump and serious. His parents chucked him under the chin, waved small toys at him, snapped their fingers, made a variety of sounds—but nothing made him smile. "They never do what you want them to do," said the Prince. "I'm sorry he's not all that smiley today. We will probably get all those child specialists saying we handled him wrong." Then he laughed. "You should have been here at half past eight."

His mother finally tickled William, gave him a string of kisses, and that did it. A grin and a gurgling kind of chuckle resulted.

The young Prince showed the television audience his white silk embroidered romper suit, but no teeth. While he was chewing on his brightly colored teething ring and rattle, the consensus among viewers was that he looked like Charles did when he was a boy, with the same impish personality, but that he had his mother's hair and his grandfather Spencer's smile.

The genealogists had never stopped tracing lines, and their latest discovery was that William might well have had a direct ancestor in the real king behind the legend of King Arthur. New research identified a fifth-century British king named Riothamus—which meant High King—referred to elsewhere as Arthur. (Arthur was William's second name.) His ancestry already had been traced back to Cedric, the first king of the West Saxons, who landed at Southampton in A.D. 495.

Before his mother carried him away, Prince William perhaps showed the signs of things to come and grabbed a photographer's finger. "He has a really strong grip," commented the cameraman.

Diana had begun to make more solo appearances again, mainly at hospitals and children's centers. At the Great Ormond Street Hospital, the children were already waiting for her on the balcony, shouting "Di! Di!" Waiting with them were nurses, doctors, and even surgeons still in their green gowns, their masks hanging loosely around their necks, who had hurried out of their operating rooms to get a quick look.

Diana's step-grandmother, Barbara Cartland, who perhaps had private reason for bitterness, nevertheless glowed about Diana. "Oh, Diana's proved her magic," said Miss Cartland in her impressive dining room. The table was covered with everything for a proper tea—delicious dark chocolate cake, superb meringues, a delicate assortment of small sandwiches.

"I went the other day to open a special room for very old people in our worst kind of hospital. Old people who are senile but not bad enough for an asylum. Mongol children who never grow up. If you give your hand to any of them, they won't give it up. These are mentally deficient people who never go out, never go anywhere. A sad, terrifying place. But they all have cut out Princess Diana's picture and tacked it on the wall. I also visit a lot of factories and all the workers have her picture over their machines. And in France they're just as mad about her as they are in America.

"She's captured the world! Maybe they see the natural kindness in her face. Oh, it's magic all right."

Miss Cartland then added, "I'll tell you something else about those two. They've got such beautiful manners. If you send them anything, they write by return mail. Beautiful manners. When you think of the amount of letters they must get, it's absolutely amazing, staggering, and yet they write by return. And Princess Diana writes a beautiful letter."

What moved most people in a crowd was not just her manners and her style but her concern. "I'm so touched that you bothered to stand out here to see me," she would tell them. "You must be frozen."

This was not something they might expect from Princess Anne or Princess Margaret or some of the other Royals. But beyond that, she talked to them, told them things about her child and her husband. In the several weeks before Christmas, she covered more royal engagements than any other Royal, twice as many as her husband. She even wrote letters to local playgroups asking if they would want her to visit them. For most of these appearances, she came alone.

When she visited the Royal Marsden Hospital, she stopped in the ward where women were all suffering from breast cancer, sat on every bed, and chatted with every woman. She always stayed much longer than scheduled.

Always there were appreciative comments: "You're beautiful, luv." "You're fantastic, darling." "We love you, Diana." She might spend a full day in the provinces, fly back in the evening just in time to dress for a charity dinner with Prince Charles. Suddenly she had been transformed into a working Princess.

"But I always find time each day for William," she told an old woman in a Coventry club. "He comes first . . . always!"

Among the most touching encounters for Diana were those in which small children gave her Christmas presents for William, mostly soft toys. William's nursery at Highgrove was a bright place with a wraparound mural, hand-painted furniture, small tables and chairs, and a tiny rocking horse. There was also a trolley bath with a convenient foldaway blue plastic tub and plastic shelves, a wicker basket trimmed with white ribbon for "bits and bobs," and three large jars painted with teddy bears. Besides a large fluffy frog, there was a music box that played "The Love Bugs."

Nanny Barbara Barnes was perfectly content to let the parents do as much as they wanted with the baby. As she put it, William was not her child, after all. And she had two rules which Diana liked: A nanny should be firm and loving, but she should not raise her voice or her hand. Butler Alan Fisher, who also loved children, had no such compunction. If the reason was strong enough, he might very well smack a Royal bottom.

Shopping was still Diana's passionate pastime and she sneaked out whenever she could, even though it became increasingly difficult to go anywhere unrecognized. Her wardrobe had now become more high-fashion. She favored strapless black taffeta that "brought back the shoulders and the bosom." She also wore knee breeches and flat shoes, looking as if she had stepped "out of the frames of nineteenth-century upper-class paintings by Lawrence and Winterhalter."

Indeed Diana embodied the very upper-class country British look of angular body, flawless complexion, minimum makeup, well-brushed and beautifully cut hair.

But she still went to Sloane Ranger shops. She'd scoot around in her Ford Escort accompanied by her detective and bodyguard, and visit the General Trading Company (where she had her wedding list and where Prince Charles still buys from the catalogue), Harvey Nichols, and Harrods for overall necessities and nearby Benetton for Italian separates. At Harvey Nichols she was seen wandering from the knick-knacks on the third floor to the men's shop to look at a

Charles & Diana

Dior tie for her husband's birthday. A few streets away, at Beauchamp Place, she visited the shop of Caroline Charles, a top designer. She was there at lunchtime, and observers saw trays of food arriving from the posh San Lorenzo Restaurant.

She bought shoes from Charles Jourdan, Peruvian hand-knit sweaters from Elizabeth Street, nightwear from Night Owls on Fulham Road, print handbags from Souleiado. All these shops were, of course, delighted to send her anything she wanted to see in the privacy of her Kensington Palace apartment. When she shopped publicly, she could count only on the natural British reserve to let her alone, even when she was recognized.

This did not include photographers. Prince Charles and Princess Diana discussed possible solutions with a London editor. Was it possible, Diana wondered, for photographers to take pictures of her before she went into a store, and then not follow her inside? The editor patiently explained why that wouldn't work: The photographers would be fired if they all came back with a picture everybody else had. Their job was to get an exclusive shot.

Even though Prince Charles could not have cared less about clothes, some thirty-six firms held royal warrants from him. The warrants had been in existence since the Middle Ages and were a mark of recognition that an individual was a supplier of goods or services to the Royal Household. They entitled the grantee to use the term "By Appointment," and to display the royal coat of arms on their company's products, on their stationery, and on their premises.

Henry VIII gave a royal warrant to Thomas Hewytt to "serve the Court with Swannes and Cranes and all kinds of Wildfoule." Other royal warrants in other years included a "Pin Maker," a "Rat Catcher," and an "Operator for the Teeth."

Some of Prince Charles's warrants were for medals (Spink & Son), shirts (Turnbull & Asser), and polo sticks (J. Salter). He preferred striped shirts or solid plain colors, nearly all of which need cufflinks. His ties were similarly plain or striped. He liked a handkerchief in his breast pocket and, often, a carnation in his buttonhole. His suits usually were single-breasted and quietly conservative. Aside from his city wardrobe, he had tweeds for the country, kilts for Scotland, safari suits for hot climates, a Norfolk suit for shooting, and a complete range of uniforms.

One of his favorite places for amusing presents was a novelty shop in Tetbury with the strange name of Tetbury Furniture Com-

309

pany. He also expanded his collection of old toilets at Homelines in London, specializing in old painted "loos" and mahogany toilet seats.

While the Prince's hobby was old toilets, the Princess liked to collect jewels, new and old. From her original delicate necklace with the gold D, she had graduated to an elegant gold and diamond pendant complete with the Prince of Wales feathers, a choker of emeralds, a diamond feather brooch, sapphire and diamond earrings, and, of course, her dazzling tiara from the Queen. She still preferred the same mannish round-faced watch she wore as a teenager, only now it was made of 18-carat gold.

Diana and the other Spencer women—sisters, mother, and grandmother—operated a sort of jewel pool, in which they shared what they had. It is doubtful, however, that Diana would have loaned any of them the sunray diamond necklace that she wore to the opening of Parliament. It was a Queen Mary heirloom and the Queen herself wore it for her birthday portrait the previous June.

For Diana, 1982 had been a year of astonishing adjustment to the world of the Royals. There were those who felt that the pressure had been too great, that she had simply "freaked out." But in her hectic round of engagements before Christmas, she showed the world that she was still the same naturally easy Diana who could say, "What a long time to sit! I've got pins and needles in my bottom."

"Her eyes were so bright that I could light my pipe at them." That was a description of Diana's ancestor, Georgiana, Duchess of Devonshire. Despite all the year's trauma, much the same would be said, two hundred years later, of Diana. A Chelsea pensioner, after Princess Diana's visit, commented, "There were many hearts broken here yesterday."

Diana herself said of the royal scene, "It's seventy percent sheer slog and thirty percent fantastic."

22

The year 1983 was destined to be Princess Diana's toughest year because it was the year she learned the full reality of the Royals' world. The heart of her lesson was that people don't like an unblemished story. "They like to see warts even if there aren't any."

The couple needed a second honeymoon. Away from royal duties, away from Britain, away from their staff, and even away from their baby. And, more than anything else, *away from the press*. The last was virtually impossible.

"I'll tell you why," said photographer Kent Gavin of the *Daily Mirror*, who has been covering the couple for a long time. "It's really very simple. Diana is the number one pinup in the world. No question about that. But she has this phobia that 'I'm private. I'm on holiday. I'm not yours.' Well, the Royal Family is never on holiday. The world wants to *know*. I really think she'd like to be just Diana Spencer, and just go round like that. Well, she can't. Never again.

"Another thing. If you check the most sensational pictures about Diana, I think you'll find that most of them were made by the foreign paparazzi. They can afford to hire helicopters and everything else to chase after Diana. And you know why? Because any exclusive picture they get is worth a bloody fortune. For example, take that skiing vacation . . ."

Charles and Diana had picked a fairytale castle perched on a 500-foot cliff in Liechtenstein, accessible only by a single road. The castle belonged to seventy-six-year-old Prince Franz Josef, a distant relative. In his bachelor days, Charles had visited the castle several times and loved the peaceful beauty of the place. There was a rumor once that Charles might marry Franz Josef's daughter Nora. Not only was the setting idyllic but the castle, with its 15-foot-thick stone walls, seemed blissfully cut off from the world.

No longer. Within an hour of their arrival the nearby Schlossle Hotel registered forty reporters and photographers from every part of Europe. The watch was on. Suddenly a royal car came down the castle road "like lightning," and most of the forty newsmen were in hot pursuit. When they caught up with the car, they discovered that "Diana" was really one of Prince Josef's chambermaids. Charles and Diana meanwhile had taken off for Laax, Switzerland.

But their escape was short-lived. The local Swiss paper got a call from one of its loyal readers who had seen them. A rented helicopter with three Swiss photographers was soon on the way. Spotting the royal couple on the Vorab glacier, they buzzed them. Diana waved her ski poles angrily. It was futile. The helicopter followed them down slopes, landing ahead of them to get pictures. Then it shadowed Charles and Diana up a ski lift, landed in time to get a picture of them on the lift together. The helicopter then put down in the car park for still another picture.

The press was now at every intersection, watching for any car, with binoculars. But Charles and Diana had already raced into nearby Austria. Austrian customs people were alerted to give newsmen and photographers a hard time at the checkpoints, delaying them as long as they could. By the time they caught up with Charles and Diana, the royal pair were lunching at a mountainside restaurant. After a long wait, Charles appeared, smiled, and said, "Now I'm going to blow my nose for everyone to photograph." And everyone did.

The Prince's personal bodyguard, Police Superintendent John Maclean, then made an agreement with the press. If they would let the Prince and Princess lunch in peace, the Royals would promise them a photo session at the end of the afternoon. The press agreed. But when they returned, Diana had reneged. She would not pose. This was her holiday. This was her private time. Why didn't they leave her alone? When she did emerge from the restaurant, she kept her head down. The Prince pleaded, "Please, Diana, don't do that. Don't be stupid. Please, darling . . . please, darling." She wasn't listening. She huddled glumly in a woolen ski hat pulled firmly over her head, her gloves hiding her face. Maclean apologized sheepishly to the press. "We haven't kept our side of the bargain, so I guess it's too much to expect you to keep yours."

On the ski slopes of Lech in western Austria, a British newspaper even hired a seventy-year-old ski expert to ski along with the royal pair and judge Diana's downhill ability. She was wearing a burgundy-red ski suit with white boots and a blue and white crocheted hat. Charles's ski suit was royal blue. The ski expert's judgment was that Diana was good, very good considering she hadn't skied for several years. Charles had fallen once, but she had stayed upright. As the expert tried to get closer to Diana, he was knocked off his feet twice by her bodyguard, once near a 200-foot precipice. He still gallantly predicted that Diana "could easily reach silver and gold medal standard by her mid-20s"—provided she had enough practice.

Their ten-day "holiday" was hardly a vacation, much less a second honeymoon. And their anguish was not over.

The British newspapers had headlined the skiing story: DIANA FLEES SKI SLOPE, CHARLES IN RAGE. SULKY DI. DIANA 80 PERCENT CERTAIN TO HAVE BREAKDOWN.

"When the Queen Mother was the Duchess of York and became Queen, she had a more gradual time to adjust because there wasn't the full power of publicity and television. Diana hasn't had that time," said a cousin. "That's why Diana almost had a couple of nervous breakdowns."

Two psychiatrists had decided they knew exactly what was going on. "If she has not already gotten sick," said Dr. Thomas Holms of Diana, "there is a real potential for her doing so." An obsessive-compulsive illness is a definite possibility." The doctor based his opinion on the Holms-Rahe stress scale which he had helped devise. Using a system of life-change units, he tabulated the degree of stress an individual undergoes adjusting to certain events. Anyone scoring between 150 and 300 points on this scale, according to Holms, stands a 50 percent chance of becoming ill in the near future. Based on her behavior at public events since her wedding, Diana had scored an alarming 407. Thus her potential for mental illness was increased to 80 percent. Her stress chart changes included marriage, pregnancy, birth of child, career change, change in work responsibilities, outstanding personal achievement, change in living conditions, revision of personal habits, change in work hours or conditions, change in church activities, change in residence, change in social activities, change in recreation, change in family get-togethers, vacation, Christmas. Added possible stress points involved trouble with "boss," change in marital arrangements, trouble with in-laws, and change in eating habits. The added points raised her score to 509.

London psychiatrist Arthur Hyatt Williams also felt compelled to advise, "If one is barely out of adolescence, one wants adulation, glamor, indulgence, but there is also the adolescent yearning for privacy, which is encroached on. Some can solve it, some cannot."

Still another analyst, Dr. Ira D. Glick, professor of psychiatry at Cornell University–New York Hospital Medical Center, saw the early years of a marriage as a period in which important tasks must be accomplished, such as establishing an identity and a system of communications as well as criteria for making decisions.

"When couples have a problem they can't solve they sometimes go public with it. In doing so, often one member of the couple is looking for an ally."

If so, who was Diana's ally now?

An observer noted that the honeymoon with the press was over and it was now time for Diana to play the role of the Ice Princess or the Wicked Fairy. Royal watcher Jean Rook of the *Daily Express* pointed out acidly that Princess Diana behaved "like a little Madam . . . like a spoilt brat" when she refused to pose for pictures at the ski resort.

"If she wants to sulk inside a woolly hat, she shouldn't have taken the Crown. What right have photographers to encroach on her 'privacy'? None, if she's in a private place. But in the eye of the public, she must acknowledge public interest.

"Because the day the British public's interest in the Royal Family ends, only God can save the lot of them!"

Discussing the subject on a BBC-TV program, Nicholas Lloyd, editor of *The Sunday People*, claimed that the press had respected royal privacy during the Christmas holidays, but that when Charles and Diana ventured onto alpine ski slopes, the press had a job to do. If the Princess had posed for pictures each morning for a few minutes, she could have avoided the furor.

The Queen's Press Secretary, Michael Shea, briskly dismissed that idea. "The press did not leave the Royal Family alone over the holidays. There were fifty journalists around Sandringham during the first two weeks of the year. And it is rubbish to say that the press would be satisfied with three minutes of pictures each morning. They would still chase the Prince and Princess during the day. They do it whether the Princess is in a public or a private place—look at the photographers who hid at a private beach in the West Indies last year to catch the Princess.

"No, I'm afraid what we saw in Liechtenstein was a measure of the standards of the lower half of Fleet Street press," said Shea.

One paper that felt guilt pangs was the *Daily Star*, which editorialized: "We have certainly lost our sense of fair play . . . At times in the past, in our enthusiasm to satisfy the public interest, we, like the rest of Fleet Street and certainly the foreign press, have gone too far in our pursuit of royal stories and pictures . . . The Queen and her family are entitled to some privacy, just like every other person in Britain . . . She [Diana] just wanted to be alone with her husband . . . .

"Fair play has always been the seedcorn of the British way of life. The Royal Family are entitled to fair play from the press.

"ENOUGH IS ENOUGH!"

The editor of one of London's most important newspapers paced his large office, his face wrinkled with obvious concern. He didn't like what he was about to say. "I sometimes feel ashamed to be in my profession," he said solemnly. "A photographer knows that if he catches a Royal in an awkward moment, or if he even catches little William doing a wink-o against a tree, he's got $25,000 in his pocket for that negative. The media concentration on the Royal Family does make life difficult for them. But it's not going to change and they must know it. It's natural for Andrew or Edward to go with girls, and it's wrong for the press to hound them.

"There's no question that the enormous publicity on Diana is creating some kind of tension among the Royal Family. I would think that Anne has her nose out of joint a little. Margaret, who has always been a problem, will now be more so—she's pushed even further into the background when she was once Number Two on the Royal Tree. Surely even the Queen must feel the lopsidedness of the situation, with Diana getting so much, compared to what the Queen gets in terms of publicity. The Queen is now regarded by the press and photographers as a middle-aged monarch, and somewhat out of it. And she doesn't smile as much as she used to. It's because she worries about everything, and she worries a lot. After all, the ultimate responsibility is hers. It's true the other Royals have a lot of duties. They do them, and work at them. But the ultimate responsibility is single-handedly hers. In a time of crisis, whether it's a coal strike, or the Falklands, or a constitutional question, she alone must face up to it. Even though she does not have the power, she has the worry, and feels the responsibility."

What the editor did not say was that while Her Majesty might perhaps resent some of the lopsidedness of the publicity—a poll had declared that Princess Diana was the most popular woman in Britain—the Queen surely was not sad to see some of the press heat deflected onto her daughter-in-law.

Several months before, a barefoot intruder, Michael Fagan, reached the Queen's bedroom in Buckingham Palace by scaling a 60-foot drainpipe.

"Get out of here at once," said the Queen in her most official voice. "Our eyes met and both of us looked dumbfounded," she related afterward. Fagan instead sat on the edge of her bed and talked about his family problems. The Queen pressed the panic button at her bedside. No one came to the rescue. She lifted a phone and said calmly, "Send someone to my room at once."

"Don't be alarmed, Your Majesty. I won't do anything to harm you," Fagan insisted, and then asked for a cigarette.

When the Queen's chambermaid arrived, she reportedly blurted, "Bloody hell, Ma'am—what's he doing in here?"

"Take him outside and give him a cigarette," said the Queen. The police finally came, and were even more embarrassed to learn that Fagan had entered the Palace grounds two weeks earlier, two days before President Reagan visited. A chambermaid had seen him then, called the police—who did not arrive until hours later. Nor were the police pleased to hear from Fagan that he had planned to cut his wrists with an ashtray in the Queen's presence.

"If the Duke of Edinburgh had been sleeping here, it would have been a different story," remarked the Queen.

That remark hit like a thunderclap. It was the first time the British public officially learned that the Queen and Prince Philip slept in separate bedrooms. It was also clear from all accounts that Prince Philip had not slept at the Palace at all that night. It made for interesting speculation.

The security scandal heightened with the revelation that the Queen's bodyguard was a homosexual being blackmailed by a male prostitute. The fact that he was a homosexual was of small concern—it was common knowledge that there was a large gay circle at Buckingham Palace.

"There are about sixty gays on the Queen's staff, about thirty with the Queen Mother, and there are still about six with Prince Charles," said a former staff member. "What's interesting is that the

Princess is particularly interested in whether somebody is or is not gay, and always asks about it."

Senior Palace officials had come up through the public school system where homosexuality was not considered unusual. Moreover, the so-called Gay Mafia was generally discreet. The shock here was that the male prostitute had threatened to take his story to the press.

Worrying about these security breaches, a thirteen-year-old schoolgirl, Joanne Dobson, wrote to the Queen offering her mongrel dog, Sonny, as a guard dog. The Queen replied promptly, thanking Joanne, but saying that her security was now under urgent review.

Reading the news that week, Diana must have reconsidered the future glory of being Queen.

Only a half mile from Buckingham Palace, a bomb exploded in the barracks of Her Majesty's Cavalry, killing and mutilating people and horses. The headlines again blared about Andrew and his porn-star playmate. Despite the extraction of a painful wisdom tooth, the Queen had to preside at a Palace garden party for 9,000 guests. Probably even more painful was the fact that she had to shake hands with Labor MP Willie Hamilton, the single worst critic of the Royal Family.

He had said of Her Majesty: "The Queen is a middle-aged woman of limited intellect." Of Princess Margaret: "Margaret is a royal floozy." Of Prince Charles: "He can be the biggest nitwit in the world." Of Princess Anne and Mark Phillips: "They are bloody parasites." Of Prince Philip: "The HP sauce on the royal fish and chips." Of the Royal Family as a whole: "If every member of the Royal Family were ditched in the Channel tomorrow, I would sleep soundly."

Willie Hamilton still had the gall to complain about his meeting with the Queen: "Her handshake was very frigid. I am very angry about it."

The psychiatrists might well have wondered what a week's worth of press attention like that might have done to Diana's stress chart. The Princess herself now partially answered that question. After ten days of fleeing the press in Europe, often driving at 100 miles an hour, refusing to be photographed, "She was damned if she was going to have her picture taken," said one of her staff. She was described as agitated, nervous, distraught, angry. Yet on her first night back in Britain, back on public royal duty, there she was sparkling and smiling again while the photographers clicked away.

One of the photographers had some advice: "She should learn the trick of her father-in-law, the Duke of Edinburgh, who would smile graciously at the camera at the same time cursing you through his teeth. We got our pictures, and he got in his abuse. Everyone was happy."

Nobody was surprised when Diana decided not to present the British press awards that year. Discussing the "incredible harassment," Press Secretary Michael Shea noted, "She is undoubtedly fed up."

Mary, the late Princess Royal, had discussed the strain inherent in being born to life within the royal circle: "None but those trained from youth to such an ordeal can sustain it with amiability and composure."

Still another psychiatrist, this one a top marriage counselor—who insisted on remaining anonymous—presented his analysis of the Princess's current mood: "Probably because of her troubled childhood, Diana is emotionally naked. All her feelings, whether of delight or dismay, are on the surface. I suspect there are an awful lot of hormones chasing around in that young lady causing her to be tearful, giggly, generally far too transparent. She is too immature to hide her feelings and may never be able to do so. . . .

"My assessment is that she does not need the adulation she receives from the public—that is already wearing thin. She needs much more love from Charles . . . What she needs from marriage is passion, compassion, and companionship . . . Personally, I would doubt that Prince Charles is all that loving. Too much of his energy goes on horseback . . . Diana needs a man who comes home at night and helps her with her baby. Someone she can cook for and look after . . . They need time together . . ."

As sensible as this advice might seem, it was simply not realistic. They were Royals. They both had jobs to do. These jobs would often take them away from each other. Along the rocky road of marriage and family and royal duty, they would have to work out their own compromises.

Gradually there was the heightened realization that this was a willful young woman with her own strong mind. When Charles tried to persuade her to pose for photographers on that ski trip, she simply refused. "She doesn't listen to a word Charles says," commented one of the photographers. Another described Charles as "unhappy and rather dazed at the turn of events."

Photographers might well have summed up the situation by saying to Diana: "You didn't know you were marrying us too, did you?"

What could Diana do?

The Queen had a dignified answer to personal attack: silence. That was partly the reason the Queen and Prince Charles did not read the sensational press.

There were exceptions. When a former member of the kitchen staff sold his story of Palace high jinks to the press, Buckingham Palace sued to stop publication. On being hired, every member of the royal household signs an agreement never to reveal what he sees or hears in the course of duty. According to kitchen worker Kieran Kenny, Prince Andrew's girlfriend Koo would "romp through the royal apartments without a care for protocol." Kenny claimed that "Koo would often stay overnight on a weekend when the Queen was away, nibbling on the Queen's favorite Bendick's Superfine Chocolate, and issuing orders to the staff." Kenny also told how "barefoot Di buttered my toast."

The Queen meanwhile had her job to do. In March of 1983 that meant a trip to the West Coast of the United States.

Princess Diana may have envied that trip. Despite her own fresh celebrity status, she still stood in awe of film stars. Her hairdresser recalled how excited she was at the idea of meeting "James Bond," Roger Moore, at a film preview. She wanted a special hairdo, and decided to wear her most dazzling dress.

Her Majesty was never nervous on any of these tours—everyone else was. An observer described Nancy Reagan acting "like a nervous schoolgirl . . . She pirouetted before the cameras for a full five minutes in her royal purple and gold awaiting the arrival of the Queen."

In Hollywood fashion, the dinner for Her Majesty was held at Sound Stage 9 at 20th Century-Fox. The Royals were seated on a dais with members of Hollywood's British acting colony and somebody said it looked "like a Last Supper painted by Sir Joshua Reynolds." Tony Richardson, who sat between the First Lady and the Queen, seemed remarkably calm. Somebody said it was because he had not been told where he would be sitting, and when he did sit down, he died of fright.

A knowing observer claimed that the Queen had been had; that the dinner was a Ronald Reagan payoff to his Hollywood supporters, and was meant to bankroll his coming campaign. Her Majesty, nevertheless, seemed to enjoy herself. She liked the Frank Sinatra songs and the George Burns jokes. "Me without a cigar is like Zsa Zsa Gabor blushing on her wedding night." And, "At age seventy-nine I played God. Anything I can do at this age is a miracle."

The usually blasé Tinsel Town was impressed by the Queen's triple-strand necklace, bracelet, and drop earrings, all in diamonds. Of her white chiffon gown, New York fashion designer Halston afterward suggested that she should have shown more cleavage.

The sour note from all these Hollywood celebrities, straining to get closer to the Queen, was that so few of them actually got to meet her. Not even Fred Astaire. They ignored a call to remain seated and all stood on tiptoe for a final look at Her Majesty as she left the dinner.

The California weather was unseasonably wet and the local Los Angeles headline read: QUEEN TURNS A GRAY DAY INTO A ROYAL BLUE EVENT. James Mason described the Hollywood dinner turnout as the typical "cattle call." Others added that the Queen had discovered that underneath the Hollywood tinsel was just more tinsel.

Reporters in conversation with the Queen are not supposed to quote her, but on this trip some brash Americans broke the rule. Asked if she would be riding horses at the President's ranch, she grinned, "Of course, that's the whole idea of the trip, isn't it?" And what would she be doing at Yosemite Park? "Well, it'll give me a chance to put up my feet a bit." She had seen *The Prince and the Pauper* on television and somebody asked if she would ever change places with a pauper. No. "I like being recognized. I like being Queen."

Among the usual picket signs that seemed to go where the Queen went, one read: GOD SAVE THE QUEEN FROM NUCLEAR ATTACK. A cheerier one added: BODY BEAUTIFUL CAR WASH SAYS WELCOME QUEEN ELIZABETH. Staff members of Her Majesty breathed a quiet sigh of relief that an American photographer hadn't requested any special pose saying, "Hey, Queenie . . ."

Back in Britain, with the press focus away from him, Prince Charles managed to slip away for a week. He had been described as "desperately keen to get away." Certainly he needed his private time as much as anyone.

What he chose to do was unexpected. He worked as a farmhand

on the 500-acre Yardworthy farm on the edge of Dartmoor in his Duchy of Cornwall, getting up at seven, milking cows, delivering a calf, building stone fences. But he would also hike two miles to the nearest public telephone each night to call his wife without worrying that the phone might be tapped. At the end of it, he said he had found it "most rewarding," even though the work had been hard and his back hurt.

The farm breakfasts had been splendid, he said, and he got to know the cows well "by their udders."

"Being on the land does help one get a sense of proportion much better than being stuck in the city . . . I think being here has restored my sanity."

Diana also restored some of her sanity by taking a few trips on her own. She visited the impoverished areas of Glasgow, despite threats from the Scottish National Liberation Army protesting her visit. (They actually sent a letter bomb that exploded in City Hall.) She also visited the home of a British rail electrician, Bert McAllen, and posed with his four children while their proud father snapped the picture. "I'm afraid that my boy Barry tried to eat the Princess's cake as she was having her tea," said Mrs. McAllen, "but she coped beautifully."

These short solo side trips into reality could only help their "rumbustious" young marriage. But still Charles and Diana needed that second honeymoon. Instead, what they had coming up was a 45,000-mile royal tour of Australia and New Zealand. Tradition had it that they would leave their baby behind for the six weeks. That was what the Queen Mother had done, and what the Queen had done. Diana was different. She was sharp and loud and clear: She would not go without her baby.

The Queen understood and sympathized. She remembered her own tears when she was a twenty-five-year-old mother saying goodbye to her children for six months. There was no royal arm-twisting, no confrontation. This was a royal tradition the Queen was happy to see broken.

The decision was entirely Diana's. And she had a simple explanation which most mothers understood: "I find I can't stop playing with him."

23

irst you must imagine that you're the Prince or Princess of Wales. You must pretend to shake hands with a certain number of people, record how much time it takes at each place to wave and collect bouquets, and literally walk every foot of ground that they will walk, noting exactly how long it takes. At every stop, you must know specifically who will be there, where they will sit or stand, what they will say, and, most of all, how much time it will take. Everything, minutely detailed, will fill hundreds of pages, take almost a year of intense preparation.

Such was the preparation of Victor Chapman, the assigned press secretary on the Australia–New Zealand trip, and Edward Adeane, Prince Charles's private secretary. Even preliminary to all this was the sorting-out of invitations to decide which institution or place to visit and why.

"My father is an industrialist," said Jane Owen. "The Queen was scheduled to come to lunch one day at his factory. Well, months before it happened, Palace representatives arrived to go into every detail of who sat where and would say what, and when, and for how long. They not only discussed exactly what food would be served, but they actually prepared the food and served it. And then, shortly before the Queen came, there was still another full dress rehearsal, again with the actual serving of the food.

"I remember when Princess Anne once went to a gypsy camp and afterward remarked how clean it was. Well, of course it was clean. Like every place on a royal tour, it's cleaned up and showcased months in advance. The Royals don't seem to realize but everything is showcased for them, everything shined and polished, everyone on their best behavior. Most of the time, they're not seeing the real world at all."

The object of Charles and Diana's trip, however, was not simply to see the real world. Their trip to Australia had major political importance. Australia, in a recent election, had given a landslide victory to the Labor Party. The new Prime Minister, Robert James Lee Hawke, talked bluntly during his campaign about cutting all ties with the British monarchy, making Australia an independent republic by the end of the century. Of the upcoming royal tour, Hawke had said, "I don't regard welcoming them as the most important thing I'm going to have to do in the first nine months of office." Then he added, "I've had the opportunity of meeting Prince Charles, and I find him a nice young bloke. I don't think we will be talking about kings of Australia forever more."

That was his softer public tone. Privately he was much more caustic. And a great many Aussies agreed. As one of them put it, "There is not much to make the monarchy stick here, is there?"

Diana had another concern: What should she wear? Temperatures would range from broiling hot in Alice to rainy chill in Tasmania to near freezing elsewhere. Besides day dresses, evening dresses, bikinis, and ball gowns, she would need summer dresses and winter dresses. Evelyn Dagley, officially known as Dresser to the Princess of Wales, not only had to make sure there were the proper hats, accessories, and jewelry for all the clothes, but she had to make sure there were enough boxes of white gloves, which get quickly soiled with the constant handshaking.

Evelyn stayed home on that trip, but sent her assistant. She still remembers the emergency call from the Princess to send six more hats!

Nanny Barbara Barnes had the responsibility for managing food and diapers. On the trip, Diana would also have her press secretary, two detectives, a doctor, a lady-in-waiting, and her hairdresser. (Shortly before the trip, her private secretary, Oliver Everett, had quit without comment. There had been rumors of rows between them.) Prince Charles had a similar retinue, including two valets, "because it's a 24-hour job."

Their hosts knew the Princess would not bring along her private drinking water as the Queen did, and that she liked simple things: mostly salads and fruits, light meals generally, with an occasional barbecue. Menus at every stop already had been printed and sent to the Palace for approval.

On all these tours, the Prince had no problem. He simply ate what was put in front of him.

Known as the smallest continent, Australia featured enormous empty spaces, mostly flat and dry; three-fifths of the population clustered in cities, many of them highly industrialized. It was a country of many contrasts, with places of extraordinary natural beauty such as the world's largest coral reef. Diana and Charles both knew Australia. Diana's mother had a summer home there where Diana stayed before her engagement announcement. Charles had gone to school there, and the friendly people had washed away his shyness.

COME AND SEE HER WHILE SHE'S HOT! said the billboard advertising the town of Alice, the initial stop on the royal tour. An oasis in the middle of a desert, Alice was hit with the worst rain in fifty years several days before the couple's arrival. Floods had wiped out the causeway connecting the airfield with their scheduled hotel, and they were switched to a small, newly built motel. Instead of a bathtub, there was a wooden tub for two, called a "love tub." The staff generally wore short sleeves and slacks and one complained, "I suppose I'll have to wear a tie now."

The trip in the Royal Australian Air Force Boeing took 23 hours. They landed in the brilliant sunshine of early morning, and as Prince William was carried off the plane somebody in the crowd roared, "Here's Billy the Kid." A royal aide reported that the baby Prince had slept intermittently during the long flight "and I only heard him cry twice."

A fly landed on his face as his mother held him. "He's got his first fly on him already," noted his father. "He's going to be brought up the hard way." The traditional "Aussie salute" is to wave at flies. They soon learned to spray instead of wave. Diana was overheard asking her lady-in-waiting, "Have you got the fly spray?" They sprayed all their clothes before wearing them.

In the baking heat the Princess kissed her son before nanny Barnes whisked him away back onto the plane to head for their temporary home, while the Prince and Princess continued the tour.

Somebody complained mildly that Prince William's feet had not touched the ground of Australia. "Goodness," muttered Diana, "he isn't the Pope, you know."

Charles & Diana

The baby's new home was in Woomargama in eastern Australia, several flying hours away. It was an Australian farmhouse surrounded by 900 acres of gently sloping hills in New South Wales, with Hereford cattle and Merino sheep. It looked somewhat like an English stately home, with its rose garden, swimming pool, and artificial lake. The home was in an isolated place, about 150 miles from the farm of Diana's mother in Yass. Ronald Reagan had stayed there when he was Governor of California.

Australian police made the decision that photographers were forbidden to come closer than 23 feet to the Royals. But from whatever distance, it became quickly apparent that no matter what anybody had read anywhere about their troubled marriage, this couple was in love. Every reporter, however cynical, instantly noted it. Charles and Diana held hands whenever they could; they were constantly looking at each other with open feeling, whispering, laughing, and enjoying each other.

Relaxing after the long flight, the Princess baked herself red alongside a pool on "Snob Hill," at a borrowed bungalow, before heading back to "the Palace in Alice." That's what the locals had tagged the motel where they were staying. In preparation for their arrival, the entire place had been freshly painted, the almost-new carpets replaced with newer ones, and the mattresses aired in the sun to remove their dampness. At the fence outside the motel, cowboys still tied their horses.

Alice Springs, population 18,000, was a railroad terminus and trading center, once a gold-mining town, now famous for the TV mini-series *A Town Called Alice*. To reach 110 children scattered over 650,000 square miles, Alice had a School of the Air to broadcast educational programs. Charles and Diana sat in a dingy studio answering children's questions. They told them that Prince William had six teeth, was too young to ride a bicycle, and that one of his favorite toys was a koala bear (although a local wildlife society quickly complained because it was made of kangaroo skin). "He also has a plastic whale that throws things out of the top—little balls." The question the Princess couldn't answer was the number of rooms in Buckingham Palace. "I haven't a clue," she admitted. The Prince of Wales wasn't sure he knew either.

"Are you the King?" a five-year-old asked.

Charles smiled slightly. "No, not yet."

325

A little girl wanted to know whether Prince William could crawl.

"No," said the Princess, "he's got the right movement, but he hasn't done it yet."

The one question neither would answer was, "Do you sleep in a double bed?"

A tour like this in the Australian outback resembled a jeweled polished crown dangling at the end of a string moving over deserts, boulders, wild landscapes, isolation, mountains, and touching down on small populated areas, briefly but just long enough to give the romance-parched people a whiff of the Royals.

Next the couple drove to a historic old telegraph station for an outdoor reception in the shade of the gum trees on the banks of the original Alice Springs water hole. The people there were a mix of cattlemen, civil servants, blacksmiths, and camel drivers—with their camels! They talked about the long drought that had turned the green pastureland into sickly yellow, then the winds that blew away the dry topsoil leaving the earth hard as steel, then floods crashing down the dry riverbeds with the force of a tidal wave.

For all those who wondered how much Diana knew, how much she still had to learn—she was learning now. The education of a Queen came from such exposure. She would learn more from listening to all these different people in different countries, as well as her own, than she had ever learned in school. She learned here, for example, that tiny Alice serviced an area larger than France, that its nearest city was 900 miles away. She also learned how to catch a bouquet of flowers before it landed on her face.

An aborigine had called it "the dead heart of Australia." Ayers Rock was a flat-topped rock, 1100 feet high and 5 miles around, a sacred monument of the mystical legends of the aborigines who say the soul can be set free from there among the wonders of "dream-time." Diana and Charles were at Ayers Rock at sunset to see the silhouetted rock formations known as the Olgas turn from red rust to ochre to shadowy orange to dark brown, then purple, and finally velvety black.

Another day of touring and they were back with William at Woomargama. Their time together now was truly private, with only one easily guarded road. The verandas were shaded by pink-flowering trees, with a lovely view of the nearby hills. In the morning they were awakened by the shrieks of thousands of wild white and sulphur-crested cockatoos. It was an area of black-eared wallabies, an occasional kangaroo, and six-foot lizards. Besides a church, school, and garage, Woomargama had two tennis courts. Its total population was 60.

What Diana didn't know was that as this was her first tour, the Palace was preparing a secret dossier on her, with almost minute-by-minute details of everything she said, did, wore, how she coped with the unexpected, what were her stresses and strains, crowd reactions to her. The file was to serve as a blueprint, a learning tool for her future tours.

The Palace scrutiny still couldn't compare to the public scrutiny, particularly by the Australian women. The Princess reportedly took along some 200 outfits, the majority made especially for the trip. In 42 days, she wore 50 outfits—almost every one of them with a British label. All of them were made of either silk or cotton. Aussie women immediately commented that it was too hot for silk, too hot for her to go bareheaded, and that the best thing to wear was a leotard.

They also observed that her dresses and skirts were too long. Diana explained that she liked to bend over to talk to children, and when she did, she did not want photographers to see what they should not see. Aussie women not only knew that she had worn three dresses before, but also where she had worn them: one at the start of her honeymoon, one at Ascot just before she got married, and one at her son's christening. When Diana entered a room for a state reception, she knew just how intently every woman there would examine her jewelry, analyze her posture, makeup, hairdo, memorize her dress.

Aussie women were quick to tell her what they felt. In a walk-about in Canberra, an Australian housewife, Jill Shoebridge, who had a fifteen-month-old son of her own, told the Princess, "I wish I had a nanny just like yours to look after my son." Diana replied quickly and seriously, "I would swap with you anytime. I wish I didn't have to leave William with his nanny. I would rather do what you are doing."

Commenting on this afterward, Jill Shoebridge said, "She must be mad."

Jill said she understood the pressure on the Princess, "that it is

327

an awful lot to have a baby as well as doing the things she has to do . . . I don't envy her royal lifestyle at all . . . I still get to see my baby every day. I do feel sorry for her."

Diana was already busy telling another woman that William wasn't sleeping well. "He's waking in the night and having a good scream. He just can't settle down to Australia time."

There was nothing perfunctory in the way Diana talked to them. She seemed genuinely delighted to see them, almost as if they were old roommates. And when she left, she said, "Well, I'd love to stay chatting all day, but you know what it's like . . ."

In contrast, the Queen had a more restrained style. Her Majesty radiated a basic decency, which cut through language barriers. She came through as "a gracious lady who stands for the old-fashioned family virtues," yet her reserve was obvious. In style, Diana came closer to the Queen Mother who seemed to regard every crowd as one vast recharge battery. The Queen Mother laid foundation stones "as if it was the best way of spending an afternoon that one could possibly imagine."

Diana seemed to have an added sensitivity for one so young. When visiting the victims of some devastating bushfires, she told one woman, "I hope you don't mind the intrusion."

What was coming through to Australians, as it did to people everywhere, was the star quality of this young woman. As usual, when she and Charles each worked one side of the crowd, it was clear whom the crowd wanted. Even after talking to Charles, one woman walked away saying to a friend, "Well, we chose the wrong side of the street, didn't we?"

Aussies saw Charles as a bit of an "ocker"—an easygoing lad, a good old boy. But the Princess was something else. The Melbourne *Herald*, the country's largest evening newspaper, showed a cartoon map of Australia with a heart superimposed over it, the words "Princess Diana" in the center. The caption read: "A permanent imprint."

"Where's Lady Diana, then?" one group asked Charles. "I'm sorry about that," he replied, "you will just have to put up with me." Then he grinned. "It's not fair, is it? You'd better ask for your money back." Elsewhere, he added, "It would have been easier to have two wives."

At one banquet, the Prince told his audience how lucky he was to be married to Diana. Sitting behind him, Diana grinned, blushed, then rolled her eyes and made a wry face. As the Prince turned to face her, he said, "It's just amazing what ladies will do when your back is turned."

Daily Mirror photographer Kent Gavin observed that out of every 100 pictures he took on this tour, 92 involved Diana and only 8 showed Charles. The Prince had smilingly said, "I know I'm going to have to get used to the backs of photographers."

"She is so popular," added Gavin, "that she is in my lens from the moment she arrives at a place until the moment she leaves."

There was a small drama of expectancy at Canberra Airport. The Aussie national question was: Will she or won't she? It concerned the wife of the Prime Minister. The world knew how bitterly anti-Royalist he was, and the question was whether his wife would make a perfunctory nod to the arriving Royals instead of curtsying. Everybody sighed with relief when she made a full and proper curtsy.

Waiting to meet them too was the Prime Minister's father, the Reverend Clem Hawke, who promptly declared, "I am still one of the Queen's men." By the time they all posed together for a picture, chatting and laughing for the camera, the mood was most friendly. Afterward, even Hawke said softly of the Princess, "She's a lovely lady." The Prime Minister returned to his office "later than expected," and freely admitted that he had "quite enjoyed himself at lunch."

If she did nothing else on this tour, Diana had captured the heart and romantic imagination of the Australian people. The tour was a triumph. She even had softened the anti-Royalist Hawke into a dove, managing a very delicate political mission with her simple, natural style.

Some said that the Queen of England had no more a part in Australian politics than the Queen of Tonga. But the feeling of affection was deep; the connecting tie, however slim, was still strong. Now here were this Princess and her Prince heightening the appeal of royalty again. The polls were clear and consistent: Monarchists led republicans by two to one.

If anybody doubted this appeal, they should have been in Brisbane. More than 100,000 people—twice as many as came to see the Queen the previous year—crammed into three narrow streets in the town center, pushed past police lines, vaulted barricades, all the time screaming Diana's name, trying to get close to her to give her flowers and presents.

"It was almost mass hysteria," said assistant police commissioner

Jim Pyne. "We just weren't expecting that many people. And they just wanted to get close to the Princess, which is why they surged forward. It was adoration." An Australian secret service man, bathed in sweat, had another description: "It was hellish."

Several people were injured with broken ribs, one with a broken nose. Old women fainted. A dozen people were taken to the hospital. Children were separated from their parents, several knocked to the ground. Six-year-old Cathy Harris was screaming in terror when her mother found her. "She just got lost in the crowd and I couldn't find her," said her mother. "And she didn't even get to see the Princess."

It was Prince Charles who sensed what was happening and pulled his wife away through a narrowing gap to the Lord Mayor's rest room. He then hovered over her with cold drinks, and called for the royal doctor. The bodyguards were distinctly rattled. The chief Australian security officer noted, "We were lucky to get away with it."

But ten minutes later, Diana was ready to go again. That night there was an official reception and she could not have looked any more cool or collected or glamorous. She had passed the rigorous royal touring test "with full marks."

Closest to her in Australia was her lady-in-waiting, Anne Beckwith-Smith, the thirty-two-year-old daughter of an Epsom horse-racing official. At the Melbourne airport, Diana threw her arms around Beckwith-Smith saying, "I just couldn't have done it without you!" As a present, the grateful Diana gave her a large diamond brooch with a D on it.

The royal couple saw a lot of children. At Newcastle, children from 300 schools gathered at the International Sports Center. A large group of them had driven across 500 miles of brown scrubland to get there. Prince Charles raised some eyebrows when he told them, "Most of you now need a long rest and several tubs of beer to recover." He also talked of his own Australian schooling at Timbertop. To another group of children, he was reading a homily written by a mother in 1897 on the formation of character ("Swearing is contemptible and foolish") when a sudden gust of wind blew away the copy of his speech and the Prince exclaimed, "Oh God, my bloody bit of paper."

At another stop, where the crowd was larger than expected, the Prince commented wryly: "Maybe you are breeding faster than statistics led us to believe."

Everywhere they went, the Prince stressed the royal connection. They made a point of visiting the town of Ballarat where Australian republicanism had had its beginnings. It was here at the Eureka Stockade uprising in 1854 that disgruntled goldminers first took up arms against the colonial administration. Police put down the uprising with the loss of thirty lives. The point of the royal visit to this particular place was not lost on the Australian people.

No matter where they were, Charles and Diana returned every few days to Woomargama to be with William and to unwind.

"What counts in making a happy marriage," George Levinger of the University of Massachusetts had said, "is not so much how compatible you are, but how you deal with incompatibility." A consensus among marital researchers seems to be that personality is less crucial to marital success than is the nature of the relationship itself. Tension in marriage, they claimed, was often due to the conflict of two deeply held needs—the desire for intimacy and the desire to establish one's identity as a separate person.

Observing the tenderness between Charles and Diana, Jane Owen insisted that "Charles falls for her all over again." Owen noted how he would come to her at a garden party, after they had been separated awhile, and take her hand and kiss it. She recalled how he physically glowed with pride at the way she did things, and talked to people, how he would sneak up and put his arm around her. Owen recalled an elderly crippled lady at a Brisbane reception who painfully struggled out of her wheelchair to stand at attention as soon as she caught sight of the Prince with his Princess. The elderly woman explained: "There was something very special between them. I felt inspired as soon as I saw them."

Those who saw them on a dance floor at a charity ball in Sydney agreed unanimously about the fun they were having together. Backed by a band, three singers sang "The More I See You, the More I Want You." At first they took four slow steps, then Charles moved into a quickstep with a series of fast whirls that delighted the watching guests. He was obviously going much faster than Diana expected and she audibly pleaded with him, "Slower, slower." But he had an impish look in his eyes, and went even faster, leaving her almost breathless as he kept spinning her around. Now she was laughing with him, both of them looking as if they had done something very mischievous. When the music stopped, Diana put her hand on her heart, still laughing, still breathless.

For Prince Charles, the whole scene was like reliving a memory. Two years earlier, he had kissed Diana goodbye and had come to Australia. He had been in this very same ballroom when the band started playing the very same music, "The More I See You, the More I Want You." More than ever then, he missed Diana. He danced with someone else then, in the same fast way, but he was thinking of Diana, and missing her. Now here they were together, dancing to the same music in the same way in the same ballroom.

The crowd in the ballroom this evening was the largest for any Sydney social function since the Queen's visit in 1954. The lavish table of food for Sydney's 400 featured two flamingoes made of lard, a koala modeled in ice, and the state crest carved from butter. Tickets marked at 45 pounds sold on the black market for 1800 pounds. Earlier, at the Sydney Opera House, Diana had delighted the people by singing the Australian National Anthem, which she had memorized. Her husband occasionally had to consult his song sheet.

When a former model rushed up to the Prince on the Australian beach to kiss him in front of the ready cameras, Charles knew it was a setup and called in the suspected photographer. "I thought, here it comes, it's going to be heavy," recalled the photographer, "but all the Prince said was, 'I must admire your taste in women—she was *beautiful!'*"

The Prince took time out for a game of polo, his first in many months. (When Charles plays polo, the Princess often wears his watch, along with her own.) He played so poorly that he publicly apologized to his wife for "loyally watching her husband make a fool of himself." Former roommate Ann Bolton also came to the game, mainly to update Diana on her love life. She had found the man she adored, she said, and had chased him to Australia. This was something Diana understood very well. Diana's news was that she was trying to teach William how to swim at the Woomargama pool.

They had another reunion in New Zealand with Charles's brother Edward. New Zealand was a country of three million people, beautiful fjords, virgin forest, hot volcanoes and warm springs, lots of parrots but no snakes—all of it settled on two main islands and some outlying ones. It was the first country to grant women over twenty-one the right to vote.

Edward was a junior tutor for two terms at Wanganui Collegiate—a posh Anglican boarding school. Wearing his newly acquired kiwi-feathered cloak as an honorary chief of the Ngati Awa tribe, Edward greeted Charles who asked, "What the hell is it you're wearing? It looks like a blanket."

Edward, sixteen years younger, idolized Charles. These were two brothers who hugged each other when they met. A modest, unassuming young man, Edward had commented on being born a Prince, in a local radio interview. "You just grow up with it and it becomes a part of you. You don't have to try. On the whole, it's good fun."

He did add that it meant living "a sort of double life." There were times, he said, "when one is alone with one's family just like anyone else—and the next moment one's trying to be polite to everybody."

One of those in New Zealand who saw the other side of Edward's double life was seventeen-year-old Alison Bell who starred with him in an amateur production of *Charley's Aunt*. "He is definitely not shy with girls," she said. "I remember after the play he came up and gave me a surprise kiss. He has lovely soft lips." She quickly added that he had beautiful old-fashioned manners and was "simply a perfect English gentleman. He is not a loud person who sits laughing with the guys. He'd rather be with the girls telling them witty jokes."

He was then nineteen, not particularly a smooth dancer, better at Scottish reels than disco. He was soon scheduled to enter Cambridge to major in archeology and anthropology, following Charles's example. With nine O levels and three A levels, Edward was regarded as the brainiest of the young Royals, and possibly also the touchiest. He had been called "Jaws," because of braces he once wore, and the Queen's "forgotten Son" because he had kept himself very private.

He had blossomed in New Zealand, just as Charles had lost his shyness in Australia. Edward called Charles "such a smashing chap" and Andrew "such a randy old sod." But he envied them both. Without friends or family for support, he had found Wanganui "a daunting prospect" at first and was lonely and reserved. After a term of it, he was confident enough to "have a go at life."

The slim, handsome six-footer soon had his own group of girls. He had been trained as a pilot, qualified on the glider, would soon fly to the South Pole. In the meanwhile he was playing rugby, skiing, mountain climbing, canoeing, and generally having fun.

The negative marks came from photographers who claimed he could be a "typical spoilt royal brat" and slightly arrogant. But he still blushed easily.

The New Zealand greeting for Charles and Diana was almost as ebullient as it had been in Australia. There were a few sour signals, however. A tattooed Maori, Te Ringa Mihaka, bared his bottom as the royal couple passed in parade. At the time, he was wearing a *piopio*, or native grass skirt, and seagull feathers. He denied a charge of disorderly conduct but said he would have pleaded guilty if the charge had been showing contempt for the royal visitors.

There were, however, many more Maori anxious to rub noses with the Prince and Princess. Diana happily "hongled" with a group of Maori youngsters, following her husband's advice about "not pressing her nose too hard." The Maori also took the royal couple on a trip in a war canoe paddled by eighty warriors.

At some events, there were protestors with picket signs, and somebody even threw red dye and eggs at their car. There was occasional rowdy jeering. The royal rule was to ignore all this with silence. The Prince did make a public reference to a series of complaining letters protesting that Prince William was being fed milk and minced kangaroos.

"In fact," he said, "we are bringing him up on grass and beer."

Prince William put on his own show in a session for photographers. Not only did he show his teeth, crawl all over the blanket, and grab handfuls of dirt, but he stood on his own two feet—with a little help. The Prince let slip his nickname for his son. He called him "Wills." "The Princess had her own comment on her son's performance: "Well, who's a little superstar, then?" He even stuck his tongue out—ironically, the traditional Maori greeting.

There were balls and dinners and dances and champagne. One embarrassing moment came when the Governor General of New Zealand proposed a toast to the Queen on her fifty-seventh birthday. The 600 carefully selected guests produced a ripple of laughter because not only had someone forgotten the champagne but also the glasses.

The amount of gifts Charles and Diana received was staggering, almost 1500 presents a day, including 140 boomerangs. The most popular present in Australia was a stuffed koala for William—he got at least 250 of them. In New Zealand, it was the kiwi, the flightless bird which is the country's national emblem. All gifts of flowers were sent to nursing homes and hospitals. Most of the other items also went to hospitals, orphanages, and other institutions in the area.

Every gift was acknowledged with a royal thank-you note within three days. The grand total was 52,500 gifts.

Somebody gave Diana a gift of crystallized sugar. She took it and said quietly, "My father adores it. I'll save it for him." Prince Charles was pleased too when a beekeeper discovered his weakness for honey and gave him an almost-lifetime supply.

A group of protestors gave Prince Charles a special platypus badge named after their favorite duckbill platypus, in gratitude for the Prince's position against a hydro-electric project which would have destroyed a favorite wilderness area.

At their final banquet, Prime Minister Robert Muldoon said that while New Zealanders no longer spoke of Britain as "home," their loyalty to "Her Majesty and the heir to the throne" remained part of their national tradition.

In a quiet aside, the Princess admitted that she was "absolutely exhausted." She had a right to be. Hers was an absolute smashing success. If the Royal Family was a firm, she was now a full member. In Australia, she had proved finally to herself not only that she could do what had to be done, but that she could do it with flair, in her own style. She now knew, too, what nobody could tell her—that a Royal's education came only from experience and exposure. What she had, what made it all possible, was a husband who was a strong and loving anchor, who was with her at every turn, the constant source of the best advice she could ever get. This was not only a marriage, this was a working partnership. In Australia and New Zealand particularly, the partnership had worked superbly well. She and the Prince were now entitled to a ten-day holiday in the Bahamas. They had paid their dues.

24

To be born a future king is a trick of Fate; to be bred and trained to be a good king is a matter of patience and wisdom and hard work.

The traditional British system of educating royalty meant private tutors plus military discipline. It was the wisdom and patience of parents that put Charles in touch with the new times, made him a Royal who could be the most intellectual king since James I, and the most cultured since George IV or Charles II.

And what about the future King William?

Prince Charles said of his son, "I want him to be honest, tolerant, and, above all, well-mannered." He amplified this: "I would like to try to bring up our children . . . to think of other people, to put themselves in other people's positions."

"If they are not very bright or very qualified," he added, "at least if they have reasonable manners, I believe they will go much farther in life than by not having them."

Queen Victoria was also a stickler for good manners, feeling that a child should know its place. Her eldest daughter, nicknamed Princess "Pussy," was so carefully supervised on this that she stopped eating and almost died. The children of Edward VII and Queen Alexandra, according to their grandmother, "ran wild." "They are such ill-bred children I cannot fancy them at all," she said.

Princess Elizabeth was a blonde, curly-haired superstar as a child. Before he became king, her father said, "My chief claim to fame seems to be that I am the father of Princess Elizabeth." Her father had not been trained to be a king, nor she a queen, but her uncle was. He was the Prince of Wales who would be Edward VIII, whose training did not persuade him to put duty above love.

Royal child-training had changed since the days of Charles's

336

grandfather, George VI. George, then known as "Bertie," had been forcibly fed from a bottle, his legs put in iron braces because he was knock-kneed. His nanny was so jealous of the time he spent with his parents that she twisted his arm before pushing him into their drawing room so that he always entered in tears. No wonder he stammered.

There would be none of this with William. If Charles wanted an honest, thoughtful, well-mannered son, Diana wanted a happy one. There would be no jealousy between her and the boy's nanny because Diana would always be there, always in charge. She would change her share of diapers, give more than her share of baths, but she had firmly decided there would be no "baby worship."

So had the Prince. What they wanted for this son who one day would be king was for him to have a full sense of emotional security. That was why Diana insisted on taking William with them when they went to Australia. "She always got her own way," Earl Spencer said of his daughter. "I think Charles is learning that now."

In matters concerning their son, Diana was the reigning monarch and Charles "the accommodating spouse."

Charles and Diana reported that they had read many books on child-rearing. They both knew exactly when he was expected to crawl, walk, talk. Charles particularly seemed a walking textbook on baby statistics. But he was sophisticated enough to add, "There were some experts who were very positive about how you should bring up children and they turned around after twenty years and said they had been wrong. Think of all the poor people who had followed their suggestions."

At age one, chubby William could barely stand, and then not for long. He weighed thirty pounds, and a few concerned pediatricians suggested a diet.

"He may be eating too many cereal-based foods with milk," observed nutrition expert Dr. Roger Whitehead.

Critics even zeroed in on the baby's clothes: "Why does this smart girl with such a great style of dressing put her baby boy in those uncomfortable, outdated smocked romper suits with tight elastic cutting into his chubby thighs?" asked writer Marje Proops.

"Suddenly you find that your child is not a malleable object," said Charles, "or an offprint of yourself, but is the culmination of goodness knows how many thousands of years and the genetic makeup of your ancestors."

"It's amazing how much happiness a small child brings to people," Diana added blissfully.

The usual rumors concerning the baby's future schooling soon circulated. The Queen reportedly had formed a small royal think-tank to help plan her grandson's education. Charles and Diana already supposedly had decided to send their son to Eton instead of Gordonstoun—where Charles had been so unhappy.

A royal observer reported other concerns: "Suppose the Princess wanted her child to go to a village school, as Princess Anne's son does. I don't imagine for one minute that the Queen would stand for that. She would be far too afraid that the child would rapidly become an object of curiosity."

Prince Charles took all this calmly, almost philosophically. "I'm sure it gives younger members of the family a wider sense of perspective just listening to older people and not dismissing them as being out of date or old-fashioned."

Just in case anybody had forgotten that William had Spencer heritage, too, fifty-nine-year-old Earl Spencer announced, "I know the Royals can seem to swallow people up when others marry in, and the other family always looks as if it had been pushed out. But that can never happen to us. Diana would not permit it to happen. William will grow up very close to the Spencer family and be influenced by them as much as by the others."

Being the products of a divorced family and a traveling family, Diana and Charles were determined that their own children would have what they had not had—a loving family life in a real home.

Despite this feeling, Charles and Diana were due to go on an eighteen-day trip to Canada in June of 1983. They reluctantly decided that it would be too short and hectic to take William along, that he might get seasick on the *Britannia* in a strong sea.

Diana was not happy. She felt trapped in an enveloping net. She could enforce their decisions about their baby at home, but she could only follow her husband's royal lead in the outside world. It was imperative that she join him in Canada. Her new edginess revived the anorexia nervosa rumor. Female thinness was simply women's attempt to look like men, insisted one lofty critic. Another claimed it was women's way of blaming their mothers for some lack of love.

Diana and her spokesmen repeatedly reiterated that she was absolutely healthy, that her appetite was just fine, and there was no monumental significance attached to her refusal of a pork tenderloin at a Cornwall lunch. Nor, she said, was she suffering from post-partum depression, "baby blues." The reason she cried easily was simply because *she cried easily.*

But she did seem much thinner, and dressed in a strapless evening gown she now revealed skinny arms and bony shoulders. She was now described as "an exquisitely beautiful but remote snow-drop."

At a London ballet charity performance, a special spotlight was trained on her until the show began. She could almost hear the audience comment: "She's very thin, isn't she?" And, "I'm not sure I like her dress."

Their trip to Canada came less than two months after the Australian tour, but what made it most pleasant was that they sailed on the *Britannia.* One of the more memorable remarks recorded aboard the yacht was Diana asking if anyone could mix her a gin drink called Pimm's. "I got particularly addicted to them on my honeymoon," she said, and then grinned. "But that's the *only* thing I got addicted to."

Since they were concentrating on the Atlantic provinces in Canada, they didn't need ninety suitcases and trunks as they had for Australia, and they had the great advantage of their Canadian press secretary, Victor Chapman, running interference for them. Chapman, a burly fifty-year-old former Edmonton Eskimos football star, once served as press secretary for Canadian Prime Minister Pierre Trudeau. He knew their pace and potential because he also had been with Charles and Diana in Australia.

"She has become a very accomplished lady," he had said of Diana. "She still has a lot to learn but she's learning fast. I can't believe the kind of stamina she has."

Some towns had started preparing for the visit months in advance. The St. Johns City Council sent letters to householders telling them to clean up their homes and yards for the upcoming visit—or face legal action. One woman was even told to paint her clapboard house. Halifax spent $16,000 on new sod of Kentucky bluegrass for a rush job on their public parks. Canadian newspapers gave the royal tour their splash headline treatment: THE ROYAL SUPERSTARS.

Only a year before, Queen Elizabeth had signed Canada's constitution, which cut the former colony freer than ever politically.

But here was this young couple tying it together again emotionally. A sample was a large hand-painted slogan: WE ADORE YOU. GIVE OUR LOVE TO LITTLE WILLIAM AND THE REST OF THE ROYAL FAMILY.

Hundreds of thousands of Canadians were caught in the grip of what was called "Di-mania."

Alice Nicholl in Dartmouth, Nova Scotia, had never been a waitress before but the fifty-seven-year-old woman begged for the job so she could get a glimpse of the royal couple when they dined on lobster in a Bridgewater High School gymnasium. She was ecstatic afterward.

"They were beautiful, sweet, and darling. I touched Charles's suit and I made the coffee he drank. It was wonderful."

They missed William's first birthday. Their thought was that he "was too young to notice." Diana went shopping for a present for him while in St. Andrews, New Brunswick. She was searching for something "he won't be able to break."

Prince Charles meanwhile had addressed a youth festival, saying how keen he was to have a companion for his son. "My wife deserves a medal for the first one." Earlier he had informed an audience, "The royal breeding program is now firmly under way." Told about all this, the Princess blushed and said, "How embarrassing."

When someone asked Diana if she was pregnant again, she replied quietly, "That's a *very* personal question." Asked again, she was more irritated. "I am not on a production line!"

Her husband would not be daunted. Apologizing for William's absence to a group of well-wishers, he promised to bring the boy with them next time and added, "Perhaps several by then, you never know." Then, with a grin, looking at his wife, "That's not a hint, I assure you."

"I try my best to embarrass her in each speech," Charles told the audience at a banquet in St. John's, Newfoundland. Referring to some of the odd names of Newfoundland towns, he had said, "I'm very sad I can't take my wife to a place called Leading Tickles." This time Diana refused to blush.

Even more embarrassing was the Premier of New Brunswick, Richard Hatfield. In introducing Charles and Diana to an audience, he was often incoherent and then said, "We have heard and read the lies. Your Royal Highness, the Princess of Wales, as it always is, today it was wonderful to meet and know the truth." The blushing Princess looked down at her toes. Then the band played a song called

"Lady Di," composed for the occasion. One of the lines in the lyric was, "The music of that smile was made by Lady Di."

Prince Charles tried to stare solemnly in the distance. Hatfield continued, "Let the flame burn to warm hope and extinguish cynicism and despair. To heat the soul that remains and remembers." Then he raised his glass in "a toast to love."

Prince Charles's reaction was: "I can only say you have left me speechless."

Diana afterward confided to her hairdresser, "I've never been so embarrassed in my life. I have no objections to things being informal, but that man went right over the top. Poor Prince Charles, he didn't know where to look." To someone else, she had commented, "It sent shivers down my spine."

Hatfield's own explanation of the evening: He had been overtired but did *not* have too much to drink.

Diana had planned to call William from Canada every day, but Professor John Morton, director of the Cognitive Child Development Clinic in London, warned it would not be a good idea. "A disembodied voice on a telephone line could be very perplexing for the boy." When talking with two Nova Scotia grandmothers, Ellen Lownds and Audrey Rector, Diana said wistfully, "I wish I had William with me. I miss him so much." Prince Charles told a crowd in Shelburne that he would send William to celebrate their tercentenary, not realizing that William would then be 101.

On Father's Day, Prince Charles found two cards addressed to him. One showed a rabbit being pulled out of a hat. The words inside: "Dad, I think you are magic. Love, Wills." The other card showed twenty-one rabbits firing cannon. Diana had written: "To Papa, a 21-gun salute, Love, Wombat."

Eva Frye drove five hours to stand in the front row during a royal walkabout. Charles asked the crowd, "Have you seen my wife?" Eva Frye seemed to answer for everybody, "Yes, she's beautiful. Don't lose her."

When people sighted Charles and Diana they didn't simply cheer—they actually screamed. "There is an element of hysteria here," reported James Whitaker of the *Daily Mirror*. "In Australia, we saw this sort of thing as the tour progressed, but here it has come right at the outset. What happens is that the emotion builds as each place tries to outdo the welcome of the one before it."

Diana had become a cult figure. "I have covered all kinds of royal tours with the Queen and Prince Philip, even with Charles before he was married, but I have never seen anything like the effect of Diana," observed Buckingham Palace official Wilfred Fielding. So great was the focus on Diana that the *Ottawa Citizen* goodnaturedly referred to Prince Charles as an "also-ran."

"We want him out of the way so we can photograph her," photographer John Shelley admitted frankly. An Ottawa reporter described public reaction as "frenzied squeals more normally reserved for a rock star rather than a member of the Royal Family." Thousands chanted, "We want Diana . . . we want Diana."

Prince Charles still had his admirers.

"I asked him if a girl might get a kiss from a visiting Prince, and he said, 'Yes you may.' Then he kissed me and I kissed him," said Judy Nousler of Halifax. "It's a thrill of a lifetime and something I'll remember all my life. My knees are still shaking."

Of course, there still were pickets, as there always were. One said: BRITISH RUBBER BULLETS KILL IRISH BABIES. Not only were Charles and Diana constantly monitored by a security camera to spot suspicious faces, but Diana was followed closely by a plainclothes woman, twenty-eight-year-old Katie Wiegert of the Royal Mounted Police, who was a karate expert. Wiegert was prepared to hurl her body in front of the Princess in case of any trouble.

In any tour it was almost obligatory to plant a tree, tour a town hall, sign a visitors' book. But Charles and Diana were also enjoying themselves. In the Klondike celebrations in Edmundston, they dressed up in period costumes—the Prince in a frock coat, silk cravat, spats and a silver-topped cane, duplicating an outfit his great-grandfather wore in Canada, and the Princess in a dress of pink silk and cream lace with a bustle and lace-up boots. Their press secretary Victor Chapman was dressed to look like Wyatt Earp with a black hat and ruffled shirt. As for the Scotland Yard detectives, they mostly looked like riverboat gamblers. The costumes had been made months in advance according to each person's measurements. Diana described the event as "a bit of a hoot."

They traveled through the city in horse-drawn coaches, then watched a spirited performance of cancan girls, joined a sing-along chorus of "Daisy, Daisy, Give Me Your Answer Do," and a number of saucier songs. Nobody sang more enthusiastically than Diana, tapping her feet, swaying to the music, and even waving her napkin in the air.

Those close enough testified that she and Charles were exchanging frequent one-liners. "If he makes a quip, she comes right back with another one," said Newfoundland Premier Brian Peckford. "They were having fun." Others observed that the Prince would slip his arm frequently around his wife's waist. "Occasionally his hand slips to her hip to steady her on the royal barge, or a canal trip, or to simply let her know he is at her side."

Even more impressive to Premier Peckford, a former social worker, was the way the Princess "sat down on every single hospital bed to talk to people. She speaks very softly. She does not raise her voice—she makes people come down to her decibel level and it is lovely."

"Diana really likes people better than animals," observed a friend. "I can't tell you how rare that is in her circle."

A small boy gave her a bouquet and she could not understand why he kept touching her dress and buttons. Nobody had told her that the boy had been blind since birth. When she knew, "she almost cried," said Peckford. Diana then invited the boy to join her after lunch. "She let him touch her leg and her shoe," said the boy's mother. "She held his hand, then he wanted her other hand and she gave it to him. She even bent down to let him touch her face to feel its shape. She knew what it is like to be a mother."

Presented with three flowers by another little girl, Diana chided her gently, "You shouldn't spend your money on me."

The only brouhaha of the tour came when there was a press party aboard the *Britannia*. Everyone there was made aware that all remarks by the Royals at the party were strictly confidential. Diana Bentley, wife of the editor of the Halifax *Daily News*, could not restrain herself. Her story was headlined THE AGONIES OF A PRINCESS. In it, the Princess referred to the British tabloid press as "the wolf pack."

"When they write something horrible," said the Princess, "I get a horrible feeling right here," she pointed to her heart, "and I don't want to go outside." Then she added, "It will probably take five or ten years for me to get used to it."

"The future Queen of England shyly confided that life as the world's most famous Royal can be pure agony," wrote Mrs. Bentley.

Diana herself put it more discreetly when she spoke of herself to her new admirer Brian Peckford. "I am finding it very difficult to cope, but I am learning. I have learned a lot in the last few months, particularly in the last three or four. I feel I am doing my job better now than I was before. I have matured a lot recently."

But she was still only twenty-two. She and Charles celebrated her birthday over breakfast in their Edmundston hotel suite. Prince Philip was then touring another part of Canada and sent a congratulatory telegram. At the opening of the World University Games, a crowd of 65,000 sang "Happy Birthday." The Prince gave her a present of jewelry, but they kept exactly what it was private between them. Rouza Hellmore, a BBC correspondent, recalled that "he had a big birthday cake for her on which was inscribed 'I LOVE YOU DARLING.'" "My perfect birthday is going home," Diana said. "I can't wait to see William."

It was the final day of their tour, and they knew what a smashing success it had been. That night they flew back to Britain, headed straight for Highgrove for a belated birthday party for their son.

Highgrove had a friendly feeling from the presence of the housekeeper, Mrs. Nesta Whitehead, and her husband Paddy, a sixty-nine-year-old Liverpudlian. A small, childless, cheerful woman, Mrs. Whitehead looked frailer than she was, and knew how to cook as well as clean. In a house with Persian rugs and parquet floors, the modern oak-lined kitchen had a surprisingly old-fashioned stove. Paddy's responsibility was the upkeep of the swimming pool as well as the cattle.

Whether they were in Highgrove or Kensington, Charles usually woke first—about 6:30. He jogged for a while, returned to eat breakfast with his wife—usually something simple like bran flakes and honey for him and Muesli for her, or perhaps just toast and coffee if they were scheduled for an official lunch.

"People can't believe that the Royal Family eats an ordinary breakfast," said a member of the household staff. "They imagine that the Royals eat caviar every five minutes."

Lunch at home would be equally simple—cottage cheese, salads, omelets. If Diana ate out with friends, she normally began with raw vegetables followed by a fish dish. If Charles ate out informally, and nobody was looking, he would try to get some Chocolate Oliver cookies for which he had a passion. In fact, he would try to get them anytime.

The Prince of Wales preferred bland food. He was particularly happy with banana and jam sandwiches, but he also liked scrambled eggs with smoked salmon, fruit puddings, and *frikadeller* (Swedish meat patties). The Princess usually drank Malvern Water, and her husband liked a Lemon Refresher, a calorie-free mix of fresh lemons and water, which he preferred to any alcohol. He almost never took a hot drink.

The one dish Diana could not resist was shepherd's pie, a dish of chopped meat topped with whipped potatoes which she called "mince 'n mash mush." She now made little use of her cooking expertise in sauces and soufflés, but she still insisted to everybody, "I have an enormous appetite despite what people say, and so has Prince William."

Prince William provided better physical evidence of this than she did. He was still a chubby child. Diana made certain to keep her early morning hours free for him, no matter how tight her schedule. So did the Prince, whenever he could. She also spent the late afternoon, from six to eight, with William. Both were there at the boy's bedtime, when they would bathe him and read to him.

One of the most unexpected contributions to an art show of one hundred portraits to aid MENCAP, the National Society for Mentally Handicapped Children and Adults, came from the Princess of Wales. It was a pencil sketch she had done while on the *Britannia* en route to Canada, showing her son in simple dungarees, partly pouting but with a determined thrusting chin.

Professionals were promptly asked to comment. "She's had a jolly good stab at that mouth, the head has form, and there's a nice sense of anatomy in that fat little wrist and the forearm," observed Ruskin Spear. "Even the profile around the edge of the head is very sensitive . . . Either she's a remarkable sort of person or she's had some training in drawing somewhere. I've taught art for twenty-five years at the Royal College of Art, and if she was a student of mine, I'd be very interested. This shows a talent worth pursuing."

Prince Charles had been painting for some time, mostly watercolors, all of them discreetly signed with the initial "C." Two of them were exhibited at the Mall Galleries near Buckingham Palace, showing a lake in Canada and a hut in Nepal. "If he had the time," said Charles Bone, president of the Royal Institute of Painters, "he would be really good."

Painting seemed to be a hobby in the Royal Family. Prince Philip had been painting in oils for years. He had put a 10,000 pound reserve price on a painting he contributed to a charity auction, but nobody bid that high. Prince Andrew specialized in landscapes, and had exhibited two Canadian views. Sir Hugh Casson, who had taught Prince Charles, said flatly of Andrew, "He's definitely an artist. He could take it up professionally. . . ." Queen Victoria kept a sketchbook all her life, and drew brutally frank pictures of her children. She rarely sketched her son Leopold because 'he's a very common-looking child.' "

Prince Charles felt differently about his child. Anyone trailing the Prince on a day of appointments heard him refer almost regularly to "My son . . ." "His private time with his family, he insisted, "was more important than anything."

Friends were astonished to see how much more relaxed and confident he now was. One of them commented, "Di seems to have softened his stiff upper lip." Another noted, "The starchy Royal has turned into a smoochy husband." "Can anyone imagine Princess Anne and Mark canoodling in public?"

Charles and Diana usually spent the weekdays at Kensington Palace and the weekends at Highgrove. It compensated for their many official evening engagements. As much as Diana relaxed at Highgrove, she really came alive at Kensington Palace. In the heart of London, this twenty-two-year-old Princess had her favorite shops, her closest friends, and her hairdresser.

Kevin Shanley usually arrived when she was still in her dressing gown and slippers, without makeup, after a leisurely morning bath, listening to the blaring of pop songs on her radio. She was letting her hair grow longer so that her tiara would fit properly. "It makes her look a bit older," said fashion expert Percy Savage, "but she's got a very pretty neck and nice shoulders."

Savage was less kind about her taste in hats and clothes. "In the beginning, I think it was pretty appalling, especially her taste in hats. Her taste and judgment is still rather young. She learned a lot from Anna Harvey at *Vogue*. She would pop in and ask, 'Do you think I should wear a blouse or a shirt?' . . . She and Anna would have breakfast together a lot; she learned an awful lot from Anna. Anna's office was always full of samples of next season's clothes which her magazine was going to photograph. She could tell Diana everything she needed to know about fashion trends. Now Diana's developing her own taste. And she's getting better at it.

"I'll tell you this much: She's done a helluva lot for the British fashion business. Five years ago we were in the doldrums, and now British fashion is beating French fashion and certainly beating American fashion. We're basically not buying much fashion from America anymore; they're buying from us. And it's all thanks to Diana. Absolutely."

"Only Mrs. Kennedy's impact on the fashion world has been comparable to Diana's," noted Bernadine Morris, fashion editor of the *New York Times*. "She's given the biggest zip ever to British fashion. For them, she's the best thing to happen since sliced bread."

In developing her own style, Diana started searching for young designers who were "with it." Arabella Pollen was not only Diana's age, but looked a lot like her. She had no formal art school training, but began designing as soon as she left school. Hers was Diana's much-photographed suit of pale banana-yellow tweed, with a brown velvet collar on a double-breasted jacket. Jasper Conran, similarly young, designed some of Diana's maternity clothes and still designs for her. His clothes are beautifully cut, chic, and classic. Conran designed a two-piece silk suit that caused considerable comment in Canada. Victor Edelstein, another young designer who had no formal art school training, specializes in evening wear that Diana likes.

Bruce Oldfield launched his own independent collection in 1975 after a solo fashion show at the Plaza Hotel in New York for Henri Bendel. His was that stunning one-shouldered dress of brilliant blue silk with its black coin dot print—softer and slimmer than her usual evening look—that she wore at a Birthright fund-raising fashion show. One of the Princess's most sensational dresses was a Hachi-designed one-shouldered dress of silver and white which she wore on her last night in Melbourne. The papers called it "a royal sizzler," and referred to her as "The Princess of Wows." Born in Japan, Hachi had lived in London for the past dozen years. He specialized in wonderfully embroidered beaded evening dresses. Jan Vanvelden, trained in Holland but now working in London, made the pretty silk outfits with serrated collars that Diana wore on her Australian tour. At the end of the tour, *Time* wrote: "She came. She wore. She conquered."

There were more new designers whom Diana favored, many more. She enjoyed discovering them. To most designers, Diana was known as "her."

"She has progressed full-tilt to glamor," observed Peter York, one of the originators of the Sloane Ranger phrase. "She realizes she is on stage. Sometimes she looks brilliant, sometimes curious; but she is always the cynosure of all eyes.

"Royal protocol demands that she observe certain proprieties, like wearing a hat, and stronger colors than she prefers. Consequently she can look older than she is, and unkind comments about her clothes must cause her distress."

The hat industry was almost dead in Britain until Diana started wearing hats. "Wearing hats gives me confidence," Diana said. John Boyd, who makes most of her hats, uses feathers, bows, plumes, cockades, and hunts for fabrics out of production to give her something exclusive. But it was the soft seductiveness of a veil that Prince Charles "adored"—according to Diana.

"One of the first formal hats Diana wore before she was married was a veiled one," noted Aaron Chubb. "Prince Charles is reported to have loved it and ever since then veiled hats have been something of a Diana signature."

The so-called "Lady Di look" that blossomed in the fall of 1983 emphasized simple-lined suits in bright blocks of colors. As Jane Owen observed, however, "she still wears many blouses, pieces of jewelry, and dresses similar to those she wore before the wedding . . . She has also retained her flair for wearing blouses that give her a soft, filmy look . . . Her clothes are royal without being boring or frumpy."

And how did she cope with chilly nights in London? Underneath her glamorous gowns and flimsy dresses, the Princess of Wales wore thermal underwear.

"I was at a party not too long ago," said Lady Elizabeth Anson, cousin of the Queen, "and I saw the Prince of Wales and I asked him where was Diana and he said she was across the room. I looked across the room and there was this young woman I did not recognize. Now, I knew Diana before she met the Prince of Wales, but the difference in her in these three years has been extraordinary."

One of the strongest defenders of Princess Diana was Donald Campbell, one of her favorite fashion designers. In the unpretentious back room of his Knightsbridge shop, he talked about her. About the statements by some that the Princess, in her new superstar status, had become aggressive, domineering, even "bitchy," Campbell was indignant.

"Look, she came to my shop before her engagement. Her sister Jane brought her. Her sister was one of my clients and so is her grandmother, Lady Fermoy. Princess Diana then was easy and charming and natural, and she's still easy and charming and natural. When I go to the Palace with my fitter to fit five garments, she receives us alone, in the nicest way and we're in and out of there within an hour. That's not just remarkable, it's doubly remarkable. And I should know. I have my share of difficult customers. Princess Diana is just an ideal customer. She's a delight."

Campbell smiles at the forever-floating rumors of anorexia. "Of course, her weight goes up and down within a range. But her waist is still the same as when she came to me. She was a size 12 then [American size 10], and she's still a size 12. She could buy my things right off the rail. She has a perfect figure. That's why she's so easy to fit."

Campbell admitted that Diana's taste was still in transition. "After all," he said, "she's only twenty-three." Diana has patronized some twenty designers who have their own styles and taste. She was obviously learning from all of them. If some did suggest things, she would listen, but still make up her own mind. "She was very definite in her selections when she first came to me, when she was only nineteen. She doesn't ask for my suggestions and I don't give her any," said Campbell. "What I do is submit about forty sketches at the start of a season, along with different material, and she will decide what she wants in what material. Or she might say, 'Can't we do something else with this material?' " If anything, added Campbell, the Princess was now even more confident of her judgments. "But she's totally unpretentious, totally unaggressive."

Campbell was amused at the vast amounts Diana reportedly spent on clothes. "Based on what I know, it's sheer fabrication. Except for a very few, British designers don't charge thousands for dresses, and the Princess wears her clothes a number of times—we get them back for alterations."

In her search for her own personal style, Princess Diana, the fashion experts claim, has made serious mistakes as well as smashing choices. "She should never wear red," said one of them. "It gives her a hard look, makes her look too much older. . . . She often gets too frou-frou, with too many bows and things." It was, they agreed, part of her wish to get away from her early Laura Ashley image. She also had to walk the fine line of dressing with the dignity of a Royal.

A longtime fashion editor predicted that Princess Diana would soon learn what photographs best. "A lot of things that appear marvelous in sketches, even appear marvelous in the mirror, will not react kindly to the camera.

"Of course, she has to wear good fabrics, and good fabrics crease. Printed things appear to crease less. So she may go in more for prints. As for color—well, color makes you stand out in a crowd. Besides, she has this gorgeous English complexion. Chic colors like sludge green and beige and black that suit the Continental woman don't suit English skin. She needs the blues and the pinks and the greens and the mauves, even though some of those colors, in high fashion, are not considered very smart. Of course, if you're young, you can wear almost anything if you've got good skin."

Diana seemed to have similar problems searching for a hair style. At the opening of Parliament, she wanted her hair "up." She added that her husband would like to see it put up, too. Her hairdresser, Kevin Shanley, disagreed, claiming it would make her look old before her time. She soon got a new hairdresser, and her hair went "up."

But hairdos were still a problem, even with her new stylist, Richard Dalton. "I once asked the Princess if she was fed up with the press reactions to all her different hairdos. She had three hairdos in one week," recalled Lady Elizabeth Anson. "The Princess had replied, 'I can't fight it. It's not fun anymore.' That's when she went back to her original hairdo."

And more criticism came in, particularly about the blonde streaks in her hair. ("Di-lights" is the name now given in Britain to highlights in the hair that look as if they happened naturally in the sun—but actually happened at the hairdresser.) She should not have it done more than once every three months, advised trichologist Glenn Lyons. "If a chemical is put in her hair too often, it will alter the whole structure of the hair. It could start to break." Her natural hair color was described as blond, tinged with red.

Prince Charles also got his share of hair advice. He should not try to cover up his bald patch, but let it go bald gracefully. Nothing would look worse than letting his hair grow long and sweeping it back over the thinning area.

Prince Charles, as mentioned, had little interest in clothes. He had let his wife enjoy herself adding a casual style to his outfits, but it was her pleasure, not his.

The nearly 100 uniforms in his wardrobe were of great importance, however. There were eight different uniforms alone for his rank as commander in the Royal Navy (ceremonial, evening, active service, tropical, etc.). There were also eight different uniforms he wore as Colonel-in-Chief of the Welsh Guards, from the scarlet tunic for the Trooping the Color to the khaki pullovers of barrack dress.

Great-uncle Lord Mountbatten was responsible for reestablishing the theatrical possibilities of Royal uniforms and persuaded Charles to see it the same way. In the era of defense budget cuts, it was Mountbatten who urged that the brilliant ceremonial uniforms of the regiments of the Household Division should not be scrapped to save money. Mountbatten also designed the naval uniform in which Prince Charles was married. He was even more protective of the medals on uniforms. When a guest once jokingly put on Mountbatten's beribboned naval jacket, Mountbatten told him gently but firmly, "You have to earn them to wear them."

Prince Charles's valet had to know what he was required to wear on which occasion, and had to transfer all the proper medals and honors to the jacket to make sure that not a single gold pip was out of place.

When Hollywood's Mr. Blackwell saw a picture of Princess Diana wearing a baggy pink sailor-style outfit at her friend's wedding and described her as a "1910 bathing beauty from a Mack Sennett movie," he also added her to his 1982 list of the world's Worst Dressed Women. Within the year, she was on everybody's list of Best Dressed.

At the end of 1983, discussing the Princess of Wales, the Royal watchers agreed: What a difference a year makes!

A year before, at the Festival of Remembrance at the Royal Albert Hall in November, she looked thin, flustered, miserable—besides arriving after the Queen. Now she was buoyant, in command, smiling. In the week before Remembrance Day, she had visited a hospital, attended a Mountbatten memorial, given a tea for thirty children, attended a concert at Royal Festival Hall, dedicated a plaque to the Falkland dead, helped celebrate an anniversary of local independent radio, among other events.

"A year ago all this would have exhausted the Princess," said one of her staff. "Now she can do two jobs a day and still be raring to go at a dinner party in the evening."

Credit for this renewed vigor was given to her regular aerobics workout at the South London studio of the Royal Ballet director, Merle Park. She felt sprightly enough to join Charles in January on his annual ski trip to Liechtenstein as guests of the Crown Prince. This time Diana willingly agreed to a photo session with photographers at the start of the holiday, if the photographers would then leave them alone. And this time Charles and Diana did have their privacy.

Diana now fully realized that photographers were part of her life and always would be. She even taught her son William to wave at the photographers. "A year ago that wouldn't have happened," commented one of her staff.

Diana had learned much of what photographers want. She had learned to pause when getting out of her limousine, looking for the photographers, flashing them a smile for their morning papers.

Now she even felt confident enough to make a solo 20-hour trip to Oslo. (The only other time she had traveled abroad alone as a Royal was to the Princess Grace Funeral.) As Patron of the London City Ballet, Princess Diana had been invited to Norway to attend its world premiere of *Carmen*. Hundreds of people had waited in sub-zero temperatures to watch her arrival at the new Koncerthus. Many were still waiting to watch her leave. She wore a blood-red silk evening dress, and Diana-watchers quickly recalled that she had worn the same dress in Canada.

She even planted a tree before leaving. Since the British Embassy ground was absolutely frozen, it took considerable elbow grease and boiling water to help get a hole dug. She arrived hatless and gloveless, "but she has left us goggle-eyed," said a Norwegian photographer. "Everyone agrees that her secret is in the eyes. They look so wondering and modest."

The secret was more than they knew. The next day—just in time to give the world newspapers a Valentine's Day headline—the Prince and Princess of Wales publicly revealed that they were expecting the birth of their second child in late September.

Back in England, Diana and Charles visited a Jaguar automobile factory. After examining the assembly line, the Prince told a worker, "Your production is going well."

The worker looked at him, grinned and replied, "Your production is going well, too, Sir."

25

The father and son were leaving "Buck Palace" to go to Greenwich for a fund-raising dinner in Prince Philip's car, which he was driving. Protocol required wearing naval uniforms. Before they got into the car, the father carefully examined his son's uniform. "You are wearing field marshal shoes with an admiral's uniform. That won't do," he said sharply. "I'll give you five minutes to get the proper shoes, or I'm leaving without you."

Prince Charles dispatched his valet on a full run to get the shoes. The valet, still racing, returned thirty seconds after the five minutes were up. Prince Philip already had departed.

This tension between father and son was not difficult to understand. Despite their basic love and mutual respect, there was also fear and envy. Fear of his father's force and temper by the son, envy of his son's position and future power by the father. The sixty-three-year-old Philip felt himself ever more deeply pushed into the shadow. Despite his obvious ability and consistent hard work for "the firm," he was the master only in his home. The public regarded him with awe more for his caustic tongue than for his royal status.

His competition and envy seemed to intrude even into minor areas. It was evident in his query to an editor, "How is my son's book doing?" Prince Charles had written a children's story for his brothers which had been successfully published, selling many more copies than a book of his father's speeches.

What riled Prince Philip even more was that he felt his son was not living up to his royal responsibilities by limiting his public performances to spend more time with his family.

It became a point of public comment when Prince Philip did not visit his new grandson, Prince Harry, for five weeks. "Prince Philip walks out of the room when Charles comes in," a royal observer reported.

What was said, and often, was that Prince Philip felt that the raunchier Andrew was more his sort of son than Charles, his eldest, that Charles was "too soft . . . too thoughtful." This is hard to accept. While Charles had not been in actual combat like his father, he had proved his courage countless times, parachuting from planes, diving under icecaps.

If Charles had a strained relationship with his father, Diana did not. Diana adored her father-in-law. Her own father, whom she deeply loved, had deteriorated badly in his illness. Prince Philip was a handsome, virile replacement. She had no awe of him as almost everyone else in the Royal Household did.

"She's a great tease," said a friend who was at one of the parties, "and it takes a well-reasoned argument to make her change her mind about something she feels strongly about. That, of course, is just the sort of person who appeals to Prince Philip."

The two got along very well indeed. It was also true that, given his distant relationship with Charles, Prince Philip was the one Royal who competed least for her husband's time. Diana has said several times, in front of her husband, that Prince Philip is the hardest working Royal.

Although Prince Philip's own formal education was limited, he had read extensively and was considered an authority in many fields. He once traveled 1500 miles to squeeze in thirty engagements and make fifteen speeches in the course of a single week. These speeches were concerned with his primary interests: scientific and technological research and development, welfare of young people, encouragement of sport, and the conservation and state of the environment. He was involved with the environment "long before it became a cliché." "Some people have a positive genius for saying absolutely nothing in the most charming language," Prince Philip once wrote. "I try to say something which is at least constructive."

His intolerance caused critic John Grigg to call him "a benevolent busybody without rival in our time." His kinder critics claim that his brashness hides a natural shyness. Other friends insist he is the greatest enemy of pomposity and cant. "There is no more ridiculous sight than a horse performing its natural functions with someone in full dress uniform mounted on its back," observed Prince Philip with some glee. Even Grigg, summing up Philip, has added, "He is a

354

dedicated and thoroughly professional prince. We are lucky to have him."

A man of unbounded energy, a member and patron of hundreds of groups, the Prince once described the kind of world he wanted to see:

"First I would like to see a stabilized world population so that we need make no further demands on land resources. I would like to see farming techniques in all countries developed in sympathy with the needs of population but to the point where no one need go hungry.

". . . Conservation is a case of now or never. Wildlife, whether in the shape of birds, animals, fish, or plants, is being threatened and eroded as never before in history. If we do not get the answer right now, there will not be a second chance.

". . . If you come to think of it, there are really only two categories of people, the good and the bad or the decent and the indecent. The only trouble is that people are not consistent. . . ."

Prince Philip has said of himself, "Perhaps I made the mistake of saying what I think." When he did, the Queen has been said to "draw breath silently." Nevertheless, nobody valued Prince Philip's counsel more than his wife.

As a member of the Privy Council, the small group of advisors to the Queen, Labor MP and Cabinet Minister Richard Crossman had a chance to see their relationship at work. The Queen and her Counsellors were having a spirited discussion when Prince Philip joined them, sitting next to the Queen, then completely taking over the conversation for a half hour, looking at his watch, and saying to the Queen, "Well, they ought to be going now."

"And out we went," recounted Crossman.

"I often think that some of the Royal Family are closer to me than they are to each other," confided a royal cousin, "because they tell me things that they don't tell each other. The Queen once told me that she felt Prince Charles was being sucked in by some charity organization and was being used. I asked her, 'Why don't you tell him that?' and she said, 'I don't want to interfere.' She would tell *me* but she wouldn't tell him. They are very, very careful about interfering in each other's lives."

In crisis, however, they draw tightly together; they are a royal wall against the world.

As he grew older and more self-confident, Prince Charles was better able to defend himself against his father. In a philosophical moment, he admitted, "My father is very wise about how one should look at life. As I got older, I began to realize that he was probably worth listening to . . ." The tantalizing word in that judgment is "probably."

"It is interesting to watch the changes taking place in myself as I grow older," said Charles. "Maybe I forget what I was like at twenty, but I'm aware now, having a son, that I should keep telling myself to try to remember what it was like so I can give him some useful advice when he is twenty."

The Prince then said that it was a tragedy the way the elderly were pushed into institutions. Because of this, "children don't benefit from having the experience of their grandparents, or elderly aunts and uncles."

"I can only speak from my own experience, but I'm sure it gives younger members of the family a wider sense of perspective just listening to older people . . ." He was, of course, thinking of his rich experience with his then eighty-two-year-old grandmother, the Queen Mother, and with Lord Louis Mountbatten.

Any expected new Royal is big news in Britain. This time, however, everybody seemed to want a girl. The rumor factory claimed that the Princess wanted a girl, the bookmakers favored a girl 4–5, the doctors had told Charles that it would be a girl, and even that a name had already been selected—Elizabeth. What threw everyone into a tizzy was the discovery that Diana had ordered twin cots for the nursery. Her grandfather, Lord Fermoy, was a twin, and so was his wife's father.

Princess Diana had her own views. She told Birthright charity organizer Mrs. Vivienne Parry, "If men had babies, they would only have one each." To another group of mothers, she confessed her morning sickness still made her miserable. "I haven't felt well since Day One." Then she added, "I don't think I'm made for the production line but it's all worth it in the end." She was determined, though, to keep up with her scheduled events as long as she could, "because I don't want to disappoint anyone."

One of her events was an honorary fellowship from Glasgow's Royal College of Physicians and Surgeons. She blushed prettily when a professor said she "relegated Cleopatra to eclipse." The professor also insisted that the Princess's motto should be "spread a little happiness as you go by."

Watching her every move, the critics never stopped. Should Diana drive so fast as she got closer to term? She drove her own flashy Ford Escort convertible. Her two back-up detectives followed in a green Range Rover, and sometimes had to speed to keep up with her. A child care specialist, Dr. Hugh Jolly, came to her defense: "There is absolutely no risk involved with a woman driving in the final stages of her pregnancy. The important thing is that she feels perfectly happy driving."

Other critics sniffed at her diet. It included royal jelly nectar, which is supposed to make you live longer, look younger, and feel fitter and sexier. She had discovered it during her first pregnancy and took it along with wheat germ oil and honey. The royal jelly was also said to help a woman feel calmer during pregnancy and help relieve morning sickness. "The main thing is to eat a well-balanced diet with carbohydrates like brown bread or potatoes, little and often," advised Dr. Barbara Pickard, researching morning sickness at Leeds University.

"My second child will never have quite the same sort of pressure or problems to put up with that poor William must confront all his life," Diana confided to a friend.

Charles and Diana were so concerned about their children being hounded by photographers that they consulted one of Fleet Street's top editors when Diana was six months pregnant with her second child. "You know, Mother called in the editors the first time, but we thought this time we'd do it ourselves. It's our problem."

All the editor could advise was for them to appeal again to the sense of decency and fairness of the leaders of the press.

William seemed to be thriving. His father gave him a floppy-maned Shetland pony for his second birthday. He swam regularly with water wings in his various pools, he had a sand box and portable swing. Nobody yelled at him, no matter what he did. That was the Wales nursery rule—no raised voices.

"He's very destructive," admitted his father. "He has to be watched like a hawk." While touring King's College Hospital, Diana noticed a decorative tank with turtles. "William would have had those over by now," she said. She held up her bouquet. "He would have pulled these apart, too.'' Even nanny Barnes said, ''He's a bit of a handful.'' A family friend added that William yelled, kicked, and screamed until he got something he wanted.

William was beginning to move fast. When he picked up one of the hairdresser's brushes, Diana warned, ''Better get that back, or it will wind up in the loo.'' He activated the security alarm system at Balmoral by pushing a button in the nursery. Diana apologized. ''It's very difficult to watch his every move.'' The staff at Highgrove had been fully alerted: ''Do not allow a single object to remain on a low table!''

Butler Alan Fisher smiled. ''Of course, he can be a rambunctious, lively little boy. But I've been in homes with lots of children, and I've never seen a little boy so beautifully mannered, so polite, and considerate. Tell him his nanny might be unhappy with something he may have done, and his little face furrows. He's a dear, little boy.''

The boy was teething. In Kensington Palace, the master bedroom and the nursery were close, on the same wide landing. When William wailed, his mother was up and running. Both the nanny and Charles had tried to persuade her to delegate, but she wouldn't. ''I do get tired,'' she admitted. At Highgrove, the nursery is farther away from their bedroom, in a separate wing, and there the nanny does take over.

Charles often offers advice on child-rearing to his wife, sometimes in public. Her comment to a friend, ''Charles knows so much about babies—he can have the next one.''

Just before her second delivery, Diana rested at Balmoral. She had stopped by to watch her husband play polo, slipped out of the royal box at the end of the game to surprise the Prince with a kiss. It was their third anniversary.

This time, for the actual delivery of her second child, it was a fully natural birth without painkillers. Diana sucked on an ice cube to prevent dehydration, a nurse rubbed cream on her chapped lips, and her husband was there again, holding her hand.

The scene outside was the same, the crowd yelling congratulations to Charles, offering him a baby pacifier, suggesting, ''Let's have another one.'' The tired Charles almost smiled. ''We've nearly got a full polo team now.'' A pretty girl volunteered a kiss, but the Prince gently refused. ''I've had enough excitement for one day.''

For grandfather Spencer, this new excitement was invigorating.

Once again he hoisted up the family standard above Althorp, absolutely delighted that William would now have a brother to play with "and fight with." He was similarly certain that his new grandson would be "a very good chap."

Despite the rumors the royal couple were in agreement and had the name ready: Henry Charles Albert David. They even added a footnote, "But he will be known as Harry."

Henry was indeed a royal name. The first King Henry was the son of William the Conqueror and reigned in the twelfth century. Shakespeare immortalized Henry V for his victory over the French in the Battle of Agincourt. The most famous of all was Henry VIII, who broke with Catholicism in the sixteenth century and set up his own church. The name Charles was of course connected with the monarchy, but also a noted name in the Spencer family. Albert was the name of Prince Charles's grandfather, George VI, as well as of Queen Victoria's husband. And David was the name of the Queen Mother's favorite brother, David Bowes-Lyon.

The *Daily Express* ran a succinct headline: WILD ABOUT HARRY.

Prince William was brought to the hospital to meet his brother. It seemed to have been an amiable meeting. Once again, the Princess decided to leave quickly. Within 24 hours, she was back in her palace.

Prince Harry reportedly had his mother's eyes and his father's ears. The new Prince was third in succession to the throne. Before Harry was born, Prince Andrew was quoted as saying that every time Prince Charles and Prince William flew in the same plane, "it scares the hell out of me."

Astrologers solemnly observed that Harry, being a Virgo, would be shrewd and practical with a dry sense of humor. They also predicted that he would be better behaved than William.

In ancient times, legend had it that a royal birth was heralded by strange sightings in the sky. When the Princess of Wales was in labor with her first child, a pilot from Gatwick sighted an object "rather doughnut-shaped and flat-bottomed." At Harry's birth, no sightings were reported.

Prince Charles got a telephone call from Helen Lightbody, who had been his own nanny. She was elderly, and she had not been invited to the christening planned for late December. She wanted to see the Prince's first-born son, William. The Prince arranged a meeting.

Diana had invited her small household staff to the private family christening. The butler, Alan Fisher, was admiring a piece of statuary when he heard a voice say, "It is beautiful, isn't it?" He said "Ma'am" before he even turned around—he knew it was the Queen. She asked about nanny Lightbody. The Queen seemed to know everything. Lightbody had been a forceful nanny, and the Queen had kept her on a tight leash. Now she wanted to know what the butler had thought of Lightbody. Fisher pondered a moment, then replied, "Well, Ma'am, if Cleopatra had had two nannies like Lightbody, she would have kept the Nile."

The Queen threw her head back and laughed.

The christening went off in proper style. Harry cried only once. Prince William took center stage right after the christening by hugging his brother and then imitating a dog. He and his cousin Zara, Anne's daughter, then raced around the legs of the Archbishop of Canterbury—to everybody's amusement. Prince Andrew and Lady Sarah Armstrong-Jones were chosen as royal godparents. Others included the royal portrait painter, Brian Organ, Diana's former roommate Carolyn Pride (now Mrs. Bartholomew), Lady Cece Vestey, and Gerald Ward, both old friends of the Prince. Lady Cece was a former nurse who married Lord Vestey, a meat and shipping magnate with probably the second largest fortune in Britain. Both were polo and racing enthusiasts. Ward was an old Etonian who farmed 2,000 acres in Berkshire. The fact that he was divorced raised some ecclesiastical eyebrows. He was forty-five, once co-owner of the Caribbean island of Mustique.

The godparent selection caused a family rift. ("Royals have rifts, never have rows," Princess Margaret once said.) The furor this time concerned the fact that Prince Charles did not select his sister as one of the godparents. His father was reported to have been in a fury about this. But Charles and Diana held their ground. Few were therefore surprised when Princess Anne and her husband, saying they had had a previous commitment to hunt rabbits, did not attend the christening.

An electric atmosphere was reported that Christmas at Sandringham. A staff member reported the "iciness" between Anne and Diana. "But at the same time, they are all pretending like mad that nothing is wrong." Anne's defenders pointed out that, after all, she had picked Charles to be godfather to her son, Peter.

Princess Anne suddenly had a surprisingly large number of supporters. Her Royal Rudeness had been magically transformed. The "go to hell" girl was now known as the Princess Who Cares and Dares. As president of the Save the Children Fund she had gone all over the world, sometimes spending as much as six months a year abroad, away from her husband and two children. She had gone to Swaziland, Malawi, Kenya, Somalia, North Yemen, even war-torn Beirut. In a single year, she had been on 244 official engagements with six overseas visits—more than any other Royal. She was in a "dark rage . . . sick to the back teeth with it all," because newspapers didn't give her a line while she was on a hazardous trip in Northern Ireland, but they all featured Diana going to a gala. Soon afterward, Princess Anne said publicly that interest in royalty had reached "a frivolous level."

Perhaps deepening her feeling was the fact that Diana seemed to have it all—youth, good looks, a happy marriage. Her own marriage had been rocky. Captain Mark Phillips, a good-looking, good-natured, successful horseman, seemed to be shunted into the shadows while his wife gained increasing acclaim for being "bloody brave."

He stayed home taking care of their 1,000-acre farm, their boy of six and girl of three, while his wife traveled around the world. They had made only 26 joint public appearances all year, spending 178 days apart. A reporter revealed that they were both in Los Angeles for the Olympics at the same time, but stayed in separate hotels.

Anne insisted on calling herself a farmer's wife, and she did work hard on the farm with her husband—when they were together. Of their marriage, he said, "We've had our ups and downs, but it's a pretty good life in the end."

Anne had a great sense of family, with a particularly strong relationship with her father. "When we were children," she said, "Charles and I used to fight like cat and dog. But the family was always there, the feeling of being in a family, and we are stronger for it, I think. And the family is still there."

Perhaps tellingly, in her 1984 Christmas speech, Her Majesty chose the theme of family unity, saying, "Above all, we must retain the child's readiness to forgive . . ." The message was not lost on Anne and Diana. As they left the church in Sandringham at the end of Christmas week, the two walked out side by side, smiling and laughing. Prince Charles and Mark Phillips joined them in a similar mood. The event was much photographed.

Within two weeks, the four followed up by sharing a pub lunch at King's Head on the Sandringham estate. Again the mood was laughing, joking. The Queen and Prince Philip soon joined them, too. The mood at the time could not have been more merry. Nonetheless, there was an eleven-year difference between Anne and Diana, and because of their dissimilar personalities they would be unlikely friends under any circumstances.

As part of her transformed public image, Princess Anne even appeared on a TV "chat show" displaying a sharp wit and an engaging sense of humor. Looking attractive in a high-necked blouse, her long hair swept back, Anne said that if the monarchy were abolished, she and her husband would have to work harder on the farm or get jobs working with horses. What advice had she given Princess Diana? One could only learn from one's own experiences and problems, Anne said, and each person reacts differently.

"You said that like a Dowager," observed her host.

"I've been practicing," parried Princess Anne.

One does not say no to the Queen. Diana not only seemed to bow to her solemn mother-in-law by smoothing over the rift with Anne, but even got on a horse—for the first time since she was a young girl. "The Queen chose a safe old gray mare to put Diana back in the saddle," and Her Majesty herself shouted instructions when the horse wandered into the undergrowth. Nevertheless, Diana was not captivated by the experience.

Even her grandchildren felt the distance of the Queen's dignity and her implied wish for strict obedience. This was no "cuddling granny." She would tolerate no screaming tantrums, no flat disobedience, "no jammy fingers on her cashmere sweater." From her they would learn respect and manners.

The press winced when Her Majesty blasted them for "harassing" the family during their annual New Year's holiday at Sandringham. A photograph on a front page showed her riding with Prince Edward, glaring sternly at the photographer who took the picture. Most of the papers were apologetic, promising to keep their staff photographers away during Royal Family holidays.

Nor could Prime Minister Margaret Thatcher stay aloof from a royal command. The Queen was furious when President Reagan sent troops into Grenada in 1984. Americans could not understand the British anger over their action, but the simple fact was that the United

States was invading the Queen's country; it was part of her Commonwealth.

The Queen, therefore, was in an understandable fury when she first heard of the invasion not from her Prime Minister, but over the radio. Her Majesty sent a curt message to the Prime Minister for an immediate meeting. Mrs. Thatcher replied that she would come to the Palace within the hour. A sharper, shorter message then came from the Queen that she wanted the Prime Minister at the Palace "*now*." Prime Minister Thatcher was there in ten minutes. The inside report was that the Queen did not even offer her a seat.

After that, the truce between the two women was polite, but uneasy. Members of Parliament asked each other in private, "What's the latest news from the battlefront?" To make matters worse, the Prime Minister once arrived at the Palace wearing the same colored dress as the Queen—which just is not done. To avert future mishaps, a Downing Street aide called the Palace asking to be notified in advance of the color of the Queen's dress, but got the cool reply that the Prime Minister need not worry "because the Queen never notices what women around her are wearing."

The Queen had been working to change her voice ever since her coronation, the upper-crust or so-called cut class pronunciation softening into what was called "standard BBC newsreader English." (Prince Charles's was still very much an upper-class accent. Princess Diana's accent had been described as "delightful" — "more in touch with the younger generation.") The Queen's voice was still somewhat high-pitched and "rather girlish." Her royal wave looked like a gentle karate chop with her hand slightly cupped.

She had traveled over a million miles on her overseas tours, usually with a minimum of six large trunks and two six-foot wardrobes for ball gowns besides boxes of shoes and hats. Two dressers accompanied her with their ironing boards and their cross-reference system for coordinating accessories. She also took along her grandmother's parasol and an attaché case filled with homeopathic remedies (which Prince Charles also did). Her traveling entourage usually numbered about forty, including ladies-in-waiting who answered the phone, paid any bills, and wrote thank-you notes.

Her Majesty used minimal makeup—a thin layer of foundation

and powder and a tiny dab of "blusher" on each cheek. Her eyebrows were unplucked and she used a rinse called Chocolate Kiss to make the gray in her hair look like dark honey.

When somebody once sympathized with all her necessary hand-shaking, she replied, "It's not as difficult as it might seem. You see, I don't have to introduce myself. They all seem to know who I am."

Her role as monarch had perhaps removed her from the main-stream of many movements. She once asked a male playwright at a reception what "all this feminism is about." The playwright strug-gled to explain and she interrupted, "I really don't understand it. I've never suffered because I'm a woman."

The Queen Mother once had told her, "Your work is the rent you pay for life." Indeed, she had worked with nine prime ministers. She could talk to West Africans more easily than she could talk to Welsh miners. She was the longest reigning monarch of this century, and a recent poll in Britain revealed that 89 percent of the people wanted the monarchy to continue.

Her concern was not only for the people of Britain, but for people throughout her Commonwealth. As head of the Commonwealth for 32 years, the Queen's stature was enormous, towering over her own ministers as well as the presidents of former colonies. Common-wealth prime ministers had direct access to the Queen without going to Downing Street. As head of the Commonwealth, the Queen was not bound by the advice of any single government. Nobody knew this better than Her Majesty, and, now, Prince Charles.

Public comment at home was sometimes mixed: "I admire the Queen, but she should remember that it's the people of this country who pay her, not the people of India."

The Queen and her heir agreed on basic principles. Prince Charles sensed deeply that he was a symbol of a family of nations. The weight resting on him was that of an intelligent, well-informed man, intent on understanding the world, who was nevertheless gagged against making political statements. If he hired a black West Indian girl on his personal staff, as he had, or a former Ghurka soldier as a valet, this caused considerable comment. Yet he did these things because he knew what they symbolized.

His two brothers were still on the sidelines. Prince Andrew had come back from the Falklands a national hero, but promptly dissipated this image in a series of escapades with lovely young women. He was still the raunchy Randy Andy to the press, who noted a comment he made to liven up a breakfast: "You know, the one thing I can never possibly imagine is my mother and father making love." And yet, in an interview, talking about his passion for photography, he displayed a rare seriousness as he showed some of his pictures. Asked if there was a theme to his pictures, he replied, "Loneliness. If you look at them all as a package, there is not much there. There is nobody in them."

Now twenty-five, Andrew had the right to marry without the Queen's permission. He was promptly ordered out to sea for the next five months.

As a personality, Andrew was somewhere in between Charles and Edward. More than his brothers, he tried to ingratiate himself with the press. Reporters were no longer surprised when the young Prince sidled up to them at a bar, offering to buy a drink, then asked how they got a particular story or a specific picture.

At twenty-one, Prince Edward was called the low-key Prince: self-effacing, hard-working, and most private. Photographers and some reporters also called him caustic, arrogant, even nasty. At Cambridge, he had followed in his brother Charles's footsteps, both as an actor and as a major in archeology, then switching to history. As the fifth in line to the British throne, he had picked as one of his second-year subjects "The Transformation of the British Monarchy."

Unlike Andrew, Edward tried to keep his girlfriends secret, and partially succeeded. At college, he took his clothes to the launderette, ate pizza with his detectives, and did his own shopping. At parties, he usually arrived late, left early. In the college theatricals, he worked "jolly hard." After Cambridge, he expected to join the Royal Marines as a second lieutenant for several years.

Nearing her middle fifties, Princess Margaret had many friends but was a lonely woman. Friends sometimes saw her having dinner alone, drinking steadily, occasionally motioning to a young man at a nearby table to join her—either for the meal or the evening. She had been born out of her time. Had she lived in a later age, the Royals might have let her marry the man she loved even if he had divorced his wife. Now there was serious concern about her health.

She had been a heavy smoker and part of her lung had been removed.

She did have pleasure and pride in her children. Her twenty-three-year-old son, David, though living in nearby Dorset, still maintained a room in Kensington Palace and often joined the Royal Family for their holidays and hunting.

Though generally a serious young man, he once turned up in Bath's Theater Royal wearing an overcoat and boots with nothing underneath, "in a silly game of forfeits." The young viscount was described as looking more like "a punk than a peer."

Regarded as a ladies' man in the Sloane Ranger set, Linley was determined to keep as clear from the "royal circus" as he could. He insisted on being called plain David Linley. "My mind and heart are in the workshop," he said. "I just want to lead my own life."

So did his sister, Lady Sarah Armstrong-Jones. She was twelve when her parents divorced and her trauma was lasting. The Queen virtually adopted her niece, making her part of country weekends, horse shows, seating Sarah next to her at assorted functions and family dinners. Like her brother, Sarah was more artistic than academic. She had studied fabrics and design and had gravitated toward the film industry. Sarah had gone with her father to India when he shot still photographs for the film *A Passage to India*, and then worked for Mountbatten's son-in-law, Lord Brabourne, a film producer. Like Diana, she had refused to go the debutante route, avoiding what she called "the dreadful chinless wonders."

As the most senior—and most likable—of the young Royals, Sarah could later opt for royal duties and get on the Civil List for a salary and expenses. But she could never be a princess unless she married a prince.

Diana reportedly made a preliminary attempt to match Sarah with her own brother, Charles. They did date. A tall, sandy-haired young man in T-shirt, dinner jacket, and goggles, twenty-year-old Charles would zoom down from Oxford in his Volvo to join his gregarious, energetic cousin. Like the Queen Mother, she had the bright smile that could light up a room, but somehow the chemistry was not right.

The press had dubbed Diana's only brother "Champagne Charlie" because he had reportedly refused to pay a bill for champagne at Boodles. The club's manager claimed "Charlie" had behaved "like a spoiled brat," and added, "We don't want obnoxious little boys here swigging drink from the bottle." In the argument, the manager also claimed that the future Earl of Althorp had blurted out, "Don't you know who I am? We can get you closed down. I am Princess Diana's brother!"

Of course it made headlines in all the papers.

Before that, little had been heard of the Viscount Althorp. He had worked as a stock exchange messenger clerk, a factory quality controller checking food in a supermarket, a bit player in a spy film. Basically, he was just a quiet history student at Magdalen College in Oxford who had had three A levels and his father's charm. His fellow students described Charles as polite at parties, always well-behaved, only occasionally arriving rigged up like a matinee idol or in "punk" battle dress.

After the Boodles fracas, Charles was involved in a "punch-up" with photographers in a midnight brawl after a party; told an interviewer, "I'm a pushover about sex"; confessed on TV that he had fantasies about taking part in Roman orgies; had another restaurant fight with waiters trying to prevent him and his friends from taking off the pants of a disc jockey named Blackburn. Finally, the young viscount told of his new ambition to have a restaurant of his own. He said he would not trade on his sister's name: "I wouldn't call it 'Diana.'"

The Palace advice was terse: Cool it.

Discussing all this in his mother's London flat in Pimlico, Charles, looking even younger than his twenty years, was apologetic and even blushed occasionally.

"The implication from all these stories," he said, "is that here is Di's brother. We all know she's wonderful, which she is. But here's this brattish little brother that lets her down."

He attributed his fights and pranks to his youth, his inexperience with the world, the fact that he was a "sitting target." He looked depressed and worried when he said, "I do feel vulnerable.

"I didn't expect to get any attention . . . I thought that after the actual wedding they'd leave the whole family alone. But because I'm young, male, and I like doing normal things, I'm more of a target than my older sisters who are married with children."

Theirs was a tight family, he said. They were all very upset but "they're very good at closing ranks . . . There's no ticking off business, though. I don't get sat down and told what to do . . . Diana wouldn't think it her business to advise me."

This very tall (6'2"), slim young man very much resembled his sister, even to the way he looked up through his eyelashes. He and Diana still were very close, saw each other often, lunched together. Charles was one of the first to get her news that she was marrying Prince Charles.

Stressing her thoughtfulness, he told of the time they were lunching in a small restaurant and one of the detectives had to wait outside in the car. "Diana just got up and filled a bowl of strawberries and cream and took it out to the man in the car because she was worried about him not eating."

The charge of arrogance had hurt him the most. "My sisters and I were brought up not to be snobby—certainly to be aware of people and not dismissive and look down on them. I've always been aware of how lucky I am not to have to worry about the gas bill."

"People expect me to be stupid," he told reporter Paula Yates. "It's the cliché image: He's got a title, he's got money, he must be stupid." He was proud of the fact that he was holding his own scholastically at Oxford.

Of his early years, he remembered endless nannies after his parents divorced. When his mother remarried, he said his stepfather "did everything to take the bumps out of it." He admired his own father greatly, saying that "he's brilliant with people." Of his stepmother, Raine, he said less.

He found it difficult to bow to his sister Diana, but "she's not bothered about it anyway." He did, though, always call Prince Charles "Sir," and regarded him as "a marvelous bloke" whom his sister thinks is "the most handsome man on earth."

It was easy to sympathize with young Viscount Althorp. He was being asked to remember constantly that his godmother was a Queen and his sister a future Queen. All *he* wanted to do was have some fun.

Prince Charles's month-long tour of African countries was primarily undertaken in his capacity as a director of the Commonwealth Development Corporation, which was involved in financing 260 projects in more than 40 countries. Zambia farmers were surprised at how much the Prince knew about farming. On a later trip to New Guinea, a land of 700 dialects, the Prince was again more of a symbol. When they made him "Number One Fellah," chief of Paradise Island,

and carried him ashore from a war canoe on a carved wooden bed, he had told them in his newly learned pidgin English: "Woroh, woroh, woroh, all man meri belong Manus. Mi hammamas tru." ("Thank you, all men and women of Manus, I'm truly filled with happiness.") As an old married man now, the Prince was able to greet the bare-breasted native girls more directly this time, without modest sidelong looks.

Diana went on neither trip with him. William was in his "terrible twos." She was also breast-feeding Harry, and he was too young to leave behind.

At the insistence of public and press, there was a birthday press conference for Prince William when he was two. Loudly and clearly, Wills said "Daddy" and "What's that?" (Diana always called her father "Daddy." Prince Charles always called his parents "Mommy" and "Poppy." William now called his father "Papa.")

"William is a splendid little character," said Prince Charles. "Very good-natured. Seems to have quite a good sense of humor. And he's very outgoing, which is encouraging. Which will be a great help to him, I think, later on." Further information given at this time was that he adored dogs, had his own Scotland Yard detectives, and seemed curious about cameras. There was no comment on the statement by the Royal Society for the Prevention of Automobile Accidents who criticized the Prince for letting Wills hold the steering wheel of their Range Rover while the Prince was driving. There was also no comment on the rumor that the Princess was "no soft touch as a mother," that she did not leave the discipline of her son to others but corrected him herself.

Following the Prince's return to England, she and Charles attended a rock concert starring Duran Duran and Dire Straits. "I've got my earplugs in my bag." She asked them, "Do you think I'm going to need them?" The money raised was in aid of the Prince of Wales Trust to help young people find jobs. As Dire Straits played one of their hits, "Romeo and Juliet," the Princess put her hand on Charles's knee and sang the words. The group dedicated one of their songs to the royal couple. "Here's to the two young lovers. Let's wish them every happiness."

Charles spent as much of his time watching the audience as he did the musicians. He would have preferred a concert of classical music or jazz or opera.

When he worked late at home in his study and Diana had gone

to bed early, the Prince listened to his own favorites. If it was too late, he had a bed made up in a side room and slept there rather than disturb Diana. According to staff people, he continued doing his exercises at night before going to bed.

Describing their marriage in general, the Queen's press secretary, Michael Shea, insisted, "There has always been a lot of laughter. It's a super marriage."

What reinforced it even more were the children. Prince Charles said, "Funny, I never realized . . . when you have children of your own, you only then discover what fun they can be." Both profoundly believed that babies must be talked to and loved. They were not parents who demanded "a clean plate" at meals. They worked on the theory that the baby's body knew what it needed. The young parents both agreed that Prince Harry was "absolutely adorable," that William's initial sibling rivalry had dissipated happily, and that they were more relaxed with their second child. He was, they said, "extraordinarily good, sleeps marvelously, and eats very well. Doesn't wake us up too much in the middle of the night. A thoroughly splendid chap.' "

Of his enlarged nuclear family, the Prince said, "We'll have to try for a girl next time."

26

just because you came from a broken home, you're not going to break up my life."

Kensington Palace butler Alan Fisher directed his outburst at Princess Diana. Within a short time, Fisher had quit.

This is not something Fisher would tell an interviewer. But it was said, and it was overheard.

What Fisher did tell the press was, "I'm a Sagittarius and the decision to go is just one of those crazy things we Sagittarians do."

What he did not tell was what really went on in their home life. He is still most discreet about it, but he does say how deeply in love the two still are. "As soon as he came home from anywhere, the first thing the Prince always asked was, 'Where's the Princess?' And we learned quickly to have a specific answer. And she was the same way about him. One of their favorite, most-used words, in public or private, was 'Darling.' Their love was obvious—the way they looked at each other and touched each other and talked so endearingly in the privacy of their home. And the way they laughed together. There was so much laughing."

The myth spawned by the press was that the butler had quit because the Princess had invaded his traditional areas of responsibility.

"Nonsense," said Fisher. "She never interfered. Nobody could have been more considerate or appreciative of what I was doing. The Princess was a nice, natural, friendly girl when I first met her, and she still is. That superstar stuff hasn't changed her at all. She's one of those rare human beings with no 'edge' to her, no 'side.'

"That doesn't mean I was happy there. I wasn't. I didn't begrudge them their quiet privacy. But there simply wasn't enough for me to do. I was bored."

Before the Prince and Princess hired Alan Fisher as their butler, the Princess warned him, "They don't pay much money."

"When he died, Bing Crosby left me fifteen dollars," said the smiling Fisher. "I can loan you five."

The Prince roared with laughter.

The Princess also asked Fisher to send her a note on what he thought were the butler's duties. Fisher wrote her that the butler's primary duty was to help create a happy home "and dodging all the thrown crockware."

Since Diana moved into Kensington Palace, Royal watchers noted the departure of some 40 employees. This was an amazing statistic, since the normal Palace turnover was small and seldom. Many of them blamed their exit on The Boss—as they called Diana. She vigorously denied it. "I just don't sack people," she said. "I am not responsible for any sackings." This was not quite true.

From a small group who would talk about it anonymously, there was a consensus that the Princess was not unhappy to see Fisher leave—however much she herself used him as a confidant. Their collective judgment was that the Princess, in her insecurity, was jealous of anyone who had a close relationship with the Prince, anyone who took too much of his time, too much of his affection. She wanted the Prince all for herself and her children.

"Check her astrology sign," said one of her closest friends. "She's a typical Cancer, a nest-builder. Her immediate family is everything to her. Nothing else matters."

A more perceptive friend traced it to Diana's parents' divorce—the mother who went away. "It's a terrible scar and it has never healed with her. I've talked to some outstanding psychologists about it, and they have two phrases that fit: 'magic gesture' and 'self-fulfilling prophecy.' Magic gesture defines Diana's feeling that if she keeps her family in close and fills them with her love, then nothing can ever separate them. The self-fulfilling prophecy is that if she does it that way, if she keeps her nest too restrictive, if she keeps her husband reined in too tightly then she will lose everything she wants to gain. Even if she doesn't want to be part of the world, he has to be, and he must break loose. Not that he can ever divorce her, but it can change their love. His love is her anchor peg. The only way she can grow out of her insecurity is to retain the knowledge that she has his love. If she does, if she has the full confidence of that, then she can grow with him, increasingly become a part of this royal world she now resents. If she does grow with him they will have a healthier marriage. But they have years of crisis ahead of them."

What she truly did not like were masses of people. She didn't even like masses of children. When she visited a school and they wanted her to pop in on every classroom, she wouldn't do it. All classes are the same, she said. She preferred people, particularly children, on a one-to-one basis. But if she had had her choice, she would have avoided other people's children entirely to stay with her own.

Another myth exploded.

Despite their love for each other, there were problems, conflicts, trouble. Most of it stemmed from the fact that she found most royal chores a bore, particularly the formal state occasions. She preferred her social scenes in small informal friendly groups with lots of dancing. When Charles was elsewhere, or too tired, she even occasionally went alone to a friend's country house for a Saturday night dance. One evening in June 1985, she kept on dancing until 4 A.M. at a country dance in Leicestershire, exhausting a whole series of bachelor partners.

One question the Princess always asked before a planned royal tour or a state occasion or special function: "Do I have to go?"

"Sadly, the Princess does not like people," the Prince told one of his closest confidantes, who later added:

"And she wants everything! She not only wants more of his time, but she wants him to change his habits and his friends. She should be building up this man. After all, he's going to be King. But she's been cutting him down, changing his image. Making him cut out hunting which is an historic royal sport. And all this nonsense about vegetarianism and spiritualism and things like that. That diminishes him with people. Makes him seem weaker. It really does. And now, for heaven's sake, she's even got him into gardening. He was never interested in *gardening!*

"I'm really worried about him. I'm worried about his happiness. I'm worried about his image. I hope she settles down and realizes what she's doing to him."

Another equally close friend of Charles was not so concerned.

"Prince Charles is not a wimp. He's giving in to her a lot because she's so young, and because of the children. There's little question that marriage and fatherhood have mellowed him. He's a thoughtful husband, but hardly a henpecked one. He has his own stubborn strength and dedicated purpose. When he disagrees with her about anything, he lets her know it. And when he's really angry, he can be very formidable."

This ended another myth. The Prince was not a doormat of a husband. In the course of family arguments, which were loud and long, the Prince's voice could be heard "three blocks away." He stated his views sharply, and without stint. He seldom gave in on anything he strongly believed. If he did give in, it was almost never without a fight, and only because he loved her, not because he was weak.

Neither was she. Her hairdresser was there during a confrontation, and he embarrassedly turned up the hairdryer to try to drown out the noise. He described the tiff in terms of heated words, but not blazing. Diana afterward joked about it. "A good job it wasn't something serious."

The Prince's friends blamed Diana for all the staff changes in their several years of marriage. There were nine major ones. Most important were the two private secretaries who came and went. A royal private secretary is a key advisor who suggests what should and should not be done, and why. Oliver Everett was in high favor when he was given the job. He had come from the British Embassy in Madrid, his quick thinking reportedly had saved the Prince's life in Florida, and he had been most helpful to the Princess in Wales. But then she turned on him, almost ignored him, was seen sobbing on her husband's shoulder saying, "Why doesn't he leave? He knows I don't like him." One explanation offered was that the Princess had overheard Everett, at the tail end of a telephone conversation, making some remark she had interpreted as belittling to her. A friend once warned her, "Don't try to overhear what people say because one day, surely, you will hear something bad about yourself." The Prince finally found Everett another job at Windsor Castle.

His successor was the unflappable Etonian bachelor Edward Adeane, a dignified libel lawyer whose family had a heritage of royal service. His father had been private secretary to the Queen.

"Adeane was invaluable to her," confided a friend of Charles. "He knew absolutely everything about all the royal minefields. It's unbelievable that she sacked him."

Others more friendly to Diana insisted that Adeane had decided to quit—not because of the Princess, but because he was making too little impact on the Prince.

The Prince had complained to an intimate friend that his wife was "consumed with motherhood." To another friend, he expressed his worries about their difference in age, his concern that she might find him stodgy. "Diana will keep Charles on the dance floor for hours on end," said a close friend, "and he refuses to quit while she wants to keep going." She would also sometimes tell him, half-jokingly, to turn to some other TV show. "It's an old man's show. You're not an old man yet."

They compromised on much. He tolerated her ballet and she tolerated his opera. He liked a small range of her favorite pop music and she liked an even smaller range of his classical favorites. She often had her *Dallas* and *Dynasty* programs taped so that she could see them at her own leisure without imposing them on him. (The Prince seemed to be succumbing, however. On a visit to a housing project in Newcastle upon Tyne, he asked one disabled couple when he saw their TV set, "Do you watch *Dynasty?* My wife has got me watching it.")

Their at-home conversation was not untypical of other young marrieds. Their untiring subject was their children. "I would like to say the Prince is a better father than the Princess is a mother—I really would like to say that," said a close friend of Charles. "But I can't. He is a wonderful father, but she's a perfect loving mother."

Besides children, they talked about their daily activities, particularly amusing stories about various people they met.

The subject of friends was a dangerous discussion area between them. She had few, and seemed to want fewer. He missed his friends. Few things distressed him more than meeting an old friend at a function and merely shaking his hand.

There were many myths about the current crop of friends of the Prince and Princess of Wales. Every such list always included the Romseys, who had inherited Mountbatten's Broadlands estate where the royal couple honeymooned and still visited. Charles and Diana also had availed themselves of the Romseys' Caribbean resort home near Eleuthera. The Princess, however, did not regard them as close friends. She was overheard referring to them as "part of the Mountbatten Mafia."

Impulsively once, the Prince told his butler to plan a large dinner party. The butler was delighted. The Prince was still buoyant about it when he announced his surprise idea to his wife at lunch. The Princess was not delighted. Later that afternoon, the Prince curtly told his butler to drop the plans for the party—they had changed their minds.

About once every two months, the Prince and Princess did have a small official dinner, usually for some top executives associated with their different special interests. At such times, the staff, which included three chefs, was instructed to "keep it moving." Such guests did not linger long.

At one of their own small official dinners the Princess held aloft the name card of a pretty woman and asked her butler, "Where should I put her?"

He knew what she was thinking. The woman was *very* pretty. He had a prompt reply, though. "You could put her in the Prince's lap and it wouldn't matter. At the end of the dinner, she will go out the door and you will still be here."

The Princess smiled, put the name card next to her husband.

Given his wife's distaste for such functions, the Prince might invite someone for lunch or a drink. At such times, the Princess would seldom appear. Guests automatically assumed that she was not at home, but most of the times she was—in her own room.

In the years of their marriage thus far there had been almost no social entertaining at their home in Kensington Palace. Nor did they go out to small dinner parties. People who had been close friends, particularly of the Prince, reported that they had called with invitations two or three times, and then simply stopped calling to save Charles and Diana the embarrassment of another refusal.

In their defense, it should be understood that protocol required them to spend many evenings away from home at banquets, fundraisers, premieres, state functions. With the arrival of an important head of state, the Prince would have difficulty giving vent to his anger. He would grasp his desk tightly with both hands and say in a quiet choked voice, "Now, Alan . . ."

If someone on staff did something of which he strongly disapproved, the Prince could bellow his anger. But if the butler was the guilty party, the Prince would have difficulty giving vent to his anger. He would grasp his desk tightly with both hands and say in a quiet choked voice, "Now, Alan . . ."

If the Prince wanted something special, a certain food perhaps, and said, "Now, Alan, do you think we could get . . ." Alan would promptly interrupt to say, "Sir, I would cross two continents and the Sahara Desert to make certain you get it . . . whatever it is." The Prince would then give his butler a warm, appreciative look.

Fisher once told the Prince, "When you give me my paycheck, you buy my service, but not my loyalty. My loyalty, which you have, is my gift."

Perhaps there was a special need in Prince Charles for surrogate fathers, since he saw so little of his own when he was growing up. Perhaps this partly explains the unique relationship of mutual affection and admiration between the Prince and his older butler.

Similarly, Diana saw Charles as her pathfinder, her ultimate protector. There is little question that wherever they were together, she was constantly looking at him for approval and direction.

At a premiere of the film *Gandhi*, the Prince was in stage center of the presentation line while Diana was shunted slightly aside. Producer Sir Richard Attenborough apologized for this, but she replied, "Don't worry, I'm used to it."

She was now also used to the outpouring of adulation. A consensus of beauty contest candidates for Miss World all agreed that Princess Diana was "obviously the most beautiful woman in the world." Polls in the United States, Japan, France, Germany, and Australia all listed Diana as the best-known Briton in the world, more popular than any pop star or prime minister or even the Queen. Syrian Defense Minister Mustafa Dias was such a Diana fan that he said, "If Mrs. Thatcher were to invite me, I wouldn't go. But if it were Princess Diana, I'd travel to England on a lame donkey."

If the press paid sharp attention to her hair styles and clothes, nothing ever exceeded their interest in the actual marriage relationship between Charles and his Princess. It was more than just Fleet Street's "ability to construct a baroque palace on the head of a pin." Dame Rebecca West described the interest as due to "the Royals' showing us magnified images of ourselves, but better."

That's why the press faithfully recorded just how often Charles and Diana touched each other in public. A report by a team of sociologists visiting cafés in seven different countries noted the number of nonsexual touches they saw in the course of three hours. In Greece, they saw more than 500, in Spain 400, in London none. It was therefore delightful to the British public that this royal couple were such frequent "touchers." (Occasionally this was not so. A bystander once saw the Prince place his hand possessively on his wife's backside. Diana gently removed it, without a smile, and openly reproved him because other people were present.)

What was not so delightful were the increased rumors that Diana, more and more, had become the overweening boss of her home. She was surely boss of the kitchen. It featured mostly vegetarian meals, with a calorie count for her of 1,500 to keep her weight at 124 pounds. She was also largely the boss of the nursery, and her children and nanny knew it.

Her social priority was for family over friends. Friends note that this did make Charles restless. The myth was that Diana had made him cut them out completely—particularly his married women friends, Lady Tryon and Camilla Parker-Bowles. The fact was that he saw them often at polo matches, big receptions, parties, and balls. Lady Tryon was a close friend of Princess Margaret. The Queen Mother was godfather to their child. At a fund-raising reception at Salisbury Cathedral, the Prince spotted them and promptly invited them to lunch at the Palace.

Those who know insist that it never could have been an impulsive gesture. The Prince automatically gets an advance list of all who will attend a function at which he will be present. He knew Lord and Lady Tryon would be on it and must have said to the Princess, "Darling, look who's going to be there. They have been friends for so long and I really feel I must make it up to them for not seeing them. Shall we invite them for lunch?"

The marvel to the few who knew of this—and it was never reported in the press—was that the Princess agreed. From their reports, it was a most pleasant lunch, the first break in the ice floe that has separated the Prince from his old friends. Inside watchers considered this a strong sign that the Princess has started losing some of her insecurity.

The press also seized on another rumor: that Diana had made her husband swear off hunting. Indeed, he had stopped, and even given his guns to his brother Andrew. Yet close friends testified that he had decided to stop long before he met her. Another myth refuted. When the mood suited him, however, he went fox-hunting again with his young cousin Viscount Linley, Princess Margaret's son.

So, indeed, perhaps the Prince was still his own man, listening to his wife when it suited him, but following his own will at other times.

His interest in spiritualism was a case in point. His friends blamed such interest on Diana. Intimates, however, insisted that she was disturbed by his interest in it and that it predated her knowing him.

It started with his serious interest in extrasensory perception, even to his urging the University of Wales, of which he is a Chancellor, to set up a professorship in parapsychology. He had been impressed by the fact that Angus Ogilvy, husband of Princess Alexandra, had been cured of crippling back pains by a faith healer. And an editor of the *Spiritualist Gazette*, Tom Johanson, insisted that Prince Charles had tried to contact his great-uncle, Lord Mountbatten, using the Ouija board. Whether he had done this at all, and if so whether he had done it seriously or out of idle curiosity, is not known.

Dr. Diana Bates claims to possess a remarkable photograph. It shows her late mother, Dr. Winifred Rushworth, Prince Charles, and Princess Diana holding hands, apparently believing they were in contact with the spiritual world.

Dr. Rushworth was a well-known psychiatrist and the author of a book on spiritualism. Dr. Bates claims to have taken notes while the Prince had consulted her mother. She also had replied to personal letters the Prince had written to her mother. The letters, she added, "are now in a very safe place."

The Prince was strongly attached to the concept of alternative medicine, again an idea of his and not Diana's. He partly believed, along with his mother, in homeopathy—the use of herbs for illness—and took along a chest full of herbs on long tours.

His belief in holistic medicine centered around treating the underlying causes of disease, the whole body rather than isolated symptoms. Discussing this with medical students at St. Mary's Hospital in London, the Prince once made the point that a woman with a headache might need social help rather than medicine because she lived alone with two small, demanding children. Addressing the British Medical Association, Charles urged doctors to explore the idea that more illness can be prevented by "developing a different attitude toward existence." Then he asked a friend, "Do they think I'm a crank?"

Nor did Diana force him into gardening. It stemmed partly from

RALPH G. MARTIN

his interest in farming, tilling his own soil, which gave him "a sense of proportion." He got more of this interest from his grandmother, who had a great love of gardening, and from his friends the Marquess of Salisbury and his wife. They advised him on constructing an ornamental garden, surrounding it with a hedge and planting an avenue of yew trees at Highgrove for screening. Charles was even seen at the controls of a mechanical digger.

With all this, he was hardly growing soft. He seemed to be playing more polo than ever, sometimes as much as five times a week. He and Diana still had their skiing holidays in Liechtenstein. And he was highly unhappy when Her Majesty stopped him from any more parachuting. He still did a lot of skin-diving exploring the hulk of the *Mary Rose*, Henry VIII's flagship.

In the constricting position of being required to bite his tongue because he was a Royal, the Prince more and more often said what he thought these days. He told architects in London that the planned National Gallery extension was "a monstrous carbuncle." He urged a conservation and development program for "liveable cities," to help counter the loss of 37,000 fertile acres in England each year. Meeting three workers in a visit to Liverpool, he described their weekly wage of 36 pounds as "daylight robbery." He was deeply concerned, he said, with young people "who think life stinks."

British Labor leader Neil Kinnock told a party conference that the Prince was more caring than Prime Minister Thatcher, that he realized "the great gap between the ordinary bloke who wants to get on with the job and the means of enabling him to do it."

In an impassioned outburst, the Prince also told a board meeting of the British Council that he was "pig sick" over the spending cutback by the Thatcher government of Council funds. The Council, of which the Prince was a patron, promoted British influence abroad.

All this reflected a Prince Charles over whom Diana had minimal influence. Her primary influence was in the home. She could change his traditional dark pinstripe suit into an informal, fashionable lightweight tweed, and she was still the only one who could tell him, "Oh, don't be so stuffy, Charles." But she was not responsible for any curtailment in his royal workload.

If he did occasionally ease off on his schedule of appointments, it was due to his own desire to share more time with his family. His speeches now had homely touches. He could tell a crowd about his

380

children: "They both have stinking colds at the moment." He amplified this by saying that William got along very well now with Harry, but "you have to watch out for flying tractors."

Diana more candidly explained William's absence one day when she visited an orphanage. "I didn't bring William today because he's a little pest. He won't do as he's told and he touches everything." He was, however, coming along nicely in other areas: He had learned the royal etiquette of shaking hands, without prompting.

On a family trip to Balmoral, Prince William suddenly discovered that he could not fly with his parents. The Queen had finally put her foot down in opposition to Diana's wishes. She decreed the need to enforce the long-standing routine of separate traveling for the new heir to safeguard the royal line of succession against accident or attack.

There was some talk that Diana was thinking of starting a nursery school for the youngest Royals, when Harry was a little older. Rumors even circulated that Baby Number Three was on the production line. Lil Hill, a mother of eleven, in Hartcliffe, Bristol, advised Charles that if he didn't want the trouble of a large family like hers, "Keep your pajamas on."

Prince Charles appeared on TV reading from his own best-selling children's story, *The Old Man of Lochnagar*. It was about a grouchy old man who leaves home in search of adventure. It began, "Not all that long ago, when children were even smaller and people had especially hairy knees, there lived an old man of Lochnagar . . ." Watching and listening at home was his son William.

Diana, meanwhile, kept up with her own work schedule, including a visit with ten mothers whose babies had died from the crib-death syndrome. She flew there in a blizzard and told them, "I couldn't get here fast enough." At another home for neglected children, the Princess was close to tears: "I can't understand how anybody can abandon their children. I love my own so much." She smiled, though, when she said motherhood was one of the toughest jobs—"hard work and no pay."

A matter of deep but quiet concern for Diana and Charles were continued IRA kidnap threats. On the top of the list were Prince Charles and his two sons.

Diana went to Wellingborough to visit a center for elderly and unemployed in a multi-racial, multi-faith, multi-cultural neighborhood. As soon as it was scheduled, security people arrived to get the names of all guests to run through their Special Branch computer. Their men paced the royal route twice, checking exactly what would happen where, what cars would be arriving, who would be carrying packages. In view of the recent death threat to kill a Royal, there would be hundreds of policemen around the center on her arrival, including sniffer dogs and marksmen.

Not only was the entire center repainted but a special bathroom was set aside for her "just in case." Its latest refinements included a mirror, a pedestal mat, a brand-new toilet seat, and a fresh toilet roll. To make certain no one else used it before her arrival, the door was taken off its hinges. Caretaker Philip Graham, who had done all the work on the bathroom, quietly confided that he hoped the Princess would have to go to "the loo" because of all the work he put into it.

During a dress rehearsal at Victoria Center, complete with practice curtseys, the director told the staff, "If she does say hello, don't behave as if the world has come to an end. Remember that she's just a young lass, just as nervous as you . . ."

One of the things Diana would not appreciate was a banner that read: HI DI HI.

The answer was yes.

But she did not have to go to the loo.

At another walkabout in a trade school, she talked to a trainee carpenter who wore a punk haircut with a two-foot pigtail dyed orange, red, black, and blonde. "It makes a pleasant change," she said, "to talk about someone else's hair—rather than having everyone talking about mine."

The Prince made his own headlines, donating blood—the first Royal ever to be a blood donor. It made news, too, when he gallantly rescued the hat of an elderly lady, or announced that he would sing with the Bach Choir and English Chamber Orchestra to celebrate the 300th anniversary of Bach's birth.

An angry concern of Diana's was a saucy poster used to promote *Penthouse* magazine, showing a Diana look-alike adjusting a half-open zipper in her trousers.

A West German magazine, *Playbock*, was even more flagrant in

She stayed 23 minutes longer than planned, went on an unprogrammed walkabout, and talked to a great many people, including a young man in the gym. "Are your girlfriends impressed with all your muscles?"

showing a fake nude picture of the Princess. The publisher later admitted, "We put Princess Di's head onto a suitable naked female body. I have no regrets."

Diana had a low tolerance for criticism. Critics said she was in a cocoon surrounded by "yes" people. Unlike Charles, Diana read all her press clippings and got incensed at many of them. While she chatted easily at walkabouts, her public utterances were restricted to a total of about a thousand words.

The royal rule is that the title of Prince and Princess can descend from George V, but only through the male line. Of his thirty-four direct descendants now living, only ten can claim those titles. When they die, their titles die with them. Their children may be Lords and Ladies, but not Princes and Princesses. The exceptions, of course, are the children of Prince Charles and Princess Diana.

Royal succession is a constant subject in the British press. Abdication is not a British tradition; the abdication of Edward VIII is still considered a scandal. In a recent poll, 61 percent of the British people voted that the Queen should not abdicate. "It would create a very dangerous and undesirable precedent," said former Tory prime minister Lord Home. "Once is enough."

The Queen sees her position almost as a religious duty. So does Prince Charles. At a recent private dinner party, the Prince candidly said that he did not expect to be King before he was in his late fifties. "The ladies of our Royal Family are traditionally long-lived," noted Lord Denning. Victoria, Alexandra, and Mary all lived into their eighties; the current Queen Mother is a vital eighty-four.

Not yet sixty, the Queen still shows remarkable energy. As she has often said, she likes being Queen. As she gets older, the Prince will probably take over many of her functions, particularly much of the overseas touring. Close observers have predicted that Prince Charles and Princess Diana might well one day preside over their own soirées and parties for the best and brightest in Britain, creating a glittering, glamorous setting reminiscent of the most memorable past.

Looking into the long-range future of the Princess, many see her as someday evolving into the charming and lovable successor of the Queen Mother. They have such similar temperaments. But long before that, she has a mature life to live. "All by herself, she has given the monarchy new magic and brought it closer to the people," said the managing director of *Debrett's Peerage*. This, however, is just the beginning.

"Being Princess of Wales is an education in itself," said Palace spokesman Michael Shea. "One day she will be talking to the head of the miners' union, and the next evening she may be seated next to the head of state at an official banquet."

The Prince's education is even more intense, more ongoing. Unknown to the public, there are constant formal lunches with leaders of British life who will discuss their needs and their abiding interests with him. "I would rather earn my bread," once said Charles X of France, "than rule like the King of England." That was said in the days of the ivory-tower approach to kingship. Prince Charles knows better than anyone that royal life is composed of duties. He jokes about the monarchy being the "oldest profession in the world," but he also sees it as a job of constant exploration. His grandmother, the Queen Mother, has said of him, "If there was anything left to discover in the world, Charles would have been an explorer."

Prince Charles knows that the Royal Family sits on top of the aristocratic pyramid in Great Britain, dependent only on the approval of the British people. They know that only in this way can they maintain their invulnerability.

In his large inner office at the *Times* in London, the unpretentious editor Charles Douglas-Home, a cousin of Diana's, discussed the monarchy as an institution that had been built up brick by brick to become the one constant factor in British politics. "Politicians come and go, and it is reassuring to them, when they lose power, to know that they will lose it to someone who may also lose it and will anyway be subject to the same constraints, the same rituals, the same accountability as they are . . . only the sovereign stands above it, an object of unchanging reverence."

Even though Her Majesty would be forced to sign her own death warrant if Parliament so decreed it, she also has the residual power to act politically in national crises, dismissing Parliament, calling new elections, selecting a prime minister when parties are in indecisive turmoil. "If there is such a crisis," said Douglas-Home, "and we had one not too long ago, and they throw the whole scrambled egg on her plate, Her Majesty has the power to resolve it.

"The monarchy is only as strong as its hold on the whole nation's imagination. Its authority is based on an illusion that it is what people want; that, as an aggregate of their wishes, it represents an expression of the power of the people. So be it."

Prince Charles knows all this. Despite the restrictive framework of his role, he has spoken out increasingly on various issues. It is not improbable that he may use the public forum of the House of Lords in the future to express more of his strong, personal views. He can say and do only as much as the public will approve. He is learning his job in the hardest possible way, but, as someone said, "He's a stayer and a winner." When he does become King, there will have been no more knowledgeable monarch.

The real adventure of Charles and Diana, the real magic, is still to come.

Epilogue

I t was so early in the morning on May 4th, 1985, in Venice's St. Mark's Square that even the pigeons had not yet arrived. The local Italian newspaper headlined: CARLO E DIANA!

First on the scene were the men with red bunting to decorate the dock. Next were some workers struggling with a long red carpet. After considerable discussion they decided it was not quite long enough, was worn at one end and would not stay flat. Finally a crew was dispatched and soon returned with a huge, impressive-looking Oriental rug to cover the worn end of the red carpet.

Barriers were erected to hold the crowds back on the short route from the dock to the Doge's Palace. A small area, dubbed The Animal Cage, was fenced off for press photographers.

People started arriving singly and in small groups, patiently taking their positions. They had a holiday look about them, and there was much laughter.

The printed schedule said that the royal yacht *Britannia* would pass by St. Mark's Square at 8:10 A.M. At first, it was a dot in the distance. As it came closer, one could see all its huge flags flying, officers and crew lining the decks. The ship was followed by a British naval escort. At exactly 8:10, the *Britannia* passed alongside the square.

The cleared area near the dock now held a scattering of pompous-looking officials and a small group of intense Secret Service men, some of them obviously British, peering at the growing crowd. A parade of uniformed Italian police, most of them looking very young, stationed themselves almost lackadaisically in front of the barriers. Then came an honor guard costumed in feathered hats with red and blue feathers, white epaulets with lots of white braid, double red stripes running down the sides of their trousers, and highly polished dress swords.

A barge arrived filled with plants to line the entrance from the dock. A young man came carrying a plastic-covered bouquet of salmon-colored roses for the Princess. (The plastic would never be removed.) A police helicopter circled the area again and again.

And, finally, as if on cue, the pigeons arrived.

Suddenly a cheer went up from the waiting crowd. The *Britannia* had berthed alongside the Grand Canal. A royal barge was en route to the dock flying the highly decorative Venetian flag as well as the British and Italian flags. The barge was escorted by a whole flotilla of small boats, but the local *vaporetto* continued its ferrying past them, obviously undeterred.

"There she is!" yelled a British tourist in the crowd, and everybody started clapping and cheering. The young Princess looked radiant, obviously delighted to be in this magical place. She smiled, waved, started shaking hands. It was a gray day but, also as if on cue, the sky seemed to brighten slightly.

Dressed in a white cotton suit with royal blue polka dots but no hat, she seemed slightly taller than the Prince, standing directly behind her. A woman reporter in the Animal Cage almost hissed, "Dreadful shoes." Diana was wearing blue shoes with high heels. No flatties.

Paparazzi threw bird food high in the air to attract pigeons around the Princess, but they were busy elsewhere.

Everything was carefully geared to a timetable and the Prince and Princess were soon whisked away to the Doge's Palace. The first scene in Venice was over.

This had been a long trip for them, a grand 17-day tour in the royal tradition. Neither of them had ever been to Italy before, except for a quick stop in Trieste for the Prince. "I have talked to my grandmother a great deal about this," the Prince said. "When she was young she spent part of the year in Italy because both her grandmothers had villas there. She often told me stories about Italy.

"I'm going to take my sketchbook with me," he continued. "I have always longed to see the light in Italy and try my hand at it—but I am very bad." Then he added, "I am a great admirer of Italian opera singers . . . I become moved very easily by the Italian operas."

387

What he remembered most vividly about the Italians in Trieste was their emotion. "The first person I talked to when I got out of the car was this elderly man who put both his arms around me and gave me a kiss on both cheeks."

Diana's dilemma was her wardrobe. It infuriated her that the press already had reported she had spent 100,000 pounds for 75 outfits and that her baggage would weigh four tons. Her dilemma was whether to dress as a fashion plate or a royal princess. The Queen steadfastly refused to accept the concept that a sovereign should look like a film star, but the world had thrust Diana into the celebrity category. The expectation was that stylish Diana was set to bowl over the Italians. She was now, after all, the key figurehead of the British fashion industry.

The paparazzi, the effervescent Italian freelance photographers, were waiting. They had taken pictures of Princess Caroline of Monaco topless and of the Pope in his swimming trunks. The word was out that they wanted to snap Diana in her underwear.

The trip had had a sunny start in Sardinia, where the royal couple flew to board the *Britannia*. Diana was greeted by chants of "*Bella, bella . . . bellissima . . . carissima!*" Her conquest was complete when she answered their greetings with a few Italian phrases of her own. The police were especially protective against paparazzi when Charles and Diana ate their spaghetti in a local restaurant "because no one can eat spaghetti elegantly."

At that restaurant in Sardinia she refused more pasta saying, "If I eat this sort of food, I'll get fat—I'll explode."

The Prince was scheduled to make a trip without her to see some secret naval equipment, but the Princess decided at the last minute to come along. "If you tell an English princess she cannot do something," said the Italian Minister of Defense, "she will insist on doing it. There is a trace of your first Queen Elizabeth in her."

For a people who had sent their own Royal Family into exile forty years before, the Italians were enormously excited about Charles and Diana's arrival, typified by the waitress in their restaurant who wrapped their glasses in napkins to take home as "precious souvenirs." Much was made of the Princess stooping to pick up a newspaper falling from the nervous hand of an elderly woman who had greeted her. "She is so gentle, so beautiful, and so democratic," said the woman still shaking with emotion.

Asked why Italian women were so taken with Princess Diana, a woman in Rome promptly answered, "Because she is young, beautiful, and lucky." And an Italian reporter called her "the most perfect of today's princesses: beautiful, silent, smiling, wonderfully still."

Italian fashion writers, however, soon pounced on her. The pink chiffon evening dress that she wore to Milan's La Scala was labeled "ugly and banal." Another source added, "She looked like a salesgirl from a department store." In her defense, a British fashion writer commented, "It's just sour grapes because she's wearing English clothes and nothing Italian." But the Italians were even more incensed when the British observers revealed that Diana had not worn a new dress for the occasion, that she had worn this same dress in Australia and Canada. A friend commented that maybe this was her way of taking revenge on all those writers who had reported on the fortune she supposedly spent on clothes for her Italian trip. Then, to show Italians that she did indeed have some new clothes, she wore a Bruce Oldfield design, a blue-gray suit with high-cut collarless jacket and a sexy skirt slit in the back.

It was reported that the Princess told an Italian designer at a reception that she had enjoyed wearing his creations before she was married but now she had to stay with British fashion and "wear the flat." She had not brought along a favorite backless dress, she said, "because people don't know where to put their hands when they are guiding you." They found it "rather embarrassing," she added, "when they touch bare flesh."

A woman asked her if her son Henry had any teeth. "Not at the last count," said Diana smiling. When she bought a pot of honey in a shop, she was asked if it was for the children. "No," she said, "it's for me."

Since one of the twenty-three staff people accompanying them was a doctor, and since one of her photographs showed a slight protrusion around her middle, Italians promptly jumped to the romantic but untrue conclusion that the Princess was pregnant again. If she wasn't, they declared, she soon would be because somebody insisted she had said, "I want from Charles a baby made in Italy."

The wildly imaginative Italians already had dubbed the royal yacht *The Love Boat*, and claimed to have photographed the couple's bed, said to be shaped like a gold-embossed boat. They also insisted the Prince had told his valet to make sure that all their beds in Italy were big, and the bedrooms soundproofed. They even revealed that the Prince and Princess would be eating aphrodisiac spaghetti.

The Prince smilingly alluded to that in a speech. "Indeed, we are informed that we shall be constantly eating a special kind of spaghetti which has magical properties!"

Not entirely overshadowed by his dazzling wife, Prince Charles had his own enthusiastic claque. "Carlo . . . Carlo . . . ," When he kissed a woman's hand, she said afterward, glowing, "I feel like a princess myself." He also kissed the head of a pensioner who said she had met the Queen in 1953. "He may have big ears," said a teenage girl, "but he is very *simpatico*."

He was equally appealing when he rescued a little girl whose fingers were caught between metal barriers when the crowd surged forth. He got a big *Bravo!* for that. But when he and Diana visited a school and he tried to entertain some of the young students, the teacher objected to the noise and Diana told him, "Darling, she wants you to stop." He apologized.

In his spare time the Prince sketched. He had invited noted British artist John Ward to join him on the Italian tour to give him some pointers. He had done two pencil drawings of an archeological site in the Sicilian port city of Syracuse, and more of the coastline. "We are now moving on to pen and wash," said Ward.

The Prince made a speech in Italian at the Town Hall in Florence. When he finished, the Princess, her eyes shining, leaned over to tell him, audibly, "Well done, darling." It was the same phrase he had used with her after she had repeated her marriage vows at their wedding. Earlier, Diana took a slip of paper from her handbag and read her Italian greeting: "*Mio marito ed io siamo molto felici di essere qui.*" "My husband and I are very happy to be here."

At a dinner in their honor the Italian aristocrat and designer Emilio Pucci compared the Princess to Botticelli's beauteous Primavera. "She has brought us a real breath of spring." Later, during a private tour of the Uffizi Gallery, the Princess sat alone on a leather-covered bench for a long time staring at the *Primavera*.

The Princess visited the Baby Jesus Hospital on the outskirts of Rome, and a little boy asked, "Is it true you have a crown?" The Princess smiled. "Yes, but I have left it behind today." At the same time, the Prince was talking to the President of the Italian Chamber of Deputies, a Communist, asking whether the Italian Communists supported the Russian invasion of Afghanistan. The reply was "No."

When the Prince and Princess visited a cemetery at Anzio, the bloody beachhead of the Italian campaign in World War II, the Princess examined the names and birthdates of the dead soldiers of the Commonwealth, and realized how many of them were her own age. "How young they all were," she said sadly.

The biggest brouhaha of the trip was the publicity flap over the proposed private papal mass. Ever since Henry VIII broke with the Catholic Church and created his own Anglican Church, there had been mild murmurings of a rapprochement. When the Pope visited Britain in 1982, Prince Charles told him, "I hope some time we can share a prayer together." The Prince thought his attendance at a private Vatican mass might be accepted in an ecumenical spirit. The Queen and her Privy Council thought otherwise. She felt that her nation of Protestants would be shocked. The Prince, after all, was the future Defender of the Faith—Anglican style. The mass was cancelled.

With all the hubbub over the proposed papal mass, it was not then noted that the Prince had attended a Catholic mass earlier in the year at Arundel, for a royal relative, the Duke of Norfolk.

Diana seemed highly nervous when she arrived to meet the Pope, but she emerged laughing. She had given the Pope a deep curtsey, and he had put her quickly at ease by asking about her children. Later, a theological student presented Diana with a bouquet. "I am afraid your beauty puts the flowers to shame," he said.

There were complaints that the Italian police assigned to protect Diana were not doing their job properly. Instead of scanning the crowds for possible danger, too many of them were openly staring at her.

"I think she is obsessed with looking slim," noted Judy Wade, a fashion expert. "That must be the reason she insists on wearing tailored, tight-fitting clothes. And why has she taken her hems up when everyone has lengthened theirs? I think the Princess picks styles that are smart, but far too old . . . they would suit her mother. Her clothes should be younger and more zippy." The same sentiment was echoed in the remark that "lamb should not be dressed as mutton."

Royal watchers noted that Diana's hair was now blonder, shorter, and curlier. Her hairdresser, Richard Dalton, commented, "I've put more highlights into her hair to give her a blonder look. It is more carefree and just right for the summer. And I've also introduced more curls, especially at the back to give her a softer, bouncier look.''

Everyone stared even harder when she wore a white collarless gabardine suit consisting of a long-line jacket with slit pockets and a slim skirt. Under it she had a white shirt and bow tie. The fashion verdict was that it made her look like an Italian waiter. In fact, during her walkabout, somebody shouted ''Waiter!'' and she looked up. ''The worst outfit of the tour,'' wrote one critic. ''Quite ridiculous.''

Her toughest critics called the trip a fashion fiasco. Everything she wore was scrutinized mercilessly. One of her aides admitted that the Princess had no prearranged plan of what to wear when, but usually made up her mind at the last minute. ''What everyone seems to forget,'' said the aide, ''is that the Princess is just like any other wife—she likes to wear what her husband thinks she looks nice in. And he loves the way she looks.''

The romantic Italians reported the couple's every loving gesture: When they visited a citrus farm and she tickled him under the nose with some lemon blossom; when they sat in the Sistine Chapel, her head resting on his shoulder, admiring the Michelangelo masterpiece; when the Prince gave her a flower and lovingly kissed her hand.

An observer caught them as they stopped to examine a self-portrait by an artist. It obviously reminded the Prince of someone. He put his arm around Diana and whispered something in her ear. She burst into a fit of giggles.

''Here comes your beauty Queen,'' the Prince had said smilingly to some students who were tolerating him but waiting for her. She was always watching him, too. ''I must leave you now and go and talk to my husband,'' she told one group at a reception, ''because, as usual, he's surrounded by women.'' To another group she added, ''I must keep my eye on him, you know.''

''They talk a lot more when they are going around together,'' commented an observer who had been trailing them throughout the tour. The driver of the Maserati which had been assigned to them had his own observations: ''They're always laughing. They're always lighthearted. They are a really happy couple.''

''Mind your head,'' the Prince warned her as he ducked under an arch in a Florentine garden.

''Why?'' she said smiling. ''There's nothing in it.''

She was putting more and more into it all the time. If there was within her a reluctance to accept the royal scene, there was no such reluctance in her feelings about Italy. The Prince earlier had talked about the Italians' ability "to make life into a kind of art form"— the way they designed and built their houses and towns, the way they used light and shade, even the way they prepared their food. While no Italian man had faced the national challenge of getting close enough to the Princess to pinch her bottom, she loved the natural, exuberant warmth of the people.

And now here they were in Venice, the most romantic setting of all. They were due to have lunch on the island of Torcello at the Locanda Cipriani Inn, next to an ancient church that featured many original Giottos. The restaurant had been closed to the public that day, but the maitre d' had promised a disappointed guest, "If you come to-morrow, you will get a better meal than the Princess gets today."

The restaurant sat at the end of a small canal so that boats could come right to the door. Hours before the royal arrival, a dozen police boats had zoomed in and out of the canal, and Italian frogmen in colorful red wet suits had carefully explored its bottom. The area in front of the hotel's entrance had been roped off and a scattering of police were in deep conversation with the men from Scotland Yard. A police helicopter circled the scene again and again.

What was remarkable was how early the crowds arrived, how patiently they waited. Among them were British expatriates and tourists. One young man, who had worked in a factory in Scotland when the Prince had paid a visit, recalled, "What impressed me was that there was a very tightly arranged schedule, but that the Prince suddenly said, 'I don't want to do this. I want to talk to the man who sweeps the floor.'"

The luncheon guests arrived first, the admirals and generals and ambassadors and their wives, each looking their elegant best. A flock of schoolchildren joined the scene. The chefs in their tall hats were in the backyard with their assistants to witness everything. The maids inside the restaurant could still be seen polishing glasses at the last minute.

When Princess Diana stepped ashore, it was difficult to believe that she was only twenty-three. She had poise, presence, complete control. Prince Charles looked slimmer and slighter than one might have expected. He had the look of someone who had done this many

many times before. By contrast, Diana's mood was exuberant, filled with the enthusiasm of someone new to the royal red-carpet treatment. Before they entered the restaurant, the Princess turned, smiled, and responded to the warm applause by waving.

When the Princess woke up the next morning aboard the *Britannia*, she saw Venice at its most festive. It was their annual Vogalanga. Almost every boat in Venice passed by the royal yacht, their crews attired in the most colorful costumes. Some boats had crews of two, others more than twenty, but each sported its own distinctly different outfit.

It was Sunday and the couple went to church. St. George's Anglican Church on the Rio di San Vio canal was a small, unpretentious church on the side of a bridge. The theme of the sermon that morning was "Do you love me above all else? Then feed my lambs and tend my sheep." When they signed the guest book, they took a whole page, writing simply "Charles" and "Diana."

When they came out, their ornately carved black gondola was waiting—it had been waiting for more than an hour, mostly under the bridge to keep it dry in the sprinkling rain. It had a black and gold seat that looked like a throne flanked with two large gold pillows backed by two cupids. A waiting Italian confided that it was the finest gondola in Venice, the same one that had been used by the Queen Mother, Prime Minister Margaret Thatcher, Sophia Loren, President Carter, and Richard Burton and Elizabeth Taylor.

The gondolier was Signor Mario de Pita. He wore a white uniform with gold buttons, a red sash with gold tassels over his hip, and a large gold seal on his arm. His nephew, who oared with him, was similarly dressed.

The crowd applauded as the Princess stepped down into the gondola. She wore an emerald green checked wool suit with a wide collar and a wide-brimmed green hat with a turned-up front. The consensus of fashion critics on this outfit was again negative. The Prince, in a sober suit, carried an umbrella just in case and glared at a reporter who asked if he would like a Cornetto ice cream cone. A year before, the Queen Mother had accepted one.

"I wanted to sing to them," said the gondolier, "but they didn't give me time."

They were both anxious to get back to the *Britannia* to greet their sons. Wills and Harry were joining them for a four-day family sail.

Diana had called them every day, but Harry was only eight months old. She never had been away from them this long. It was an emotional reunion with tears and hugs and kisses, all to an applauding audience crowded along the dock.

When an interviewer asked the Prince for a judgment on Italy, he turned to his wife. "What do you think, darling?" She talked about the warmth of the people "who have made us feel at home."

Whatever way it had begun, the Prince and the Princess now had a fully shared marriage. However little Diana may enjoy her royal chores, this is her life and her duty, and she accepts it. If she no longer regards her life as a Cinderella story, many millions of people all over the world are still fascinated by the living fairy tale.

Living fairy tales depend on people's hunger for myth and magic. For Charles and Diana, and for their children, the future hinges on how much the monarchy can extend its reach and still maintain its mystique and its magic.

The great difficulty in providing sources for a book on the Royal Family is that so few people within the royal circle are willing to be quoted. A great many of them were willing to talk to me, largely because they had read some of my earlier books, particularly *Jennie: The Life of Lady Randolph Churchill*. In other cases, we shared mutual friends. But they asked not to be quoted or acknowledged for a simple reason: If they were, they would no longer be part of that royal circle.

There are, however, many people I can credit. Most valuable were Michael Shea, Press Secretary to the Queen, and Assistant Press Secretary Victor Chapman, who concentrates on the Prince and Princess of Wales. They were particularly helpful in suggesting some of the myths that might be destroyed, and people who might help destroy them. I am grateful to that elegant gentleman, Sir Martin Gilliat, Private Secretary to Queen Elizabeth the Queen Mother, who not only shared his memories with me, but arranged for my meeting with the Queen Mother. Sir Laurens van der Post, one of Prince Charles's closest advisors and friends, offered valuable perceptions and suggestions.

The Dowager Lady Patricia Hambleden, Lady-in-Waiting to the Queen Mother, could not have been more gracious with her time and recollections. The Rt. Hon. William Deedes, a member of the Privy Council as well as editor of the *Daily Telegraph*, was particularly acute in his observations. So was Kenneth Harris, editor of the *Observer*, who has had exclusive interviews with so many members of the Royal Family. Charles Douglas-Home, editor of the *Times*, gave me a special insight, especially with regard to the royal relations with the Commonwealth.

Dale, Lady Tryon, a longtime personal friend of Prince Charles, gave me an entirely different insight, correcting many of the romantic myths about the Prince. So did Barbara Cartland, Princess Diana's wise and gracious step-grandmother. Lady Elizabeth Anson had warm and witty anecdotes about her royal cousins.

Alan Fisher, former butler to the Prince and Princess of Wales at Kensington Palace, was reluctant to be acknowledged, but his contribution to this book is so obvious that I feel no hesitation in expressing my gratitude. William Lewisham, stepbrother to Princess Diana, was most helpful.

I am particularly grateful to Stephen Barry, former valet to Prince Charles, who gave me so unstintingly of his time, recalling so much that was never published in his own two books on the Royal Family.

John Barratt, Private Secretary to Lord Louis Mountbatten for many years, was invaluable in destroying more myths. So were Dick Francis, Peter Ffrench-Hodges, Una Mary Parker, Donald Campbell, Jill Churchill, Heather McConnell, John Rendall, Patricia Behr, Michael Wall, Allen Warren, Alan Schwartz, Rouza Hellmore, Jonathan Rendell, and Jill Thornton.

I owe a special debt to Percy Savage, who gave me not only his own keen observations, but introduced me to some pivotal people. Anthony Holden's memories and suggestions were also most valuable.

Of that special breed of royal watchers, the two most perceptive and most helpful were Audrey Whiting and Jane Owen. Not only was their material fascinating, but I do believe they have total recall. Kent Gavin, that noted photographer, was similarly helpful in destroying another myth or two. So was Stephen Handleman of the *Toronto Star*, Ann Barr, formerly with *Harpers & Queen*, as well as Sue Carpenter, Inga Seward of *Majesty* magazine, and Gordon Honeycombe.

My special thanks to Cyril Kersh, Managing Editor of the *Sunday Mirror*, and the Chief Librarian, Harry Cox, who could not have been more helpful. I must similarly thank Jeffrey Care at the *Observer* Library, Jane Astell of the BBC, and Stella Mummery of the Central Office of Information.

There is a large list of books about the Royals, but the majority seem to repeat the much-manufactured myths. The best among them, for me, were *Prince Charles* by Anthony Holden (Atheneum, 1979). *Majesty* by Robert Lacey (Harcourt Brace Jovanovich, 1977), *Diana* by Penny Junor (Fireside, 1982), *The Spencers of Althorp* by Georgina Battiscombe (Constable, 1984), *Mountbatten* by Philip Ziegler (Collins, 1985), *Royal Service* by Stephen P. Barry (Macmillan, 1983), *Royal Secrets* by Stephen P. Barry (Villard, 1985), *The Official Sloane Ranger Handbook* by Ann Barr and Peter York (Ebury, 1982), *Elizabeth R* by Elizabeth Longford (Hodder & Stoughton, 1983), *Prince Philip* by Basil Boothroyd (McCall, 1971), *The Year of the Princess* by Gordon Honeycombe (Michael Joseph, 1982), *Diana, Princess of Wales: The Book of Fashion* by Jane Owen (Colour Library, 1983), *The Queen*

Mother by Ann Morrow (Granada, 1984), *Yet Being Someone Other* by Laurens van der Post (Penguin, 1982), *Book of Celebrities* by Barbara Cartland (Quartet, 1982), *Family Royal*, by Audrey Whiting (W. H. Allen, 1982), and *American Ancestors and Cousins of the Princess of Wales* by Gary Boyd Roberts and William Addams Reitwiesner (Genealogical Publishing Company, 1984).

The newspaper files of the *Observer*, the *Mirror*, the *Times* of London, and the *New York Times* were especially valuable. I am also grateful to the staff at the Library of the British Museum as well as at the Westport Public Library. My thanks also to Stewart Grainger of the British Information Services.

My dear and old friends Paul S. Green, Ernest Leiser, Jack Raymond, and Andrew A. Rooney were there to help me when I needed help. So were Ed Antrobus, Merle Miller, Joyce and Allen Andrews, Jane Bradford, Martin Gilbert, Ed Plaut, Naomi Roth, Elinor Green, Dr. Murray Krim, Harriett and John Weaver, Dr. Howard Gotlieb, Alan Williams, Deni Auclair, Fenya Slatkin, Edie Frankel, Michael Sissons, Myrna Blyth, Bob Levey, and Maybelle and Walter Buhler. As always, dear Ruth and Larry Hall were there to read the proofs of the book—as they have for so many of my books.

The most valuable person in organizing all my material and helping with research and editorial comment was my daughter Tina. My daughter Elizabeth also provided excellent research. For following through on research in London, I am most thankful to Alan Collings, Carolyn Forte, and Robert Andrews. For help here in the United States, I am grateful to my dear friend Olga Barbi.

The original idea for this book came from another dear friend, Phyllis Grann. Phyllis was also the editor of my early novel *Skin Deep*, and of *The Woman He Loved*. Joan Sanger, my editor on this book, proved again how superb she is both as an editor and as a friend. My thanks to Mary Kurtz for her excellent copyediting of the manuscript, as well as to Gypsy da Silva, Director of Copyediting, and Ron Lief for their guidance and efficiency in handling very tight production schedules. I'm also appreciative to Joe Freedman for his fine design of the book. Mari Walker, once again, as on all my books, had the tough job of typing my taped interviews and deciphering my notes. And my wife, Marjorie Jean, as always, was the first to read and criticize and enrich my book, as she has enriched my life.

The Royal Family—Select Tree

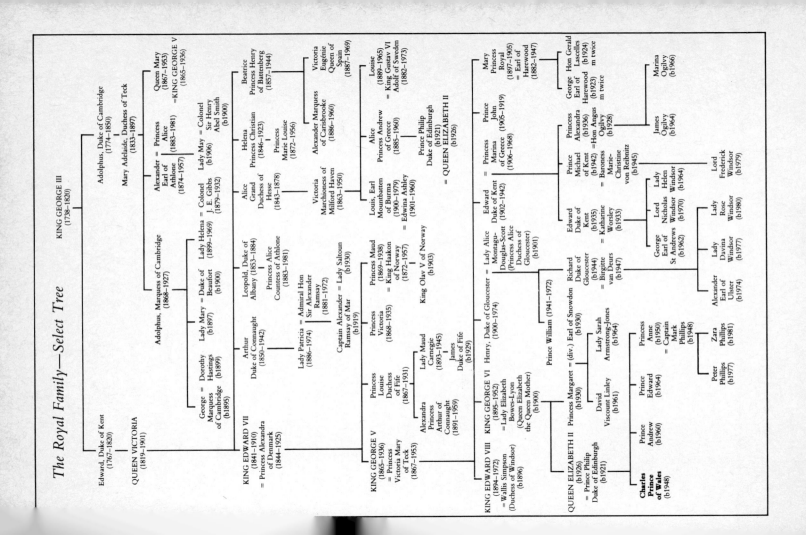

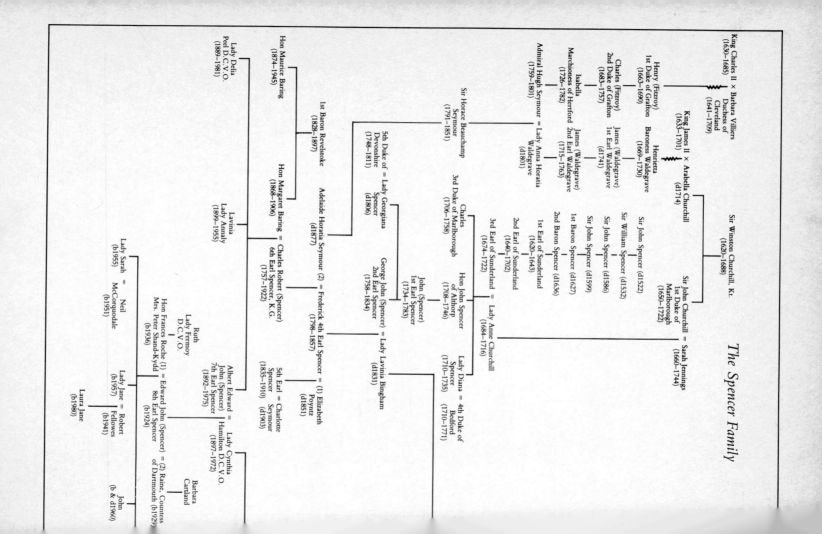

The Spencer Family

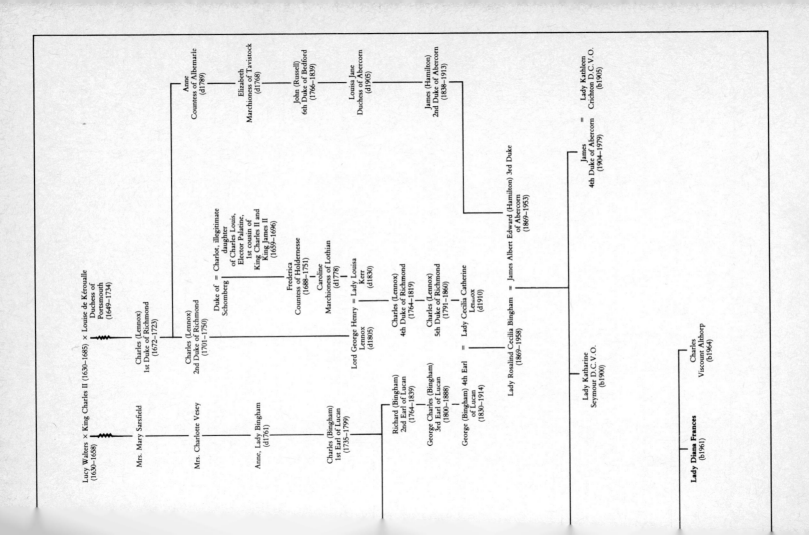

Lucy Walters × King Charles II (1630–1685) × Louise de Kéroualle
(1630–1658)   Duchess of
                                                   Portsmouth
                                                   (1649–1734)

Mrs. Mary Sarsfield

Charles (Lennox)
1st Duke of Richmond
(1672–1723)

Mrs. Charlotte Vesey

Charles (Lennox)
2nd Duke of Richmond
(1701–1750)

Anne, Lady Bingham
(d1761)

Duke of = Charlot, illegitimate
Schomberg   daughter
               of Charles Louis,
               Elector Palatine,
               1st cousin of
               King Charles II and
               King James II
               (1659–1696)

Frederica
Countess of Holdernesse
(1688–1751)

Caroline
Marchioness of Lothian
(d1778)

Anne
Countess of Albemarle
(d1789)

Elizabeth
Marchioness of Tavistock
(d1768)

John (Russell)
6th Duke of Bedford
(1766–1839)

Louisa Jane
Duchess of Abercorn
(d1905)

James (Hamilton)
2nd Duke of Abercorn
(1838–1913)

Charles (Bingham) 1st Earl
of Lucan
(1735–1799)

Lord George Henry = Lady Louisa
Lennox   Kerr
(d1805)   (d1830)

Charles (Lennox)
4th Duke of Richmond
(1764–1819)

Charles (Lennox)
5th Duke of Richmond
(1791–1860)

Richard (Bingham)
2nd Earl of Lucan
(1764–1839)

George Charles (Bingham)
3rd Earl of Lucan
(1800–1888)

George (Bingham) 4th Earl
of Lucan
(1830–1914)

= Lady Cecilia Catherine
  Lennox
  (d1910)

James Albert Edward (Hamilton) 3rd Duke
of Abercorn
(1869–1953)

Lady Rosalind Cecilia Bingham = James Albert Edward (Hamilton) 3rd Duke
(1869–1958)   of Abercorn
                                   (1869–1953)

James
4th Duke of Abercorn
(1904–1979)

Lady Kathleen
Crichton D.C.V.O.
(b1905)

Lady Katharine
Seymour D.C.V.O.
(b1900)

Lady Diana Frances
(b1961)

Charles
Viscount Althorp
(b1964)

Select Family Tree of Frances Eleanor Work, Mrs. Burke Roche, American Great-Grandmother of The Princess of Wales

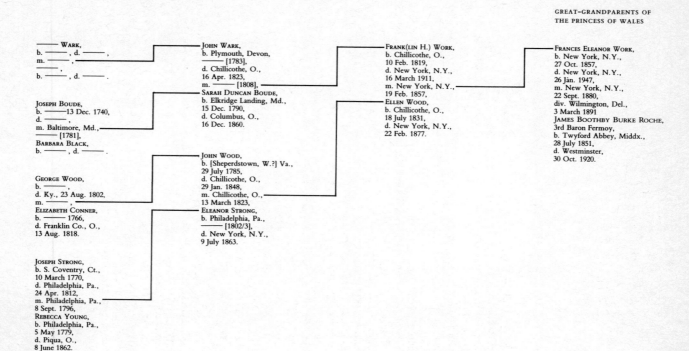

———— WARK,
b. ———— , d. ———— ,
m. ———— ,
———— ,
b. ———— , d. ———— .

JOHN WARK,
b. Plymouth, Devon,
———— [1783],
d. Chillicothe, O.,
16 Apr. 1823,
m. ———— [1808],

SARAH DUNCAN BOUDE,
b. Elkridge Landing, Md.,
15 Dec. 1790,
d. Columbus, O.,
16 Dec. 1860.

JOSEPH BOUDE,
b. ————13 Dec. 1740,
d. ———— ,
m. Baltimore, Md.,
———— [1781],
BARBARA BLACK,
b. ———— , d. ———— .

FRANK(LIN H.) WORK,
b. Chillicothe, O.,
10 Feb. 1819,
d. New York, N.Y.,
16 March 1911,
m. New York, N.Y.,
19 Feb. 1857,
ELLEN WOOD,
b. Chillicothe, O.,
18 July 1831,
d. New York, N.Y.,
22 Feb. 1877.

JOHN WOOD,
b. [Sheperdstown, W.?] Va.,
29 July 1785,
d. Chillicothe, O.,
29 Jan. 1848,
m. Chillicothe, O.,
13 March 1823,

ELEANOR STRONG,
b. Philadelphia, Pa.,
———— [1802/3],
d. New York, N.Y.,
9 July 1863.

GEORGE WOOD,
b. ———— ,
d. Ky., 23 Aug. 1802,
m. ———— ,
ELIZABETH CONNER,
b. ————1766,
d. Franklin Co., O.,
13 Aug. 1818.

JOSEPH STRONG,
b. S. Coventry, Ct.,
10 March 1770,
d. Philadelphia, Pa.,
24 Apr. 1812,
m. Philadelphia, Pa.,
8 Sept. 1796,
REBECCA YOUNG,
b. Philadelphia, Pa.,
5 May 1779,
d. Piqua, O.,
8 June 1862.

FRANCES ELEANOR WORK,
b. New York, N.Y.,
27 Oct. 1857,
d. New York, N.Y.,
26 Jan. 1947,
m. New York, N.Y.,
22 Sept. 1880,
div. Wilmington, Del.,
3 March 1891
JAMES BOOTHBY BURKE ROCHE,
3rd Baron Fermoy,
b. Twyford Abbey, Middx.,
28 July 1851,
d. Westminster,
30 Oct. 1920.

Index

Spencer, Albert Edward John ("Jack"), seventh Earl, 17–19, 41–42

Spencer, Charles, Viscount Althorp, 35–39, 229, 253–54, 272, 366–68

Spencer, Cynthia Hamilton, Countess, 16–18, 34–36, 38, 41, 122

Spencer, Lady Cynthia Jane, *see* Fellowes, Mrs. Robert

Spencer, Diana, Duchess of Bedford, 14–15, 236

Spencer, Edward John ("Johnny"), eighth Earl (formerly Viscount Althorp), 12, 17–19, 36–42, 44–46, 86–89, 93, 94, 158, 159, 162, 163, 164, 174, 192, 197, 205, 207, 212, 214, 217, 244, 246, 248, 252–53, 255, 256, 272, 285, 287, 291, 300, 306, 335, 337, 338, 354, 358–59, 367–69, 372

Spencer, Lady Frances, *see* Shand-Kydd, second Mrs. Peter

Spencer, Honorable G. C., 230

Spencer, Georgiana (Duchess of Devonshire), 14

Spencer, Henrietta (Lady Bessborough), 14

Spencer, Father Ignatius, 47

Spencer, Raine, Countess (formerly Countess Dartmouth), 34, 41–42, 45–46, 86–88, 94, 160, 163, 192, 197, 205, 252, 253, 255–56, 291, 368

Spencer, Sarah, Duchess of Marlborough, 14

Spencer, Lady Sarah Lavinia, *see* McCorquodale, Mrs. Neal

Spiritualist Gazette, 379

Spock, Benjamin, 15

Sporting Life (magazine), 34

Stark, Koo, 304, 319

Steel, David, 262

Stephen, Beverly, 220

Stern (magazine), 66

Stevens, Delphine, 283

Stevenson, Adlai, 15

Stone, Sandra, 126

Strathmore, Earl and Countess of, 26

Streisand, Barbra, 115–16

Strong, Joseph, 15

Suenens, Joseph Cardinal, 113

Sunday Standard (India), 153

Sunderland, Earl of, 289

Supertramp (rock group), 227

Swaziland, King of, 231

Tailor & Cutter (magazine), 130

Taylor, Elizabeth, 276, 394

Te Ringa Miraka, 334

Tennant, Lady Anne, 268–69

Teresa, Mother, 154

Teviot, Lord, 244

Thatcher, Margaret, 164–66, 219, 362–63, 377, 380, 394

Thomas, George, 80, 262

Thompson, Janet, 35

Thompson, William Hale ("Big Bill"), 126

Three Degrees (rock group), 128

Thurn und Taxis, Princess Gloria von, 13

Timbertop, Geelong School (Australia), 67–69, 124

Time magazine, 347

Times (London), 20, 60, 82, 100, 150, 171, 173, 181, 196, 218, 244, 286, 292, 296, 384

Tirson, Geoffrey, 213

Tito, Marshal, 187

Tonga, King of, 198, 230

Toronto Star, 114

Tower of London, 84, 286, 295

Townend, Peter, 157

Townsend, Peter, 59–61

Travolta, John, 194, 247

Trinity College (Cambridge), 71–74, 81, 83

Trudeau, Margaret, 115

Trudeau, Pierre, 115, 239

Truman, Harry S., 33

Tryon, Lord Tony, 123–24, 230, 238, 378

Tryon, Lady Dale ("Kanga"), 97, 123–25, 133, 147, 149, 162, 230, 238, 298, 378

Tucker, Sophie, 266

Tudor, Arthur, 190, 236

Valentino, Rudolph, 15

Van Buren, Abigail, 304

About the Author

Ralph G. Martin is the author of more than two dozen books, including the two-volume biography *Jennie: The Life of Lady Randolph Churchill*; *The Woman He Loved: The Story of the Duke and Duchess of Windsor*; and *A Hero for Our Time: An Intimate Story of the Kennedy Years*. He lives in Westport, Connecticut.